ANNUAL REVIEW OF
INFORMATION
SCIENCE AND
TECHNOLOGY

VOLUME 33 1998

ISBN: 1-57387-065-X
ISSN: 0066-4200
CODEN:ARISBC
LC No. 66-25096

ANNUAL REVIEW OF
INFORMATION SCIENCE AND TECHNOLOGY

Volume 33, 1998

Edited by

Martha E. Williams
University of Illinois
Urbana, Illinois, USA

asis

Published on behalf of the
American Society for Information Science
by Information Today, Inc.

 **Information Today, Inc.**
Medford, New Jersey

ISBN: 1-57387-065-X
ISSN: 0066-4200
CODEN: ARISBC
LC No. 66-25096

Published and distributed by:
Information Today, Inc.
143 Old Marlton Pike
Medford, NJ 08055-8750

for the

American Society for Information Science
8720 Georgia Avenue, Suite 501
Silver Spring, MD 20910-3602, U.S.A.

Distributed in Europe by:
Learned Information Ltd.
Woodside, Hinksey Hill
Oxford OX1 5BE
England

ARIST Production staff, for ASIS:
Charles & Linda Holder, Graphic Compositors
Cover design by Sandy Skalkowski
Printed in the U.S.A.

Contents

I
Planning Information Systems and Services   1

II
Basic Techniques and Technologies   85

Preface

PUBLISHING HISTORY

This is the 33rd volume of the *Annual Review of Information Science and Technology* (*ARIST*). It was produced for the American Society for Information Science (ASIS) and published by Information Today, Inc. ASIS initiated the series in 1966 with the publication of Volume 1 under the editorship of Carlos A. Cuadra, who continued as Editor through Volume 10. Martha E. Williams has served as Editor starting with Volume 11. ASIS is the owner of *ARIST*, maintains the editorial control, and has the sole rights to the series in all forms.

Through the years several organizations have been responsible for publishing and marketing *ARIST*. Volumes 1 and 2 were published by Interscience Publishers, a division of John Wiley & Sons. Volumes 3 through 6 were published by Encyclopaedia Britannica, Inc. Volumes 7 through 11 were published by ASIS itself. Volumes 12 through 21 were published by Knowledge Industry Publications, Inc. Volumes 22 through 25 were published by Elsevier Science Publishers B.V., Amsterdam, The Netherlands. With Volume 26 Learned Information, Inc., assumed the role of publisher of *ARIST* for ASIS. In 1995 Learned changed its name to Information Today, Inc.

POLICY

ARIST is an annual publication that reviews numerous topics within the broad field of information science and technology. The contents vary from year to year; no single topic is treated on an annual basis. Inasmuch as the field is dynamic, the contents (chapters) of the various *ARIST* volumes must change to reflect this dynamism. *ARIST* chapters are scholarly reviews of specific topics as substantiated by the published literature. Some material may be included, even though not backed up by literature, if it is needed to provide a balanced and complete picture of the state of the art for the subject of the chapter. The time period covered varies from chapter to chapter, depending on whether the topic has been treated previously by *ARIST* and, if so, on the length of the interval from the last treatment to the current one. Thus, reviews may cover a one-year or a multiyear period. The reviews aim to be critical in that they provide the author's expert opinion regarding developments and activities within the chapter's subject area. The review guides the reader to or from specific publications. Chapters aim to be scholarly, thorough within the scope defined by the chapter author, up to date, well written, and readable by an audience that goes beyond the author's immediate peer group to researchers and practitioners in information science and technology, in general, and ASIS members, in particular.

PURPOSE

The purpose of *ARIST* is to describe and to appraise activities and trends in the field of information science and technology. Material presented should be substantiated by references to the literature. *ARIST* provides an annual review of topics in the field. One volume is provided each year. A master plan for the series encompasses the entire field in all its aspects, and topics for each volume are selected from the plan on the basis of timeliness and an assessment of reader interest.

REFERENCES CITED IN TEXT AND BIBLIOGRAPHY

The format for referring to bibliographic citations within the text involves use of the cited author's name instead of reference numbers. The cited author's surname is printed in upper case letters. The reader, wishing to find the bibliographic references, can readily locate the appropriate reference in the bibliography (alphabetically arranged by first author's last name). A single author appears as SMITH; co-authors as SMITH & JONES; and multiple authors as SMITH ET AL. If multiple papers by the same author are cited, the distinction is made by indicating the year of publication after the last name (e.g., SMITH, 1986), and if a further distinction is required for multiple papers within the same year, a lower case alpha character follows the year (e.g., SMITH, 1986a). Except for the fact that all authors in multi-authored papers are included in bibliographic references, the same basic conventions are used in the chapter bibliographies. Thus, the reader can easily locate in the bibliography any references discussed in the text.

Because of the emphasis placed on the requirement for chapter authors to discuss the key papers and significant developments reported in the literature, and because *ARIST* readers have expressed their liking for comprehensive bibliographies associated with the chapters, more references may be listed in the bibliographies than are discussed and/or cited in the text.

The format used for references in the bibliographies is based on the *American National Standard for Bibliographic References*, ANS Z39.29. We have followed the ANSI guidelines with respect to the sequence of bibliographic data elements and the punctuation used to separate the elements. Adoption of this convention should facilitate conversion of the references to machine-readable form as need arises. Journal article references follow the ANSI guide as closely as possible. Conference papers and microform publications follow an *ARIST* adaptation of the format.

As the information world becomes more networked and as publishing becomes increasingly electronic, more publications are appearing on the Internet with no complementary hard copy version. In such cases the only option for citing the publication is a cite to the uniform resource locator (URL). Unfortunately, most of these publications are not permanently archived, and many of the sites (e.g., World Wide Web (WWW) sites) are not maintained or updated, and they do not retain permanent addresses. Some move to other servers, and others die as sponsorship or funding wanes. The *ARIST* staff verifies all cited URLs during the course of editing chapters, but by the time this volume is published some URLs will undoubtedly no longer be valid. While *ARIST* has always required page numbers for quotations, electronic documents do not consistently have explicit pagination noted; thus some quotes from URLs are cited without page numbers.

STRUCTURE OF THE VOLUME

In accordance with the *ARIST* master plan, this volume's eight chapters fit within a basic framework: I. Planning Information Systems and Services; II. Basic Techniques and Technologies; and III. Applications. Chapter titles are provided in the Table of Contents, and an Introduction to each section highlights the events, trends, and evaluations given by the chapter authors. An Index to the entire volume is provided to help the user locate material relevant to the subject content, authors, and organizations cited in the book. An explanation of the guidelines employed in the Index is provided in the Introduction to the Index. A Cumulative Keyword and Author Index of *ARIST* Titles to this and all prior volumes follows the Index.

DATABASES AND ABSTRACTING AND INDEXING
SERVICES COVERING *ARIST*

ARIST as a whole and/or individual chapters are included in a number of abstracting and indexing (A&I) journals both within the United States and internationally. Databases that both cover *ARIST* and are available through major online services in the United States are:

BIOSIS (Biological Abstracts)
Current Contents
ERIC (Educational Resources Information Center)
Information Science Abstracts
INSPEC (Computer and Control Abstracts)
Library Literature
LISA (Library and Information Science Abstracts)
Social SciSearch (Social Sciences Citation Index)

Publishers of other A&I journals and databases who would like to include *ARIST* in their coverage are encouraged to contact the publisher for a review copy and notify the editor who will add the database name(s) to this list when appropriate.

Appreciation

Appreciation is expressed to many individuals and organizations for their roles in creating this volume. First and foremost are the authors of the individual chapters who have generously contributed their time and efforts in searching, reviewing, and evaluating the large body of literature on which their chapters are based. The *ARIST* Advisory Committee Members and *ARIST* Reviewers provided valuable feedback and constructive criticism of the content. The Dialog Corporation plc generously provided the authors with online access to databases. Appreciation is expressed to all of the members of the editorial staff and *ARIST* technical support staff who are listed on the Acknowledgments page.

Martha E. Williams

Acknowledgments

The American Society for Information Science and the Editor wish to acknowledge the contributions of the three principals on the editorial staff and the technical support staff.

Linda Schamber, Copy Editor

Debora Shaw, Index Editor

Linda C. Smith, Bibliographic Editor

Technical Support Staff

Laurence Lannom, Technical Advisor

Mary W. Rakow, Technical Advisor

Linda C. Smith, Technical Advisor

Sheila Carnder, Assistant

Linda Holder, Compositor

Advisory Committee for *ARIST*

Blaise Cronin

John Hearty

Peter Hernon

Mark T. Kinnucan

Katherine W. McCain

Ronald E. Rice

Karen J. Sy

Amy J. Warner

Judith E. Weedman

Contributors

Anne R. Diekema
Syracuse University
4-206 Center for Science and
    Technology
Syracuse, NY13244

Elin K. Jacob
Indiana University
Main Library 005F
Bloomington, IN 47405

Anita Komlodi
University of Maryland
41421 Hornbake Library
College Park, MD 20742

Tomas A. Lipinski
University of Wisconsin at
    Milwaukee
Enderis Hall
P.O. Box 413
Milwaukee, WI 53201

Gary Marchionini
University of North Carolina
100 Manning Hall
Chapel Hill, NC 27599-3360

David M. Nichols
Lancaster University
Lancaster LA1 4YR
England

Douglas W. Oard
University of Maryland
Hornbake Library, South Wing,
    Room 4117J
College Park, MD 20742

Robin P. Peek
Simmons College
300 The Fenway
Boston, MA 02115

Jeffrey P. Pomerantz
Syracuse University
4-206 Center for Science and
    Technology
Syracuse, NY13244

Debora Shaw
Indiana University
Room 012 Library
Bloomington, IN 47405

Michael B. Twidale
University of Illinois
501 E. Daniel
Champaign, IL 61820

Sherry L. Vellucci
St. John's University
8000 Utopia Parkway
Jamaica, NY 11439

Sheila Anne Elizabeth Webber
University of Strathclyde
Livingston Tower
Glasgow G1 1XH, UK

Chapter Reviewers

Marcia Bates

David Becker

Wesley T. Brandhorst

Pauline Cochrane

Blaise Cronin

Raya Fidel

John Hearty

Margaret T. Fischer

Peter Hernon

Mary Ellen Jacob

Paul B. Kantor

Mark T. Kinnucan

Lois Lunin

Katherine W. McCain

Ronald E. Rice

Nancy Roderer

Tefko Saracevic

Thomas Surprenant

Karen J. Sy

Peter J. Vigil

Mickie A. Voges-Piatt

Amy J. Warner

Judith E. Weedman

ASIS and Its Members

For over 50 years the leading professional society for information professionals, the American Society for Information Science is an association whose diverse membership continues to reflect the frontiers and horizons of the dynamic field of information science and technology. ASIS owes its stature to the cumulative contributions of its members, past and present.

ASIS counts among its membership some 4,000 information specialists from such fields as computer science, management, engineering, librarianship, chemistry, linguistics, and education. As was true when the Society was founded, ASIS membership continues to lead the information profession in the search for new and better theories, techniques, and technologies to improve access to information through storage and retrieval advances. And now, as then, ASIS and its members are called upon to help determine new directions and standards for the development of information polices and practices.

I

Planning Information Systems and Services

Section I includes two chapters, "Information Ownership and Control" by Tomas A. Lipinski of the University of Wisconsin in Milwaukee and "Pricing and Marketing Online Information Services" by Sheila Anne Elizabeth Webber of the University of Strathclyde in the United Kingdom.

According to Tomas A. Lipinski, the development of the National Information Infrastructure (NII) opens new avenues for information products and services. As these information products and services are developed and marketed, the producers of those products and services naturally want to protect their proprietary interests in the underlying information. This commodification of information is exhibited in recent attempts to extend legal protection to basic facts (long considered to be noncopyrightable) and other public domain information. Through a combination of administrative policy, court cases, and Congressional activity, the public information space is slowly being reduced. The Clinton Administration set into motion Congressional action that, in conjunction with judicial developments, may work to limit public information space. In his introduction, Lipinski focuses on disturbing trends in information ownership which lead in that direction. He reviews the legislative, judicial, and regulatory documents as well as statements from the administration's work on NII.

The first two major sections of the chapter are titled "Policy Statements and Background" and "Restricting Movement in the Creative Space." In the latter section copyright is discussed and we see that the individual's right to use copyrighted works seems to become more tenuous when the works are digitized. Copyright can be enforced by electronically marking each copyrighted work (digital watermarking) and tracking the use of that work, and also by use of an electronic key/ password encryption that renders the document unreadable so only authorized users can open the document. The last two major sections

1

are "Loss of Factual Information Space," which concerns developments in contract and misappropriation law that reduce the right to use factual information and "The Loss of Virtual Space," which includes linking to and framing material on Web sites. The chapter points out the relative influences of technology, and the Internet in particular, in fostering entrepreneurship and fueling the contention between the public and private sectors regarding information and data rights.

Sheila Anne Elizabeth Webber's insightful chapter on "Pricing and Marketing Online Information Services" opens by defining online as remotely held electronic information services accessed through networks. She discusses pricing primarily in the context of marketing, as a part of the marketing mix. The emphasis is on the type of information content of interest to the professional and business sector. The literature covered is largely from 1991 through 1997. Webber discusses relevant changes in the marketing context, and issues of value relating to price. She summarizes other literature reviews and surveys on pricing and discusses how ongoing trends affect pricing. The first trend is the effect of the information chain on pricing issues and strategy, including the relationship between producer and host and the roles of vendor and information professional. The second is the effect of public sector involvement on the information industry. More recent influences are also reviewed, notably the effect of the Internet and the effect of consumer online services (aimed at individual, not corporate, customers) on the pricing of traditional online products.

In conclusion, Webber highlights movement toward traditional pricing, toward price discrimination, and toward both the aggregation and disaggregation of prices. She observes that although certain trends are discernible, the pricing of online products is still complex and problematic.

1 Information Ownership and Control

TOMAS A. LIPINSKI
University of Wisconsin, Milwaukee

INTRODUCTION

This chapter reviews recent legal developments in United States information policy related to digital information, particularly on the Internet. Although the range of information policy is topically broad (BURGER), this review focuses on disturbing trends in which information ownership is slowly encroaching on public uses of information or on public information space, that is, control and ownership of information versus public access to and use of information. Rather than concentrate on the work of others in discussing similar problems, this chapter reviews the actual documents of regulatory, judicial, and legislative information policy: statements from the Clinton administration's work on the National Information Infrastructure (NII), via the recent leading court cases and legislation in the 105th Congress (with one or two exceptions). These are primary sources of information policy that allow the reader to understand how current information policy is developing in response to the challenges of new technologies (CATE ET AL.). Secondary sources are commentators' analyses of these documents, which are cited for illustrative or reinforcement purposes and to assess the importance of present information policy development.

There are many avenues from which one can observe this loss of public information space (use and access rights to information beyond mere copyright concepts). In addition to the obvious copyright issues within the sphere of intellectual property rights, this chapter examines related areas such as renewed interests in limiting information access through the doctrine of misappropriation, contract and license, developments in information trespass, and tort. This chapter does not intro-

Annual Review of Information Science and Technology (ARIST), Volume 33, 1998
Martha E. Williams, Editor
Published for the American Society for Information Science (ASIS)
By Information Today, Inc., Medford, NJ

duce these concepts, but rather reviews significant developments in these areas to support a thesis that suggests a dangerous trend. As information becomes more valuable and marketable, others will attempt to own and control it, resulting in a loss of that information by the public at large, or at least making use of the information more costly. Commentators such as KARNOW and JOHNSON & POST trace this development to the characteristics of digital information: because digital information is mutable and not bound by physical dimensions, traditional concepts of possession fail; as a result, information owners attempt to exert property rights enforced through the legal system. Information is viewed as property, that is, subject to ownership and control vis-à-vis legal mechanisms. Striking a balance between these ownership rights and the space in between (public domain and fair use rights) is one of the most important issues for users in the NII environment (CREWS). Negotiation of these rights occurs in three types of information space. (1) Creative information space is where the most traditional uses of information ownership mechanisms such as copyright operate. (2) Factual information space involves new developments in the use of contract and misappropriation law that erode the right to use basic factual information. (3) Virtual information space includes information uses in unique NII environments, such as the linking to and framing of Web site material.

POLICY STATEMENTS AND BACKGROUND

Although *Intellectual Property Rights in an Age of Electronics and Information*, prepared by the Office of Technology Assessment (OTA) (U.S. CONGRESS. OFFICE OF TECHNOLOGY ASSESSMENT) in 1987, predates this discussion, it established a benchmark from which subsequent policy statements developed. Unlike recent documents discussed below, it does not recommend specific legislative responses. It does, however, identify various alternatives to accommodating intellectual property rights in an age of new technology. These alternatives include: marketplace solutions, judicial remedies, legislative amendment or revision of existing protection and use schemes, the adopting of sui generis legislation (legislation that creates or combines new legal rights rather than making existing law, such as copyright, apply), and alternatives to traditional intellectual property rights protections. All approaches are evident in the following three sections of this chapter. Alternatives to traditional copyright protections are subsequently reviewed by FLEISCHMANN, GOLDSTEIN, LITMAN (1989), MILLS, and SAMUELSON (1990). Each commentator exhorts the shortcomings of existing copyright initiatives in digital environments and demonstrates the review, consistent with this chapter, of legislative and judicial developments in assessing policy alternatives. The OTA report also spends considerable time discussing the impact of technology on intellectual property (primarily copyright) protection mechanisms. New technologies often force the extension of protection mechanisms into areas not originally contemplated by policy makers. The report also observes that courts are ill suited to deal with new problems because the particular legal issues may be defined by the litigants.

The Clinton administration is charting a new course in information policy and information ownership. Its first articulation is contained in the blueprint for the NII: *The National Information Infrastructure: Agenda for Action* (INFORMATION INFRASTRUCTURE TASK FORCE, 1993). The Information Infrastructure Task Force (IITF) recognized the conflict between owners and users of information and stated that the public interest in promoting access to information must be balanced with the need to ensure the integrity of intellectual property rights and copyrights. Part of the plan is to develop new mechanisms to reimburse copyright holders in a digital environment. These would include digital watermarking, encryption, tracking, and personal identification number (PIN) access. The problems of protecting copyright in the NII are discussed by GROSSO and KALIL. Without these protections, copyright owners and developers would be unwilling to venture into the NII.

The first Clinton administration report to review specifically the existing boundaries of intellectual property rights and make concrete recommendations is the *Intellectual Property and the National Information Infrastructure: A Preliminary Draft of the Report of the Working Group on Intellectual Property Rights* (INFORMATION INFRASTRUCTURE TASK FORCE, 1994). Otherwise known as the Green Paper, it recognizes the shortcomings of the existing copyright law. The Green Paper recommends changes to the copyright law in order to make clear its applications to Internet environments. For example, the definition of transmission should be expanded to include transfer over the Internet. Further, the development of copyright management and tracking technology is encouraged. The report reflects the dominance of private sector and ownership interests outweighing public access interests. Finally, the role of public institutions is observed in that "public libraries and schools, and the access to information that they provide, have been important safeguards against this nation becoming a nation of information 'haves' and 'have nots'" (INFORMATION INFRASTRUCTURE TASK FORCE, 1994, p. 133).

In the following year, the final version of the report, known as the White Paper (INFORMATION INFRASTRUCTURE TASK FORCE, 1995), was issued. It reiterates many points contained in the Green Paper, but in more detail. It also includes the text of actual legislation to implement the recommendations of the Working Group on Intellectual Property. Various stakeholders each found something to dislike in the final document. While the White Paper argues against a blanket exception for the use of copyrighted works by nonprofit institutions, libraries and archives are recognized as the only entities exempt from contributory infringement. The thorny issue of online service provider (OSP) immunity is left undecided; the authors of the White Paper do not recommend a safe harbor for OSPs given the uncertainty of the law. In addition, the IITF spends considerable time discussing various electronic copyright management options using digital signatures or watermarks. Recommendations include defining the distribution right to include transmission in digital environments and protecting the right of libraries to make digital copies of copyrighted works in certain circumstances, such as ensuring access for the visually impaired. The IITF also advocates closing loopholes in the criminal copyright law (*United States v. La Macchia*, discussed below) and promoting technological protections such as copyright management information systems. The impact of the White Paper on copyright information policy cannot be overestimated, as the next section demonstrates.

RESTRICTING MOVEMENT IN THE CREATIVE SPACE

A number of developments both in case law and in legislation introduced into Congress would restrict the movement of copyright users within the creative information space. In a nondigital environment the Supreme Court has attempted to carve out traditional fair uses of copyrighted material, as well as define uncopyrightable subject matter and material in the public domain. Material for which copyright protection has lapsed is also deemed to be in the public domain. Applying these standards, lower court cases have found users liable for copyright infringement in digital environments. However, where creative spaces still exist, recent copyright revision legislation in Congress attempts to redefine those spaces and close perceived copyright loopholes. In cases such as *CAMPBELL V. ACUFF-ROSE MUSIC, INC.*, the rights of users to take qualitatively significant aspects of copyrighted works for purposes of parody (rap group Two Live Crew taking the signature guitar riff of Roy Orbison's "Pretty Woman") was protected by the Supreme Court. Likewise, the Court's decision in *FOGERTY V. FANTASY, INC.* (awarding attorneys' fees to the prevailing party, not just a prevailing plaintiff as was the prior practice) might also be viewed as a triumph for users of creative works. The decision discourages litigation against copyright infringers unless the plaintiff expects to succeed in the court. It does, however, make it more difficult for holders of copyrights on less lucrative works to police their works because they may not have the financial resources to risk litigation to enforce their copyright (i.e., the losing party in copyright litigation pays both parties' attorneys' fees as a result of *Fogerty*).

The use of copyrighted works in the NII environment remains largely undefined and uncertain, according to commentators such as CASTAGNOLI. Also, NII copyright issues need to be resolved before the Clinton administration NII plan can proceed. Other commentators claim that existing legal schemes are capable of defining what use is allowed and what is a copyright infringement in light of existing legal parameters. LASTER discusses some misconceptions regarding digital and Web environments and suggests that doctrines such as copyright and misappropriation should apply in both the NII (digital) and print environments.

Recent Litigation Applying Copyright to the Internet

PLAYBOY ENTERPRISES V. FRENA and *CENTRAL POINT SOFT-WARE, INC. V. NUGENT*. The *Frena* decision in 1993 was an early and leading case in defining creative space in online environments. The case involved a bulletin board operator who scanned *Playboy* and *Penthouse* centerfold images onto a bulletin board service (BBS). The plaintiff claimed both copyright infringement (scanning and loading the images onto the bulletin board, then making the images available via email) and trademark infringement (the *Playboy* bunny logo was used without permission and misused when it was placed on the *Penthouse* images). The important holding in the cases is that the placing of the images onto a BBS was a display and a distribution for copyright purposes, that is, it usurped two of the copyright owners' exclusive rights.

This case exemplifies the play between the courts and Congress as makers of information policy: new technologies and new technology products and services create information policy vacuums. The entity that addresses the issue first establishes the information policy under which owners and users must operate. In *Central Point Software, Inc. v. Nugent*, the BBS operator was also found liable for direct copyright infringement. The case involved facts similar to those in *Frena* in that the BBS operator uploaded and downloaded copyrighted materials without permission. More important, the BBS operator encouraged others to do the same.

As a result of the *Frena* and *Nugent* decisions, it became clear that copyright applies to Internet technologies in the same way it applies to traditional reproduction or information technologies. Fair use of copyrighted material (creative space) is limited in the online environment in the same way as in the print environment. This interpretation is consistent with evaluations by COX and by LASTER, and the review of court cases in *The Copyright Law Journal* (COPYRIGHT LAW JOURNAL, THE).

TASINI V. NEW YORK TIMES CO. In this simple contract dispute, the question for the district court was whether the existing contract between authors and distributors should be interpreted to include or anticipate new means of dissemination, that is, through online data-bases such as DIALOG and LEXIS. If the electronic publishing rights were not transferred to publishers and disseminators by the original contract, then the authors of the news stories still retained those rights. New contracts would have to be negotiated and new revenue generated and owed to authors. The legal question is whether the copyright laws allow for the transferred rights interpretation rather than a retained rights interpretation and whether the copyright law restricts contracts to rights in the same media, unless otherwise stated in the contract. The court interpreted the contract to include electronic distribution rights and interpreted the copyright law to allow similar contracts in other media. According to CENDALI & REYES, the *Tasini* decision can be read narrowly as merely expanding in a new technology the long-recognized practice of publishers transferring paper periodicals to microfilm. But the decision also can be read broadly as sanctioning any form of distribution of a collective work (e.g., a database) as long as the selection or arrangement of the original version is sufficiently preserved. The question for policy makers is whether this should be the interpretation. One possible effect of the decision is suggested by Cendali and Reyes: it encourages publishers of collective works who were previously fearful of copyright infringement to consider packaging their works in a NEXIS or CD-ROM format because the rights have been released by the original contract. While initially this might benefit the public at large through increased electronic access, that access will not come without a price. Further, once individual authors realize that their works can now be exploited this way, new contracts will contain clauses covering electronic publishing. Any increases in the cost of obtaining the publishing rights from the author will undoubtedly be passed along to the consumer.

   SEGA ENTERPRISES V. MAPHIA I (1994) (Maphia I) and SEGA ENTERPRISES V. MAPHIA II (1996) (Maphia II). Unlike *Frena* and *Nugent, Maphia I and II* involved a BBS operator who did not himself actually use, copy, or display copyrighted software and video games on the BBS, but encouraged others to do so. The case is important because it illustrates the copyright problems that result from making technology available so others can infringe on the space of copyright holders. The Maphia BBS operator was found liable for contributory infringement (a concept of judicial creation that assigns liability when one facilitates infringement through the provision of copying technology). This case raises an important and unresolved issue: should BBS operators be held liable if they only provide the technology, as in the case of online service providers (OSPs), who provide Internet access but do not actually load copyrighted materials without permission? In *Maphia I*, a preliminary injunction was issued against Maphia and the operation of the illicit board ceased. At the trial in *Maphia II*, the court concluded that indeed the operator of the Maphia board was liable for contributory infringement, that is, providing the copying technology. However, because the plaintiffs could not prove that the Maphia BBS operator either uploaded or downloaded the software himself, the court had no recourse but to conclude that Maphia was not responsible for direct copyright infringement. This case impacts the creative space because it suggests that actual copying by a defendant is not required to violate the copyright law. All users need to be aware of their limitations on the use of the creative space and on the limits placed on movement in that space vis-à-vis the doctrine of contributory liability. These concerns become acute in the digital environment because of the power of technology to facilitate copyright infringement. The authors of the White Paper (INFORMATION INFRASTRUCTURE TASK FORCE, 1995) state that the only entities statutorily exempt from contributory infringement are libraries and archives.

RELIGIOUS TECHNOLOGY CENTER (RTC) V. LERMA. The litigation began when a former member of the Church of Scientology placed copyrighted church material on the Internet. (RTC is an official arm of the Church of Scientology). The documents were used in an attempt to discredit the church. Typically the church does not publish its documents, but its documents are protected by copyright nonetheless. In *Religious Technology Center v. Lerma,* as in *Playboy Enterprises v. Frena,* the court found that the fair use doctrine is limited, even on the Internet. Lerma (the individual who posted the church documents) was found liable for copyright infringement when he posted copied church documents without permission. However, the more important case in a series of copyright infringement cases was that against the BBS operator, Netcom.

In *RELIGIOUS TECHNOLOGY CENTER V. NETCOM ON-LINE COMMUNICATIONS SERVICES, INC.* the defendant, Netcom, argued that as an OSP and not the reproducer of any copyrighted materials (as was Lerma), it could not be liable for copyright infringement. The court concluded that while there could be no claim of direct copyright infringement (denial of a motion to dismiss the lawsuit), the case could proceed on the issue of OSP contributory infringement. Next, Netcom claimed it had no knowledge of the infringing post, nor did it possess any way to verify the claims of the church. The court stated that if these assertions were borne out by evidence at trial, Netcom would not be liable for contributory infringement either.

The court reasoned that Netcom was like the owner of a copying machine who lets others make copies; assigning liability to Netcom for direct infringement would create too many separate acts of infringement and eventually lead to unreasonable claims of liability. The parties settled their dispute in 1996. Neither side admitted any liability or wrongdoing. According to GOODIN, the case "may signal a growing recognition among Internet and on-line service providers that they could be liable for infringing material that subscribers post on their services." Cases like *Netcom* raise an important policy question that is still unresolved: who should be responsible for copyright compliance? Holding OSPs responsible means that OSPs either assume the role of copyright police or restrict posting on their sites and BBSs for fear of litigation. This may discourage Internet product and service development.

UNITED STATES V. LA MACCHIA. A loophole was also identified as a result of this litigation: copyright law criminalizes willful (intent is not an element of civil copyright) infringement only when made for purposes of commercial advantage or financial gain (UNITED STATES CODE). La Macchia ran Cynosure, an unauthorized software exchange BBS. He did not charge users to access his board, nor did he make any profit from the software downloaded and uploaded on his board because he did not offer the software for sale. La Macchia was not charged with criminal copyright infringement and the criminal wire fraud charges against him were dismissed because there was no financial gain. In dismissing the suit, the judge observed that La Macchia's actions failed to meet the financial gain elements of either a criminal copyright violation or wire fraud, but urged Congress to close the legal anomaly. The software industry condemned the result and lobbied hard for legislation reform (SOFTWARE PUBLISHERS ASSOCIATION). Support was also present in the Clinton administration's White Paper. As a result, legislation was introduced in both the 104th and 105th Congress to close this loophole (SHERMAN & ECKENWILER). The success of these efforts is described below.

Recent Analysis of Policy Alternatives

In spite of administrative statements such as the White Paper (IN-FORMATION INFRASTRUCTURE TASK FORCE, 1995) and some congressional activity, the ability to use copyrighted information in digital environments, particularly the Internet, is being defined by the courts on a consistent case-by-case basis. The courts have begun, albeit in piecemeal fashion, to articulate a fair use standard and determine where responsibility for infringing lies (WEIMER). Although Congressional responses have been limited, the 105th Congress may have more success in obtaining passage of White Paper legislative proposals. Furthermore, support or criticism of congressional initiatives may depend on whether one is a copyright owner or user. Several White Paper recommendations articulated in reform legislation are reviewed by RUPP-SERRANO on the basis of three criteria: equity, flexibility, and implementation feasibility. Rupp-Serrano views the White Paper and the legislation deriving from it as favoring industry and copyright holders, not users. She also states that legislative leadership is necessary because courts are unable to deal adequately with the applications of new technologies to old law. As a result, Rupp-Serrano views amendments to copyright laws such as H.R. 2441 and S. 1284 (companion bills), Information Infrastructure Copyright Act of 1995 (U.S. CONGRESS, 104TH, 1995a, 1995b), measures that would preserve fair use protection for libraries and archives in the digital environment, as necessary and positive steps.

KIRKWOOD takes a more conservative approach, stating that a balance between copyright users and copyright owners can be achieved by ensuring a safe environment for the release of copyrighted works in digital environments. Making the digital environment safe requires several changes in copyright law. Kirkwood recommends the removal of legal impediments to criminal prosecutions of copyright infringement (the *United States v. La Macchia* scenario). He also favors granting limited immunity to OSPs in order to encourage OSPs to develop and offer new information services and products. Without such immunity, OSPs might be forced to undertake expensive and counterproductive (from an access provider's viewpoint) monitoring of content. MORRIL & EATON argue that existing law should be applied to the problem of OSP liability; that if the requisite notice and knowledge of the infringing posting exist (as in *Netcom*), the OSP should be liable. A shared liability approach, in which both direct infringer and OSP operator are held accountable, is also discussed by KAMARCK. Other commentators, such as STUCKEY, view OSP liability as applicable only if there has been direct copying by the OSP or actual knowledge of copying (contributory infringement). Alternatively, TICKLE views the OSP vicarious or strict model as analogous to the lessor/lessee relationship of a landlord and tenant. If there is control over the original infringer's actions coupled with a financial benefit (revenue stream) to the OSP, then vicarious or strict liability may also apply. These then are the three ways (direct, contributory, and vicarious or strict) to infringe copyright. Given the proper supporting facts, each could be applicable to an OSP.

A standard consistent with the purposes of copyright law to encourage information creation and dissemination would hold the OSP responsible only if the OSP knew or had reason to know of the infringing action and possessed a realistic ability to monitor the activity. This strategy would also prevent the possible negative effect of the OSP liability model; otherwise OSPs may not allow some BBSs or pages to exist. Safe harbors such as take-down periods for removing infringing postings are supported by industry groups (FENSTER). The landlord/tenant analogy is also applied to OSP liability by SHULMAN, who analyzed OSP liability in light of *FONAVISA V. CHERRY AUCTION*, in which a swap meet director and organizer was found liable for the trading of infringing material. Fonavisa possessed more than 38,000 counterfeit recordings of music and made them available for sale or trade. Thus Shulman concludes that the OSP would be found liable under existing copyright law. However, she also supports congressional action to define the limits of that liability. Revision is necessary to prevent slowing the growth of digital information products and services. Similar concerns as a result of the *Fonavisa* decision are raised by STEPHENS & SUMNER, who conclude that OSP liability should be limited to situations of actual knowledge, with a safe-harbor period for removal of the copyrighted material.

KIRKWOOD uses a dance-hall analogy: if the dance-hall owner takes a share of the door or gate proceeds, then copyright liability should be shared between the dance-hall owner and members of the band who play copyrighted music without permission. Likewise, an OSP that charges fees for others to operate BBSs and home pages on its system should share liability. This is the result under current case law. But it is argued that this result is not conducive to the development of new Internet products and services. Another supporter of the dance-hall analogy is DOBBINS, who argues for the balance of owners and society, not necessarily owners and users. He proposes a primary purpose test, in which the OSP would be responsible only if the primary purpose of the posting is to infringe copyright. He also would assess whether OSP control over the infringing activity is exercisable in practice. Unlike RUPP-SERRANO, Dobbins says courts are in the best position to deal with problems on a case-by-case basis. He says placing the burden of monitoring transactions on OSPs would create in essence a vicarious or strict liability that would undermine the utility of BBSs, Web sites, and other services on the Internet.

Copyright Management Information and Technological Solutions

The right of individuals to use copyrighted works (movement within the creative information space) in digital environments is threatened by technologies that shift copyright enforcement efforts from the OSP to the individual. This is done in one of two ways. First, identifying the use, fair or otherwise, of copyrighted information through tracking technology is one alternative. The tracking is accomplished by electronically marking each copyrighted work, called digital watermarking in the White Paper. The second option is to use some form of electronic key encryption. In order to access the documents, an electronic key or password must be provided by the user. The key (without which the document is unreadable) is obtained through paying an access fee.

Watermarks, keys, and other copyright monitoring mechanisms are known as copyright management information (CMI). LENZINI & SHAW see the development of a mediating industry to facilitate CMI in the same way the Copyright Clearance Center (CCC) exists to help copyright users obtain permission and pay the proper use fees. The CCC is in essence a copyright licensing intermediary. If industry proponents have their way in eliminating the liability of digital intermediaries, such as OSPs, individual users may instead be targeted as defendants in copyright infringement suits. CMI mechanisms enable copyright owners to trace infringement with relative ease. The ramification for an individual user of copyrighted material in digital environments is considerable. For example, if any use of copyrighted material can be tracked online, there is concern that a protected use may come to include viewing or reading the material on a computer screen. This scenario is discussed by LITMAN (1995). Because the transaction cost of enforcing each separate copyright use will be greatly reduced, the problem of copyright free riders (those who take content for personal use or for use in a competing product) may be solved. One danger expressed by both BAND & KENNEDY and ELKIN-KOREN is that these mechanisms might also render concepts such as fair use obsolete.

As discussed earlier, the White Paper (INFORMATION INFRA-STRUCTURE TASK FORCE, 1995) presents mechanisms for tracking the use of copyrighted works in digital environments. Digital watermarks or codes would be embedded in copyrighted works and would function as tracking, identification, and use signatures. Any use of a work could be logged, as is done with print documents through the Copyright Clearance Center. Information identifying the work as copyrighted could be used to alert users of the current status of a work, protected or in the public domain, who the author is, along with other information such as a royalty fund account number. In an electronic key encryption system, only registered or authorized users possess the keys. The lock-and-key mechanism was accepted as part of the settlement in *FRANK MUSIC CORP. V. COMPUSERVE, INC.* In *Frank,* music publishers alleged that a CompuServe BBS connected to the Internet allowed users to submit or copy previously recorded songs. The BBS included more than 941 songs, representing more than 384 music publishers. The statutory damages would have totaled close to $69 million. Instead, the settlement proposes the digital licensing of sound recordings in online networks. Users who wish to copy songs from the BBS would need a personal identification number (PIN). The settlement demonstrates both the technological feasibility of electronic solutions and the desire of copyright owners to couple electronic tracking mechanisms with a compulsory licensing scheme (i.e., anyone who has paid for the key or PIN can download the music). According to

RAYSMAN & BROWN (1996), the proposed licensing scheme could develop into an industry standard.

Legislative Alternatives in the 105th Congress

OSP liability issues. Congress has not yet identified which electronic marking systems are to be adopted and how CMI systems are to be implemented. Congress prefers instead to let the marketplace determine which products and services will best meet copyright owners' needs. However, pending legislation would make it a violation of copyright law to knowingly remove any CMI or to market or import products or services for circumventing a CMI system. S. 1146, Digital Copyright Clarification and Technology Education Act of 1997 (U.S. CONGRESS, 105TH, 1997e) prohibits the removal or alteration of CMI with the intent to induce infringement. The selling of copyright management circumvention devices is also prohibited in related legislation S. 1121 (U.S. CONGRESS, 105TH, 1997j) While generally supported by copyright owners, these measures are viewed by BAND & KENNEDY as having the potential to curb the development of encryption technology and may in effect "override existing law on fair use."

S. 1146, above, and H.R. 2180, On-Line Copyright Liability Limitation Act of 1997 (U.S. CONGRESS, 105TH, 1997i), contain provisions designed to protect OSPs from liability for contributory infringement, if the systems they maintain have copyrighted material placed on them by users. If the OSP is not legally liable, then copyright holders are forced to attack infringers directly by suing them. In a CMI environment, identifying individual infringers could be done with relative ease. As SCHRADER (1997) points out, suing individual infringers raises the cost of enforcement (many lawsuits against individuals versus one lawsuit against the OSP). It also means that more individuals are likely to be sued as recovery from the "deep pocket" of the OSP is precluded. In this way, the creative space for use of copyrighted materials is also curtailed. Both bills, H.R. 2281 and S. 2037 (U.S. CONGRESS, 105TH, 1998b, 1998c) are now part of the Digital Millennium Copyright Act of 1998. The House passed H.R. 2281 in August 1998 and the Senate passed S. 2037 shortly after introduction in May 1998.

S. 1146 provides a safe harbor for material residing on the system, such as on a BBS, but the information must be removed "expeditiously" once the OSP receives proper notice of its illegality. Like current copyright law, S. 1146 exempts employees and agents of nonprofit libraries and archives, who are assumed to have a reasonable interest in the fair use of materials. Instead of safe harbor, H.R. 2180 offers immunity if the OSP does not initially place, alter, endorse, or advertise the material, or gain financial benefit from its residence on the system, or know that it is infringing. It does not necessarily exempt the OSP from contributory infringement but limits its liability to injunctive relief if the OSP otherwise meets the circumstances noted above. Generally, S. 1146 is broader than other proposals in that it includes provisions for active transmission and storage. It also applies to a broader range of OSP and Internet products and services such as site-linking and navigational aids. These differences are reviewed by STUCKEY.

Copyright term extension. Support or criticism of legislation that restricts the ability of copyright users to move within the creative space may depend more upon whether one views users' rights in digital environments as inadequate (typically a user's perspective) or too broad (typically a copyright holder's perspective). However, proposed legislation to lengthen the period of copyright protection can only be viewed as strengthening the position of copyright holders against those of copyright users. When the length of a copyright is extended, it takes that much longer before the work falls into the public domain and can be used freely. The longer the duration of the copyright, the more years the copyright holder has to profit from the revenue stream generated by the work's use. Companion bills were introduced in the 105th Congress to extend the term of copyrighted works by 20 years. (The current duration of works created on or after January 1, 1978 is for the life of the author plus 50 years) H.R. 604 and S. 505, Copyright Term Extension Act of 1997 (U.S. CONGRESS, 105TH, 1997b, 1997c) contain exceptions for nonprofit library and archive use of copyrighted materials during the extension period, 20 years. The exception is inapplicable if (1) the work is "subject to normal commercial exploitation," that is, there is still a market for the work beyond that of the rare book trade, (2) if a copy of the work can be obtained at a "reasonable price," or (3) the owner indicates to the library that either of the other two circumstances exists. It is suggested that the exemption for libraries and archives might be pointless in digital environments where works are always available for legitimate copy and purchase through digital copyright clearinghouses. The impact of term extension is discussed by SCHRADER (1995). Because copyright holders believe that there is always a benefit (revenue stream) in having their works protected for a longer period of time, there appears little point in having library and archive exceptions tied to commercial viability. The work would still be valuable, hence the exception would not apply. Copyright extension legislation is another example of a measure that curtails the use of copyrighted works by others, or makes that use more costly. A number of recent case developments regarding the use of copyrighted material in digital environments are discussed in the section on the loss of virtual space.

Criminal copyright infringement without financial gain. H.R. 2265, No Electronic Theft (NET) Act of 1997 (U.S. CONGRESS, 105TH, 1997g), and a similar bill, S. 1044, Criminal Copyright Improvement Act of 1997 (U.S. CONGRESS, 105TH, 1997d), would amend the copyright act by changing the elements required for criminal copyright infringement for financial gain. The new definition of financial gain is expanded to include the receipt of anything of value including copyrighted works such as software traded (uploaded and downloaded) on a BBS. This legislation, advocated by the White Paper (INFORMATION INFRA-STRUCTURE TASK FORCE, 1995), is an attempt to close the *United States v. La Macchia* loophole where copyrighted software was exchanged and traded, but not sold, on the Cynosure BBS. LOUNDY says this legislation "creates a potential chilling effect and upsets the constitutional balance provided by the Copyright Act" (p. 5). On the other hand, closing another avenue for copyright abuse may lower the transaction costs of copyright enforcement, thus reducing the cost of copyrighted works to legitimate users. The problem of controlling or recovering transaction costs in copyright enforcement is discussed by MERGES. This bill became law with the signing of Public Law 147 (U.S. CONGRESS, 105TH, 1997h).

LOSS OF FACTUAL INFORMATION SPACE

Policies, whether judicial, legislative or administrative, that curtail the public's right to use public domain material hamper the creative process. Materials such as federal government publications, facts (names and dates), basic scientific data, other uncopyrightable works, and works for which the copyright has expired are within the definition of public domain material. Generally, these works may be used without fear of legal (copyright) restriction. Attempts to remove factual and other basic data from the public domain, according to SUGARMAN & WEBB, are not only questionable from a legal perspective but also result in "bad policy." Unfortunately, recent judicial and legislative developments suggest a slow but alarming trend toward curtailing the ability to use factual information. As new technologies develop, new information product and service markets are created. Information owners and developers become more possessive of the information under their control, claiming a proprietary right not only in the marketing of the information product or service, but also in others' use of the underlying information. Use is restricted unless compensation is received.

BRANSCOMB (1994) views the struggle for control of the legal information infrastructure (the legal framework defining ownership and user rights in information-related issues) as the critical challenge of the coming millennium. Although Branscomb focuses primarily on privacy issues, she does spend considerable time discussing the owner-ship of factual information in light of intellectual property law. She agrees that developments in information products and services are making the underlying information so valuable that others attempt to control and profit from it. This underlying information is typically public domain information like facts or scientific data that are unpro-tected by copyright. Information owners are constantly searching, through the process of information policy making, to expand their control beyond the legal limits of traditional copyright into alternative areas such as contract and licensing, misappropriation, and sui generis (a specific right created by legislation). Although these new restrictions apply only to specific products or services, the overall trend is that more information is subject to an owner's control and restriction.

The United States Supreme Court decided one of the major copy-right decisions of the decade in *FEIST PUBLICATIONS, INC. V. RU-RAL TELEPHONE SERVICE CO.* The case resolved the ownership dispute between rival publishers of essentially the same telephone directory white pages. The Court held that a telephone directory could be copyrighted as a compilation if it met these criteria: original selec-tion, coordination, and arrangement. The decision is important for several reasons, including the statement that originality is a constitu-tional requirement for copyright. The court stated that facts are never copyrightable, rather the selection, coordination, or arrangement of uncopyrightable facts is protected as a compilation. In stating this, the court rejected the "sweat of the brow" doctrine created by the lower courts to reward the compilers of uncopyrightable information. An originality standard applies now to databases and other factual compi-lations, although that standard of minimum creativity is admittedly rather low. In essence, this allows extraction of unprotected facts that can be incorporated into new compilations that may also be copy-righted. As a result, the *Feist* decision opens the way for new entrants into database markets (remote, CD-ROM, or otherwise). Similar impli-cations of *Feist* are described by LEWIS and by WILLIAMSON (under-lying facts and alphabetic arrangement of names are not copyright-able), and the impact of *Feist* on subsequent database litigation is described by BURKE. Unfortunately, data compilers believe their eco-nomic interests are threatened because, under *Feist*, all of the underly-ing information could be captured, extracted, and republished or used in a new work. The underlying facts are never protected by copyright, even if the original database or compilation was created through in-tense labor or investment. This interpretation is consistent with RUBIN. Such advances for user rights are creating a reactionary climate in Congress. Pending legislation, if passed, would overturn the effect of the *Feist* decision and replace database protection under a modified misappropriation protection scheme.

Protecting Page Numbers and Other Factual Information

The West Publishing litigation. One example of the broad range of information in which entrepreneurs claim a proprietary interest is the controversy over ownership of reporter page numbers and other elements of legal case citations. For years West Publishing Company has claimed a copyright on the page numbers in legal case reporters such as the *Federal Supplement* and the *Federal Reporter*. West is also the only comprehensive publisher of these cases, a fact incorporated into standard legal citation rules. The page numbers are embedded in the case citations in a style known as star pagination. As the online database market developed in the early 1980s, a competitor, LEXIS-NEXIS, began embedding the West reporter page numbers (corresponding to the print version) in the digital version of its cases. West sued and won in *WEST PUBLISHING COMPANY V. MEAD DATA CENTRAL, INC.* Since 1988, West Publishing licenses the use of its page numbers to LEXIS-NEXIS. Unfortunately, West has refused to license its star pagination to other legal database and CD-ROM developers and has also maintained its stance on the validity of its copyright claims. As a result, the legal database market has been dominated by these two companies. In effect, West controls a monopoly over the case reports, while the text of judicial opinion is public domain (SCHEFFEY; WYMAN). The monopoly problem was exacerbated when Thomson Corporation bought West Publishing and merged to form the West Group.

Small developers of CD-ROMs and databases have recently sued West. In *OASIS PUBLISHING COMPANY, INC. V. WEST PUBLISHING COMPANY*, the West copyright claim was upheld. The parties have settled and in an agreement reached in July 1997, West now allows Oasis to use its star pagination (GATLAND). However, in other star pagination litigation, *MATTHEW BENDER & CO. AND HYPERLAW, INC. V. WEST PUBLISHING COMPANY*, the West Publishing Company copyright claim was rejected. Parts of a West reporter, including the case outline (headnotes) and syllabus, are also protected by copyright (*CALLAGHAN V. MYERS*). Recent attempts by competitors to scan those elements into competing products without permission have not met with support in the courts (*WEST PUBLISHING COMPANY V. ON POINT SOLUTIONS, INC.*).

Consent Decree and Final Judgement. The U.S. Department of Justice became involved tangentially in the dispute when its Antitrust Division reviewed the West-Thomson merger. The merger was approved and a proposed agreement, a Consent Decree, was issued (U.S. DEPARTMENT OF JUSTICE). The Consent Decree contained provisions for the compulsory licensing of West page numbers on a graduated basis that would begin with 4 cents per thousand characters of text the first year of the agreement and peak at 9 cents per thousand characters in the seventh and subsequent years. One contributor to the public comments indicated that it would cost a CD-ROM or database developer $632,000 a year just to license the full text of the *Federal Supplement* with star pagination. In March 1997, a Final Judgement was interred in the Justice Department review of the West-Thomson sale, approving the merger (*U.S. V. THOMSON CORPORATION AND WEST PUBLISHING COMPANY*). In order to prevent a monopoly in American legal publishing, the newly formed West Group was to divest itself of a number of publishing assets. More important, the licensing phase-in fee for use of West's star pagination was retained. Rates would be adjusted in accordance with changes in the Labor Producer Price Index for Finished Goods. However, West has agreed not to charge small publishers a license fee until December 31, 2003, unless, of course, the Supreme Court adjudicates the West Publishing copyright claim favorably toward West Publishing (WISE). In addition, LEXIS-NEXIS was given the option to continue the 1988 settlement-license agreement with West for another five years. The option is exercisable for up to one year. As an addendum to the Final Judgement, if the net sales of West Group do not exceed $25 million in any given year, then for that year the West Group may elect to defer the collection of the license fees until the Supreme Court adjudicates the copyright pagination claim. Any fees so deferred go into an escrow account.

Sports Scores and Misappropriation

The misappropriation doctrine arose because copyright cannot extend to underlying facts. It is traced to the *INTERNATIONAL NEWS SERVICE (INS) V. ASSOCIATED PRESS* decision. After Associated Press (AP) wire service stories were distributed for publication to various newspapers across the country, the stories were posted on bulletin boards outside AP offices for the public to read. INS, a competing firm with far less resources, regularly sent its employees to read the stories posted on the bulletin board and rewrite the information in their own words for publication in INS affiliate papers. Often the INS stories hit the presses before the AP stories. The value of the AP distributions was severely compromised. The Supreme Court held that the behavior of INS was actionable and created the tort of misappropriation. The court observed that the nature of the "news element—the information respecting current events contained in a literary production—is not the creation of the writer, but is a report of matter that ordinarily are publici juris; it is the history of the day." (p. 234). The actor in the event (the driver of a car involved in an accident or the defendant in a newsworthy crime) does not create news for copyright (as the author of a story does) simply by being involved. The court realized that although there was no violation of copyright, information was still taken, and harm resulted.

The Supreme Court in *Feist* reiterated the uncopyrightability of factual information while also discussing the INS case. However, while focusing on the relationship between the two competitors, the court ignored the effect on the consumer: the information becomes less available. This concern did not escape Justice Brandeis, who in his INS dissent warned that "the rule for which the plaintiff contends would effect an important extension of property rights and a corresponding curtailment of the free use of knowledge and of ideas" (*INTERNATIONAL NEWS SERVICE (INS) V. ASSOCIATED PRESS*, p. 263). Most recent cases of misappropriation have involved information or entertainment industries. According to KARJALA, after *Feist*, the misappropriation doctrine should be expanded to fill the void in protection for factual information *Feist* created, even though this role is admittedly "contrary to its [*Feist's*] spirit" (p. 888). That prediction, in spite of Justice Brandeis's warning, is coming to pass, at least in light of recent controversies.

The controversy in *NATIONAL BASKETBALL ASSOCIATION (NBA) V. MOTOROLA, INC. AND SPORTS TEAM ANALYSIS AND TRACKING SYSTEMS, INC.* arose because Motorola created a subscription service whereby individuals with pagers could receive real-time updates on NBA games drawn from television and radio broadcasts of games in progress. The NBA claimed that the Motorola service misappropriated the NBA's proprietary news interest in professional basketball games. In response, the defendants claimed that their actions were protected by the *Feist* decision, which holds that copyright protection is not available for facts, such as game scores or other news information.

In 1997, the Second Circuit Court of Appeals held that Motorola did not unlawfully misappropriate the NBA's property. The court limited the INS application to "hot-news" situations. The information is protected only when all of the following apply: (1) the news or information is gathered at a cost, (2) the information is time-sensitive, (3) the (mis)use of the information is viewed as free-riding on the plaintiff's efforts, (4) the plaintiff and defendant are in direct competition for similar products and services, and (5) the ability of other parties to free-ride would reduce the incentive to produce the information. This is essentially a cost-benefit analysis. It encourages factual news information to be collected and disseminated (albeit at a cost to consumers and profit to producers). This in turn produces a social benefit, which is worth the cost of granting economic property rights in the information to the producers.

The NBA game score litigation provides another example of a new technology (pocket pagers) creating new market space, space over which the originator of the information, the NBA in this case, attempts to exert ownership rights. The case exemplifies how the control of factual event data (e.g., game scores) is being expanded through the use of legal doctrines beyond that of traditional copyright. The problem has since subsided as the NBA now posts game updates on its own Web page, Gamestats. If Motorola were to collect its information from Gamestats and use it on a competing Web site, it would likely be free-riding under the Second Circuit Court ruling.

The NBA cases demonstrate the issue under discussion: whether information that is created because of an action or activity or merely discovered should be given property attributes and held by the actor or discoverer with attendant proprietary rights. In these cases, the extension of the misappropriation doctrine provides a monopoly over factual information (SHURE). Unfortunately, lawsuits of this nature are likely to increase as commercialization forces proprietors or would-be proprietors of information to seek new ways to exploit and control information.

Contract and License Restrictions
on the Use of Factual Information

The case of *PROCD, INC. V. ZEIDENBERG* is another example of information entrepreneurs who seek other legal mechanisms to protect their interests when copyright protections are not available. ProCD sold a CD-ROM containing national business and residential telephone listings. The defendant, Zeidenberg, purchased a copy of the CD-ROM and, in keeping with the law expressed in *Feist*, extracted the unprotected names and addresses, created his own search software, and loaded the contents onto the Internet.

The district court viewed the legal basis of that conflict to be that of copyright and, relying on *Feist* (uncopyrightability of facts; underlying information in a database is unprotected), ruled in favor of Zeidenberg. However, ProCD based its claim on a contract. When Zeidenberg accessed the data (names, telephone numbers, and addresses), he "clicked" his affirmation on several user screens. These assents represent his willingness to be bound by the terms of a contract similar to those in a software license agreement. On appeal, the Seventh Circuit Court rejected every point of the district court opinion. The Seventh Circuit Court decision explicitly permits a publisher to employ a private contract to protect uncopyrightable information that would otherwise be available for reuse or republishing under fair use or other provisions of the copyright law. In the words of Judge Easterbrook: "Copyright is a right against the world. Contracts, by contrast, generally affect only their parties; strangers may do as they please, so contracts do not create 'exclusive rights'" (p. 1454). Thus the court validated both the use of shrink-wrap licenses (activated by opening the package) to protect software and the use of web-wrap or click-on licenses for Web-based materials. Unlike earlier cases cited by the ProCD court, the shrink-wrap license was upheld because "Zeidenberg inspected the package, tried out the software, learned of the license, and did not reject the goods" (p. 1452).

The most important point made by Judge Easterbrook is that users can bargain away their copyright fair use or other privileges if they choose to do so. The implications are both enormous and dangerous. One can foresee a future where books and other material would be shrink-wrapped, with warnings and contract provisions restricting use beyond that of traditional readership or copyright. These possibilities are stated by ELKIN-KOREN and by TALBOTT. The *ProCD* scenario offers two models of policy attitudes toward factual information: a freedom-of-contract noncopyright model (i.e., parties may freely contract away their fair use rights; contract law supersedes copyright) versus a public domain copyright model (i.e., copyright law overrides any private agreement such as a contract). The public domain copyright model is criticized by O'ROURKE. Others, such as SAMUELSON (1995) and SIMMONS, caution that copyright could become obsolete or least mostly replaced or supplemented by other legal doctrines such as contract. Because software and other information products are being sold by license, purchasers have one of two options: either agree to the terms of the license or forgo purchase. There is a danger if such transfer mechanisms are applied to basic information products and services such as books or CD-ROMs. The implications of mass-market licenses are also criticized by MCMANIS.

Creating Ownership Rights in Factual Databases

The *Feist* case continues to generate controversy; it is not surprising that legislation has been introduced to extend protection to the underlying information of some databases that *Feist* sought to remove and place in the public domain. The impact of *Feist* is unclear in the legal literature (STRONG; *UNIVERSITY OF DAYTON LAW REVIEW*). Two competing approaches to database protection are developing, as outlined in the 1997 U.S. COPYRIGHT OFFICE *Report on Legal Protection for Databases*. One is a sui generis approach, creating special protections for databases, and the other finds new legal recourse for database protection in existing doctrines such as misappropriation (BAND & KENNEDY).

H.R. 3531, Database Investment and Intellectual Property Antipiracy Act of 1996. H.R. 3531 (U.S. CONGRESS, 104TH, 1996a) is an example of a sui generis approach and is in direct opposition to the law established in *Feist*. H.R. 3531 rewards database compilers for their efforts in collecting otherwise unprotected (read uncopyrightable) information. The bill creates a new form of protection for databases. Use or extraction of all or a substantial part of a protected database is prohibited. The prohibited use can be either qualitative or quantitative. The period of protection is 25 years from January 1 following the date on which the database is first made available to the public. Use of an insubstantial part is permitted, as is the independent collection, assembling, or compilation of the information from sources other than the protected databases. An insubstantial part is defined as a use that does not diminish the value of the database, conflict with normal exploitation of the database, or adversely affect the market (real or potential) for the database.

Although H.R. 3531 died in the 104th Congress, it is a sui generis approach that exemplifies legislation promoted by certain entities to protect their proprietary interests. The sui generis approach is reviewed favorably by AUSTIN, who offers several refinements to H.R. 3531 for introduction in the 105th Congress. The refinements include narrowing the definition of database, which would protect only databases subject to free-riding (taking content for use in a competing product). Austin would also reduce the 25-year term to only 4 years. This would allow for a reward for the original database compiler, but not monopolize use of the information for an extended period of time. He would also incorporate some type of compulsory licensing scheme for use of the underlying information. As DEUTSCH notes, this would give economic rights and incentives to producers who make substantial investments in creating databases.

H.R. 2652, Collections of Information Antipiracy Act of 1997. H.R. 2652 (U.S. CONGRESS, 105TH, 1997a) is an example of expanding existing protection schemes to new products such as databases. The bill takes a misappropriation approach to protecting information and closes the copyright loophole opened by *Feist*. It rewards the efforts of the original compiler, but only when others are profiting from it. MAYBERRY states that it will strangle academic and scientific research permanently by removing most collections of information from the public domain. The NBA hot-news exception is recognized. One goal of legislation is to protect the financial investment of database compilers from free riders, who expend little effort to collect or discover the data but later extract the data into a new and competing product. H.R. 2652 adopts a misappropriation standard and prohibits the extraction or use in commerce of all or a substantial part of the database, when the database (or other collection of information) was compiled at "investment of substantial monetary or other resources." There must also be market harm; for example, insubstantial uses are allowed, as are nonprofit uses that do not harm the actual or potential market for the product. Privatization of government information is prohibited. This bill uses the Second Circuit Court's analysis in the NBA litigation as a model for weighing the costs and benefits of fact data protection.

The misappropriation aspect of H.R. 2652 (the bill uses the word "misappropriation" but in essence offers the same protections as H.R. 3531) and the sui generis protection of H.R. 3531 are two alternatives for protecting factual works. Another approach is to adopt some type of compulsory license fee, as advocated by the Justice Department in the West page number controversy discussed earlier. The licensing scheme is also advocated by GINSBURG, who says the license should depend not on the information itself, but on how the information is used (as with existing music licensing under BMI or ASCAP). LEMLEY states that licensing in the NII environment would work only to the disadvantage of users and the public. The trend toward protectionism, according to GORDON, discourages more creativity than it induces; Gordon would base recovery on a restitution theory (replacement or recovery for a loss suffered, i.e., lost sales) that assesses the value of any unjust enrichment. R.A. EPSTEIN supports protections only for information limited in value by its immediacy, the so-called hot-news exception. DODD would apply a conversion theory (wrongful possession of author's property, i.e., the database information itself) to unfair taking of ideas or other intangible assets. Dodd also sees intellectual property laws as inadequate and in need of reform. AUSTIN says that benefit to the public for access to factual information in databases outweighs the loss of some factual information that would result from increased ownership protection when owners and authors lack adequate incentives to collect, compile, and market the information.

One bright spot is the introduction of H.R. 3048, the Digital Era Copyright Enhancement Act of 1997 (U.S. CONGRESS, 105TH, 1997f), which would override the *ProCD* decision and cases like it that attempt to limit access to and use of information through legal mechanisms beyond those of copyright (LOUNDY; PALENSKI). H.R. 3048 prohibits contracts or other legal mechanisms designed to limit the use of uncopyrightable material such as the telephone numbers in *ProCD*. Section 7 of H.R. 3048 voids contract provisions that limit the reproduction, adaptation, distribution, performance, or display of uncopyrightable material or that abrogate or restrict the limitations on exclusive rights contained in the copyright laws (fair use, software loaning, the first-sale doctrine, and the library and archive reproduction exceptions).

There was no action involving H.R. 3048 in the second term of the 105th Congress. However, H.R. 2652 was passed by the House in May 1998 and a version was introduced in the Senate in 1998 as S. 2291 (U.S. CONGRESS, 105TH, 1998a) and did not pass.

THE LOSS OF VIRTUAL SPACE

Beyond copyright, other developments can be characterized as threatening the loss of virtual space. One issue involves linking (connecting one Web site to another) and framing (importing part of one Web site into another). In recent linking and framing litigation, courts are under pressure to use existing legal concepts to interpret new technological situations. Linking often results in a loss of movement between Web sites, the virtual space. Another issue is online defamation litigation, in which early court cases prompted congressional action that may make it more likely for individuals to be sued for posting or sending defamatory materials online. The fear of lawsuit could result in some loss of virtual information (free speech) rights.

Linking and Framing on the Web

Linking involves moving a user to a new Web site; most problems arise when the home or first page is skipped. Some Web site owners take the position that their property rights are violated when another site moves (links) a visitor to their site without permission. Linking does not typically involve copyright issues, but other property issues such as trespass, possible unfair trade practices, or trademark dilution. In framing, the viewer never leaves the original site. The importation of portions of other sites without permission is more easily seen as taking or copying and may involve copyright or misappropriation.

The legal and policy problems of these acts are reviewed in the legal literature by practitioners including GAHTAN, HARTNICK (1997a, 1997b), and MAIZENBERG. JACKSON reviews direct, contributory, and vicarious or strict copyright liability alternatives and concludes that linking only fits the contributory infringement model. The direct link is akin to dialing a phone number to reach a voice mailbox or an answering machine with a copyrighted message of the day. Linking should not be copyright infringement, according to ROSENOER, because there is "no copyrightable expression in a hypertext link" (p. 10) nor should simply viewing the site be an infringement. STUCKEY says framers may be liable for copyright infringement because the framed site (either a collection of framed sites or the incorporation of framed sites) may constitute a derivative work for which permission is required from the original site owner. SMITH indicates that liability for framing is less clear. The owner of a Web site with links to other sites possesses a protectable interest analogous to the publisher of the telephone directory. Jackson sees in this analogy possible liability for framing, because then it is as if the new Web site captures (copies) not only the raw unprotected factual information but also its selection, coordination, and arrangement (the requirements for copyright in a factual compilation, i.e., a database).

TICKETMASTER CORP. V. MICROSOFT CORP. The questions involving linking were raised in the *Ticketmaster* litigation. Ticketmaster sued Microsoft because Microsoft linked to an internal page on the Ticketmaster site. The internal link bypassed introductory pages of the Ticketmaster site that contained paid advertising and took users directly to the ordering information area. Microsoft lost the case and discontinued its internal linking on July 9, 1997.

One analogy used in linking cases to illustrate the property rights issue is residential: instead of knocking on the front door or gate (the home page or first page of the site), a visitor moves immediately into the house or yard. The linked site claims that a trespass has been committed. A counterargument is that the door or gate is left open or unlocked, inviting unannounced guests. This interpretation is more consistent with the nature and purpose of Web sites, especially sites that do not charge users to move beyond the first page. Usually the ownership claim is economic: Web site owners want to sell advertising space and expect users to see it. There is also a loss of integrity in nonadvertising content when initial pages are skipped. Another successful trespass claim, involving unwanted electronic junk mail or advertising posted to email accounts, was *EARTHLINK NETWORK V. CYBER PROMOTIONS, INC.* M.N. EPSTEIN predicts more such cases, as it is far from clear whether the controlling law is trespass, copyright, or something else.

WASHINGTON POST V. TOTALNEWS, INC. The practice of framing was raised when TotalNews, rather than collect the news on its own, appropriated information from the *Washington Post* Web site. The *Washington Post* claimed copyright infringement of its creative text, misappropriation of factual information, and trademark infringement of certain *Washington Post* features incorporated into the TotalNews site. In June 1997 the dispute was settled. Similar cases have occurred in other countries, such as *SHETLAND TIMES LTD. V. DR. JONATHAN WILLS AND ZETNEWS LTD.* in Scotland, and have also been settled.

The importation to the second site of the framed material is akin to the original INS misappropriations, according to RAYSMAN & BROWN (1997). M.N. EPSTEIN notes that the problem is exacerbated if the site is accessed as a paid subscription. FREELING & LEVI suggest that a possible loss of revenue from advertising or user fees may be the determining factor in a judicial analysis. KUESTER & NIEVES argue that a First Amendment right to free speech might supersede any rights of economic return. In *ACLU V. MILLER*, the court found unconstitutional a statute that made it a crime to transmit a trade name, mark, logo, seal, or symbol that would falsely state or imply that a person had permission to do so. The statute applied to electronic mailboxes, home pages, and other electronic storage banks or points of access. As of this writing, no pending legislation directly addresses the problems of Web site linking and framing. In other words, a judicial standard is not likely to be set in the near future.

Defamation and the Impact of Cybertorts

Cybertort is the label given to the genus of cases involving defamation in online settings. Typically, cases arise where one party has posted a defamatory and injurious message about another party on a bulletin board system (BBS). The policy issue here, as in the OSP copyright cases, is who should be legally responsible, the individual who posted the message or the entity that controls its appearance on the BBS. Identifying the responsible party may relate less to potential harm from the defamation and more to who is best able to absorb the cost of the injury, or in the alternative, who is in the best position to monitor postings for defamatory content. As in the copyright arena, OSPs have argued that they should not be viewed as Internet police simply because the technology exists for them to do so. Policy development has progressed much further in defamation than in copyright. DECARLO, for example, says traditional defamation law should be modified for the online environment. OSPs and BBS operators should be held responsible only if they are able to identify the defamer or original poster, remove the message, and offer a right of reply. DeCarlo argues that this will keep abusive language to a minimum without discouraging the free exchange and debate that have become the hallmark of the Internet.

Shifting responsibility away from OSPs may nevertheless alter communication among individuals. First, as one avenue of recovery—the OSP—is closed to defamed plaintiffs, they will be forced to seek compensation from the individuals who defamed them. The threat of litigation may make individuals less likely to speak. Second, if OSP immunity is tied to identifying the defamer, then issues of subscriber privacy arise (these issues are important but beyond the scope of this review). An early proponent of protection for the individual is WEBER, who identifies the danger of increased individual litigation if immunity is granted to OSPs. Weber says that a right to reply to any defamatory statement should be offered by the OSP in return for immunity. He places great faith in the power of the online BBS to reach, and thereby correct, any harm. He argues that it would be poor policy to adopt a low-fault or no-fault standard. Making OSPs liable simply because they are in a position to police their BBSs is not a rationale. Finally, Weber says that holding OSPs responsible for the messages posted on their BBSs will have a discouraging effect on online speech because the OSPs will be unwilling to let certain controversial BBSs operate or Web sites exist.

Cybertort litigation. Two early cases that later prompted Congressional response were *CUBBY, INC. V. COMPUSERVE, INC.* and *STRATTON OAKMONT, INC. V. PRODIGY SERVICES CO.* In *Cubby,* the OSP was found not liable for a defamatory message because the court determined Cubby served more as a conduit (like a newsstand, bookstore, or library) than as a content provider (like a newspaper, book editor, or publisher). Stratton Oakmont, however, was found liable because evidence offered at trial suggested that it acted more like a newspaper publisher by providing some editorial functions, such as the use of screening software, and by representing itself as a "family network." Other courts have reached opposite results in deciding whether a BBS is more like a newspaper or more like a newsstand. In *STERN V. DELPHI INTERNET SERVICES CORP.*, a New York State court held that a BBS that posted an image of radio personality Howard Stern was in fact a "news disseminator" (conduit) for purposes of an exception to state misappropriation law and thus was not liable for its posting. Under New York misappropriation law, a news disseminator is insulated from liability if the person whose image is appropriated is newsworthy. Howard Stern at the time had announced his candidacy for governor and the BBS was established to debate his suitability for the state's highest office. In *IT'S IN THE CARDS V. FUSCHETTO*, a Wisconsin State Court of Appeals held that a BBS was not a periodical for purposes of the Wisconsin defamation statute. Wisconsin law requires a retraction request preceding any filing of a lawsuit if the defamation appeared in a "periodical." *It's in the Cards* raised this lack of retraction request as a defense. The Wisconsin Court of Appeals determined that a BBS was not a periodical for purposes of the statute and therefore that restriction was not necessary and the suit could proceed.

Good Samaritan provisions and OSP immunity. Congress was not impressed with how the courts were developing the law of online defamation. In response, it added a "good Samaritan" provision, section 230, to the Telecommunications Act of 1996 (U.S. CONGRESS, 104TH, 1996c), which exempts from civil liability any provider of an interactive computer service that made a good-faith effort to block objectionable material. The good Samaritan provision is intended to protect providers who employ blocking or screening software to protect children from harmful (obscene or indecent) materials. The Conference Report specifically states that "one of the specific purposes of this section is to overrule *Stratton-Oakmont v. Prodigy* and any other similar decisions which have treated such providers and users as publishers or speakers of content" (U.S. CONGRESS, 104TH, 1996b, p. 194). More important, since its passage, two courts have referred to section 230 when analyzing the claims against America Online, Inc. In *ZERAN V. AMERICA ONLINE, INC.*, a federal district court found that section 230 insulated the OSP against liability. In *DOE V. AMERICA ONLINE, INC.*, a Florida State court also concluded that section 230 protects an OSP from any liability.

OSPs are sued when one or two circumstances exist. Either the identity of the individual poster of the message is not known, so suit against an individual is precluded, or the possibility of a rich recovery makes suing a "deep pocket" more attractive (KURZ). Under section 230, the only party able to be sued in an online defamation case is the individual poster of the message, not the BBS operator or OSP. The practical result is likely to discourage free expression of personal opinions on the Internet.

CONCLUSION

As technology opens new markets for information products and services, the opportunities to own and control the underlying information will increase. Intellectual property law and other laws exist to encourage and reward investments in information. It is also the public policy of this country to reserve a public information space. The delicate balance between control and access is in flux. This chapter reviews creative, factual, and virtual aspects of this public information space that are currently under attack as information entrepreneurs attempt to expand their control and ownership rights. As ownership and use disputes filter through the courts, some resolution is obtained. In addition, Congress, urged by Clinton administration initiatives and judicial developments, is also defining the limits of public information space. If these trends continue, the result may be increased market space (more information products and services available, but at cost) and a loss of public information space. It is hoped that this chapter serves to outline the areas of conflict and present a variety of positions, viewpoints, and alternatives.

BIBLIOGRAPHY[1]

ACLU V. MILLER. 1997. 977 F. Supp. 1228 (N.D. Ga. 1997) (Northern District of Georgia).
AUSTIN, WESLEY L. 1997. A Thoughtful and Practical Analysis of Database Protection under Copyright Law, and a Critique of Sui Generis Protection. Law-Technology. 1997; 30(2): 1-36. ISSN: 0278-3916; OCLC: 07231557.

---

[1]Note: case citations are to standard legal reporters. U.S. (United States Reports), F. 2d and F. 3d (Federal Reporter Second and Third), F. supp. (Federal Supplement), Wis. 2d (Wisconsin Reports, Second), N.W. 2d (Northwestern Reporter, Second).

BAND, JONATHAN; KENNEDY, JOHN. 1998. Battle Lines Form Over WIPO Copyright Bills. National Law Journal. 1998 January 26; 20(22): C5, C7. ISSN: 0162-7325; OCLC: 04161259.

BEAL, KARA. 1998. The Potential Liability of Linking on the Internet: An Examination of Possible Legal Solutions. Brigham Young University Law Review. 1998 Spring; (2): 703-739. ISSN: 0360-151X; OCLC: 02243706.

BRANSCOMB, ANNE WELLS. 1994. Who Owns Information: From Privacy to Public Access. New York, NY: Basic Books, Inc.; 1994. 241p. ISBN: 0-465-09175-X, (cloth); 0-465-09144-X (paper).

BRANSCOMB, ANNE WELLS. 1995. Lessons from the Past: Legal and Medical Databases. Jurimetrics Journal of Law, Science and Technology. 1995 Summer; 35(4): 417-448. ISSN: 0022-6793; OCLC: 12395021.

BURGER, ROBERT H. 1993. Information Policy: A Framework for Evaluation and Policy Research. Norwood, NJ: Ablex Publishing Corp.; 1993. 193p. ISBN: 0-89391-890-3 (cloth); 1-56750-018-8 (paper).

BURKE, EDMUND B. 1995. Database Copyrights. EDUCOM Review. 1995; 30(2): 56-57. ISSN: 1045-9154; OCLC: 11314334.

CALLAGHAN V. MYERS. 1888. 123 U.S. 617(1888).

CAMPBELL V. ACUFF-ROSE MUSIC, INC. 1994. 510 U.S. 510 (1994).

CASTAGNOLI, CHARISSE. 1996. Evaluating Existing and Implied Licenses for On-Line Distribution Rights. The Acquisitions Librarian. 1996; 15: 111-121. ISSN: 0896-3576; OCLC: 17009807. Reprinted in: Strauch, A. Bruce, ed. Current Legal Issues in Publishing. New York, NY: Haworth Press; 1996. 111-121. ISBN: 1-56024-804-1.

CATE, FRED H.; HAMMOND, ALLEN S.; MCCONNELL, BRUCE W.; NELSON, MICHAEL; OBUCHOWSKI, JANICE; ROTENBERG, MARC. 1995. Information Policy Making. Federal Communications Law Journal. 1995; 48(1): 57-92. (Panel discussion). ISSN: 0163-7606; OCLC: 04099879.

CENDALI, DALE M.; REYES, RAMON E., JR. 1997. Freelancers Reeling in Fight Over Online Rights: Unless Congress Takes Action, Authors May Be Denied Pay for Electronic Publishing Rights. National Law Journal. 1997 October 20; 20(8): C2-C3. ISSN: 0162-7325; OCLC: 04161259.

CENTRAL POINT SOFTWARE, INC. V. NUGENT. 1995. 903 F. Supp. 1057 (E.D. Tex. 1995) (Eastern District of Texas).

COPYRIGHT LAW JOURNAL, THE. 1994. Recent Cases and Developments. The Copyright Law Journal: An Analysis of Current Cases and Developments Affecting Intellectual Property Rights. 1994; 3(5): 57-58. ISSN: 0884-4437; OCLC: 10898636.

COX, JOHN. 1996. Copyright Economic Rights and Moral Rights. The Acquisitions Librarian. 1996; 15: 123-128. ISSN: 0896-3576; OCLC: 17009807. Reprinted in: Strauch, A. Bruce, ed. Current Legal Issues in Publishing. New York, NY: Haworth Press; 1996. 123-128. ISBN: 1-56024-804-1.

CREWS, KENNETH D. 1995. Copyright Law and Information Policy Planning: Public Rights of Use in the 1990s and Beyond. Journal of Government Information. 1995; 22(2): 87-99. ISSN: 1352-0237; OCLC: 29785232.

CUBBY, INC. V. COMPUSERVE, INC. 1991. 776 F. Supp. 135 (S.D.N.Y. 1991) (Southern District of New York).

DECARLO, KEAN J. 1997. Tilting at Windmills: Defamation and the Private Person in Cyberspace. Georgia State University Law Review. 1997; 13(2): 547-580. ISSN: 8755-6847; OCLC: 11383007.

DEUTSCH, ANDREW L. 1997. Congress to Consider Data Base Bill. National Law Journal. 1997 October 20; 20(8): C3-C5. ISSN: 0162-7325.

DOBBINS, M. DAVID. 1995. Computer Bulletin Board Operator Liability for Users' Infringing Acts. Michigan Law Review. 1995; 94(1): 217-241. ISSN: 0026-2234; OCLC: 01757366.

DODD, JEFF C. 1995. Rights in Information: Conversion and Misappropriation Causes of Action in Intellectual Property Cases. Houston Law Review. 1995; 32(2): 459-499. ISSN: 0018-8694; OCLC: 01752338.

DOE V. AMERICA ONLINE, INC. 1997. CL 97-631AE (Fla. Cir. Ct. Palm Beach Co. June 26, 1997) (Florida Circuit Court of Palm Beach).

EARTHLINK NETWORK V. CYBER PROMOTIONS, INC. 1997. BC 167502 (Los Angeles County Super. Ct.) (Los Angeles County Superior Court.) (Consent decree entered April 18, 1998).

ELKIN-KOREN, NIVA. 1997. Copyright Policy and the Limits of Freedom of Contract. Berkeley Technology Law Journal. 1997; 12(1): 93-113. ISSN: 1086-3818; OCLC: 33930600.

EPSTEIN, MARK N. 1997. Hotlinking & Framing Pitfalls. Intellectual Property Today. 1997 December 28. Available in LEXIS-NEXIS, LEGNEW Library.

EPSTEIN, RICHARD A. 1992. International News Service v. Associated Press: Custom and Law as Sources of Property Rights in News. Virginia Law Review. 1992; 78(1): 84-128. ISSN: 0042-6601; OCLC: 00826179.

FEIST PUBLICATIONS, INC. V. RURAL TELEPHONE SERVICE CO. 1991. 449 U.S. 340 (1991).

FENSTER, JULIE R. 1996. Fault-Based Libel and Copyright Infringement Liability for On-Line Content Providers and Bulletin Board Operators as "Information Distributors." St. John's Journal of Legal Commentary. 1996 Summer; 11(3): 654-657. ISSN: 1049-0299; OCLC: 13432620.

FLEISCHMANN, ERIC. 1988. The Impact of Digital Technology on Copyright Law. New England Law Review. 1988; 23(Summer): 45-65. ISSN: 0028-4823; OCLC: 01759770.

FOGERTY V. FANTASY, INC. 1994. 510 U.S. 517 (1994).

FONAVISA V. CHERRY AUCTION. 1996. 76 F. 3d 259 (9th Cir. 1996) (Ninth Circuit).

FRANK MUSIC CORP. V. COMPUSERVE, INC. 1995. 93 Civ. 8153 (S.D.N.Y. 1996) (Southern District of New York) (settled November 7, 1995).

FREELING, KENNETH; LEVI, JOSEPH E. 1997. Frame Liability Clouds the Internet's Future: Lawsuit Protests Web Programming Trick. New York Law Journal. 1997 May 19; 217(95): S5. ISSN: 0028-7326; OCLC: 02255104.

GAHTAN, ALAN. 1997. Inappropriate Use of Frames May Constitute Infringement. Cyberspace Lawyer. 1997; 2(2): 2-4. ISSN: 1088-0593.

GATLAND, LAURA. 1997. Status Report: West Settles Copyright Suit. ABA Journal. 1997 October; 83: 37. ISSN: 0747-0088.

GINSBURG, JANE C. 1991. Creation and Commercial Value: Copyright Protections of Works of Information in the United States. In: Dommering,

Egbert J.; Hugenholtz, P. Bernt, eds. Protecting Works of Fact: Copyright, Freedom of Expression and Information Law. Boston, MA: Kluwer Law and Taxation Publishers; 1991. 41-58. ISBN: 90-654-4567-6. Earlier version appeared as Creation and Commercial Value: Copyright Protection of Works of Information. Columbia Law Review. 1990; 90(7): 1865-1938. ISSN: 0010-1958; OCLC: 01564231.

GOLDSTEIN, PAUL. 1989. Copyright Law and Policy. In: Newberg, Paula R., ed. New Directions in Telecommunications Policy. Durham, NC: Duke University Press; 1989. 70-100. ISBN: 0-8223-0916-5.

GOODIN, DAN. 1996. Scientology Case Helps Define On-Line Liability. The Recorder. 1996 August 26: 1. Avail. in LEXIS-NEXIS, LEGNEW Library.

GORDON, WENDY JANE. 1992. On Owning Information: Intellectual Property and the Restitutionary Impulse. Virginia Law Review. 1992; 78(1): 149-281. ISSN: 0042-6601; OCLC: 00826179.

GROSSO, ANDREW. 1994. The National Information Infrastructure: Implications of the Information Superhighway for Commerce, Security, and Law Enforcement. Federal Bar News and Journal. 1994; 41(7): 481-488. ISSN: 0279-4691; OCLC: 07905080.

HARTNICK, ALAN J. 1997a. "Framing": Internet Equivalent of Pirating? New York Law Journal. 1997 April 4; 217(64): 5. ISSN: 0028-7326.

HARTNICK, ALAN J. 1997b. "Framing": Internet Equivalent of Pirating? (part 2). New York Law Journal. 1997 April 11; 217: 5. ISSN: 0028-7326.

HAYES, DAVID L. 1998. Application of Copyright Rights to Specific Acts on the Internet. The Computer Lawyer. 1998 August; 15(8): 1-23. ISSN: 0742-1192.

INFORMATION INFRASTRUCTURE TASK FORCE (IITF). 1993. The National Information Infrastructure: Agenda for Action. Washington, DC: National Telecommunications and Information Administration; 1993. 26p. NTIS: PB 93-231272.

INFORMATION INFRASTRUCTURE TASK FORCE (IITF). 1994. Intellectual Property and the National Information Infrastructure: A Preliminary Draft of the Report of the Working Group on Intellectual Property Rights (Green Paper). Washington, DC: Government Printing Office; 1994 July. 141p. OCLC: 31154413.

INFORMATION INFRASTRUCTURE TASK FORCE (IITF). 1995. Intellectual Property and the National Information Infrastructure: The Report of the Working Group on Intellectual Property Rights (White Paper). Washington, DC: Government Printing Office; 1995 September. 239p. OCLC: 33320572.

INTERNATIONAL NEWS SERVICE (INS) V. ASSOCIATED PRESS. 1918. 248 U.S. 215 (1918).

IT'S IN THE CARDS V. FUSCHETTO. 1995. 193 Wis. 2d 429, 535 N.W. 2d 11 (Ct. App. 1995) (Wisconsin Court of Appeals).

JACKSON, MATT. 1997. Linking Copyright to Homepages. Federal Communications Law Journal. 1997; 49(3): 731-759. ISSN: 0014-9055.

JOHNSON, DAVID R.; POST, DAVID G. 1997. The Rise of Law on the Global Network. In: Kahin, Brian; Nesson, Charles, eds. Borders in Cyberspace: Information Policy and the Global Information Infrastructure. Cambridge,

MA: MIT Press; 1997. 3-47. ISBN: 0-262-61126-0 (paper); 0-262-11220-5 (cloth).

KALIL, THOMAS. 1995. Public Policy and the National Information Infrastructure. Business Economics. 1995; 30(October): 15-20. ISSN: 0007-666X; OCLC: 01537881.

KAMARCK, MITCHELL D. 1996. Understanding Copyright Liability in Cyberspace: A Primer. Cyberspace Lawyer. 1996; 1(9): 2-4. ISSN: 1088-0593; OCLC: 34505029.

KARJALA, DENNIS S. 1992. Copyright and Misappropriation. University of Dayton Law Review. 1992 Spring; 17(3): 835-928. ISSN: 0162-9174.

KARNOW, CURTIS E.A. 1997. Future Codes: Essays in Advanced Computer Technology and the Law. Boston, MA: Artech House; 1997. 276p. ISBN: 0-89006-942-5.

KIRKWOOD, R. CARTER. 1997. When Should Computer Owners Be Liable for Copyright Infringement by Users? University of Chicago Law Review. 1997; 64(2): 709-735. ISSN: 0041-9494; OCLC: 02123921.

KUESTER, JEFFREY R.; NIEVES, PETER A. 1998. Hyperlinks: A Form of Protected Expression? National Law Journal. 1998 January 26; 20(22): C10-C12. ISSN: 0162-7325; OCLC: 04161259.

KURZ, RAYMOND A. 1996. Internet and the Law: Legal Fundamentals for the Internet User. Rockville, MD: Government Institutes; 1996. 247p. ISBN: 0-86587-506-5.

LASTER, DANIEL. 1997. Copyright, Trademark, and Database Issues. In: Lee, Lewis C.; Davidson, J. Scott, eds. Intellectual Property for the Internet. New York, NY: John Wiley & Sons, Inc.; 1997. 131-149. ISBN: 0-471-16703-7.

LEMLEY, MARK A. 1995. Shrink Wraps in Cyberspace. Jurimetrics Journal of Law, Science and Technology. 1995; 35(3): 311-323. ISSN: 0022-6793.

LENZINI, REBECCA T.; SHAW, WARD. 1996. Facilitating Copyrights: The Role of the Middleman. The Acquisitions Librarian. 1996; 15: 129-133. ISSN: 0896-3576; OCLC: 17009807. Reprinted in: Strauch, A. Bruce, ed. Current Legal Issues in Publishing. New York, NY: Haworth Press; 1996. 129-133. ISBN: 1-56024-804-1.

LEWIS, GERARD J., JR. 1992. Copyright Protection for Purely Factual Compilations under Feist Publications, Inc. v. Rural Telephone Service Co.: How Does Feist Protect Electronic Data Bases of Facts? Santa Clara Computer and High-Technology Law Journal. 1992; 8(1): 169-207. ISSN: 0082-3383; OCLC: 11765510.

LITMAN, JESSICA. 1989. Copyright Legislation and Technological Change. Oregon Law Review. 1989; 68(2): 275-361. ISSN: 0196-2043.

LITMAN, JESSICA. 1995. The Exclusive Right to Read. Cardozo Arts and Entertainment Law Journal. 1995; 13: 29-54. ISSN: 0736-7694.

LOUNDY, DAVID J. 1998. The Good, Bad, Ugly of Copyright Law Rewrites. Chicago Daily Law Bulletin. 1998 January 8; 144(5): 5. ISSN: 0362-6148.

MAIZENBERG, DAVID. 1997. Disclaimers and Hyperlinks. Cyberspace Lawyer. 1997; 2(1): 10-11. ISSN: 1088-0593; OCLC: 34505029.

MARKE, JULIUS J. 1997. Database Protection Acts and the 105th Congress. New York Law Journal. 1997 March 18; 217(5): 5. ISSN: 0028-7326.

MATTHEW BENDER & CO. AND HYPERLAW, INC. V. WEST PUBLISHING COMPANY. 1997. 1997 U.S. Dist. LEXIS 6915 (S.D.N.Y. 1997) (Southern District of New York).

MAYBERRY, JODINE. 1998. Copyrights: Database Protection Legislation. Computer Law & Online Industry Litigation Reporter. 1998 January 6; 15(7): 7. Available in the LEXIS-NEXIS LEGNEW Library.

MCMANIS, CHARLES R. 1997. Do Not Support "Privatizing" of Copyright Law. National Law Journal. 1997 October 13; 20(7): A24. ISSN: 0162-7325.

MERGES, ROBERT P. 1997. The End of Friction? Property Rights and Contract in the "Newtonian" World of Online Commerce. Berkeley Technology Law Journal. 1997; 12(1): 115-136. ISSN: 1086-3818; OCLC: 33930600.

MILLS, MARY L. 1989. New Technology and the Limitations of Copyright Law: An Argument for Finding Alternatives to Copyright Legislation in an Era of Rapid Technological Change. Chicago-Kent Law Review. 1989; 65(1): 307-339. ISSN: 0009-3599; OCLC: 01554167.

MORRIL, MARK C.; EATON, SARAH E. 1996. Protecting Copyrights On-Line: Copyright Liability for On-Line Service Providers. Journal of Proprietary Rights. 1996; 8(4): 2-6. ISSN: 1041-3952; OCLC: 18757754.

NATIONAL BASKETBALL ASSOCIATION (NBA) V. MOTOROLA, INC. AND SPORTS TEAM ANALYSIS AND TRACKING SYSTEMS, INC. 1996. 931 F. Supp. 1124 (S.D.N.Y. 1996) (Southern District of New York), 939 F. Supp. 1071 (S.D.N.Y. 1996); rev'd 105 F. 3d 841 (2nd Cir. 1997) (Second Circuit).

O'ROURKE, MAUREEN A. 1997. Copyright Preemption after the ProCD Case: A Market-Based Approach. Berkeley Technology Law Journal. 1997; 12(1): 53-91. ISSN: 1086-3818; OCLC: 33930600.

OASIS PUBLISHING COMPANY, INC. V. WEST PUBLISHING COMPANY. 1996. 924 F. Supp. 918 (D. Minn. 1996) (Minnesota District); No. 96-2887 (8th Cir. 1996) (Eighth Circuit) (settled 7/24/97).

PALENSKI, RONALD J. 1998. Tech-Related Bills Pile Up in Congress. National Law Journal. 1998 February 2; 20(23): C1, C14. ISSN: 0162-7325.

PLAYBOY ENTERPRISES V. FRENA. 1993. 839 F. Supp. 1552 (M.D. Fla. 1993) (Middle District of Florida).

PROCD, INC. V. ZEIDENBERG. 1996. 86 F. 3d 1447 (7th Cir. 1996) (Seventh Circuit).

RAYSMAN, RICHARD; BROWN, PETER. 1996. Internet Copyright Developments. New York Law Journal. 1996 January 9; 215(6): 1. ISSN: 0028-7326.

RAYSMAN, RICHARD; BROWN, PETER. 1997. Dangerous Liaisons: The Legal Risks of Linking Web Sites. New York Law Journal. 1997 April 8; 217(66): 3. ISSN: 0028-7326; OCLC: 02255104.

RELIGIOUS TECHNOLOGY CENTER V. LERMA. 1996. 1996 U.S. Dist. LEXIS 15454 (E.D. Va. 1996) (Eastern District of Virginia).

RELIGIOUS TECHNOLOGY CENTER V. NETCOM ON-LINE COMMUNICATIONS SERVICES, INC. 1995. 907 F. Supp. 1361 (N.D. Cal. 1005 1995) (Northern District of California) (settled 8/22/96).

ROSENOER, JONATHAN. 1997. Cyberlaw: The Law of the Internet. New York, NY: Springer-Verlag Press; 1997. 362p. ISBN: 0-387-94832-5.

RUBIN, E. LEONARD. 1997. U.S. Fails to Guard Data Base Henhouse: Other Nations Seek to Protect Compilations of Facts, But Congress Lays an Egg in Failing to Take Up Legislation to Circumvent "Feist." National Law Journal. 1997 June 8; 19(41): B7, B18. ISSN: 0162-7325; OCLC: 04161259.

RUPP-SERRANO, KAREN J. 1997. Copyright and Fair Use: A Policy Analysis. Government Information Quarterly. 1997; 14(2): 155-172. ISSN: 0740-624X.

SAMUELSON, PAMELA. 1990. Digital Media and the Changing Face of Intellectual Property Law. Rutgers Computer and Technology Law Journal. 1990; 16(2): 323-341. ISSN: 0735-8938; OCLC: 08496275.

SAMUELSON, PAMELA. 1995. Will the Copyright Office Be Obsolete in the Twenty-First Century? Cardozo Arts and Entertainment Law Journal. 1995; 13(1): 55-68. ISSN: 0736-7694; OCLC: 08791727.

SCHEFFEY, THOMAS. 1996. A Crack in the West Monopoly? New Jersey Law Journal. 1996 December 2; 146(9): 1. ISSN: 0028-5803; OCLC: 01759865.

SCHRADER, DOROTHY. 1995. Copyright Proposals for the National Information Infrastructure. Washington, DC: Congressional Research Service; 1995. 18p. CRS order no. 95-1166 A.

SCHRADER, DOROTHY. 1997. Online Service Provider Copyright Liability: Analysis and Discussion of H.R. 2180 and S. 1146. Washington, DC: Congressional Research Service; 1997. 16p. CRS order no. 97-950 A.

SEGA ENTERPRISES V. MAPHIA I. 1994. 857 F. Supp. 679 (N.D. Cal. 1994) (Northern District of California).

SEGA ENTERPRISES V. MAPHIA II. 1996. 948 F. Supp. 923 (N.D. Cal. 1996) (Northern District of California).

SHERMAN, CARY; ECKENWILER, MARK. 1995. Bill Criminalizes Copying Irrespective of Motive: Willful Infringers of Certain Copyrights Could Be Prosecuted Even Absent Their Financial Gain. National Law Journal. 1995 October 23; 18(8): C14-C15. ISSN: 0162-7325; OCLC: 04161259.

SHETLAND TIMES LTD. V. DR. JONATHAN WILLS AND ZETNEWS LTD. 1996. Scotland Court of Session, 1 EIPLR 723 (Oct. 24, 1996) (settled Nov. 11, 1997) (Case history available WWW: http://www.nytimes.com/library/cyber/law/112797law.html and settlement terms available WWW: http://www.shetland-times.co.uk/st/daily/dispute.htm).

SHULMAN, MARY ANN. 1997. Internet Copyright Infringement Liability: Is an Online Access Provider More Like a Landlord or a Dance Hall Operator? Golden Gate University Law Review. 1997; 27(3): 555-600. ISSN: 0098-6631; OCLC: 02242221.

SHURE, JON. 1996. NBA v. AOL: Erecting Toll Booths on the Information Highway. New Jersey Lawyer. 1996 September 23: 3. ISSN: 1090-689X.

SIMMONS, EDLYN S. 1995. Intellectual Property and the Internet: "You Can't Sell It If You Give It Away." Searcher. 1995; 3(1): 38, 40-41. ISSN: 1070-4795; OCLC: 28109010.

SMITH, GRAHAM J.H. 1997. Internet Law and Regulation. 2nd edition. London, England: FT Law and Tax; 1997. 308p. ISBN: 0-7520-0468-9.

SOFTWARE PUBLISHERS ASSOCIATION. 1995. Software Publishers Association Position Statement on the La Macchia Decision. PR Newswire. 1995 January 5. Available in the LEXIS-NEXIS NEWS Library.

STEPHENS, KEITH; SUMNER, JOHN P. 1997. Catch 22: Internet Service Providers' Liability for Copyright Infringement over the Internet. Computer Lawyer. 1997; 14(5): 1-8. ISSN: 0742-1192; OCLC: 10292308.

STERN V. DELPHI INTERNET SERVICES CORP. 1995. 165 Misc. 2d 21, 626
N.Y.S. 2d 694 (N.Y. Sup. Ct., New York County, 1995) (New York Superior
Court).

STRATTON OAKMONT, INC. V. PRODIGY SERVICES CO. 1995. 23 Media
Law Reporter 1794 (N.Y. Sup. Ct., Nassau County, 1995).

STRONG, WILLIAM S. 1994. Database Protection after Feist v. Rural Telephone Co. Journal of the Copyright Society of the U.S.A. 1994; 42(1): 39-67.
ISSN: 0886-3520; OCLC: 08107929.

STUCKEY, KENT D. 1997. Internet and Online Law. New York, NY: Law
Journal Seminars Press; 1997. 1 volume. OCLC: 35317560.

SUGARMAN, ROBERT G.; WEBB, NADJA. 1996. If Idea Is in Public Domain,
Don't Complain. National Law Journal. 1996 October 14; 19(7): A22.
ISSN: 0162-7325; OCLC: 04161259.

TALBOTT, JAMES N. 1997. Facts, Copyright, Unfair Competition and Contracts; Will NBA v. Motorola Lead to Shrink Wrap Television? The Entertainment and Sports Lawyer. 1997; 15(2): 7-12. ISSN: 0732-1880.

TASINI V. NEW YORK TIMES CO. 1997. 972 F. Supp. 804 (S.D.N.Y. 1997)
rehearing denied 981 F. Supp. 841 (S.D.N.Y. 1997) (Southern District of
New York).

TICKETMASTER CORP. V. MICROSOFT CORP. 1997. 97-3055 DDP (C.D. Cal.
1997) (Central District of California).

TICKLE, KELLY. 1995. The Vicarious Liability of Electronic Bulletin Board
Operators for the Copyright Infringement Occurring on Their Bulletin
Boards. Iowa Law Review. 1995; 80(2): 391-418. ISSN: 0021-0552.

U.S. CONGRESS. 104TH CONGRESS, 1ST SESSION. 1995a. Information
Infrastructure Copyright Act of 1995: House Bill 2441, 104th Congress, 1st
Session. Washington, DC: Government Printing Office; 1995 October 3.

U.S. CONGRESS. 104TH CONGRESS, 1ST SESSION. 1995b. Information
Infrastructure Copyright Act of 1995: Senate Bill 1284, 104th Congress, 1st
Session. Washington, DC: Government Printing Office; 1995 October 2.

U.S. CONGRESS. 104TH CONGRESS, 2ND SESSION. 1996a. Database Investment and Intellectual Property Antipiracy Act of 1996: House Bill 3531,
104th Congress, 2nd Session. Washington, DC: Government Printing
Office; 1996 May 23.

U.S. CONGRESS. 104TH CONGRESS, 2ND SESSION. 1996b. Telecommunications Act of 1996; Conference Report to Accompany Senate Bill 652, House
Report no. 458, 104th Congress, 2nd Session. Washington, DC: Government Printing Office; 1996 January 31. 214p.

U.S. CONGRESS. 104TH CONGRESS, 2ND SESSION. 1996c. Telecommunica-
tions Act of 1996: Public Law 104, 104th Congress, 2nd Session. United
States Statutes at Large. 1996; 110: 56-161. Washington, DC: Government
Printing Office; 1996.

U.S. CONGRESS. 105TH CONGRESS, 1ST SESSION. 1997a. Collections of
Information Antipiracy Act of 1997: House Bill 2652, 105th Congress, 1st
Session. Washington, DC: Government Printing Office; 1997 October 9.

U.S. CONGRESS. 105TH CONGRESS, 1ST SESSION. 1997b. Copyright Term
Extension Act of 1997: House Bill 604, 105th Congress, 1st Session. Washington, DC: Government Printing Office; 1997 February 5.

U.S. CONGRESS. 105TH CONGRESS, 1ST SESSION. 1997c. Copyright Term Extension Act of 1997: Senate Bill 505, 105th Congress, 1st Session. Washington, DC: Government Printing Office; 1997 March 20.

U.S. CONGRESS. 105TH CONGRESS, 1ST SESSION. 1997d. Criminal Copyright Improvement Act of 1997: Senate Bill 1044, 105th Congress, 1st Session. Washington, DC: Government Printing Office; 1997 July 21.

U.S. CONGRESS. 105TH CONGRESS, 1ST SESSION. 1997e. Digital Copyright Clarification and Technology Education Act of 1997: Senate Bill 1146, 105th Congress, 1st Session. Washington, DC: Government Printing Office; 1997 September 3.

U.S. CONGRESS. 105TH CONGRESS, 1ST SESSION. 1997f. Digital Era Copyright Enhancement Act of 1997: House Bill 3048, 105th Congress, 1st Session. Washington, DC: Government Printing Office; 1977 November 7.

U.S. CONGRESS. 105TH CONGRESS, 1ST SESSION. 1997g. No Electronic Theft (NET) Act of 1997: House Bill 2265, 105th Congress, 1st Session. Washington, DC: Government Printing Office; 1997 July 25.

U.S. CONGRESS. 105TH CONGRESS, 1ST SESSION. 1997h. No Electronic Theft Act: Public Law 147, 105th Congress. 1st Session. United States Statutes at Large. 1998; 111: 2678-2680. Washington, DC: Government Printing Office; 1998.

U.S. CONGRESS. 105TH CONGRESS, 1ST SESSION. 1997i. On-Line Copyright Liability Limitation Act of 1997: House Bill 2180, 105th Congress, 1st Session. Washington, DC: Government Printing Office; 1997 July 17.

U.S. CONGRESS. 105TH CONGRESS, 1ST SESSION. 1997j. WIPO Copyright and Performance and Phonograms Treaty Implementation Act of 1997: Senate Bill 1121, 105th Congress, 1st Session. Washington, DC: Government Printing Office; 1997 July 21.

U.S. CONGRESS. 105TH CONGRESS, 2ND SESSION. 1998a. Collections of Information Antipiracy Act: Senate Bill 2291, 105th Congress, 2nd Session. Washington, DC: GPO; 1998 July 10.

U.S. CONGRESS. 105TH CONGRESS, 2ND SESSION. 1998b. Digital Millennium Copyright Act of 1998: House Bill 2281, 105th Congress, 2nd Session. Washington, DC: GPO; 1998 October 20. (formerly named WIPO Copyright Treaties Implementation Act. House Bill 2281, 105th Congress, 1st Session. 1997 July 29).

U.S. CONGRESS. 105TH CONGRESS, 2ND SESSION. 1998c. Digital Millennium Copyright Act of 1998: Senate Bill 2037, 105th Congress; 2nd Session. Washington, DC: GPO; 1998 May 6.

U.S. CONGRESS. OFFICE OF TECHNOLOGY ASSESSMENT. 1987. Intellectual Property Rights in an Age of Electronics and Information. Washington, DC: Government Printing Office; 1987. 300p. (OTA-CIT-302). NTIS: PB 87-100301.

U.S. COPYRIGHT OFFICE. 1997. Report on Legal Protection for Databases: A Report of the Register of Copyrights. Washington, DC: Government Printing Office; 1997 August. 111p. ISBN: 0-16-049211-4.

U.S. DEPARTMENT OF JUSTICE. ANTITRUST DIVISION. 1996. Public Comments and Plaintiff's Response, United States of America v. The

Thomson Corporation and West Publishing Company (Consent Decree). Federal Register. 1996; 61(199): 53,386-53,457.

U.S. V. THOMSON CORPORATION AND WEST PUBLISHING COMPANY. 1997. 1997 U.S. Dist. LEXIS 2790 (S.D.N.Y. 1997) (Southern District of New York).

UNITED STATES CODE (U.S.C.). 1994. 17 U.S.C. 506 (Criminal Offenses).

UNITED STATES V. LA MACCHIA. 1994. 871 F. Supp. 535 (D. Mass. 1994).

UNIVERSITY OF DAYTON LAW REVIEW. 1992. Copyright Symposium Parts I and II: Copyright Protections for Computer Databases. CD-ROMs and Factual Compilations. University of Dayton Law Review. 1992; 17(2-3): 323-730, 731-1117. ISSN: 0363-2148; OCLC: 02429606.

WASHINGTON POST V. TOTALNEWS, INC. 1997. 97 Civ. 1190 (S.D.N.Y. 1997) (Southern District of New York).

WEBER, JEREMY STONE. 1995. Defining Cyberlibel: A First Amendment Limit for Libel Suits against Individuals Arising from Computer Bulletin Board Speech. Case Western Reserve Law Review. 1995; 46(1): 235-278. ISSN: 0008-7262; OCLC: 01553468.

WEIMER, DOUGLAS REID. 1997. The Copyright Doctrine of Fair Use and the Internet: Caselaw. Washington, DC: Congressional Research Service; 1997 June 27. 6p. CRS order no. 97-656 A.

WEINREB, LLOYD L. 1992. Custom, Law, and Public Policy: The INS Case as an Example of Intellectual Property. Virginia Law Review. 1992; 78(1): 141-147. ISSN: 0042-6601; OCLC: 00826179.

WEST PUBLISHING COMPANY V. MEAD DATA CENTRAL, INC. 1986. 700 F. 2d 1219 (8th Cir. 1986) (Eighth Circuit).

WEST PUBLISHING COMPANY V. ON POINT SOLUTIONS, INC. 1994. 1994 U.S. Dist. 20040 (N.D. Ga. 1994). (Northern District of Georgia).

WILLIAMSON, ROBERT MARK. 1992. Copyright in Fact Works: Identifying Protected Elements. Thurgood Marshall Law Review. 1992; 18(1): 69-105. ISSN: 0749-1646; OCLC: 08824103.

WISE, DANIEL. 1997. Some Decision Reports Denied Copyright Protection. New York Law Journal. 1997 May 21; 217(97): 1. ISSN: 0028-7326.

WYMAN, JAMES H. 1996. Freeing the Law: Case Reporter Copyright and the Universal Citation System. Florida State University Law Review. 1996; 24(1): 217-281. ISSN: 0096-3070; OCLC: 01774925.

ZERAN V. AMERICA ONLINE, INC. 1997. 958 F. Supp. 1124 (E.D. Va. 1997) (Eastern District of Virginia), affirmed 129 F. 3d 327 (4th Cir. 1997).

2 Pricing and Marketing Online Information Services

SHEILA ANNE ELIZABETH WEBBER
University of Strathclyde
United Kingdom

INTRODUCTION

The difficulty of setting prices for online information services is a perennial theme. Paschal's comment (BLAKE, 1994) that the current pricing models are "absolutely ridiculous" is fairly typical. BERRY & YADAV ask readers to "consider, for instance, computerized on-line information services, which are notorious for their complicated pricing schemes" (p. 46). A review of the literature presents a picture of both vendors and customers frequently baffled and defeated in their attempt to set prices that are both profitable and comprehensible.

Nevertheless, there has been progress, or at least change. The literature reflects a more business-like business, and an increasingly big business. Separate industries, including online services, document delivery, journal publishing, primary and secondary publishing, World Wide Web publishing, software, and even broadcast media, are converging. The same players are delivering information through a multiplicity of media. This is causing customers to compare and question prices, and vendors to try out pricing models that formerly belonged to other media: online priced like cable TV, journals priced like online, databases priced like advertising-supported freesheets. The catalyst for much of this development has been the Internet.

With these changes as background, this chapter aims to place the pricing of online information in the broader context of marketing, and highlight some important issues and trends. Pricing is viewed primarily as part of the marketing mix, as opposed to viewing it from an economics standpoint.

Annual Review of Information Science and Technology (ARIST), Volume 33, 1998
Martha E. Williams, Editor
Published for the American Society for Information Science (ASIS)
By Information Today, Inc., Medford, NJ

In her chapter for the 1991 *Annual Review of Information Science and Technology* (*ARIST*), SPIGAI summarizes pricing developments for books, serials, CD-ROM, and online, concentrating on 1986 through 1990 and reflecting on the impact these developments had on libraries. This chapter concentrates on online services, here defined as remotely held electronic information services accessed via networks. The emphasis is on the type of information content of interest to the professional and business sectors and primarily on literature from 1991 through 1997.

The pricing of CD-ROM products is not dealt with specifically. A number of articles in the bibliography mention both CD-ROM and online, and a few recent articles on CD-ROM pricing have been included (GRASHOFF; HAWKINS; ROWLEY & BUTCHER) to supplement those cited by SPIGAI.

Serials pricing has a substantial literature of its own: a good starting point is BAILEY's regularly updated bibliography on scholarly publishing. Pricing of serials has been seen as separate from pricing of online information, but for electronic journals, this is an increasingly artificial distinction. For example, KING & GRIFFITHS include delivery of full-text documents via online hosts in their consideration of the economics of scholarly publishing. One aspect of electronic journal article pricing is addressed in the context of aggregation and disaggregation, or bundling and unbundling of information objects, below.

This chapter considers changes in the marketing context and issues of value relating to price, and summarizes other reviews of online pricing. It then highlights trends affecting pricing: first, ongoing trends concerning the effect of the information chain on pricing issues, and the question of public-sector involvement in the industry, and second, more recent trends concerning the effect of the Internet and consumer online services. Then it highlights three important pricing trends: promotional pricing, price discrimination, and price aggregation and disaggregation.

The following terms are used throughout the chapter: Information professionals covers both librarians and information scientists. Online host identifies an organization that mounts data, not necessarily produced by that organization, on a computer for remote access by others. Vendor is used to mean any organization that supplies products or services to others, normally for a fee. Customer is applied to users, or recipients, of products or services. End-user identifies the ultimate user of information (normally, within an organization). Consumer online services are services aimed at individual, as opposed to corporate, customers.

THE MARKETING CONTEXT

A number of trends reflected in the marketing literature are relevant to pricing electronic information services. These concern marketing generally, services marketing, marketing of high-technology products, and international marketing. These topics are addressed in this section.

With more general acceptance of the importance of marketing has come questioning of some of the underlying principles of traditional marketing. BRADY & DAVIS, for example, talk of marketing's mid-life crisis. While their discussion focuses on tangible consumer goods, they highlight a number of general factors such as the need to take a total system approach. This involves researching and meeting customers' requirements up to the point of use. Marketing textbooks now stress that marketing is an all-pervading philosophy that should be practiced by everyone in the organization. The customer's needs are paramount, and the organization should strive to develop a distinctive relationship with each client.

ARNOLD (1990) discusses relationship marketing in his *ARIST* review of the literature of electronic information marketing. This has become a buzz phrase of the mid-1990s (see, e.g., CRAM), although Arnold and other writers have pointed out that the concept is scarcely new. However, the topic is now being addressed explicitly by those writing about information marketing (e.g., WALKER), where the Internet is seen as an enabling mechanism for creating one-to-one relationships. With increased emphasis on individual relationships, one might expect to see more price differentiation and negotiation as products and services are modified to meet individual needs.

The traditional producer-oriented marketing mix has been defined as the four Ps: product, price, promotion, and place. GRONROOS sees a paradigm shift away from marketing theory based around the marketing mix, and toward a paradigm centered on customer-oriented relationship-building. LAUTERBORN suggests the replacement Cs: customer needs and wants, cost to the customer of satisfying those needs and wants, communication, and convenience. The replacement of price by cost to the customer seems useful in relation to online information. Particularly in the early days of online, the costs of telecommunications (see SILK) hardware and software, as well as the investment of the customer's time in training etc., were usually a bigger part of the cost than the database price.

On the whole, forcing a burden of costs onto the customer is not a good idea, although once the customer has made a big investment in switching costs (e.g., training for and setting up a new system), the investment itself tends to encourage loyalty. KIERZKOWSKI ET AL.

mention this phenomenon in the context of software and hardware systems, and of various Internet services. Information professionals are proud of their skill in getting the best out of a particular system, and online hosts may risk cutting loyal customers loose when they change or simplify systems. JACSÓ (1996a) describes his reaction to CompuServe's pricing changes (from a flat-fee/unlimited-use charge for basic services with additional premium charges, to a flat-fee charge covering only five hours per month but including more databases). He sought out, and in many cases found, free alternatives on the Internet, and urges other searchers to consider "jumping ship" likewise.

Services Marketing

BERRY & YADAV begin their marketing article on the pricing of services with the blunt statement, "The pricing of services in the United States is a mess" (p. 41). Thus the online industry is not alone in being unable to find a solution to the pricing dilemma. The emphasis in the earlier marketing literature on discussion of marketing tangible consumer products, as opposed to business-to-business services (which most online services were until recently), may have made it more difficult to perceive the parallels between marketing online services and marketing other types of services. The term business here refers to any organization.

The particular problems associated with services marketing are well documented in marketing literature. ROWLEY (1995) sees electronic information as a mixture of product and service. Online information exhibits the characteristics of a service more strongly than some other forms of electronic information. With tangible products, alternatives for pricing can be related to tangible features (e.g., apples may be priced by weight or by unit). The more tangible information products are also more likely to have a pricing mechanism relating to the physical product (e.g., price per book or CD-ROM disk).

Key problems of service marketing, as described by KOTLER and many others, are: (1) intangibility, because the product cannot be handled or previewed, and customers incur expense rather than gaining possession of goods; (2) variability, because the involvement of a human in the transaction means that no two products are alike; (3) perishability, because spare capacity cannot be stored for future use, and pricing may be used to even out demand; and (4) inseparability of production and consumption, because, for example, search results are tailored for individuals as they develop their online strategies.

The first problem, intangibility, and last, inseparability of production and consumption, make it particularly difficult for customers to estimate in advance the value to them of a particular purchase. This uncertainty makes the purchase riskier and may discourage customers from trying the product. The intangibility and variability of the information product make it more difficult for customers to compare prices beforehand, which is a usual (and for customers, reassuring) part of a sales transaction. These factors also make research techniques such as conjoint measurement (a technique often used when setting prices for tangible products) more difficult to use successfully.

BERRY & YADAV propose three strategies for pricing services for value: (1) satisfaction pricing, or recognizing and reducing customers' perceptions of uncertainty through service guarantees, benefit-driven pricing, and flat-rate pricing; (2) relationship pricing, or encouraging long-term relationships through, for example, contracts and price bundling; and (3) efficiency pricing, involving identification of activities in the service chain, and reduction or elimination of those that do not add value for the customer. Subsequent sections of this review present evidence of increasing use of these strategies in the online industry.

As an example of benefit-driven pricing, BERRY & YADAV cite ESA-IRS's move away from charging for connect time and toward charging for information delivered. They also mention a law firm that moved away from the equivalent of connect-time charging by offering a flat-rate fixed annual fee to a particularly large client. Pricing is seen as part of relationship building, since price reductions can be used to initiate a relationship that can then be cemented by long-term contracts. Price bundling, or aggregation, can also build relationships, since the vendor is affecting a wider range of the customer's activities and has the opportunity to learn about the customer. Berry and Yadav note that AT&T, by offering credit-card services to existing telephone customers, was able to combat customer defections from both services.

The literature gives some indication that business-to-business products and professional services (HANNA & DODGE) are more likely to be cost-based in their pricing than tangible consumer goods. Because online information is a service that, until recently, was primarily sold business-to-business, the cost-orientation of early pricing strategies in the online industry is perhaps unsurprising, even if it makes "little sense" (VARIAN).

Marketing High-Technology Products

Some characteristics are common to high-technology marketing in general, such as the fact that supply-side marketing dominates early market stages. These characteristics can also be applied to the online industry, where they can affect pricing. For example, the product may be so innovative that customers are unaware they need it, which makes it more difficult to gauge how they will value it.

In the literature, pricing of electronic information content is sometimes discussed at the same time as pricing of software (e.g., in BAKOS & BRYNJOLFSSON). One might attribute this partly to a woolliness about defining the concept of information (a concept comparatively few non-information scientists define, despite the fact that they make different assumptions about what is encompassed by information). However, there are also obviously characteristics in common, such as the high cost of initial production and low cost of reproduction, and the fact that customers may need to experience the product before being able to estimate the product's value to them. CAHILL suggests that pricing in the electronic information industry may follow the pattern of the software industry, with decreasing prices or increasing functionality for the same price.

Because online information services are distributed via telecommunications networks, policy in this area (e.g., European Union directives concerned with the competitiveness of the telecommunications market) influences online information pricing and affects the total cost to the customer. There is an extensive literature on telecommunications pricing. Many articles focus on issues that arise from its role as a public good and from regulation (e.g., research on strategies for local telephone calls). TAYLOR provides a recent review of the issues and the research. He discusses a number of points that are also applicable to online information pricing. For example, he looks at the value of a phone call in terms of the opportunity cost of not making the call, pointing out that making a phone call may be a way of earning income rather than of consuming it.

International Marketing

The online industry has from the start been an international industry, and as such is subject to the impact of linguistic, cultural, and political factors. As data networks have developed and interconnected, culminating in the Internet, cross-border data flow has become increasingly common. The international nature of online services affects pricing, as it does other parts of the marketing mix. The value of the same information to customers in country X may not equal its value to customers in country Y. If country X customers find that the information is not in their language, is priced in a foreign currency, and does not cover their local news, the value to them will be less.

At the same time, the cost to customers may increase because they may be paying more in telecommunications charges and taxes than customers in the information service's home country, and they may have to expend more time and money to get training or support. WHITE mentions the high bank charges for cross-currency transactions, and notes the fact that some major European countries do not commonly accept credit cards, which he feels could inhibit the use of consumer online services. Services based in the United States, for example, may assume that credit-card use is as ubiquitous abroad as it is in their home country, and effectively bar international customers by offering only credit-card payment.

Increasing availability of interconnected data networks has decreased the cost to customers, tending to even out the telecommunications cost differences between countries. A 1982 study by EUSIDIC (SILK), surveying host and telecommunications costs in European countries, showed that the biggest difference was between countries that were or were not connected to the EURONET packet-switched data network (e.g., at that time a search from Portugal on ESA-IRS cost about twice as much as a search from Italy or the Netherlands because of telecommunications costs).

As an international distribution channel, the Internet has brought mass-market pricing to data networks. QUELCH & KLEIN note that it also allows both increased customization of pricing, and increased cross-border price comparisons by customers. This may mean that information producers and online hosts are discouraged from practicing price discrimination (differentiation) by country when setting standard prices. Customers are already shopping around internationally for the lowest-priced software packages and audio CDs. This may cause problems where an online host or information producer has an agency agreement that includes freedom to determine local pricing strategy.

The Internet is seen by QUELCH & KLEIN, and by many others, as a means of facilitating international marketing. It can improve speed of response (including speed of implementing price changes), access, and customer service (e.g., customer-support information or Web browser search interfaces in several languages), thus increasing value to overseas clients.

Nevertheless, basic issues of value (and therefore price) cannot be resolved by the existence of the Internet alone. The value of the information content is still going to be affected by the language and the coverage of the information, and how these relate to the needs of individual customers in their home countries.

INFORMATION VALUE

In the marketing literature, the favored approach is to match price to the customer's perception of the product's value. To fit in with the concept of relationship marketing, the prices "must reflect the learning that has taken place in the relationship" between vendor and customer (CRAM, p. 151). A recurring theme in recent comments by those in the information industry is also that pricing must be related to benefits and value.

There is an extensive literature on the value of information. It is outside the scope of this review to explore the issue of value in depth, but it is fundamental to the question of price, and some points are highlighted here. SARACEVIC & KANTOR provide a recent summary of some views. They identify three research approaches: (1) normative value, involving the application of rigorous models involving information uncertainty and/or utility; (2) realistic value, measuring the effect of information on outcomes; and (3) perceived value, involving subjective valuation by information users. The perceived value approach is usually applied in the price-setting process in a marketing context, although information producers (and information professionals) might undertake studies that adopt one of the other approaches (sometimes hoping to produce results that affect customers' perceptions of value).

Frustration at customers' lack of appreciation of information's value often surfaces when information professionals discuss the question. For example, JAMIOLKOWSKI of PsycINFO says pricing must begin with the perceived value of the product to customers, but continues, "If more customers were aware of how much it costs to publish a database, in relation to the value derived, their perception of database prices would be more tolerant and help counter the long-held attitude that all information should be 'free'" (p. 101). However, few marketing textbooks would recommend simply emphasizing high production costs, a practice that might instead be seen as a sign of inefficiency unless high production costs were linked to benefits such as improved features desirable to customers. If a vendor wishes customers to part with their money, it should price products in a way that relates to customers' perceptions of value (whatever prejudices cloud those perceptions), not the perceptions of value the vendor thinks customers ought to have.

The extent to which product substitution is possible tends to affect the value of a product and thus its price. FISHBURN ET AL. note that although information content producers typically have a monopoly, it is not perfect, because a similar product may be an acceptable substitute. For example, the U.K. MONOPOLIES AND MERGERS COMMISSION investigated a possible monopoly of historical news by the *Financial Times* (FT), and judged that the FT did not have a monopoly. Testimony submitted to the Commission (e.g., from user groups) said that the news in the FT newspaper could have been obtained from other sources. This seems to indicate that customers will consider substitutes for even highly branded products.

NAGLE notes that a key influence on price sensitivity is the number of similar products of which the customer is aware. The customer may not, of course, know about all the substitutes. Additionally, when the product has to be experienced before people can decide whether it is an acceptable substitute, price competition is not likely to be fierce. SAFFADY's (1996) comparison of the undiscounted connect-time cost of 74 databases offered by three or more hosts demonstrates the wide variety of prices offered for a single source. Saffady found a difference of more than 50% in hourly rates, between highest and lowest charge, for 44 databases. For 48 databases, there was a difference of more than 50% for display charges. Despite this range in pricing, price competition between online services is seldom discussed in the literature.

The range in pricing could also reflect the importance of other parts of the marketing mix (e.g., product) in making purchase decisions about online services. It could partly reflect the difficulty of comparing multipart prices (a host may try to avoid price comparison by deliberately taking a complex approach to pricing). The fact that multipart pricing is common is obvious if one examines any of the surveys mentioned in the next part of this chapter, where it is highlighted by commentators such as ROWLEY (1993).

The work undertaken to identify criteria for assessing the quality of online databases is relevant in this context. BASCH includes a number of articles summarizing developments in this area, many involving user groups such as the Southern California Online Users Group (SCOUG) and the European On-Line User Group (EUROLUG). The various sets of criteria all include value to cost as one element, together with elements that could be related to the product and place parts of the four Ps of the marketing mix.

In the EQUIP study (WILSON), for which 989 questionnaires were received from about 600 individuals in 12 European countries, respondents ranked ten database quality criteria. Overall, the price-related criterion ranked sixth, below criteria such as coverage, accuracy, and timeliness, implying that respondents did not simply choose the cheapest database. JAMES mentions a study carried out by UMI in which school librarians, public librarians, and university librarians ranked attributes of quality and service above the attribute of low price. He also stresses that an information producer must concentrate on the value-added features desired by customers, rather than those the producer thinks desirable. He lists some features, particularly reliability and currency, that add value to UMI products.

REVIEWS OF ONLINE PRICING IN PRACTICE

SPIGAI summarizes trends in the literature from 1986 through 1990. This section concentrates on post-1990 material, and some significant earlier items (mainly European) not covered by Spigai. Market research into pricing is undoubtedly being carried out by online hosts and information producers, but in an increasingly competitive environment one only receives tantalizing glimpses of it in the published literature.

The process of tracking basic price data over time is not straightforward because of the ephemeral nature of price lists: libraries, individual customers, and even vendors tend not to retain out-of-date lists. In particular, information about discounted prices is hard to gather retrospectively, as it may not be recorded in price lists. The *Clover Comparative Cost Chart for Online Files* (first published by Clover Publishing in the United Kingdom (U.K.), and now published by Effective Technology Marketing as *ONLINE FILES: COMPARATIVE COST ANALYSIS*) provides information on a good range of hosts/databases covering the period from 1989 on. Earlier in the 1980s, as noted by SPIGAI, some issues of *Online Review* (now *Online & CD-ROM Review*) carry price lists. SAFFADY's (1979; 1985; 1988; 1992; 1996) series of analyses of online costs also provides useful data, and some individual studies may include detailed lists of one type of price (e.g., TINCKNELL on Dialog's KWIC format).

Some useful early studies from the U.K. survey both the North American and the European scene. PRATT details the prices of online databases between 1973 and 1975. This early list demonstrates that connect time was the most popular form of pricing. The pay-as-you-go approach predominated, although some data services for the corporate sector (e.g., Data Resources Inc.) levied more substantial up-front subscriptions. LEXIS also levied a monthly fee, although this was related to the computer terminals that at that time were part of the LEXIS package.

MULLER & WILSON provide a summary of pricing issues, and the types of costs and prices applying to databases and their printed equivalents in 1986. They tried to identify price competition between hosts mounting the same databases. They found that although Dialog was most often in competition with other hosts, DataStar and DIMDI had lower prices. A move from connect-time to transaction pricing was seen as desirable. DUNN & BOYLE of the Chemical Abstracts Service (CAS) comment at around the same time that pricing by connect time is poor marketing because the charge does not reflect the value to the customer.

There have been some general reviews of pricing policy. BYSOUTH edited a collection of articles, from the late 1970s and early 1980s, on the economics of online. It provides a good perspective on that era. The collection includes a survey of the royalties received by database producers, articles on costing and pricing from Harry Collier and Art Elias (both frequent commentators in this field), and articles on online costs from a customer perspective.

DUCKITT & MAY report on a one-day meeting organized by the U.K. Online User Group in 1988, at which hosts, information producers, and information professionals shared their views about online charging policies. After summarizing presentations from the participants, Duckitt and May analyze the viewpoints of the three groups. There seemed to be no support for connect-time charging as a policy, but producers and hosts were reluctant to make radical changes in case they upset an industry that was then relatively small and young. The diversity of need even among information professionals was stressed. The latter felt that the hosts should be taking the initiative in introducing new pricing strategies. They appreciated the value of information. Online hosts and information producers needed to spend more time researching the needs of their market.

In terms of simplifying pricing structures, little progress appears to have been made between 1988 and 1994, when the U.K. MONOPOLIES AND MERGERS COMMISSION published its report investigating a possible monopoly by FT Profile. The report provides a summary of pricing of historical news databases and notes that, because of the variety of pricing mechanisms and structures, comparison of prices between hosts is problematic. In a telephone survey of 146 online users, 61% said they found it difficult to compare prices. Tables in the report illustrate this complexity, and detail the discounts offered on the Textline database.

ROWLEY (1995) summarizes the various strategies that have been used for pricing online and CD-ROM products and ROWLEY (1993) provides examples of charges for specific hosts. BUCHER reviews the pricing structures of (mostly European) hosts. He highlights instances of high annual and monthly subscriptions or minimum charges (e.g., for the German host GENIOS), which are being used deliberately to help position services at the premium end of the market. He discusses arguments for and against pricing according to connect time, hits, and search terms. Bucher notes that, since 1993, STN has allowed its customers to choose between two pricing structures for bibliographic databases. He sees a trend toward billing for information and toward fixed-price deals for large-scale customers.

COLLIER (1993) reviews strategies and pricing mechanisms. He identifies four pricing methods: (1) connect time, (2) an amalgamation of connect time and other elements, (3) subscription, and (4) payment according to quantity of data retrieved. Disadvantages and advantages are perceived for each option. He stresses that pricing should reflect value to the customer and notes that pricing must be a marketing decision. Because of the perceived shortcomings of online pricing in the past, he recommends that new entrants to the market view others' pricing with suspicion.

UNRUH & SCHIPPER identify connect time plus display charge as the traditional model for pricing (in 1991), and then discuss alternatives such as pricing linked to computer resource costs, or to number of searches or search sessions, and fixed-fee/unlimited-use pricing.

In one of the few surveys on online pricing, NELSON surveyed information producers in 1994 and received 62 usable returns (an 18% response rate). He found that print accounted for more revenue than any other format, followed closely by electronic file licensing, but that 90% of respondents expected print revenues to decline proportionally. Nelson provides a table showing the pricing mechanisms used by respondents: 93% were using connect-time charging, 84% were charging by online hits, 54% had flat-fee or subscription plans, 25% charged on search terms in some way, and 11% used transmission speed as a factor. Nelson notes that there was a lack of consensus as to the effect of technological developments on searching behavior.

SAFFADY (1996) provides a substantial review of costs and prices of online services. He gives examples of fixed and variable costs associated with online searching, and make comparisons with his surveys of previous years (SAFFADY, 1979; 1985; 1988; 1992; he does not appear to recalculate previous years' prices to account for inflation). He makes useful observations concerning trends in pricing mechanisms. His survey is referred to in various sections of this chapter, as is that of NELSON.

WEBBER concludes that larger and more commercial companies are being more assertive in their pricing policies, and that the Internet and consumer online hosts are influencing strategy. She describes some recent trends including the increasing use of fixed-use contracts and unit pricing, price discrimination, optional feature pricing, product bundling pricing, promotional pricing, and value pricing (providing more for less money).

The question of production-cost allocation across media is still sometimes discussed. MULLER & WILSON note in 1985 that, although the online product had by that time shifted from being a byproduct of print to a product of equal importance, costs still tended to be calculated on a marginal basis. UNRUH & SCHIPPER outline issues concerning the costs of different publishing media, and difficulties in deciding how to allocate the costs of data creation to different products. JAMIOLKOWSKI of PsycINFO reflects more current thinking in striving for an across-the-media pricing strategy, looking at consumption of the product in all media on one purchaser's site.

ONGOING ISSUES: THE INFORMATION CHAIN
AND PUBLIC POLICY

This section examines issues that have influenced pricing strategy from the start of the online industry, and which continue to be important. The first set of issues concerns the life cycle and distribution chain for an information product. The process can be very complex, and the pricing of information is affected by the relationship between different parts of the chain. The relationship between information producer and online host, and the role of other intermediaries in the chain, is considered. This section ends with an examination of the effect on pricing of the involvement of the public sector.

Intermediaries in the Information Chain

Relationship between information producers and hosts. One of the distinguishing factors of the electronic information industry is the way in which information producers seek to influence the product delivered by hosts to customers and set conditions for its use. Unlike vendors of, for example, raw materials for manufactured products, which are concerned with transfer of ownership under simple purchase agreements, information producers are concerned with intellectual property and normally operate under licensing agreements. The information pricing process is more difficult, as conflicts may arise between database producer and database host about the strategy to be employed. Most notable was the dispute between the American Chemical Society (ACS) and Dialog (BUSINESSWIRE; KABACK). This concerned two problems: (1) the scheme that ACS used to determine royalty payments for the Chemical Abstracts Service (CAS) database, and (2) withdrawal by ACS of the abstracts in the CAS database from all versions except those mounted by the host, STN International, which is part-owned by ACS. As a consequence, Dialog was unable to provide CAS abstracts, which are preferable to references with only bibliographic information. Regarding royalties, Harry Boyle, manager of marketing services for CAS, points out that CAS's license dictated how licensees (hosts) must pay for use of the data, and not how licensees must charge their customers (PEMBERTON). Nevertheless, the complexity of the pricing scheme imposed by CAS scarcely made the pricing process easier.

In situations like this, hosts have expressed the view that information producers are standing in the way of customer-oriented pricing. Comment in print is likely to be muted in order not to upset existing partnerships, except where conflicts such as the one above lead to frankness. Heinz Ochsner of DataStar (OWEN) states in 1996 that while fixed pricing is the best strategy, he has doubts as to whether information producers will find it acceptable.

Information producers, in turn, have expressed concern about the lack of control they have over the pricing of their products by online hosts. NELSON found that 57% of those he surveyed thought they had little or no control over pricing. Satisfaction was higher with the way they were recompensed by hosts. One third were moderately satisfied, 25% moderately dissatisfied, and 25% neutral. Concerns were reflected in the comments, for example, "I cannot over-emphasize the power of the online vendors (services)—especially since the DIALOG/DataStar buyout was completed" (p. 85). Another database producer complained about having to pay to access its own data on the host system.

ARNOLD (1989) expresses the view that "information providers who rely on third parties to distribute their information in electronic form have little influence on prices" (p. 6). Analyzing factors affecting costs and pricing two years later, ARNOLD (1991) predicts that primary authors will become more powerful, offering direct access to data, demanding more in terms of license fees, and in some cases not appreciating the role that secondary publishers can play in the information chain.

Disintermediation is taking place in a number of industries. For example, some companies in the financial services industry have cut a layer in the distribution chain and saved overhead costs (of staff and physical premises), thus giving leeway for price cuts. Writing about business in general, QUELCH & KLEIN see the role of intermediary businesses changing with the advent of the Internet because customers can buy directly from producers. They emphasize that the added value of the intermediary will lie in collecting, collating, interpreting, and disseminating information rather than collecting and distributing goods.

BRODWIN & KLINE foresee a healthy future for the large online hosts, providing they can produce integrated services that have an impact on a customer's whole company. The authors highlight the depth and breadth of content, sophisticated search engines, and long-term customer relationships. However, they predict problems for middle-tier players (like SilverPlatter), which have neither the breadth of a Dialog nor the focus and depth of a niche information publisher.

James E. Coane of Telebase Systems (WICKS) sees publishers, under pressure to lower prices, going directly to customers, bypassing the traditional online host. QUINT (1995) envisions authors and information producers taking advantage of forthcoming electronic payment mechanisms to sell directly to customers. John Weeks of market research publisher Mintel (LYON, 1997a) also sees a move away from using third-party hosts and expects only hosts that originate their own content to survive. He describes how Mintel is withdrawing from traditional online hosts so as to gain control over its product and pricing, by offering its own service via CD-ROM and the Internet and offering pay-per-view and subscription services.

A shortening of the information chain may result in lower prices to customers for an individual product. However, it should be noted that this may also result in an increase in the total cost to customers, because customers must spend more time evaluating and aggregating information to answer all their information needs.

Information producers that are still working with hosts may develop closer relationships with those hosts. Bill O'Conor of Disclosure (ABELS) sees a growing sense of partnership between producers and hosts, and says it is no longer a case of just "send me my royalty check" (p. 239). When KIRSCH of Infoseek Corporation talks about "partner publishing," the high-profile emphasis on partnership reflects the current vogue for strategic alliances and virtual corporations.

Information professionals and infomediaries. The online industry was primarily business-to-business for many years, and even now, in terms of revenue, the business-to-business sector is more significant. Business-to-business, or industrial, marketing is generally characterized by shorter distribution chains and a longer negotiation phase than consumer product marketing. Information professionals fit into this chain, bringing more expert knowledge of the product and its alternatives than end-users. BAKOS & BRYNJOLFSSON note that this is often the case with such agents in the buying chain.

GARMAN (1995) observes that the apparent trend toward price simplification leaves less scope for skilled searchers to "beat the system" on one host. However she (and others) say that being able to choose the best value option between different vendors is still a role that information professionals can fill. This is demonstrated by, for example, JACSÓ's (1996b) comparison of search costs on Dialog, OCLC's EPIC, and OVID.

It is interesting to observe in the literature the extent to which information professionals have clamored for pricing change, exchanged hints to "beat the system," and lobbied to get better deals. From the early days of online services, various articles (e.g., LOMIO) have explained cunning ways to circumvent the latest pricing changes. An example is the flurry of articles that appeared when Dialog lowered connect-time charges but introduced a pay-per-view fee for browsing titles and index terms (BATES; FLETCHER; MILLER). In this case, the customers won: the pay-per-view fee was scrapped.

From a modern marketing perspective, it is alarming how some information vendors, presented with what was effectively free market-research feedback from customers, maintained a defensive or dismissive attitude for many years. The current breed of information vendors must be customer-oriented. Information professionals continue to exchange views, not only through their existing professional networks, but also through Internet discussion lists.

The role of the information professional and library consortium in negotiating site licenses is discussed in the section on aggregation below. This trend can be linked to the rise of the infomediary predicted by HAGEL & RAYPORT. They define an infomediary as "a business whose sole or main source of revenue derives from capturing customer information and developing detailed profiles of individual customers for use by selected third-party vendors" (p. 56). In particular, they see a role for customer-oriented infomediaries, which help customers exploit the value that exists in their own customer profiles. Customers are portrayed as increasingly unwilling to yield detailed information about their habits and preferences. Existing purchasing brokers are seen as potential infomediaries.

While HAGEL & RAYPORT focus primarily on the consumer market, their discussion is interesting considering the growth in the number of library consortia (see below). The INTERNATIONAL COALITION OF LIBRARY CONSORTIA stresses that consortia and libraries must have the right to share management information about the use of electronic products. A key area of study in the economics of information is that of information asymmetry, when the customer and vendor of a product have different amounts of information about the product. Normally the vendor knows more about the product and its value than the customer does, and therefore has more control of the pricing market. Information professionals may start to make more aggressive use of the data about customer experiences that would help alleviate the asymmetry.

Public Sector, Private Sector

A number of legal and political factors may affect prices. HANNA & DODGE provide an overview of general legal issues related to pricing. Some countries have laws against price collusion; for example, the Treaty of Rome inhibits price discrimination between European Union countries. Intellectual property and data protection laws, foreign policy (e.g., banning trade with a particular country), and taxation (e.g., policy on whether online services are liable to value-added or sales tax) are also relevant to the pricing of an information product.

The focus in this section is on the area of official policy concerned with the involvement of the public sector in the information industry. A number of early entrants into the online information market were from the nonprofit sector. They supported missions dedicated to the public good, and were unaccustomed to marketing practices (see, e.g., EAST). In 1984, FLOWERDEW ET AL. identify information's attributes as a public good as one of the complications in pricing information.

Although the electronic information services market is now dominated by commercial hosts and database producers, there are still some important players from the nonprofit sector, and some for-profit market sectors are likely to have been influenced by their involvement with nonprofit organizations early on. Companies (for profit) may be concerned that, because high-value information is low-priced for public-good reasons, customers will be unwilling to pay commercial high prices for similar information (produced by for-profits), even when they value it highly. These companies may also perceive unfair competition from the public sector.

An obvious example is the MEDLINE database. The U.S. National Library of Medicine (NLM) was an early entrant into the electronic services market, and the MEDLINE database remains a market leader. Even before it became available free on the Internet in 1997, BROERING notes in 1992 that few medical libraries access the more expensive biomedical databases and that MEDLINE is ubiquitous. BUNTROCK, writing in 1984, says NLM refused to make service enhancements because MEDLINE was so inexpensive that customers would be able to afford the inefficiencies of the service. This seems to ignore the total cost to customers, forgetting that customers invest their own time in searching.

The NLM pricing scheme, described by KENTON in 1984, included charges for connect time, characters printed, disk accesses, interactions, searches, and citations printed. Its mixture of charges for computer transactions and for output reflected the concerns of a public-sector organization that did not have to recover the cost of data creation through operation of its online services, but did have to cover computing expenses. The NLM wanted to be "more equitable," and seemed genuinely concerned that the charges would seem fair to both information user and information producer. However, many elements of the price were unrelated to the value being derived from the online search, and the charges were fiendishly difficult to predict.

As recently as 1993, the NLM's director, Donald Lindberg, when announcing reductions in NLM database prices, says, "Congress has urged us to increase the usage of the Library's extremely valuable databases and suggested that we ensure that costs not be an inhibiting factor" (INFORMATION TODAY, p. 64). Complaints of unfair competition from commercial producers led to an official investigation into MEDLINE in the early 1980s. The investigators concluded that MEDLINE was achieving its objectives and stimulating the market for health-care information; but they did order the introduction of discriminatory pricing, so that non-U.S. customers (who had not contributed taxes to MEDLINE's production) paid more than U.S. customers.

SILLINCE & SILLINCE discuss the provision and development of molecular databases, exploring the issue of whether this information should be classified as a public good (and subsidized by government) and the implications for price and access. They also address the implications for data quality and for scientific research.

Public-good information services may find themselves between a rock and a hard place: commercial rivals are concerned that their prices will be undercut and customers are concerned about freedom of access and appropriate use of public funds. EAST also notes that managers in nonprofit organizations are less able to maneuver and diversify to meet the needs of the market. These factors, together with the public-service mission of a government agency, are bound to influence pricing policy and practice.

SPREHE conducted a detailed study of the costs and prices of some National Technical Information Service (NTIS) products, some of which were electronic. The objective of NTIS is to cover its costs. Decisions to price products potentially below cost-recovery levels were made either to increase sales volumes or to compete with the Government Printing Office (GPO). Some decisions were made to support cross-subsidy of products. Sprehe asked seventeen people from the information industry whether they felt NTIS's prices were too high and in general they did not. There was the possibility that the costs were too high. Sprehe highlights the problems of a government agency in marketing its services, such as limited control over staffing costs and bureaucratic procedures.

As commercial hosts and database producers became more dominant in the information industry (observed by EAST in 1986), and governments in countries such as the U.K. turned toward a market philosophy, the influence of and debate about public-sector players became less heated. Recently, however, the availability of public-good information on the Internet, cheap or free, in increasingly large quantities, has revived the issue. The amount of information available varies from country to country, and policies in the area of, for example, freedom of information, impact what information is provided.

An article by DATABASE PROMOTION CENTER, JAPAN discusses the issue in the context of Japan's five-year project for the Promotion of Government Informatization, which will increase the flow of free electronic information from the government. There are fears that this will result in a dramatic drop in the use of priced commercial databases. The article refers to the huge range of free U.S. public-sector information on the Internet, highlighting the example of the free Electronic Data Gathering, Analysis, and Retrieval (EDGAR) database.

EDGAR contains information filed by public companies with the U.S. Securities and Exchange Commission and, following consumer pressure, has been made available free on the Internet. SMITH & STEINMAN address the question of how EDGAR is impacting commercial information producers, and how it compares to their products. Like KARP, they note the limited search options and clumsy output format of the free database, and the incompleteness of the database. (In 1996, when both articles were published, not all companies were filing electronically.)

The SMITH & STEINMAN and KARP articles both quote representatives of the company Disclosure Inc. who emphasize their own product's international coverage, retrospective data, time-saving, and other value-added features. The articles provide quotations from customers, who give speed and ease of access, readability, and linked document delivery services as reasons for using the priced service. Some users indicate that their preferred source varies, depending on how quickly the information is needed. The articles suggest that the decision to offer unpriced EDGAR information has led to increased value to the consumer, with the priced products enhanced in order to meet the competition. The free service is also perceived as fulfilling a promotional function for the priced services, creating awareness in a new market.

Based on the example of EDGAR, it seems that competition from a free source may have a beneficial effect for customers in encouraging database producers to add value to their products in order to differentiate them. COLLIER (1997) sounds a note of caution, however, making the point that free databases may satisfy the needs of the many occasional or less serious users, and thus leech away profits from the added-value versions.

CURRENT TRENDS IN PRICING STRATEGY

This section starts with a discussion about customers' requirements for pricing strategies. It goes on to identify forces influencing pricing strategy, notably the Internet. Subsequent sections highlight three key trends: aggregation and disaggregation of products, promotional pricing, and price discrimination.

Information vendors have their own pricing objectives, which vary according to the missions of the parent organizations and their overall marketing objectives. However, an important question often touched on in the literature is: what do customers want from pricing structures, and what do vendors think customers want?

This is not a question for which there seems a simple answer. Pat Tierney of Dialog (WICKS) says that Dialog's parent company, Knight-Ridder, conducted focus groups on pricing in various parts of the world and found no consensus on a preferred pricing model, although in the course of the article it becomes evident that certain customer groups did have preferences (e.g., information brokers preferred transactional pricing). Dialog's HOCK also mentions this lack of consensus in his paper presented at the 1994 American Society for Information Science (ASIS) Annual Meeting. OAKLEY ET AL., in a report on the future of information content sponsored by the European Commission, say there is "little reliable information on how companies would prefer to pay for information services" (p. 106).

As guiding principles, a few words, such as fair, equitable, predictable, comprehensible, and straightforward recur in the literature. A willingness to pay for quality and to pay prices that reflect value is also expressed. Increased customer efficiency or productivity are also seen as desirable. It is a rare host or database producer that does not mention at least one of these principles when announcing price changes.

DUCKITT & MAY note that U.K. users who participated in a workshop on pricing in 1988 wanted comprehensible pricing structures and were willing to pay for value. In 1991, UNRUH & SCHIPPER quote DIALOG's Roger Summit as saying that in the future, pricing needs to be understandable and predictable to the customer, and that pricing has to relate to the perceived value of the information. A 1998 report commissioned by the JOINT INFORMATION SYSTEMS COMMITTEE proposes a new pricing model for access to datasets by U.K. universities. It identifies fairness, encouraging use, predictability, and simple and well-defined as key principles for the new pricing scheme.

It is interesting to note that, in 1998, there is still no agreement about what pricing structure actually is most predictable and straightforward. In the press release announcing abolition of Dialog connect-time charges in 1998 (DIALOG CORPORATION, THE), Dan Wagner cites customers' desire for a "more predictable pricing structure" as one reason for removal of the charges. However, Michael Foster, Reuters' director of business information, explains that Reuters is pricing its advanced service by connect hour (and its simpler version on a per-seat basis) because "we've always argued that it's important to keep pricing models straightforward and easy to understand if you want to grow your market" (LYON, 1998, p. 21).

Effect of the Internet on Online Services Pricing

A major recent influence on pricing of online services is the Internet. From the perspective of the four Ps model of the producer-oriented marketing mix, the Internet affects the types of product offered, the place (channel for distribution and use), and the types of promotion; therefore it is also likely to affect the price. The Internet has lowered costs, which are normally influential in pricing decisions. For example, Pat Tierney of Knight-Ridder says that using Web browsers as an interface decreases development and software costs, and John Regazzi of Engineering Information (Ei) sees the Internet as a low-cost distribution channel (WICKS). These lower costs mean it is easier for new companies to enter the online information services industry. This leads to increased competition among vendors.

KIRSCH highlights the expectation of Internet users that information will be cheap or free, and views these users as a mass market for which lower prices are appropriate. COLLIER (1997) expresses the view that, because the Internet has its roots in academia (where information is perceived as free) and the U.S. (where the advertising culture is strong), it is not surprising that users expect information to be funded by someone else (often an advertiser).

One of the most prominent casualties in 1997 was the online service NewsNet. Andrew Elston, NewsNet's president (O'LEARY, 1998), says changes brought about by the Internet contributed significantly to the demise of the service. He explains that customers were scanning free news sites and then using NewsNet to fill in the gaps, rather than visiting NewsNet to get everything. In other words, customers were becoming their own content aggregators.

FURNEAUX of Cambridge Scientific Abstracts lists twelve possible Internet pricing options: (1) free, (2) free to print subscribers, (3) regularly priced subscriptions for the full archive, (4) subscriptions with user surcharge, (5) subscriptions for unlimited site access, (6) multiple subscriptions with multifile discounts, (7) collections of files, (8) consortia pricing, (9) price per search, (10) transactional pricing, (11) advertising, and (12) sponsorship. He also lists seven factors that can influence electronic pricing decisions: (1) cost of sale, (2) price of the product in other media, (3) competition and what the market will bear, (4) previous prices, (5) brand, (6) estimates of the level of migration by customers to the new medium, and (7) the role of agents and other intermediaries in the information chain.

RANDALL mentions three current pricing models for Web-based content: (1) advertising-supported, which is simple to manage and apparently familiar to content producers; (2) subscription, which is appropriate for high-value content; and (3) pay-per-use, which is seen as unpopular because the necessary concomitant is a user-friendly, micro-payment mechanism that does not currently exist. Hybrid models also exist.

RANDALL proposes four scenarios for future development of the Internet, each of which results in different business models. In the first scenario, content producers negotiate with communities that bundle and license services. In the second, content aggregators derive significant revenue from advertising, and exploit the detailed information they have gathered about customers. In the third, content producers use a range of pricing strategies, based on usage transactions. In the final scenario, advertising supports many services, but there is also a range of priced services, and the choice is bewildering for customers. Randall comments that there is no logic in the way companies charge for their services and that companies providing information content are not profitable. He suggests strategies for content aggregators and specialist journals.

Effect of Consumer Online Pricing on Other Online Services

Consumer online services, which developed significantly because of the Internet, are also identified as an influence on business and professional online services. The term consumer online is used here to identify online services that explicitly target the consumer market, such as America Online (AOL).

A trend toward lower-priced services for end-users was noted by CSP INTERNATIONAL in 1986. Regina Brady (ABELS) draws attention to the fact that CompuServe was founded in 1969, although it was not launched fully until 1979. Brady also describes CompuServe's pricing structure, which was then based on the principle of unlimited access to basic services for a flat monthly fee, with connect-time and hit charges applied on other services. WHITE notes in 1996 that it is difficult to predict the price sensitivity of the emerging consumer online market.

In terms of pricing strategy, consumer hosts seem to be following the same path as traditional hosts, but in highly compressed form. After starting with subscriptions based on fees that vary according to amount of connect time used, they are moving to flat-fee unlimited-use pricing. By early 1998, both AOL and Microsoft Network (MSN) had adopted this strategy. This appears partly to be in response to the flat-fee pricing used by Internet service providers (ISPs). Donal Smith of FT Information (OWEN), among others, notes that it is becoming difficult for consumer hosts to differentiate themselves from the many other Web sites on the Internet that offer information.

For AOL, the move to flat-fee pricing resulted in a doubling of connect hours (BUTTERBAUGH). This pricing strategy may have the additional benefits of attracting and retaining customers who find the flat-fee option to be good value, and of potentially increasing nonsubscriber revenue streams. The latter may come from a boost to advertising because of increased hit rates on the AOL site, and from purchases from AOL's business partners on the AOL site. Traditional hosts and information producers, working with ASCII text and in a mainly business-to-business environment, do not have the same options to open alternative revenue streams within the core service.

In WICKS, John Regazzi of Ei and Andrew Elston of NewsNet both observe that customers expect hosts' prices to match those of consumer online services, and James E. Coane of Telebase Systems agrees that hosts must respond to the challenge and meet the customers' desire for innovative products at lower cost. QUINT (1994) describes a search on Dialog that cost $84.14 and yielded only bibliographic citations. She found that some of the material was available more cheaply on CompuServe and comments that prices must come down in order to keep old and new clients. KRUMENAKER notes that some information producers offer not only lower prices, but also more data when they migrate to consumer online services.

PROMOTIONAL PRICING

Promotional pricing involves using price as a promotional tool: for example, free samples and introductory offers. CRAM advises, "Never use price as a promotional weapon" (p. 152) as one of his rules of relationship pricing. However, a number of the reasons he cites for avoiding this strategy concern inventory stock levels, which are not a problem for online information. Some of the other grounds he cites, including the fact that promotional pricing can damage the company's value image or start price wars, have been raised as concerns in the online information services market.

Another deterrent to the use of free samples has been the fact that information can be seen as a satiation good: if a specific piece of information is supplied, it is unlikely to be required by the same customer again (unlike, e.g., a bar of chocolate, when sampling may lead to demand for more in exactly the same form). A counterargument is that customers may gain confidence in the whole product (the database, journal, online host, author) through their satisfaction with the sample; this will make them return to the same product when they have a similar information need. Sampling can probably be classified as satisfaction pricing in BERRY & YADAV's terms. It can certainly help build a brand and overcome the intangibility problem of information

With the Internet helping to reduce distribution costs for information, the use of promotional pricing is increasing and some types of information are making a shift from being products to being promotional tools. Traditional online services sometimes offered a few free hours of use to new customers, or a short period of free time on new databases, and publishers have offered the first issues of a journal free, in order to encourage customers to experiment with the product. In a discussion among U.K. academic librarians, recorded in JOINT INFORMATION SYSTEMS COMMITTEE, the value of free online trials is emphasized, along with the need to allow adequate time for serious evaluation of databases to take place. This practice is becoming far more widespread with traditional hosts, possibly due to the influence of consumer hosts distributing generous free trial passwords.

BROERING urges database producers to provide databases at low cost to academic medical institutions, on the grounds that if medical students use databases when they are in medical school, they will demand them in the workplace later. This also applies to other parts of the educational market, such as free provision of LEXIS to law students.

The educational discount strategy has been extended by electronic publishers, exploiting the fact that distribution costs for an electronic service are low and free publication can be sustained by the publisher for a longer period. FURNEAUX mentions free access to electronic publications as a means of building traffic prior to introducing fees or advertising. In some cases, the publisher has not announced in advance that the publication will eventually be priced. WEBBER describes the way in which The UnCover Company (whose core business is document delivery) introduced its free e-mailed table-of-contents service and let it run for almost a year before introducing charges. To some extent, this lack of advance notification reflects a genuine uncertainty on the publisher's part as to whether to opt for an advertising-supported or subscription-supported strategy.

Another strategy is a multi-tier approach to services. WEBBER notes that loss leaders are common in many sectors (e.g., selling bread at a loss, and pricing up other products that shoppers are less likely to cost-compare). She discusses the way in which information producers may provide free basic information on the Internet, hoping to attract high numbers of visitors, some of whom will go on to buy more sophisticated priced services. For example, Quote.Com and Electronic Share Information offered share prices for companies quoted on their local stock exchange free, and charged for other services. According to JANAL, this strategy enabled Quote.Com to approach the break-even point after four months of operation. WILLIAMS mentions provision of free access to bibliographic data, with priced access to full-text documents, as a positive opportunity for database producers.

This newly free information may be information that was formerly priced. TALWATTE notes that some players may intentionally devalue some information in order to establish their place on the Web. Talwatte's own company, Dun & Bradstreet, followed this model in mounting databases of basic company information as promotion for its full company information services.

POYNDER gives examples of hosts linking their online services to free news sites (e.g., GENIOS linking from its own top business paper

Das Handelsblatt), thus using the frequently updated news as promotion to raise awareness of the traditional online service. Poynder expresses surprise that more media owners have not adopted this strategy. The Financial Times' (FT) Donal Smith agrees that closer integration will be adopted for the free FT.COM Web site and priced FT Profile. Also from FT, Paul Maidment (GIBSON) envisions a future FT Web site consisting of advertising-supported free content, subscription services providing customized material, and pay-per-document archival services. He adds, however, that no one yet knows what business models will be successful on the Internet.

DIGITAL PUBLISHING STRATEGIES (1996) reports the views of various information producers on the Internet, in particular those with news sites. Most expect to maintain free content in order to attract people to the site, then identify value-added services that can be priced. Strategies include: (1) finding pockets of high-value content; (2) updating content to encourage repeat visits; (3) using intelligent agents to personalize the site and increase customer loyalty; and (4) creating multi-publisher communities with a strong brand image, including advertising-supported areas, priced classified advertising, priced premium services, and electronic commerce. The report also includes comments on the effect of a free online publication on print versions. All the contributors claim there has been no adverse effect on sales of print versions, and some note that the audience for the two media is different (e.g., a different age range), so a new market is being addressed by the Web versions.

The transition from core product to promotional tool has taken place for a number of information sources. JACSÓ (1996c) mentions the use of the UnCover database of free bibliographic citations, which raises awareness of the priced UnCover document delivery service and makes it easy for people to order documents from UnCover. He also discusses the use of free samples of text or audio on the Internet, and suggests that others could follow these models profitably.

However, some of these services provide information for which people have been prepared to pay traditional online services, such as bibliographic data for books, journal tables of contents, or current news stories. The case of NewsNet has already been mentioned. It is likely that the availability of, for example, free bookshop databases like Amazon.Com and free tables-of-contents databases have had an impact on priced bibliographic databases.

All the above strategies have benefited from the fact that any service providing useful information on the Internet receives free publicity. Compilers of directories or subject-based sites provide links to the free information. Print and electronic magazines and journals describe useful new sites. More importantly, by attracting more visitors to the site, businesses improve possibilities of increasing their advertising revenue.

Advertising-Supported Information Products

SPIGAI observes that advertising made up less than 1% of revenue for electronic information providers in 1989. With the Internet, this is changing. Printed consumer magazines and newspapers derive a large part, or all, of their income from advertising. It is interesting that database producers (particularly search engines) have also taken the advertising route. This is like Dialog's Dialindex being supported by advertising: an idea that would have been ridiculed only a few years ago. Today, it would be less of a surprise. In 1997, Yahoo! was the top advertising-supported site for the second year running, with $53.2 million in sales. Excite was second and Infoseek third. "The search engines remain almost a default buy among Web advertisers simply because they consistently offer the largest audience at one location on the Web," according to *ELECTRONIC ADVERTISING & MARKET-PLACE REPORT.*

REID (p. 271) says that

> guides, directories and pointers-to-others have never had it so good. It is inconceivable that book cataloguing would be a bigger business than book writing, or that TV Guide would ring up more revenue than the TV broadcast industry. But markets reward what's rare, context is rare on the Web, and Yahoo! and its competitors have fared well as a result.

Reid sees Yahoo! differentiating its product through hierarchical organization and indexing of material.

Firms pay for their articles to be included in the Mondaq site described by BLAKE (1998), in order to promote their services. The database is available free on the Web or via traditional online hosts. BLAKE notes that this business model—charging information producers but not information users—is very different from that of the traditional online world. Directory producers, however, are familiar with this strategy.

COTTRELL describes how Thomas Register (approaching its centenary in print form) provides free Web access, while charging manufacturers for enhanced entries in the Web directory, whereas it charges both directory users and manufacturers for the print version. The publishers express the view that enough print customers will remain loyal; the Thomas Register Web site does highlight the extra data and value available through the priced print versions.

A description of GTE SuperPages Web-based yellow pages directory (*INTERACTIVE CONTENT*) describes how almost all revenue comes from advertising (mostly enhanced business listings). BRUNER identifies some of the ways that Yellow Pages directories on the Internet, free to users, may derive income: from (1) advertisements, (2) Web-page creation for listed businesses, (3) providing content for other sites, or (4) becoming a shopping service (facilitating trade between the customer and a listed business). To this might be added (5) government subsidy, a factor also with the White Pages directories available for some countries. While some of these databases were not previously available on traditional online services, they at least provide information that competes with existing online priced directories.

Two key issues concerning the use of advertising revenue to support an information product (and thus cut its price to customers) are first, the possible influence advertisers might have on editorial content, and second, the effect on the total cost to the user. Advertising revenue has long provided significant income to printed consumer magazines and newspapers, and the influence of advertisers is as relevant to electronic media as it is to print. Important as this first issue is, it is outside the scope of this chapter.

The second issue, that of the effect on total cost to the user, is worth consideration here because some publications that are advertiser-supported on the Internet can be seen as substitutes for traditional online services. Most of the Internet news sites that helped kill NewsNet, for example, were supported by advertising. FURNEAUX of Cambridge Scientific Abstracts also mentions advertising as a means of supporting electronic publications aimed at technical and professional markets.

A key factor could be the extent to which customers perceive the addition of advertisements as an increased cost to them, particularly if more intrusive ads (such as interstitials, which take over the screen for a short period) are used. It is possible that home users may be more tolerant of this than those using the Internet at work (not to mention their employers). This issue is much debated in Internet advertising discussion lists and articles. OAKLEY ET AL., in the 1997 report on content prepared for the European Commission, also note the need to save time in the modern world, and the short attention span of the modern reader/viewer.

Push services with electronic ads are also seen as potentially costing more time than print ads. Vancil of Individual Inc. (LYON, 1997b) contrasts Individual's services with those of advertising-supported news services. He sees the content of the latter as too shallow to command a price, and emphasizes Individual's depth of coverage, facilities for tailoring profiles, retrospective coverage (for some services), and value added by human editors in selecting and digesting material.

PRICE DISCRIMINATION
AND PRODUCT DIFFERENTIATION

Price can be used to discriminate between different sectors of a market (e.g., academic, industrial), sizes of customer account, benefits (e.g., currency), or geographic regions. It is easiest to practice discrimination* by using a market characteristic that makes the sector easy to include or exclude. There may be a public-good element to price discrimination, such as educational discounts for schools. If the cost of the additional usage by a school is also low to the information vendor, this strategy also makes commercial sense. The different groups may form market segments with differing levels of price elasticity. A school may not be able to stretch its budget to the higher price, while a company is likely to accept that it should be charged more than a school (whereas it might demand the same low price if this were being offered to other customers in the private sector).

Quantity discounts and price discrimination by particular market sectors were used as pricing strategies from quite early in the life of the online industry. In 1986, CSP INTERNATIONAL notes instances of multi-tier pricing and discounting for non-prime-time searching (the latter being one way to overcome the perishability problem of services by encouraging people to even out their demands on the system). MULLER & WILSON provide a brief report on the types of discount scheme offered by hosts to frequent users in the mid-1980s. U.K. MONOPOLIES AND MERGERS COMMISSION gives a table comparing volume discounts on the database Textline from a number of hosts.

In NELSON's 1994 survey of information producers, all but ten out of 62 respondents offered discounts or differential pricing: most common were discounts on volume, discounts to academic customers, and discounts to those also taking the printed product. Respondents did not foresee major strategy changes within the next five years (i.e., to 1999). The two main reasons given for offering discounts were revenue maximization and customer satisfaction. In the academic context, the motive of educating future customers was also mentioned. Strategy varied according to the size of database produced: while only 50% of companies producing small databases offered some kind of pricing differential, all of the larger information producers did so.

SAFFADY (1996) gives examples of discounts available for a number of online hosts, noting the use of educational/academic discounts, member discounts, off-peak discounts, discounts in return for guaran-

---

*It should be noted that, in marketing terms, discrimination is seen as a neutral, not a pejorative word.

teed minimum payment or advance payment, volume discounts, and discounts for subscribers buying a product in more than one medium.

Discrimination by geographic area is becoming less prevalent: beyond legal restrictions (for example, in the European Union), services are more likely to be pressured directly by customers who are accustomed to surfing for information internationally and may see no reason for pricing and availability to differ from country to country. However, where there is a significant difference in willingness to pay (e.g., in a developing country) and the costs of additional consumption are low, it makes sense to set differing price rates.

VARIAN discusses discrimination of products by creating versions with different combinations of quality and price. This can be desirable where customers are willing and able to pay differing amounts for the same product, but the producer cannot easily exclude those who could pay more from buying the cheaper product. An example often given in this context is airline travel. Business travelers will pay more for the same product (an airline seat) than nonbusiness travelers. If there were simply two tariffs, one for business and one for nonbusiness travelers, then this might be circumvented (with employees encouraged by their company to buy tickets as individuals) and might also cause resentment. Therefore airlines have evolved a tariff scheme whereby improved quality (represented by, e.g., flexibility of travel time or improved quality of in-flight service) is matched by increased price. The customers self-select themselves into categories with more, or less, willingness to pay (WTP). The aim of the producer is to ensure that those with a greater WTP choose the high-price/high-quality package.

VARIAN points out that in order to ensure that customers with high WTP choose the higher-priced product, the quality of the lower-priced product has to be sufficiently low. As one example of the strategy, he gives the PAWWS Financial Network, which offers 20-minute delayed quotes at a sixth of the price of real-time quotes. Varian shows evidence that, in situations where there are not just two distinct markets with differing WTP, it is effective to have three versions: customers are more likely to gravitate toward, or trade up to, the middle-priced product. From the profitability point of view, it is important to set the middle and top options at a high enough level of price and quality. A further point made by Varian is the desirability of having control over the interface used for information content, because this may facilitate the cost-efficient creation of different versions.

WEBBER notes that hosts have often tried to discriminate between information professional and end-user markets by providing lower-priced, cut-down versions, such as fewer databases and fewer search options, for end-users (e.g., BRS After Dark). The hosts also developed similar services targeted at specific user groups (e.g., BRS Colleague, LEXIS-NEXIS' Company Quick Check).

Pat Tierney of Knight-Ridder (WICKS) distinguishes between end-users, who want subscriptions, and information professionals, who are acting as intermediaries and want transactional pricing. RANDALL, in proposing four scenarios for the future development of the Internet, also sees professional and business users as being more willing than individual consumers to pay on a transactional basis. Similarly, FISHBURN ET AL. say market behavior indicates that per-use plans appeal to businesses more than to individual consumers. As has been mentioned, Reuters (LYON, 1998) has essentially discriminated by type of customer by creating different version/price combinations to appeal to different target groups (low functionality with a charge per end-user for business people; high functionality with a charge by connect time for information professionals/researchers).

By identifying loss leaders and free samples, and repackaging the information for different audiences, both established players like The Dialog Corporation and new entrants like Quote.Com increase the layers of products derived from the same sources, but offering different sets of benefits. The same data may be differentiated in price through various options for access, selection, and delivery method. GOLDSTEIN foresees more market segmentation in pricing, with prices suited to individual needs.

Dow Jones' Tim Andrews (COPLER) stresses differentiation by adding value. "Customers don't expect everything on the Web to be free, but they do expect value" (p. 59). He notes that Dow Jones has enhanced the *Wall Street Journal* site (often cited as a shining rare example of a successfully priced Web newspaper) by adding context and interactivity. Andrews says the company consciously sought to differentiate Dow Jones Interactive from free search engines such as Alta Vista, emphasizing information quality and time savings for the customer. Michael Kolowich (BJØRNER) of the NewsEdge Corporation says explicitly that he expects companies to be looking at the cost of news overall instead of the price of news and therefore be willing to pay for news services that are more highly targeted at user needs.

Where there is public-sector involvement, pricing models may still be adapted to small-scale customers with no reduction in functionality. For example, one of the key stimuli for proposals to change the pricing model for access to datasets by U.K. universities was the inability of smaller institutions to afford the one-price flat-fee rates that had been the norm (JOINT INFORMATION SYSTEMS COMMITTEE). The final recommendation in this report is for a tiered pricing scheme.

Where there is no such public-good stimulus, however, there is no obligation to take full account of the small-scale customers' needs. A number of important online hosts and information producers have stated they are aiming at large-scale customers: for example, Donald McLagan (BJØRNER) of NewsEdge Corporation notes that its services definitely target large organizations. NewsEdge does try to provide a number of versions to suit different customers, but these versions may have significantly less content and be less convenient (e.g., the ad-heavy NewsPage, with only a five-day archive, aimed at individuals).

Exploring the ethics of such discrimination is beyond the scope of this chapter, but it can be said that it raises serious concerns (e.g., about disempowerment). The imposition of a monthly minimum charge by Dialog in June 1998 raises questions about whether smaller organizations will effectively be starved for access to a broad range of information sources (because they cannot afford the minimum charge), and whether this is socially acceptable.

Significant development of product/pricing packages was aimed at academic libraries in the 1990s; this is discussed in the section on disaggregation below.

AGGREGATION AND DISAGGREGATION OF PRICES

Bundling of goods is familiar in the information world, where customers may pay one price for an object such as a collection of print articles in a journal or company profiles on a CD-ROM. Given that valuing one information object is such a tricky business, setting a value on different combinations (bundles) of objects becomes even more difficult. In her examination of informativeness as a way of evaluating how well information services meet the needs of their communities, TAGUE-SUTCLIFFE (pp. 26-28) describes the problems of aggregating a sequence of records, or a sequence of customers of the same record. She points out that even the same record may not have the same level of informativeness for the same person at different points in time.

BAKOS & BRYNJOLFSSON analyze pricing strategies based on aggregation or disaggregation of information products, including both software and content. Aggregation includes bundling different products together; site licensing, or making one sale to different customers; and subscription, or selling one or more products across a period of time. Aggregation is a useful strategy when the marginal costs of each additional user are low, as tends to be the case for online information products. An obvious benefit of aggregation is saving on the cost of transacting individual sales. Additionally, Bakos and Brynjolfsson show that for large aggregations (many different products or many different customers bundled together), there will be more concentration on the mean valuation of the product, whereas in the whole population there will be a larger range of different individuals valuing different products at a high or low rate. Aggregating products or customers maximizes both income to the information producer and benefit to the information user. However, aggregation of services becomes less profitable when many customers have zero valuation for a given product in a bundle, and thus are less willing to pay for the entire bundle.

Site licensing tends to be transacted through an agent or intermediary. BAKOS & BRYNJOLFSSON point out that, on the one hand, the agent may have imperfect knowledge of the valuation of the products by end-users. On the other hand, in the case of experience goods (i.e., products that can be valued only by experiencing them), the agent may be able to draw on her/his greater experience with the product in order to make a better valuation on end-users' behalf than end-users could make themselves. This may well be the case when an information professional is negotiating a site license for a database. Site licenses often involve negotiation. The agent may deliberately represent end-users' valuation of the product as being less than it is in order to gain a more favorable price from the database producer. Either database producer or agent may also attempt to build a more accurate picture of an end-user's valuation by analogy with other end-users' valuations, through examining usage records, etc.

BAKOS & BRYNJOLFSSON identify four types of costs associated with bundling: (1) costs of producing the elements to go in the bundle; (2) distribution costs; (3) binding costs (e.g., costs of making many different records or databases for searching as one product); and (4) menu costs (costs of administering multiple prices). The authors seem to view the first two types of costs, production and distribution, as the more significant, although it could be said that for an online host, the binding costs are also particularly significant. They conclude that an optimal pricing strategy often includes both aggregation and disaggregation of products.

The move toward combinations of bundling and unbundling seems to be a notable development. For example, MACKIE-MASON & JANKOVICH describe a pricing experiment being carried out by Elsevier, 1996-1998, in which 1200 journals were made available electronically to academic institutions near the University of Michigan, with the aim of testing user reaction to different bundles. The authors say there are hundreds of possible bundling strategies. In the end they fixed on three options: (1) traditional subscription per journal; (2) individual (unbundled) article; and (3) unlimited access to a set of n articles selected by the user, with the option of buying increments of n articles. The authors see Elsevier aiming for a pricing model based on the value of the product to specific customer groups (implying price discrimination); the number of customers making use of products; and how often each customer uses the product.

Aggregation

The move toward fixed-fee pricing in the past few years can be considered a form of aggregation because this strategy bundles many transactions in one price. NELSON says 54% of the information providers in his 1994 survey had flat-fee or subscription plans, and that 65% of his respondents predicted they would use this form of pricing by 1999. As a recent example, Dialog (DIALOG CORPORATION, THE) announced further fixed-fee packages together with abolition of connect time as part of its pricing changes in 1998. O'LEARY (1993) describes some trends, giving the opinion that "flat rate pricing is the only way for online to fight back" against CD-ROM and tape leasing. He observes that "when online services have access to multiple databanks, one of which is flat-rate, the connect-rate databanks are spurned"(p. 35).

SULLIVAN & HEARTY of OCLC say that from OCLC's experience, "there is no question about the desire for fixed annual fee pricing. . . . Libraries still use pay-as-you-go models because the price for fixed annual fee access is perceived to be too high" (p. 99). They describe a simultaneous logon model, which they recommend for more general application, because it caters to both larger and smaller institutions.

FISHBURN ET AL. present a pricing model that indicates fixed-fee pricing is likely to be more profitable than per-use pricing, providing customers attach well-defined values to products and know how much of a product they are likely to consume. They point to AOL's move to fixed-fee pricing under pressure from its customers. They cite research (mostly from the telecommunications industry rather than the information content industry) showing that customers prefer subscription pricing, even quite often when they would profit financially by paying per use, for three reasons: (1) insurance against unexpectedly high bills; (2) overestimate of usage; and (3) the desire to avoid the hassle factor of having to think about costs every time the service is used. BERRY & YADAV say subscription plans also help develop relationships between vendor and customer.

The move toward fixed-fee pricing also may be influenced by the widespread use of CD-ROM. Current debate on appropriate pricing of site licenses to access online journals and datasets is influenced by experiences with pricing networked CD-ROM and magnetic tape. UNRUH & SCHIPPER provide a brief summary of pricing options for these media. The National Library of Medicine's scheme (GINTER), introduced in 1993, was typical in that its fixed charges took into account both demographics (e.g., number of customers) and past usage of the system. Ginter notes that, a year after its introduction, usage had increased 286%.

GILES-PETERS reports how, in 1990, the service CSIRO Australis shifted to flat-rate charging (minimum 50 hours usage) for its scientific databases. He found that usage did not change dramatically, but notes that some customers were reluctant to pay in advance for a service they were not sure they would use. Large organizations reacted by centralizing their accounts, so CSIRO had fewer subscriptions. The average number of databases used per searcher increased, as did the average number of hours used per searcher. Given the date of the experiment, it is likely that the promotion to and response from end-users was not as great as it would be now; indeed, Giles-Peters refers to the "mythical end-user."

In these examples, fees are fixed individually for each organization, or a flat fee will buy a fixed (and substantial) amount of usage. Fixed-fee/unlimited-use options are less popular with online hosts and database producers. In 1990, Reuters ceased to offer its flat-rate option for Textline, partly because it felt that large-scale customers were getting the services too cheaply. This was not a popular decision, and some commentators questioned whether it was the correct marketing strategy (*DATABASE SEARCHER*). Unlimited-use contracts are now more common in the academic sector.

A significant development is the rise of the library consortium, which can be viewed as aggregation of customers because consortia often negotiate deals that also aggregate products, including bibliographic databases, datasets, and journals. In many countries the buying power of the academic market is static or declining: while the actual demand is elastic, the budgets available to pay for the demand are inelastic. Pricing strategy of hosts and database producers in recent years is therefore geared toward gaining a larger market share. Public-sector bodies tend to have rigid budgeting cycles. Academic libraries are comfortable with committing their budgets in advance of usage; because this is what they typically do with journals, a fixed fee fits their budgeting patterns. Academic librarians may be encouraged to cut some other information sources in order to fund enhanced and distributed access to electronic journals or databases. They also have probably underestimated the cost of promoting and administering the service, while the host or database producer can achieve a saving in administrative costs by passing some of the administrative burden (training, allocating passwords, etc.) to the intermediary.

A fixed-fee strategy is less appropriate for the private-sector library market, because funding of information services by commercial companies is (theoretically at least) more elastic. Therefore one may observe information providers such as the Institute for Scientific Information (ISI) practicing price discrimination as well as aggregation.

In the United Kingdom (U.K.), a number of database producers (starting with ISI) have offered unlimited-use subscriptions to academic institutions, negotiated nationally by the Joint Information Systems Committee. The popularity of these options is shown in the substantial ongoing survey of U.K. academic library expenditures undertaken by EAST ET AL. Between 1988 and 1994, mean expenditures for end-user online services (chiefly Bath Information and Data Services (BIDS) and OCLC FirstSearch) increased from less than £1,000 (about $1,650) per university to more than £10,000 (about $16,500), while expenditures for mediated online services declined slightly.

Nevertheless, EAST ET AL. express the view that one-rate flat-fee charging is inappropriate because potential users at nonsubscribing institutions are excluded from access. They propose a rate related to potential volume of usage. This model is used by commercial hosts: for example, FLETCHER describes in detail the options introduced by Dialog in 1994. A couple of years after the report by EAST ET AL., a study commissioned by the JOINT INFORMATION SYSTEMS COMMITTEE recommended that there be three to five tiers of subscription, with institutions allocated to a tier according to a number of criteria, such as institutional size, the nature of the institution relative to the dataset, and special factors such as the presence of a relevant academic department.

Disaggregation

BAKOS & BRYNJOLFSSON discuss disaggregation, or unbundling, of information products. Disaggregation can be more profitable when distribution costs are low, customers are highly heterogeneous in their valuation of the product, or marginal costs of each additional usage are high. The first two conditions are likely to apply to a number of products. The example is given of a newspaper, for which disaggregated distribution of individual print articles is not likely to be profitable, but delivery of individual articles on the Internet may be. The authors see the Internet as a low-cost distribution mechanism that makes disaggregation of products more attractive, and they see the advent of technologies to enable micropayments as being of key importance.

One obvious pricing trend has been that away from connect time (a form of aggregation) and toward display charges. In his detailed analysis of prices, SAFFADY (1996) notes that while connect-time charges increased steadily from 1979 to 1992, the average connect-time rate for the sample of hosts and databases examined fell 3% annually between 1992 and 1996. Comparing Dialog databases by subject grouping, he shows that connect-time prices for general reference, humanities, and social sciences databases are lower than those of other subject groupings. Sci-tech databases (notably commercial patent and pharmaceutical files) have the highest connect-time prices. Saffady contrasts this with the decline in connect-time prices for business news databases from 1992 through 1996. He does not speculate on the reasons for these differences, but they could well reflect the fact that searchers of business databases are likely to be satisfied only if they find information, so a weighting toward display charges will probably represent value to the customer while maintaining revenue to the vendor. However, a patent searcher might well be pleased if a long complicated search yielded little or no return, so connect-time pricing could both represent value to the customer and protect revenue to the vendor.

SAFFADY (1996) notes both the increase in the number of databases with display charges (while 73% of Dialog files had display charges in 1984, 99% had them in 1996), and the increase in the price charged for displays. Looking at average display charges for each host from the 1980s through 1996 is not very meaningful, because most host systems have dramatically increased the number of full-text databases during this period, and thus the offerings are not comparable. SAFFADY (1996) does compare display charges for some individual databases through the years. While some have increased the amount of full text (and therefore might be justified in increasing the cost of a full record), many that did not augment their records nevertheless made steep increases in display charges.

NELSON notes with surprise that 46% of the information producers responding to his survey expected connect-time prices to increase, with only a third expecting a decline. They forecast a slight move away from display charges, though not as significant a decrease as that forecast for connect time as a pricing mechanism. Nelson comments that pricing is likely to continue moving away from traditional models, especially connect time, which will be replaced in part by a combination of other methods that focus more on value of information received.

The move toward increased weighting of display charges has generally been identified as a way of reflecting value to users (see WICKS), but even this is not a clear-cut issue. For example, QUINT (1997), in her detailed analysis of the effect of the steady rise of the cost of Dialog format 3 (basic bibliographic details) coupled with a previous rise in the cost of the KWIC format, concludes that "this pricing has no logic, that I can see, in value delivered" (p. 23), despite a decrease in connect-time charges over the period. This seems to indicate how careful information vendors must be in fine-tuning their pricing, and how they cannot assume that users (especially trained information professionals) will accept untested vendors' assurances about value and simplicity.

Skepticism about the benefit of the shift from connect-time to display charges may be justified. SAFFADY's (1996) calculation of the total cost (display and connect-time) of the same hypothetical search across 38 Dialog databases in 1979 and 1996 showed that, on average, costs increased 12.4% a year. The annual increase from 1992 through 1996 is

14.25%. Although connect-time prices had fallen, the increase in hit charges more than offset this. SAFFADY observes that the trend toward information-based pricing has enormous implications for online search techniques.

Searchers are indeed likely to change their search habits to maximize value. For example, Marino Saksida of ESA-IRS (GARMAN, 1990) notes changes in searching habits following ESA-IRS's replacement in 1989 of connect-time charges by file-entry charges. Additionally, with information-based pricing, the price of searches that yield no hits will decrease, so that the total cost of all searches (both successful and unsuccessful) might not increase.

CONCLUSION

While there are some general trends in online pricing, there seems to be no general solution to the pricing conundrum. Some trends (e.g., toward flat fees) seem to indicate greater simplicity in pricing mechanism. However, even as this article was being completed, The Dialog Corporation announced the introduction of the DialUnit, a pricing mechanism that recalls per-search charges and charges for Central Processing Unit (CPU) time. Complicated multipart pricing continues. Vendors' increasing sophistication in using price as part of the marketing mix may in fact lead to a wider range of pricing strategies aiming at different market segments. This could make prices of online products more, not less, difficult to evaluate and compare.

The effect of the Internet as a low-cost distribution channel and the entry of more players into the online market seems bound to prolong this era of change. There will certainly also be more changes in the pricing of electronic journal and magazine articles. The one consolation is that, in this continuingly complex environment, there seems to be more need than ever for alert, informed information professionals who can steer end-users to the best pricing deals.

BIBLIOGRAPHY

ABELS, EILEEN G. 1996. Pricing of Electronic Resources: Interviews with Three Vendors. Journal of the American Society for Information Science. 1996 March; 47(3): 235-246. ISSN: 0002-8231; CODEN: AISJB6.

ARNOLD, STEPHEN E. 1989. Online Pricing: Where It's at Today and Where It's Going Tomorrow. Online. 1989 March; 13(2): 6-9. ISSN: 0146-5422.

ARNOLD, STEPHEN E. 1990. Marketing Electronic Information: Theory, Practice, and Challenges, 1980-1990. In: Wlliams, Martha E. , ed. Annual Review of Information Science and Technology: Volume 25. Amsterdam, The Netherlands: Elsevier Science Publishers B.V. for the American Society for Information Science; 1990. 87-144. ISSN: 0066-4200; ISBN: 0-444-88531-5; CODEN: ARISBC.

ARNOLD, STEPHEN E. 1991. Pricing: An Old Problem with New Worries. NFAIS Newsletter. 1991 August; 33(8): 103-105. ISSN: 0090-0893; CODEN: NFNLA6.

BAILEY, CHARLES W., JR. 1998. Scholarly Electronic Publishing Bibliography. Version 21. Houston, TX: University Libraries, University of Houston; 1998 September 18. Available WWW: http://info.lib.uh.edu/sepb/sepb.html.

BAKOS, YANNIS; BRYNJOLFSSON, ERIK. 1998. Aggregation and Disaggregation of Information Goods: Implications for Bundling, Site Licensing and Micropayment Systems. In: Hurley, Deborah; Kahin, Brian; Varian, Hal, eds. Internet Publishing and Beyond: The Economics of Digital Information and Intellectual Property; [Proceedings]: 1997 January 23-25; Cambridge, MA. Cambridge, MA: MIT Press; 1998. ISBN: 0-262-58159-0. Available WWW: http://www.gsm.uci.edu/~bakos/aig.pdf.

BASCH, REVA, ed. 1995. Electronic Information Delivery: Ensuring Quality and Value. Aldershot, England: Gower; 1995. 264p. ISBN: 0-566-07567-9.

BATES, MARY ELLEN. 1995. Search Strategies for Dialog's View Fee. Online. 1995 January/February; 19(1): 22-31. ISSN: 0146-5422.

BERRY, LEONARD L.; YADAV, MANJIT S. 1996. Capture and Communicate Value in the Pricing of Services. Sloan Management Review. 1996 Summer; 37(4): 41-51. ISSN: 0019-848X; CODEN: SMRVAO.

BERTHA, EVA. 1997. Comparisons of Pricing Structures of Information on Various Electronic Media. FID News Bulletin. 1997 June; 47(6): 175-180. ISSN: 0014-5874.

BJØRNER, SUSANNE. 1998. The Desktop Data/Individual, Inc. Merger. Online. 1998 March; 22(2): 28-34. ISSN: 0146-5422.

BLAKE, PAUL. 1994. Interview: Allen Paschal. Monitor. 1994 June; (160): 12-16. ISSN: 0260-6666.

BLAKE, PAUL. 1998. Why Publishers Pay to Offer Their Data for Free. Information World Review. 1998 April; (135): 27-28. ISSN: 0950-9879.

BRADY, JOHN; DAVIS, IAN. 1993. Marketing's Mid-Life Crisis. McKinsey Quarterly. 1993; (2): 17-28. ISSN: 0047-5394.

BRODWIN, DAVID; KLINE, DAVID. 1998. Information Publishing Enters a Post-Web World. Upside. 1998 February; 10(2): 102-105. ISSN: 1052-0341. Available WWW: http://www.upside.com/.

BROERING, NAOMI C. 1992. Strategies for Pricing Site Licenses. NFAIS Newsletter. 1992 June; 34(6): 61-62. ISSN: 0090-0893; CODEN: NFNLA6.

BRUNER, RICK E. 1997. Yellow Pages See Green on the Net. Advertising Age. 1997 June 2; 68(22): S6. ISSN: 0001-8899.

BUCHER, RAINER. 1993. Einigermassen undurchschaubar: die Preispolitik der Online-Anbieter. [Somewhat Opaque: Pricing Policy of Online Vendors.] Cogito (Germany). 1993; 9(4): 5-7. ISSN: 0178-8728.

BUNTROCK, ROBERT E. 1984. Cost Effectiveness of On-Line Searching of Chemical Information: An Industrial Viewpoint. Journal of Chemical Information and Computer Sciences. 1984; 24: 54-57. ISSN: 0095-2338.

BUSINESSWIRE. 1993. Dialog Announces Resolution of Dispute with the American Chemical Society and Settlement of Litigation. Businesswire. 1993 October 29. Available on Dialog: File 610 Businesswire.

BUTTERBAUGH, SEAN. 1997. Report: AOL Strategy May Be a Pandora's Box. Media Daily. 1997 January 10. Available on Dialog: File 16 IAC PROMT.

BYSOUTH, PETER. 1987. The Economics of Online. London, England: Taylor Graham; 1987. 229p. (Foundations of Information Science: volume 2). ISBN: 0-947568-14-X.

CAHILL, DENNIS J. 1996. Further Issues in Pricing Strategies for Electronic Information. Pricing Strategy and Practice. 1996; 4(1): 34-38. ISSN: 0968-4905.

COLLIER, HARRY. 1993. Strategies in the Electronic Information Industry: A Guide for the 1990s. 2nd edition. Calne, England: Infonortics Ltd.; 1993. 120p. ISBN: 1-87369-907-7.

COLLIER, HARRY. 1997. The Question That Won't Go Away. Digital Publishing Strategies. 1997 April; 1(8): 16. ISSN: 1365-0688.

COPLER, JUDI. 1997. Behind the Scenes at Dow Jones. Database. 1997 June; 20(3): 55-60. ISSN: 0162-4105.

COTTRELL, DONNELLA. 1997. Persistence Pays Off. Internet World. 1997 December; 8(12): 49-50. ISSN: 1064-3923.

CRAM, TONY. 1994. The Power of Relationship Marketing: How to Keep Customers for Life. London, England: Pitman; 1994. 254p. ISBN: 0-273-60907-6.

CSP INTERNATIONAL. 1986. The Global Structure of the Electronic Information Services Industry. London, England: The British Library; 1986. 58p. (British Library Research Papers no. 1). ISBN: 0-7123-3091-7.

DATABASE PROMOTION CENTER, JAPAN. 1996. Databases in Japan 1996. Tokyo, Japan: Database Promotion Center, Japan; 1996. 120p. OCLC: 28211544.

DATABASE SEARCHER. 1990. Reuters Pricing Controversy in Europe. Database Searcher. 1990; 6(6): 25. ISSN: 0891-6713.

DIALOG CORPORATION, THE. 1998. The Dialog Corporation Drops Connect Time Charges. Mountain View, CA: The Dialog Corporation; 1998 May 1. Press Release. Available WWW: http://www.dialog.com/.

DIGITAL PUBLISHING STRATEGIES. 1996. Summit Presents Practical Views on Internet Publishing. Digital Publishing Strategies. 1996 October; 1(2): 6-9. ISSN: 1365-0688.

DIGITAL PUBLISHING STRATEGIES. 1997. End-Users Won't Pay for E-products. Digital Publishing Strategies. 1997 June; 2(6): 13. ISSN: 1365-0688.

DUCKITT, PAULINE; MAY, NIGEL. 1988. Online Charging Policies: A UKOLUG Report. London, England: UK Online User Group; 1988. 19p. Available from: British Library Document Supply Centre, Boston Spa, Wetherby, Yorkshire, England, shelfmark Q025.52.

DUNN, RONALD D.; BOYLE, HARRY F. 1984. On-line Searching: Costly or Cost-Effective? A Marketing Perspective. Journal of Chemical Information and Computer Sciences. 1984; 24(2): 51-54. ISSN: 0095-2338; CODEN: JCISD8.

EAST, HARRY. 1986. Non-Profit Organisations in the UK Online Database Market. Aslib Proceedings. 1986 September; 38(9): 327-334. ISSN: 0001-253X.

78   SHEILA ANNE ELIZABETH WEBBER

EAST, HARRY; LEACH, KATHRYN. 1997. A Survey on Attitudes to the
Pricing of JISC-Funded Databases. London, England: City University,
Department of Information Science, Database Resources Research Group;
1997 February. Available WWW: http://www.soi.city.ac.uk/informatics/
is/drrg/attitu97/attitu97.html.
EAST, HARRY; SHEPPARD, ELAINE; JEAL, YVETTE. 1995. A Huge Leap
Forward: A Quantitative and Qualitative Examination of the Development
of Access to Database Services by British Universities 1988-1994. London,
England: University of Westminster; 1995. 119p. (British Library R & D
Report 6202; Centre for Communications and Information Studies Policy
Paper no. 5). OCLC: 33244361.
ELECTRONIC ADVERTISING & MARKETPLACE REPORT. 1998. Web Ad-
vertising Revenue Totals $597.1 Million for 1997, Up 152.6% from 1996.
Electronic Advertising & Marketplace Report. 1998 Jan 27. Available on
Dialog: File 16 IAC PROMT.
FISHBURN, PETER C.; ODLYZKO, ANDREW M.; SIDERS, RYAN C. 1998.
Fixed Fee Versus Unit Pricing for Information Goods: Competition, Equi-
libria and Price Wars. In: Hurley, Deborah; Kahin, Brian; Varian, Hal, eds.
Internet Publishing and Beyond: The Economics of Digital Information
and Intellectual Property; [Proceedings]: 1997 January 23-25; Cambridge,
MA. Cambridge, MA: MIT Press; 1998. ISBN: 0-262-58159-0. Available
WWW: http://ksgwww.harvard.edu/iip/econ/odlyzko.html.
FLETCHER, LLOYD ALAN. 1994. DIALOG Price Restructure Evaluation:
Tentative Steps on the Road to Value-Based Pricing. Searcher. 1994
October; 2(9): 44-60. ISSN: 1070-4795.
FLOWERDEW, ANTHONY DAVID JOHN; OLDMAN, CHRISTINE M.;
WHITEHEAD, CHRISTINE M.E. 1984. The Pricing and Provision of
Information: Some Recent Official Reports. London, England: The British
Library; 1984. 96p. (Library and Research Report no. 20). ISBN: 0-7123-
3029-1.
FURNEAUX, MARK. 1997. Pricing Models for Electronic Access. NFAIS
Newsletter. 1997 July; 39(7): 88-89. ISSN: 0090-0893; CODEN: NFNLA6.
GARMAN, NANCY. 1990. Online Pricing: An Interview with Marino F.
Saksida of ESA-IRS. Online. 1990 January; 14(1): 30-34. ISSN: 0146-5422.
GARMAN, NANCY. 1995. The Pricing Conundrum. Online. 1995 January/
February; 19(1): 6-7. ISSN: 0146-5422.
GIBSON, PAUL. 1996. FT Information Launches Free Company Reports.
Information World Review. 1996 December; (120): 27. ISSN: 0950-9879.
GILES-PETERS, LEA. 1991. What Price Information: Flat Price or Flat Broke?
In: Raitt, David I., ed. Online Information 91: Proceedings of the 15th
International Online Information Meeting; 1991 December 10-12; London,
England. Oxford, England: Learned Information; 1991. 399-407. ISBN: 0-
904933-79-2.
GINTER, KAREN A. 1994. Fixed Fee and the Internet: A Formula That Works.
National Library of Medicine News. 1994 July/August; 49(3): 1, 3. ISSN:
0027-965X.
GOLDSTEIN, MORRIS. 1990. In Search of Pricing Equity. NFAIS Newsletter.
1990 March; 32(3): 25, 27. ISSN: 0090-0893; CODEN: NFNLA6.

GRASHOFF, TUDOR. 1995. Costs and Revenues. CD-ROM Professional. 1995 January; 8(1): 24-35. ISSN: 1049-0833.

GRONROOS, CHRISTIAN. 1994. From Marketing Mix to Relationship Marketing: Towards a Paradigm Shift in Marketing. Management Decision. 1994; 32(2): 4-20. ISSN: 0025-1747. Available WWW: http://www.mcb.co.uk/services/conferen/feb96/relation.mar/new_phil/backgrnd.htm.

HAGEL, JOHN, III; RAYPORT, JEFFREY F. 1997. The New Infomediaries. McKinsey Quarterly. 1997; (4): 55-70. ISSN: 0047-5394.

HANNA, NESSIM; DODGE, H. ROBERT. 1995. Pricing Policies and Procedures. London, England: Macmillan; 1995. 216p. ISBN: 0-333-61125-X.

HAWKINS, DONALD T. 1996. Information Metering: Paving the Way for Pay-Per-View Information. Online. 1996 July/August; 20(4): 36-41. ISSN: 0146-5422.

HOCK, RANDOLPH E. 1994. The Moving Target: Selling Online Services in the Late 1990s. In: Staying in Business in the Information Business [The Economics of Information: American Society for Information Science(ASIS) 57th Annual Meeting; 1994 October 17-20; Alexandria, VA.] Garden Grove, CA: InfoMedix; 1994. Audio cassette. (G2390-42B.)

HYAMS, PETER. 1996. Lovely Idea, But Unlovely Pricing. Monitor. 1996 February; (180): 2-3. ISSN: 0260-6666.

INFORMATION TODAY. 1993. National Library of Medicine. Information Today. 1993; 10(2): 64. ISSN: 8755-6286.

INTERACTIVE CONTENT. 1998. Yellow Pages: Crowded Online Field. Interactive Content. 1998 January 1. Available on Dialog: File 16 IAC PROMT.

INTERNATIONAL COALITION OF LIBRARY CONSORTIA (ICOLC). 1998. Statement of Current Perspective and Preferred Practices for the Selection and Purchase of Electronic Information. New Haven, CT: ICOLC; 1998 March. Available WWW: http://www.library.yale.edu/consortia/statement.html.

JACSÓ, PÉTER. 1996a. The Online Bottom Line: Changes in CompuServe's Pricing Scheme: Surprise, Surprise. Online. 1996 May/June; 20(3): 51-54. ISSN: 0146-5422.

JACSÓ, PÉTER. 1996b. Watching Your Online Bottom Line. Online. 1996 July/August; 20(4): 50-51. ISSN: 0146-5422.

JACSÓ, PÉTER. 1996c. Who's Gonna Pay the Piper for Free Online Databases? Database. 1996 June/July; 19(3): 8-9. ISSN: 0162-4105.

JAMES, JONATHAN. 1994. Quality vs. Price: Assessing the Trade-Offs. NFAIS Newsletter. 1994 September; 36(9): 97-99. ISSN: 0090-0893; CODEN: NFNLA6.

JAMIOLKOWSKI, NANCY. 1991. The Age of Pricing. NFAIS Newsletter. 1991 August; 33(8): 101-102. ISSN: 0090-0893; CODEN: NFNLA6.

JANAL, DANIEL S. 1998. Online Marketing Handbook. 2nd edition. New York, NY: John Wiley; 1998. 450p. ISBN: 0-471-29310-5.

JOINT INFORMATION SYSTEMS COMMITTEE. 1998. Report from the Charging Working Group of the CEI. Bristol, England: NISS; 1998. Available WWW: http://www.jisc.ac.uk/pub97/charging.html.

KABACK, STUART M. 1991. An Unsuitable Situation. Database. 1991; 14(3): 6-8. ISSN: 0162-4105.

KARP, RICHARD. 1996. My Pal EDGAR. Barron's. 1996 March 11; 76: 12-13. ISSN: 1077-8039.

KENTON, DAVID. 1984. The Development of a More Equitable Method of Billing for Online Services. Online. 1984 September; 8(5): 13-17. ISSN: 0146-5422.

KIERZKOWSKI, ALEXA; MCQUADE, SHAYNE; WAITMAN, ROBERT; ZEISSER, MICHAEL. 1996. Marketing to the Digital Consumer. McKinsey Quarterly. 1996; (3): 5-21. ISSN: 0047-5394.

KING, DONALD W.; GRIFFITHS, JOSÉ-MARIE. 1995. Economic Issues Concerning Electronic Publishing and Distribution of Scholarly Articles. Library Trends. 1995 Spring; 43(4): 713-740. ISSN: 0024-2594.

KIRSCH, STEVEN T. 1995. Selling Information on the Internet. In: Williams, Martha E., ed. Proceedings of the 16th National Online Meeting; 1995 May 2-4; New York, NY. Medford, NJ: Learned Information, Inc.; 1995. 217-222. ISBN: 1-57387-004-8.

KOTLER, PHILIP. 1997. Marketing Management: Analysis, Planning, Implementation and Control. 9th edition. Upper Saddle River, NJ: Prentice-Hall; 1997. 1 volume. ISBN: 0-13-243510-1.

KRUMENAKER, LARRY. 1994 Platform Blues: The Cozy World of Online Starts to Shatter. Searcher. 1994 October; 2(9): 22-26. ISSN: 1070-4795.

LAUTERBORN, BOB. 1990. New Marketing Litany: Four Ps Passe: C-words Take Over. Advertising Age. 1990 October; 61(41): 26. ISSN: 0001-8899.

LOMIO, J. PAUL. 1985. The High Cost of NEXIS and What a Searcher Can Do about It. Online. 1985 September; 9(5): 54-56. ISSN: 0146-5422.

LYON, JO. 1997a. The Death of the Online Host? Information World Review. 1997 January; (121): 23. ISSN: 0950-9879.

LYON, JO. 1997b. Getting Intimate with Individual. Information World Review. 1997 March; (123): 17. ISSN: 0950-9879.

LYON, JO. 1998. Matching News with Needs. Information World Review. 1998 March; (134): 21. ISSN: 0950-9879.

MACKIE-MASON, JEFFREY K.; JANKOVICH, ALEXANDRA L. L. 1997. PEAK: Pricing Electronic Access to Knowledge. Library Acquisitions Practice and Theory. 1997 Fall; 21(3): 281-295. ISSN: 0364-6408.

MILLER, CARMEN. 1994. DIALOG's New Answer-Based Pricing. Online. 1994 September/October; 18(5): 49-52. ISSN: 0146-5422.

MULLER, PETER H.; WILSON, ROY. 1985. Pricing Policies for Parallel Publishing. Oxford, England: Elsevier; 1985. 74p. ISBN: 0-946395-15-2.

NAGLE, THOMAS. 1984. Economic Foundations for Pricing. Journal of Business. 1984; 57(1 part 2): S3-S26. ISSN: 0021-9398.

NELSON, MICHAEL L. 1995. Database Pricing: A Survey of Practices, Predictions, and Opinions. Online. 1995 November/December; 19(6): 76-86. ISSN: 0146-5422.

O'LEARY, MICK. 1993. Flat Rate Online: A New Online Era Begins. Online. 1993 January; 17(1): 34-38. ISSN: 0146-5422.

O'LEARY, MICK. 1998. The End of NewsNet. Online. 1998 January; 22(1): 49-54. ISSN: 0146-5422.

OAKLEY, BRIAN; KUETER, DEREK; O'HEA, KIERAN, eds. 1997. The Future of Content: Discussions on the Future of European Electronic Publishing:

Version 1. Luxembourg: TECHSERV under contract to the European Commission; 1997. 162p. Available from: European Commission DG XIII/ E, Rue de la Loi 200, B-1049, Brussels, Belgium.

ONLINE FILES: COMPARATIVE COST ANALYSIS: a Unique Guide to the Costs of Searching the World's Major Online Databases. 1993-. Humberston, England: Effective Technology Marketing. ISSN: 0967-6090. [Formerly (1989-1992): Clover Comparative Cost Chart for Online Files. ISSN: 0959-5619]

OWEN, TIM. 1996. Internet Poses No Threat to Online Business, Hosts Claim. Information World Review. 1996 December; (120): 7. ISSN: 0950-9879.

PEMBERTON, JEFFERY K. 1988. Online Interviews Harry Boyle on CAS's New License Policy . . . Effects on Searching/Prices. Online. 1988 March; 12(2): 19-25. ISSN: 0146-5422.

POYNDER, RICHARD. 1997. It's the Brand, Stupid. Information Today. 1997 May; 14(5): 14-15, 30. ISSN: 8755-6286.

PRATT, GORDON, ed. 1976. Information Economics: Costs and Prices of Machine-Readable Information in Europe. London, England: Aslib; 1976. 115p. ISBN: 0-85142-078-8.

QUELCH, JOHN A.; KLEIN, LISA R. 1996. The Internet and International Marketing. Sloan Management Review. 1996 Spring; 37(3): 60-75. ISSN: 0019-848X; CODEN: SMRVAO.

QUINT, BARBARA. 1994. $84.14. Information Today. 1994 October; 11: 7-9. ISSN: 8755-6286.

QUINT, BARBARA. 1995. Pricing for the Masses. NFAIS Newsletter. 1995 December; 37(12): 133, 135-136, 138. ISSN: 0090-0893; CODEN: NFNLA6.

QUINT, BARBARA. 1997. Out of Cite: The High Cost of Dialog's Format 3. Searcher. 1997 March; 5(3): 16-23. ISSN: 1070-4795.

RANDALL, DOUG. 1997. Consumer Strategies for the Internet: Four Scenarios. Long Range Planning. 1997; 30(2): 157-168. ISSN: 0024-6301.

REID, ROBERT H. 1997. Architects of the Web: 1,000 Days That Built the Future of Business. New York, NY: John Wiley; 1997. 370p. ISBN: 0-471-17187-5.

ROWLEY, JENNIFER. 1993. How Much Will My Search Cost? A Review of the Changing Policies of the Online Hosts. Online & CD-ROM Review. 1993; 17(3): 143-148. ISSN: 0309-314X.

ROWLEY, JENNIFER. 1995. Issues in Pricing Strategies for Electronic Information. Pricing Strategy and Practice. 1995; 3(2): 4-13. ISSN: 0968-4905.

ROWLEY, JENNIFER; BUTCHER, DAVID. 1996. Pricing Strategies for Business Information on CD-ROM. Journal of Information Science. 1996; 22(1): 39-46. ISSN: 0165-5515.

SAFFADY, WILLIAM. 1979. Online Bibliographic Searching: Costs and Cost Justification. Library Technology Reports. 1979; 15(5): 567-653. ISSN: 0024-2586.

SAFFADY, WILLIAM. 1985. The Availability and Cost of Online Search Services. Library Technology Reports. 1985; 21(1): 1-111. ISSN: 0024-2586.

SAFFADY, WILLIAM. 1988. The Availability and Cost of Online Search Services. Library Technology Reports. 1988; 24(3): 289-502. ISSN: 0024-2586.

SAFFADY, WILLIAM. 1992. The Availability and Cost of Online Search Services. Library Technology Reports. 1992; 28(2): 115-268. ISSN: 0024-2586.

SAFFADY, WILLIAM. 1996. The Availability and Cost of Online Search Services. Library Technology Reports. 1996; 32(3): 337-451. ISSN: 0024-2586.

SANSOM, CLARE. 1996. Investing in the Future of the Online Community. Information World Review. 1996 November; (119): 33-34. ISSN: 0950-9879.

SARACEVIC, TEFKO; KANTOR, PAUL B. 1997. Studying the Value of Library and Information Services: Part I: Establishing a Theoretical Framework. Journal of the American Society for Information Science. 1997 June; 48(6): 527-541. ISSN: 0002-8231; CODEN: AISJB6.

SILK, J.A. 1982. Comparative Costs of Online Searching in European Countries. Wembley, England: EUSIDIC; 1982. 18p. (EUSIDIC Technical Note No. 2). OCLC: 11392535.

SILLINCE, JOHN A.A.; SILLINCE, MARIA. 1993. Market Pressure and Government Intervention in the Administration and Development of Molecular Databases. Journal of the American Society for Information Science. 1993; 44(1): 28-39. ISSN: 0002-8231; CODEN: AISJB6.

SMITH, E.I.; STEINMAN, JEFF. 1996. EDGAR on the Internet: Delight and Dilemma. In: Williams, Martha E., ed. Proceedings of the 17th National Online Meeting; 1996 May 14-16; New York, NY. Medford, NJ: Information Today, Inc.; 1996. 347-355. ISBN: 1-57387-026-9.

SPIGAI, FRAN. 1991. Information Pricing. In: Williams, Martha E., ed. Annual Review of Information Science and Technology (ARIST): Volume 26. Medford, NJ: Learned Information, Inc. for the American Society for Information Science; 1991. 39-73. ISSN: 0066-4200; ISBN: 0-938734-55-5; CODEN: ARISBC.

SPREHE, J. TIMOTHY. 1996. Are the National Technical Information Service's Prices Too High? Government Information Quarterly. 1996; 13(4): 373-391. ISSN: 0740-624X.

SULLIVAN, JOHN; HEARTY, JOHN A. 1994. Pricing Information for End Users. NFAIS Newsletter. 1994 September; 36(9): 97, 99. ISSN: 0090-0893; CODEN: NFNLA6.

TAGUE-SUTCLIFFE, JEAN. 1995. Measuring Information: An Information Services Perspective. San Diego, CA: Academic Press; 1995. 206p. ISBN: 0-12-682660-9.

TALWATTE, GEHAN. 1997. What Price Information? In: Raitt, David I.; Blake, Paul; Jeapes, Ben, eds. Online Information 97: Proceedings of the 21st International Online Information Meeting; 1997 December 9-11; London, England. Oxford, England: Learned Information; 1997. 277-279. ISBN: 1-900871-21-1.

TAYLOR, LESTER D. 1994. Telecommunications Demand in Theory and Practice. Revised edition. Dordrecht, The Netherlands: Kluwer Academic Publishing; 1994. 406p. ISBN: 0-7923-2389-0; LC: 93-14522.

TINCKNELL, BRUCE. 1997. Searching Smart Costs Extra: KWIC Format Charging at Dialog. Searcher. 1997 March; 5(3): 44-55. ISSN: 1070-4795.

U.K. MONOPOLIES AND MERGERS COMMISSION. 1994. Historical On-line Database Services: A Report on the Supply in the UK of Services Which Provide Access to Databases Containing Archival Business and Financial Information. London, England: HMSO; 1994. 96p. (Cm 2554). ISBN: 0-10-125542-X.

UNRUH, BETTY; SCHIPPER, WENDY. 1991. Information Distribution Issues for the 90s. Philadelphia, PA: National Federation of Abstracting and Information Services; 1991. 156p. ISBN: 0-942308-30-1.

VARIAN, HAL R. 1997. Versioning Information Goods. In: Hurley, Deborah; Kahin, Brian; Varian, Hal, eds. Internet Publishing and Beyond: The Economics of Digital Information and Intellectual Property; [Proceedings]: 1997 January 23-25; Cambridge, MA. Cambridge, MA: MIT Press; 1998. ISBN: 0-262-58159-0. Available WWW: http://ksgwww.harvard.edu/iip/econ/varian.html.

WALKER, BECKI. 1995. Relationship Marketing: The Cornerstone of Distribution Planning. CD-ROM Professional. 1995; 8(1): 48-50. ISSN: 1049-0833.

WEBBER, SHEILA ANNE ELIZABETH. 1995. Online Pricing: Changing Strategies in a Changing World. In: Raitt, David I.; Jeapes, Ben, eds. Online Information 95: Proceedings of the 19th International Online Information Meeting; 1995 December 5-7; London, England. Oxford, England: Learned Information; 1995. 1-12. ISBN: 0-904933-94-6.

WHITE, MARTIN. 1996. The Market Prospects for Consumer Online Services in Europe. In: Raitt, David I.; Jeapes, Ben, eds. Online Information 96: Proceedings of the 20th International Online Information Meeting; 1996 December 3-5; London, England. Oxford, England: Learned Information; 1996. 313-319. ISBN: 1-900871-04-1.

WICKS, WENDY K. 1995. Yes, We Have No Pricing Panaceas: The Industry Speaks. NFAIS Newsletter. 1995 December; 37(12): 133-137. ISSN: 0090-0893; CODEN: NFNLA6.

WILLIAMS, MARTHA E. 1994. The Internet: Implications for the Information Industry and Database Providers. Online & CD-ROM Review. 1994 June; 18(3): 149-156. ISSN: 0309-314X.

WILSON, TOM. 1994. EQUIP: A European Survey of Quality Criteria for the Evaluation of Databases: Report on the Questionnaire Survey. Sheffield, England: The Cura Consortium; 1994. 13p. Available from: the author, T.D.Wilson@sheffield.ac.uk.

II

Basic Techniques and Technologies

Section II contains four chapters, three of which are first-time chapters for *ARIST*. Gary Marchionini of the University of North Carolina and Anita Komlodi of the University of Maryland discuss "Design of Interfaces for Information Seeking," Elin K. Jacob and Debora Shaw of Indiana University investigate "Sociocognitive Perspectives on Representation," Sherry L. Vellucci of St. John's University covers the topic "Metadata," and Douglas W. Oard of the University of Maryland and Anne R. Diekema of Syracuse University write about "Cross-Language Information Retrieval."

In their chapter on the "Design of Interfaces for Information Seeking," Gary Marchionini and Anita Komlodi discuss the fact that the tremendous and rapid advances in technology have driven the research on and development of user interfaces. Interfaces exist at the juncture of the information seeker (user) and the enabling technologies. The organization of their chapter is based on three generations of research and development on technology, information seeking, and interface design that roughly map to the 1970s, 1980s, and 1990s.

The chapter is structured to "provide a perspective on the mutually dependent advances of technology, research on information-seeking, and human-system interaction." It provides a summary of developments in the first two generations of user interfaces—those that have been treated in previous *ARIST* chapters; and then it focuses on the third generation of interface design and development looked at from the vantage points of multidisciplinarity and interactivity. Marchionini and Komlodi conclude their chapter by observing that the user interface research of the late 1990s is headed toward widespread access to information objects and that this access is a part of the larger information activities of life.

In their chapter, "Sociocognitive Perspectives on Representation," Elin K. Jacob and Debora Shaw discuss research on the cognitive aspects of formal systems of knowledge representation. Major sections cover cognition, particularly in information science, and representation of objects, information, or data. The authors recognize the theoretical foundations established by Jesse Shera in the 1960s and the need for effective retrieval. They delineate four fundamental research questions: (1) "How does language influence the individual's cognitive representation and organization of information?" (2) "What effect does the need to communicate have on the individual's symbolic representation and/or cognitive organization of information?" (3) "What patterns or structures of cognitive organization are shared by individuals or by groups of individuals?" and (4) "How can retrieval mechanisms be designed to facilitate, augment, or mimic these natural patterns of cognitive organization?"

Jacob and Shaw outline the origins and theoretical foundations of the cognitive viewpoint, assessing its strengths and weaknesses; describe recent efforts to shift the focus from representation as an individual cognitive phenomenon to the social origins of representation within discourse communities; and review research that exemplifies a sociocognitive approach to investigating processes of representation.

In their concluding section, the authors say that representation is an essential component of the process of document acquisition, organization, storage and retrieval and that eventually sociocognitive research "will support the supervening goal of efficient and effective retrieval by facilitating the development of representational languages and organizational structures that reflect the needs of specific language games or of specific knowledge domains or linguistic communities."

Sherry L. Vellucci presents the chapter on "Metadata." Metadata is data about data: data that describes attributes of a resource, characterizes its relationships, supports its discovery and effective use, and exists for the most part in an electronic environment. Parallel and independent metadata schemes have developed as communities responsible for creating or providing access to networked electronic resources developed their own methods for organizing the resources.

Vellucci reviews a variety of metadata schemes used in the library and information science communities, and examines their background, development, and implementation. Some of the schemes were developed within a specific subcommunity or domain, for example, IAFA Templates, MARC, Text Encoding Initiative (TEI) Headers, Encoded Archival Description (EAD), Computer Interchange of Museum Information (CIMI), Government Information Locator Service (GILS), and Content Standards for Digital Geospatial Metadata (CSDGM). The content and syntax of each metadata type varies depending on the special-ized needs of its users.

The desire to convert and exchange metadata across domains has led to collaborative projects to define and test standards for metadata content, and to design architectures that will allow the necessary interoperability of data in a networked environment. The Dublin Core Metadata Element Set, developed within an international and interdis-ciplinary environment, is a primary example of a basic set of metadata elements. Higher-level architectural structures such as the Warwick Framework and the Resource Description Framework are under devel-opment to provide a container architecture that will enable metadata interoperability while preserving the integrity of distinct metadata sets.

The chapter on "Cross-Language Information Retrieval" (CLIR) by Douglas W. Oard and Anne R. Diekema addresses a timely problem, especially within the context of the Internet, which is accessible by anyone in any discipline from virtually anywhere in the world. The problem of cross-language retrieval is not new; it was quickly recog-nized in the 1960s as search and retrieval of computer-readable (but monolingual) databases became a reality. Then as now, cross-language information retrieval was seen to be a function that would facilitate the effective search for, exchange of, and retrieval of information.

The chapter by Oard and Diekema reviews research and practice in CLIR that allows users to state queries in their native language and retrieve documents in any other language supported by the system. CLIR can simplify searching by multilingual users and, if translation resources are limited, can allow monolingual users to allocate those resources to the more promising documents.

This review begins with an examination of the literature on user needs for CLIR. The chapter largely follows the retrieval system model (document preprocessing, query formulation, matching, selection, and delivery). Each section highlights the unique requirements imposed on one or more stages of the model in cross-language retrieval applica-tions. The matching stage is covered in somewhat more detail, reflect-ing the volume of research and publication in the literature. The authors describe evaluation techniques and conclude with observations regard-ing future directions for CLIR research.

3 Design of Interfaces for Information Seeking

GARY MARCHIONINI
University of North Carolina
at Chapel Hill

ANITA KOMLODI
University of Maryland

INTRODUCTION AND PERSPECTIVE

Understanding the information-seeking process and developing systems and strategies for supporting it are central goals of information science. Research in the organization and communication of information is best informed by studies of the interactions among people and external information sources. However, information technology has advanced so rapidly in the second half of the twentieth century that it dominates research and development in information seeking. The linchpin of the interactions between information seekers and these technologies is the user interface. The interactions among human physical, cognitive, and affective subsystems and the external world are defined by the juxtaposed boundaries where these physical and conceptual constructs meet. These conjunctions of boundaries are called interfaces. Interfaces serve as the communication channels through which information seeking proceeds. Defining and building interfaces that support information seeking is thus a fundamental problem in information science, and there is a rich history of work on the topic in this field as well as in human factors and human-computer interaction (HCI).

The centrality of user interface design to information science is reflected by the inclusion of chapters on the topic in four of the first eight volumes of *ARIST* (DAVIS in 1966; LICKLIDER in 1968; BENNETT in 1972; and MARTIN in 1973). Four subsequent volumes devoted chapters to different aspects of user interface design. The most recent chapter, by SHAW in 1991, noted the rapid developments in the field and the importance of user interfaces to information science progress. This chapter provides a link to the earlier work and focuses on the current

Annual Review of Information Science and Technology (ARIST), Volume 33, 1998
Martha E. Williams, Editor
Published for the American Society for Information Science (ASIS)
By Information Today, Inc., Medford, NJ

state of user interface design for information seeking. The goals of this chapter are to frame the evolution of interfaces for information seeking, provide a status report for current research and development, and suggest research directions. The fields of HCI and human factors are broad and rich; we focus on interface designs that support information seeking. We do not cover the considerable body of work related to interfaces for information systems (e.g., text processing, graphics, programming, etc.) within the information science literature. The field of computer supported collaborative work (CSCW) is an offshoot of HCI; the reader is referred to the TWIDALE & NICHOLS chapter of this volume for the social aspects of interfaces and human-computer interaction. Within the research and development devoted to interfaces for information seeking, we focus specifically on conceptual interfaces and give only broad coverage to physical interfaces. The chapter is organized to (1) provide a perspective on the mutually dependent advances of technology, research on information seeking, and human-system interaction; (2) provide a brief summary of developments in the first two generations of user interfaces that have been addressed in previous *ARIST* chapters; and then (3) focus on the current third generation of interface development considered from multidisciplinary and interactivity perspectives.

Technology Push and Interdisciplinarity

In the last third of this century the workplace has been transformed by information technology. The impact of technology on information processing is nicely summed up by William Wulf's appeal to Gordon Moore's law as the driving force for engineering innovation: "Anything that is changing at that rate just can't be ignored" (in TALBERT, pp. 37-38). The rapid evolution of technical development is reflected in hardware and software, in the user interfaces that link people to systems, and in the information industry that supports information-seeking activities. Because information technology strongly determines the ways that people interact with information, there are inherent commonalities in information science and the emerging field of human-computer interaction. The influence of technology in pushing research and development in information seeking and interface design is summarized in Figure 1. Three generations of technology, roughly mapped onto the final three decades of the twentieth century (the first generation also includes much of the 1960s), have had strong influences on the creation of new information products and services and the evolution of human interactions with information. Figure 1 provides a perspective on how information-seeking research and interface-design research developed in parallel, both driven by technological developments. This perspective serves as a framework for this chapter.

	Technology R & D	Information Seeking R & D	Interface Design R & D
1970s	Mainframe Custom Programs File management	Users: professional intermediaries Context: workplace Content: pointers Tasks: single, batch-oriented Interactivity: 　Structure: fielded files 　Rules: discrete, sequential	Users: programmers/experts Context: workplace Content: ASCII characters Tasks: specialized, iterative Interactivity: 　I/O: dumb terminal 　Style: command line/menu
1980s	Personal Computers Application Packages DBMS, Adv. IR	Users: literate end users Context: workplace/home/public Content: full text Tasks: multiple, sequential Interactivity: 　Structure: relational, hierarchical 　Rules: iteration	Users: literate end users Context: workplace/home Content: graphical Tasks: multiple, coordinated Interactivity: 　I/O: GUI/WIMP 　Style: direct manipulation
1990s	Distributed Systems WWW Hypermedia, Adv. IR+browsing	Users: universal access Context: ubiquitous Content: multimedia Tasks: integrated Interactivity: 　Structure: network objects 　Rules: customizable, parallel	Users: universal access Context: ubiquitous Content: multimedia Tasks: integrated, distributed Interactivity: 　I/O: multiple 　Style: enhanced direct manipulation

Figure 1. Three generations of research and development on technology, information seeking, and interface design

Information-seeking research takes into account users, tasks and knowledge domains, information systems, and contexts. In the 1970s, interfaces were designed mostly for users who were highly specialized professionals. In the 1990s, interfaces evolved to support casual, literate end users (i.e., average educated citizens) to the current emphasis on universal access for all users. Similarly, content has expanded from highly technical areas such as medical and scientific research to now include all areas of human interest. In this chapter, we also discuss the evolution from bibliographic data to full text and multimedia objects. As costs dropped, networking improved, and small mobile units became available, people were able to conduct electronic information seeking from the workplace to homes and public spaces. The types of plans and actions users take to meet their information needs have evolved from a focus on discrete batch-oriented steps to a focus on integrated subtasks that allow people to more directly attend to their larger information needs. Also, the hardware and software advances gradually made computationally heavy tasks possible. Of particular importance for information seeking were the data management advances that allowed theoretical information retrieval (IR) approaches proposed in the first generation (e.g., LUHN; SALTON & MCGILL; and others) to be implemented. Those fundamental insights led to systems such as Personal Library Software, which is used in many commercial services, and more recently to the different search engines on the World Wide Web (Web).

The interface design research and development column in Figure 1 reflects similar expansion for users and contexts, movement from character-based to multimedia-based interfaces, a similar progression of more integral subtasks, development of new, specialized physical interface devices for input and output, and a progression of interaction styles from batch-oriented command styles to directly manipulable visualizations. This framework highlights the parallel development of information seeking and interface design research—both mutually dependent on technology developments—and illustrates the many interdisciplinary overlaps.

Literature Trends

The importance of interface design is reflected in the research literature. Over the past 30 years, many new journals devoted to HCI have appeared, conferences devoted to HCI research have increased enormously, and specialized funding programs have been developed by government agencies and foundations. We conducted searches to follow the user interface literature both in information and library science and in computer science. The searches were carried out in four databases through the DIALOG service: Library and Information Science Abstracts (LISA), Information Science Abstracts, National Technical Information Service (NTIS), and INSPEC (The Database for Physics, Electronics and Computing).

The first two databases, which cover the library and information science literature, both have international coverage and contain biblio-graphic data and abstracts. LISA contains records from more than 500 journals and other publications from 60 countries, including informa-tion about ongoing or recently completed research. Information Science Abstracts monitors more than 300 journals, as well as books, conference proceedings, research reports, and patents. The last two databases cover computer science literature. NTIS is the source of information for gov-ernment-sponsored U.S. and worldwide scientific, technical, engineer-ing, and business-related information. INSPEC covers the literature of international computers and control and information technology, among other topics.

Both computer science databases were significantly larger in number of records and subject coverage than the library and information sci-ence databases. INSPEC was the largest with 5 million records in July 1997. NTIS had 500,000 unrestricted technical reports, Information Sci-ence Abstracts contained 165,000 citations, and LISA had 130,000 in July 1997.

The same search for the phrase "user interface" was conducted in all four databases for 1968 through 1997. The data from 1997 are not included because the literature had not been fully indexed at the time of the searches. The results are presented in Figure 2 by the ratio of hits to

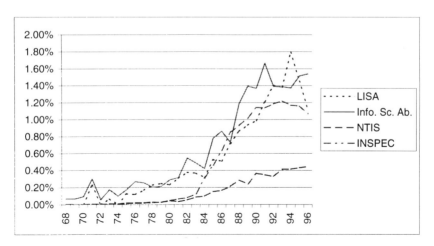

Figure 2. Literature search on "user interface": Ratio of number of hits to total number of records in databases 1968-1996

the total number of records from that year in the database. In all four databases, three phases can be observed. From the end of the 1960s until the beginning of the 1980s the literature was very small and very slowly increasing. Between 1980 and 1990 the amount of user interface literature increased rapidly, leveling off in the early 1990s. The absolute number of records shows this trend even more dramatically.

An additional search was conducted in the Association for Computing Machinery Digital Library, which at the time of the searches contained 95% of all ACM journals and proceedings from 1991 in full text and the bibliographic data of all ACM journal articles from 1985 on. This search showed similar overall trends, but a more erratic pattern due to the much smaller base of records. The number of papers with "user interface" in the text increased steadily, dropped considerably in 1994, returned to the previous level in 1995, and dropped slightly in 1996. We speculate that the drop in 1994 was due to the rise of the Web, which captured the attention of researchers in technical areas and in its earliest forms strongly affected user interface design by eliminating the basic design paradigms (e.g., multiple windows), interaction models (e.g., statefulness), and widgets (e.g., sliders).

User-Centered Interface Design

The field of human-computer interaction has developed as a confluence of people and work in psychology (the human factors community), computer science, and information science. In his 1968 *ARIST* review of "man-computer communication," LICKLIDER devotes the bulk of his chapter to hardware developments, especially the time-sharing breakthroughs of that time and bemoans the Tower of Babel of programming languages and lack of attention to human intelligence instead of artificial intelligence. Only five years later, BENNETT in his 1972 *ARIST* review on the user interface in interactive systems is able to discuss basic interaction metrics (response time and ease of use) and include results from several empirical studies of users other than programmers using a variety of retrieval systems. Bennett focuses on the nature of interactivity by identifying four components of interactive systems and giving examples of how they interact in some early online environments such as INTREX (MARCUS ET AL.) and DIALOG (SUMMIT). These four components of interactive systems—task, user, terminal, and content—draw upon progress in many disciplines and remain central today, although most researchers would add a context component (e.g., NARDI). This interdisciplinary approach to interactivity is fundamental to both human-computer interaction and information science and inextricably binds them in a mutually-reinforcing manner.

Good histories of the HCI field can be found in a chapter by BAECKER ET AL. and a recent paper by SHACKEL (1997). Four pioneers defined four themes—interaction, human augmentation, usability, and multimedia—that resonate in the interface design community today. These early visionaries in the computing field recognized that people are central to practical computing systems and established the primary challenges of interface design. In 1968 LICKLIDER was concerned with the symbiotic relationship between humans and computers—the nature of interactivity. He envisioned digital libraries used by ordinary citizens and argued for designers to consider user needs throughout the design process. In 1963 ENGELBART articulated the vision that computing could be used to augment the human intellect and demonstrated his phronetic genius by leading design teams that created new devices (mouse) and interactive tools (collaborative authoring and hypertext systems) that underlie human-machine interactions today. SHACKEL (1959) launched the European tradition of usability testing based on ergonomic factors, and SUTHERLAND (1963; 1968) demonstrated the potential of graphical displays with his Sketchpad system and the original head-mounted display. These pioneers put their theories into practice through prototypes and working systems and inspired a generation of scientists and innovators by insisting that humans and their tasks must be central when information technology is designed.

User interface development has had both academic and industrial components. Designs take into account users, tasks, and technology and develop according to a user-centered design process guided by empirically determined principles and guidelines, and informed over multiple iterations by usability testing. This process of invention, testing, and revision facilitates the flow of ideas from academic settings to the marketplace as seen in products and services such as Netscape, Yahoo, and Lycos. Helpful advances in design process have come from psychology-based studies that focus on human behavior. NORMAN provides cogent examples of how people take cues from the environment during interactions and contributes a framework for user interaction in which user goals drive execution (intention, action sequence, and physical sequence) and evaluation (perception, interpretation, comparison) cycles. This framework is especially applicable to the design of user interfaces that support iterative searching that depends on intermediate results. More specific to user queries, Landauer's group conducted many empirical studies of how people name concepts. For example, DUMAIS & LANDAUER summarize experiments that illustrate that novices formulate rather simple queries and discuss the interactions between popularity of terms in command languages and the specificity users need when doing their individual tasks. Subsequent work (e.g., GOMEZ ET AL.) demonstrates the long-recognized need for rich indexing if query interfaces are to support user natural-language queries.

A long history of task analysis research informs interface design. There are two primary approaches to identifying user needs and building principles for design. (1) The cognitive engineering approach is best illustrated by CARD ET AL. (1983), who developed the GOMS (Goals, Operators, Methods, and Selection rules) model for user interaction as a formal theory upon which precise user performance could be predicted. The basic model grew out of many carefully controlled text-editing experiments and was the first formal model of human-computer interaction. The original GOMS model depends on error-free, sequential user behavior and does not take into account user learning as the task progresses; however, many researchers have created adaptations that address some of these strong constraints. John and Kieras, who have both independently applied GOMS-like models in complex interface design work, provide an excellent summary of the various GOMS models (JOHN & KIERAS, 1996a; 1996b) and an empirical comparison of four models applied to the task of paragraph editing embedded in a larger collaborative writing task.

(2) An alternative to the cognitive engineering approach is more holistic and considers the user and task as situated in a larger milieu. This approach is best illustrated by the work of Carroll and his colleagues who advocate phased designs appropriate to users' varying needs. In a seminal chapter, CARROLL & ROSSON (1987) define the "paradox of the active user" arising out of peoples' needs to get their work done rather than learn new systems and describe peoples' tendencies to learn new systems through analogy. They stress that these are not flaws in human learning that designers should aim to remedy, but important properties upon which user-centered design should be based. From this perspective, they propose "training wheels" designs that are extensible, use progressive disclosure of features as users gain experience, provide undo features and guided explorations, and minimize dependency on metaphors that constrain learning of new features. This holistic approach to users and tasks also gives rise to scenario-based design and user testing (CARROLL & ROSSON, 1992).

Another aspect of interface design that gets broad attention in the research literature is the specification of the design process itself. The importance of planning, testing, and teamwork in software engineering is demonstrated in the classic essays of BROOKS, whose experiences in building large-scale systems influenced recognition of the need for interface design. SHNEIDERMAN (1998b) articulates a design model that integrates psychological research, computer science principles, and technical tools as the basis for 15 years of interface designs in his laboratory. This model is based on theories and models of HCI and empirical research and aims to incorporate iterative usability testing, user interface management systems, and guideline documents to develop successful designs. NIELSEN offers a practical volume on usability testing, and HIX & HARTSON present a practical guide to the user-centered design process.

Information Seeking in Electronic Environments

Information seeking is a process in which humans engage to purposefully change their state of knowledge. The process is inherently interactive as information seekers direct attention, accept and adapt to stimuli, reflect on progress, and evaluate the efficacy of continuing. Information seeking is thus a cybernetic process in which knowledge state is changed through inputs, purposive outputs, and feedback. Information seeking is, however, a strictly human process that requires adaptive and reflective control over the afferent and efferent actions of the information seeker. We distinguish information seeking from information retrieval (IR) in that IR does not demand persistence or continuous human attention, that is, retrieval may aim to yield an intermediate value that is applied and then forgotten. IR also may be automated and embedded in the larger information-seeking process. Progress during an information-seeking episode is thus a product of information seeker attributes, informational environment attributes, and the communication channel over which information flows.

A rich literature relates to information seeking, including numerous *ARIST* chapters on user needs. We provide a terse summary of key work leading to the current focus on human interaction with analog and digital information. Early studies of information-seeking behavior demonstrated that users progress through different stages as they recognize and articulate an information need. TAYLOR's classic four stages (visceral, conscious, formalized, and compromised) illustrate the long-standing research focus on question articulation, and DERVIN helped the field focus more on the communication of needs as the essential aspect of information seeking. BELKIN (1980) focused attention on the information seeker's initial state of mind by proposing his anomalous state of knowledge framework and then moved beyond theory to apply the framework as a basis for system design. BATES (1979a; 1979b) created a taxonomy of practical strategies and tactics that information seekers could use during searching; the taxonomy also served as the basis for interface design recommendations (BATES, 1990). Work by BATES (1989), MARCHIONINI (1995), and others added empirical legitimacy to systems that support and depend on user browsing strategies. This is most obviously manifested in today's point-and-click interaction style on the Web. BORGMAN (1984) explained user information-seeking behavior by examining users' mental models for the retrieval system and knowledge domain, and KUHLTHAU extended the model of information seeking as a cognitive process with an affective dimension all embedded in a task context.

SARACEVIC has recently summarized the current view of information seeking as an interaction between people and information. Based on models developed by BELKIN (1996) and INGWERSEN, this view integrates factors and processes where the interface connects resources (both informational and computational) and the user (user characteristics, user query, and environment) at different temporal (as interaction progresses) and conceptual (surface/behavioral, cognitive, and situational) levels. Thus, information-seeking research currently rests on the foundational work done with users and information systems and focuses on the nature of interactions with information.

In many respects, this evolution in information-seeking research has been driven by technological developments that reveal the details of the information-seeking process by dramatically speeding up the pace of iterations and broadening the scope of access. Users must make more decisions, more quickly, and these decisions must be precisely specified. MARCHIONINI (1992; 1995), adopting this view of information seeking as a dynamic, interactive process, pointed out that most system and interface designs focus on the query aspects of the larger information-seeking process and argued that designers should take a more integral view when designing user interfaces. As Figure 1 suggests and the sections that follow demonstrate, the research paths for information-seeking and user-interface design reflect parallel evolutions that are rooted in a phenomenon common to both—interactivity. In both cases, interaction has increased, user options have increased, and discrete subprocesses have become more integral.

The state of interfaces for information seeking today reflects mutually dependent developments in information-seeking research and human-computer interaction, which both have been strongly driven by technological progress. The end of the century sees an installed base of user interfaces that depend on multiple input devices (keyboard and mouse), graphical displays on screens partitioned into multiple window regions, and interaction styles that require selections (point and click) and browsing strategies more than commands and queries. These interfaces are applied in a vast, distributed network of information resources that are increasingly full text rather than bibliographic and include multimedia and active resources such as simulations and executable programs. Research and development suggest that these trends will continue as designers leverage new input/output devices, ubiquitous access, and advanced visualization techniques to support (1) more directly manipulable interfaces that allow information seekers to integrate analytical search with browsing strategies, (2) alternative and customizable interfaces to meet the needs of diverse user populations, and (3) information seeking as a process seamlessly embedded in larger work processes. The path toward this state is marked by key developments in early generations of user interface research and development.

FIRST- AND SECOND-GENERATION USER INTERFACES

The computer systems augmenting information seeking in the 1960s to the 1980s evolved from batch-oriented systems with machine-centric interfaces (programming) to interactive systems with novice-user, graphical user interfaces (GUIs). This progress was driven by advances in hardware (from large mainframes to personal computers), architecture (from time-sharing to client-server), software (from customized programs to general applications packages), data structures (from file management to database management), and interfaces (from character-based interfaces to graphical user interfaces). The early systems supported only analytical search strategies for well-defined, text-based bibliographic information and thus required considerable sophistication to use. Over the two generations, there was an unmistakable trend toward supporting broader communities of users, richer information objects, and more interactive search strategies, culminating in the late 1980s with graphical interface designs for browsing in hypertext environments. Two main types of applications most clearly illustrate these trends in information-seeking interfaces: online IR from databases, and online public-access catalogs (OPACs). The interfaces for these types of systems typically allowed users to retrieve information from a specific database or collection and mainly supported query formulation.

Online Information Retrieval System Interfaces

The first systems allowing remote searching of databases were developed in the late 1960s as time-sharing became viable. The first services were batch searches run on data stored on tapes. In the early 1970s GECHMAN reported a movement toward interactive searching and predicted development of more refined search capabilities. An excellent volume stemming from a 1971 American Federation of Information Processing Societies (AFIPS) workshop on interactive searching illustrates the early interest in interfaces for interaction (WALKER). This volume includes papers about the pioneering systems of the period such as NASA/RECON, the precursor to DIALOG; AIM/TWX, the precursor to Medline databases and the Grateful Med interface; and other novel systems that served as foundations for commercial or research systems (e.g., BASIS-70 and INTREX). A key unifying theme was techniques to support interactive IR by users working at terminals remotely connected to systems in real time. By 1974, interactive online searching had become common and M. E. WILLIAMS in her *ARIST* chapter examined software for database searching and reviewed both batch and online database searching software, some of which included user aids such as online thesauri.

The 1970s saw continued development of robust commercial services for online retrieval and the continued evolution of experimental systems. HAWKINS reviews the history of these services until 1981, including interface aspects. He comments that most online searches require a human intermediary because of the complexity of the interfaces and the differences between systems. Intermediated searching was typical of the 1970s, although several authors cited in the chapter predict the growth of end-user searching. Hawkins treats the evaluation of searches and searchers, the reference interview and search strategy formulation as part of the user-side interface, which we (the authors) consider part of the conceptual interface.

The first intermediary interfaces automated logon procedures, selection of files and systems, and other housekeeping tasks. Experimental systems went far beyond this to support user query formulation. The NLM CITE system (DOSZKOCS) had one of the first interfaces to provide search support by allowing natural-language input of search queries. The system picked out the search terms from the queries and carried out a weighted search of the terms. The system also allowed relevance feedback and query modification. The interface was menu-driven rather than command-based, showing a trend toward easier dialogue methods to support end users. A different theme of development built upon artificial intelligence techniques to automate the intermediation process. KEHOE traces the history of the INTREX research project at MIT begun in 1964 as one of the first initiatives to automate intermediation. INTREX led to the CONIT and later IIDA interfaces and the Sci-Mate (SAARI & FOSTER) front end in the 1980s. These are but a few examples of the many projects from this period that aimed to create natural-language gateways to online services. The 1970s saw the development of commercially viable systems that provided basic support for professional intermediaries to execute sophisticated queries and experimental systems intended to support broader user communities.

The 1980s saw the spread of personal computers and a focus on end users in information-seeking system interface research and development. This trend started with the emergence of online public-access catalogs that provided end-user access to bibliographic data of library holdings. Online information services started to supply gateway or front-end software to support this new user group. MISCHO & LEE define gateway software as packages that take care of housekeeping tasks such as logging onto a database. Front-end interfaces aim to make the search transparent for the user by taking care of some of the search steps such as database selection and translation of queries into the syntax of the database. MEADOW ET AL. presented front-end research and early work on user needs and professional search strategies, culminating in the OAK interface. Commercial database vendors started to provide front ends; DIALOG's In-Search (NEWLIN) and BRS's After Dark (JANKE) were good examples. These interfaces supported the end user better and tried to incorporate the expertise of human intermediaries in the interface.

The more powerful computational platforms of the 1980s also allowed designers to build interfaces for systems that used advanced IR techniques that supported non-Boolean queries and returned ranked results. One example of a system that addressed user interface issues as well as implementing powerful retrieval techniques is the OKAPI system. The OKAPI text-retrieval system was developed through a series of research projects (ROBERTSON) focusing on user information-seeking behavior, user-system interaction, and systems design. The OKAPI systems are designed for non-expert end users. The search queries are entered in free-text form and then parsed into word-stems. The system searches based on a best-match function with term weights and produces a ranked list of documents. The user can provide relevance feedback based on these results and perform a relevance feedback search. The search process can be iterated through several cycles. Different variations on these options were implemented and tested.

VICKERY & VICKERY reviewed many of the interfaces developed for online systems that were organized around different steps of the process of searching online bibliographic databases. They list 13 steps in the online search process and discuss 12 functional requirements for online interfaces. This in-depth analysis begins with a user who already has a query and does not address the extraction and use of information found in the search. Thus, their extensive bibliography on the topic reflects the IR field's focus on query formulation, reformulation, and results inspection.

Online Public-Access Catalog Interfaces

The 1980s delimit the era of online public-access catalogs (OPACs), which emerged as extensions of library circulation systems or as separate tools developed to provide user access to bibliographic information. VIGIL makes a distinction between online information services and OPACs. The difference lies in the search language: online systems support sophisticated queries and allow users to combine sets and reuse results of previous queries, while OPACs allow novice users to enter only the most basic queries. OPACs are also more suited for known-item searches and less for subject searches, which are better supported by online databases. User studies of OPACs found that users have more difficulty with subject searching (BORGMAN, 1986; LARSON).

HILDRETH in his 1985 *ARIST* chapter reviews the history of OPAC interfaces. The first public-access systems appeared in the late 1970s with limited functionality. The real growth of OPACs started after 1980 when many libraries started to develop their own OPAC interfaces or urged the commercial library automation system vendors to develop OPAC subsystems. The emphasis in these systems was on public access. The first large-scale OPAC studies were conducted in the early 1980s (e.g., HILDRETH, 1982). User studies found that OPACs were very popular among users despite the difficulties of using them.

HILDRETH (1984) defines three generations of OPACs based on search/access, interaction/dialogue mode, display format/content, and operational assistance. The three generations show development from restricted known-item searches to subject searching, more powerful search capabilities, and interactive search refinement. The searching capability developed from character-by-character matching (similar to card catalog use) to Boolean searching, keyword access, and other more flexible searching methods. The interfaces progress from command-driven to multiple dialog modes offering both menu-driven interfaces for novice users and command-based dialogs for expert users. Hildreth predicts that future third-generation OPACs will include powerful search capabilities and intuitive user interfaces that provide point-of-need help and instructions.

BORGMAN (1986) summarizes findings from IR user studies and concludes that users of online IR systems and OPACs experience similar problems when searching. She defines two types of knowledge used in searching: knowledge of the mechanical and the conceptual aspects of searching. Later BORGMAN (1996) refines this model to include semantic knowledge of how to implement a query in a given system. In her 1986 article she summarizes problems users have with the mechanical and the conceptual aspects of searching and identifies sources of problems. In her 1996 article she states that OPACs are still hard to use. She suggests that human factors knowledge should be applied to IR screen design and identifies further research areas such as standardization of command languages and screen displays, error correction algorithms, and the development of front-end or automated intermediary systems.

During the later 1980s and early 1990s, several OPAC interfaces were developed. Children were studied as information seekers and OPAC interfaces were designed to suit their needs. BORGMAN ET AL. in 1995 summarize related research and describe studies conducted on the Science Library Catalog Project. This system provides a Dewey Decimal Classification-based graphical browsing interface that allows hierarchical browsing without the use of a keyboard. BUSEY & DOERR describe another interface designed for children, the Kid's Catalog. This interface incorporates ideas from the Science Library Project and user studies of children's information-seeking behavior. It provides multiple access points to the materials to accommodate different developmental stages. BookHaus (PEJTERSEN) is another effort to design a graphical OPAC interface. This system is especially interesting because, like a physical library interface, it provides alternative conceptual interfaces for users and tasks. For example, the children's collection and search service is distinguished from adult fiction and nonfiction interfaces. The ACCESS system at the Library of Congress provides a touch-panel direct-manipulation interface with context-sensitive hypertext help (MARCHIONINI ET AL., 1993). HYPERCATalog developed at LIBLAB in Sweden (HJERPPE) applies hypertext links across related objects in the OPAC interface.

More recent OPACs continue to leverage GUI-based techniques and advanced IR techniques. BEHESHTI ET AL. describe the Public Access Catalog Extension (PACE) interface. This system provides a graphical browsing interface simulating images of books and library shelves to help users browse through the catalog. User testing showed that the graphical browsing display provided the same user performance as the character-based display, but users overwhelmingly preferred the graphical browsing display. Just as experimental online search systems were implemented in practical settings, the ongoing work on the CHESHIRE system (LARSON ET AL.) is the basis for working OPACs while continuing to serve as an experimental platform for OPAC research. Cheshire aims to incorporate advanced IR and interface research to provide a GUI interface to multimedia objects using a Z39.50-compliant architecture that leverages both SGML markup and a probabilistic retrieval engine.

Clearly, astounding advances in information-seeking capabilities were made in these first two technological generations. This summary highlights only two application areas and ignores studies of intermediary and reference interviews, searching behavior, user-modeling techniques, search-engine functionalities, and other related areas of research that influence user interfaces. However, this discussion illustrates the trend toward highly interactive interfaces that provide universal and ubiquitous access to a variety of information objects.

THIRD-GENERATION USER INTERFACES

The current generation of research and development in user interfaces that support information seeking is mainly influenced by ongoing technical developments that give more computational and communicational power per unit cost, practical portable devices, funding for digital library research, and especially the development of the World Wide Web. These developments are leading to a global information economy in which all the world's citizens will depend on access to electronic resources.

Users

As computers and telecommunications costs drop, larger portions of the population take advantage of information technology. Today, the Web links people of all ages and backgrounds around the globe. The interest in global cooperation and expansion of the information technology marketplace has led to a growing call for universal access to electronic information resources. The Web has accelerated efforts to develop multilingual interfaces, which improve as underlying research in machine translation and multilingual text retrieval progresses. Some systems retrieve documents in one language for queries expressed in a different language, for example SPIDER (SHERIDAN & BALLERINI) retrieves Italian documents with German queries. Others provide glosses (rough translated summaries) in the same language as the query for documents in a second language. See OARD & DIEKEMA in this volume for a full treatment of cross-language retrieval.

Efforts to provide universal access have led to novel physical interfaces for a variety of users with special needs. Various approaches to interfaces for blind or visually impaired users have been developed, including musical tones (MEREU & KAZMAN), speech-based web browsers (RAMAN), and screen magnification and cursor-control facilities for low-vision users (KLINE & GLINERT). One group has even developed a user interface management system that allows interface designers to create parallel interfaces for sighted and blind users (SAVIDIS & STEPHANIDIS). Other researchers have focused on building and testing interfaces for the elderly. For example, OGOZALEK found that elderly users preferred a multimedia version of a pharmacopoeia to a text-only version and WORDEN ET AL. demonstrated that use of area cursors (larger than normal activation areas) and sticky icons (decreasing cursor movement speed on and near icons, which in effect makes the icon region kinesthetically larger) decrease target selection times by as much as 50%. A long history of interface designs specialized for children in educational settings (BORGMAN ET AL.;

DRUIN & SOLOMON) have led the development of OPAC interfaces for children.

The absence of an appropriate interface for one's needs is as much a disadvantage as the lack of computers for information access. As computing becomes more ubiquitous, a fundamental challenge is to develop alternative interfaces that allow users to select and customize interfaces that best suit their personal needs. DILLON & WATSON argue for more studies of individual user differences beyond task and system experience, so designers may more fully take such differences into account when designing interfaces. Designers currently provide users with an array of preference-setting options and wizards that allow users to model specific subtasks. The current debate about intelligent agents that automatically adapt to users and perform independent of user control (e.g., automatic query expansion and web-based filtering robots) versus rich alternatives under strict user control are best exemplified by the CHI '97 panel debate featuring Pattie Maes and Ben Shneiderman. These perspectives are well represented in publications such as MAES and SHNEIDERMAN (1998a; see also BELKIN, 1996). The history of computing has been a litany of systems that depended on the outstanding abilities of humans to adapt to the environment, and unsuccessful efforts to automate intellectual activities. Applied wisdom suggests that designers should aim to give people control over powerful tools in a symbiotic manner to optimize human abilities to think, create, and reflect, and computer capabilities to store, display, and retrieve. Users may welcome or reject increasing numbers of mental prosthetics, but they should always be free to make the choice and to maintain full control.

Toward Ubiquitous Access

Information seeking is always embedded in the larger tasks of work, learning, and play. Driven by distributed, mobile, inexpensive technologies, the world is approaching WEISER's vision of ubiquitous computing. In such a context, people can design information modules that fit into an infrastructure where information objects and the physical tools to create, access, and manipulate them are always present and assumed as an essential element of the environment. Freeing people from the tethers of office workstations will allow electronic information seeking to be embedded in their larger life activities. The vision depends on an information environment where context is unbounded, all types of content are available, and the tasks and information interactions are integrated with and customized to user needs and preferences.

Multimedia. Improvements in computational power, mass storage, and bandwidth in recent years allow even modest workstations to deliver multimedia information. Digital libraries of texts, images, sound recordings, animations, and video as well as a variety of active templates and programs are emerging, although much interface design research is needed to make these materials accessible and usable. Most multimedia access depends on linguistic cataloging to create MARC-like records for access. See DUGGAN for an overview of access, TURNER for a comparison of user and indexer term assignment, and MOSTAFA for a review of still-image retrieval. These approaches are now augmented by a variety of signal-processing and computational techniques to distinguish multimedia objects. The fundamental design challenges are deciding what levels of representation to use and what control mechanisms to provide to users.

The challenges of locating, skimming, and using image and video objects have been addressed on several fronts. Still-image and video indexing based on visual attributes such as color, luminosity, and motion (see GUPTA ET AL. for an overview) have been integrated into digital library solutions such as Informedia at Carnegie Mellon University (WACTLAR ET AL.) and Blobworld at the University of California at Berkeley (WILENSKY), and in collaborative learning communities such as the Baltimore Learning Community (BLC) (ROSE ET AL.). The Informedia interface allows speech query or typed text input and displays video skims that allow users to quickly extract the gist of television news clips. The Blobworld interface uses image segmentation based on combining color and texture features to allow users to provide relevance feedback for key parts of a still image. The early prototypes of the interface allow users to assign weights to a variety of visual attributes and leverage the Cheshire (LARSON ET AL.) retrieval engine. The BLC Project interface allows teachers to preview video clips by displaying a textual bibliographic record along with a choice of video surrogates. Users may choose the slide-show video surrogate that displays key frames at rates they control, or the storyboard surrogate that displays static key frames. The video display tool is embedded in a larger dynamic query search interface that closely couples queries and results to provide visual overviews for the entire multimedia corpus, which also includes still images, web sites, audio clips, and integrated instructional modules.

Some designers have proposed visual languages for query specification in image databases. NISHIYAMA ET AL. developed an interface that allows users to select icons, colors, and image attributes to pose queries for still images. The SageBook system (CHUAH ET AL.) allows users to sketch and edit queries as part of a larger multimedia system. Interfaces to support video browsing are under construction in several quarters. RORVIG demonstrated a video abstracting technique to rapidly scan NASA videos, and KOMLODI & MARCHIONINI conducted empirical studies of interface design parameters such as display rates, number of concurrent displays, and storyboard layouts. To preserve bandwidth in a video meeting environment, YAMAASHI ET AL. provided an interface that allows users to select from among multiple video windows, one of which presents full-resolution views while others present low-resolution views. Several color-based query systems that allow users to specify color attributes and use relevance feedback to refine image retrieval are in practical use. For example, IBM's Query by Image Content (QBIC) system is used in the art slide collection at University of California Davis (HOLT ET AL.). Other systems use a combination of user query techniques. For example, BESSER describes the Berkeley Image Database System that provides access to multiple collections and supports linguistic descriptors as well as visual attribute queries, and MOSTAFA & DILLON report empirical results that demonstrate the efficacy of combining linguistic and visual query attributes.

The bulk of the work on audio interfaces has been related to speech input, which becomes more essential as personal digital assistants (PDAs) and digital cell phones are more commonly deployed. SCHMANDT and his MIT colleagues have led the best ongoing work on audio data. YANKELOVICH ET AL. provide an excellent overview of the issues related to speech-based user interfaces and argue that speech interfaces should be created with speech behavior in mind rather than trying to translate graphical interfaces into speech-based interfaces. FERNSTROM & BANNON have developed a sonic browsing system that gives users a starfield display to interactively retrieve music. RESNICK & VIRZI provide an analysis of the design space for selection-based audio interfaces such as phone menus and PDAs. ARONS created the SpeechSkimmer system that allows users to choose the level of skim desired by using joystick or touchpad controls. Given the amount of work being done on multimedia at the time of this review, there is certain to be a plethora of new interface designs in the near future.

Multiple I/O and network objects. The addition of the mouse to keyboard-based input provided a user acceptance path for multiple input devices and portended the current developments in interfaces that give users multiple input and output (I/O) mechanisms for interacting with information. JACOB ET AL., as part of an NSF workshop to define HCI research directions, summarize HCI research related to I/O devices and provide a framework for research on multiple and multimodal devices, including those that gather inputs automatically. The trends are toward coordinated, multiple input devices, including those that monitor human physiology (e.g., heartrate, electrical activity) and behavior (e.g., eyetracking). Early work on the efficacy of touch panels (POTTER ET AL.) has been augmented with the development of specialized interface devices that use lipreading for enhancing speech (PETAJAN ET AL.), facial displays for input and output (WALKER ET AL.), baton-based controls for music (BORCHERS), pointing/gesturing alternatives (GRAHAM & MACKENZIE), and gesture-to-speech conversions (FELS & HINTON). The development of PDAs has been facilitated by a long stream of work on pen-based input that includes handwriting recognition (e.g., RHYNE & WOLF), pen-based shorthands and selections (e.g., KURTENBACH & BUXTON), and speech input techniques (e.g., SCHMANDT). All these specialized devices suggest alternatives for different tasks and users, and opportunities for multimodal interactions, but a key challenge is how to integrate the various techniques in a single design. User-selectable alternative interface designs seem most promising in this regard.

Interfaces to control remote effectors (telepresence) or virtual objects (virtual reality or VR) have attracted considerable attention for applications ranging from remote surgery to education, information retrieval, and entertainment. SPRING and NEWBY provide overviews for VR issues in information science. The primary metaphor of VR and telepresence is entering a world or controlling objects in remote places. Ubiquitous access brings computational power wherever one is, rather than projecting oneself through technology. This perhaps culminates most radically in wearable computing. Early developments at MIT and Carnegie Mellon University have led to a variety of applications and a symposium on wearable computing at MIT in October 1997. The applications range from "rememberance agents" that remind users about things to do based on context, and "nomadic radio" that keeps one in constant communication, to job-specific devices that assist technicians in tight spaces (BASS ET AL.). Although present implementations for general use are clumsy and intrusive (e.g., small video monitors attached to glasses, single-hand input devices, and computer systems strapped to the waist), users can surely expect easily wearable devices and clothing that monitor their physiology and provide on-demand access to information resources wherever they are.

Information-seeking research has broadened in the recent past as a result of technology push. Multimedia retrieval challenges and Web-based resources allow information seekers to focus on information objects at many levels of granularity rather than only at the document or bibliographic pointer levels. For a given conceptual object such as an article in an electronic journal, the unit of information-seeking analysis may be the entire paper, an abstract or outline, a concordance or term-frequency distribution, a set of hyperlinked references, a list of all subsequent references to the paper, or a co-citation map display that contextualizes the paper in a larger information space, not to mention active displays for figures or program code attached to the paper.

Because these views of the document can be automatically generated, information seekers will come to expect (and be expected) to specify the granularity for both search and display. Given the expertise required of professional intermediaries using online systems such as DIALOG to field-delimit queries and specify print formats, significant interface challenges lie ahead for end users seeking information in the Web. For example, a query to the Library of Congress American Memory site may yield a hit list that mixes finding aids, entire image collections, and specific images or manuscripts. MARCHIONINI ET AL. (1998) developed result displays that indicate the different granularities of objects available for each hit and the granularity level that yielded the hit. This kind of added-value display of results requires that part-whole and other relationship links be computable (or be manually added in the corpus).

The design challenges of many levels of information object granularity are exacerbated by distributed systems. Remote objects require naming that, unlike one's personal file directory schemes, is not solely dependent on a single user. For example, compare managing the bookmarks in a Web browser with managing the different files on an office workstation. Thus, new standards for naming or new intermediary naming services will be needed—a problem well-recognized by the digital library community (e.g., see ARMS ET AL.)—along with interfaces that support the entire range of user sophistication.

Enhanced direct manipulation and customized views. Perhaps the most important development for information seeking is the continued integration of the query and results steps in the information-seeking process and closer coupling of interactivity factors. This integration is driven by several parallel developments: empirical and technical reinforcement of user browsing as an important information-seeking strategy, advances in information visualization techniques, and interface designs that incorporate multiple levels and alternative representations for information objects. Interfaces springing from these developments enhance users' ability to directly manipulate information objects and allow users to choose and customize interfaces best suited to their needs.

Browsing has always been recognized as important in libraries, but work in the first two generations of electronic information seeking was almost exclusively concerned with analytical searching that depends on carefully planned queries and precise reformulations. BATES's (1989) berrypicking model of searching, empirical studies of end-user behavior (MARCHIONINI, 1995), and recent work by PIROLLI & CARD on information foraging illustrate the interest in supporting browsing in search systems. Browsing becomes much more important in multimedia databases and in digital libraries where consistent metadata are not available across all information objects. See CHANG & RICE for a review of browsing research and SPINK & LOSEE for a review of the importance of feedback in information retrieval. Hypertext systems, which served as the technical force for more interactive search in the 1980s, used embedded menus (SHNEIDERMAN, 1998b) and button selections to make navigation (a form of browsing) the primary user control mechanism for seeking information. The Web has multiplied this effect so that Web-based searching combines query specification and link selections. This combination of analytical and browse strategies is perhaps most strongly illustrated in GOLOVCHINSKY & CHIGNELL, who have developed systems in which queries and links are synonymous. In their VOIR interface, users iteratively select newspaper articles, which are used as queries to return new displays of articles that may again be used in a relevance feedback cycle to find the best articles to meet needs. These examples represent only a few of the different approaches to integrating analytical search and browsing strategies to get beyond the current point-and-click interface default.

Improved hardware has led to new work in information visualization. J.G. WILLIAMS ET AL. review progress in scientific visualization techniques. Here we focus on how such techniques are applied to user interfaces to support more interactive information seeking. The problem of displaying many related objects in limited display areas was addressed by FURNAS, who proposed using fisheye views of information spaces so users could focus on information objects of interest while maintaining their context. Other work aims to provide high-level overviews of information spaces through use of visual abstractions. LIN has used a Kohonen feature map algorithm to create semantic maps that allow users to visualize a high-dimensional document space in two dimensions, where size of region represents frequency (importance) of concepts and region proximities correspond to semantic similarity. CHEN ET AL. have also used Lin's approach in their digital library interfaces. Other researchers have concentrated on giving users the ability to customize visualizations for information spaces. KORFHAGE and his group have developed the GUIDO and VIBE systems that use points of interest (POIs) as visual objects users may specify to view the document space. The POIs represent any objects (e.g., a query, a profile, a relevant document) to which the user wants to compare the documents in the corpus.

To help users better understand and manipulate the results of queries, HEARST created the Tilebars interface that gives a visual display for the frequency of each query term by text section for each hit. This is a very effective visualization for understanding not only which documents are relevant in a list, but also for considering the most relevant sections in each document. This interface also illustrates how information seekers may gain views of results at different granularities. NA-

TION ET AL. created the WebTOC interface to allow users to see a table of contents view of a collection or object, including the size and data type for each component. The LIFELINES interface (PLAISANT ET AL.) allows users to visualize information chronologically along easily rescalable lines displaying color-coded attributes. Leveraging interactive systems and clustering algorithms, CUTTING ET AL. developed the SCATTER/GATHER interface that allows users to select clusters from a display produced by a clustering algorithm, gathering them into a subset that is then used to recluster the database.

Two strong threads in user interface research for information seeking are to improve the direct manipulation interfaces of earlier days to closely couple queries, results, and interactions, and to augment linguistic interfaces with visual features. In most cases, these threads were integrated into advanced information-seeking systems.

The work of Card and his colleagues at Xerox PARC provided a sequence of these interfaces. These interfaces included the Perspective Wall (CARD ET AL., 1991) that used 3D perspective to allow users to visualize large document spaces; cone trees, cam trees, and the Hyperbolic Browser interfaces that allow users to see and directly manipulate thousands of information objects; and the Web Book and Web Forager (CARD ET AL., 1996) that use a book metaphor for web browsing. In a second ongoing line of research, headed by Shneiderman at the University of Maryland, a series of dynamic query interfaces were developed for a variety of applications. Dynamic query (DQ) interfaces (AHLBERG ET AL.; SHNEIDERMAN, 1998b) provide visual displays for the corpus and control widgets such as sliders and selection buttons for probing the corpus, that is, for dynamically querying the interface in an exploratory way where the query and results are tightly coupled. The visual display, in many cases a starfield display, maps information objects onto a grid defined by two key attributes. The attributes may be redefined according to user needs and the display is immediately updated as control widgets are adjusted. In effect, users may issue scores of queries by moving a slider for an attribute of interest and watching the starfield update for each slider movement. A variety of applications have been implemented using the DQ approach, including finding homes (WILLIAMSON & SHNEIDERMAN), films (AHLBERG ET AL.), NASA research documents (DOAN ET AL.), Library of Congress digital collections (MARCHIONINI ET AL., 1998), and multimedia instructional resources (ROSE ET AL.). The key requirement for this type of interactivity is having all the attribute data immediately available. For very large collections, a hierarchical set of starfield displays is provided that allows network transfer of the appropriate partition of metadata for each starfield display. FOX ET AL. have developed the Envision system that represents information objects and their frequencies on a grid layout that supports dynamic query interactions.

These interfaces provide users with opportunities for examining information objects (whether these are entire corpora or specific documents) at multiple levels and from specialized viewpoints. Interface mechanisms such as MAGIC LENS tools have been applied to dynamic query designs (FISHKIN & STONE). In such implementations, filters for key attributes are built into lens tools that users can grab and pass over displays as query operators. The filtered results show through the lens, thus allowing users to perform rapid, exploratory probes of the corpus. Several researchers have created interfaces that allow users to view complex hierarchical objects or find structure in object collections. An example of the former is described by MUKHERJEA ET AL., who developed algorithms to display alternative hierarchical views for hypermedia based on clustering; users can select from several different visualization options. SHIPMAN ET AL. used studies of how people arrange text fragments into categories as the basis for the VIKI interface that suggests composite groupings for objects to facilitate exploration. A highly generalized mechanism for managing multiple levels of abstraction in a direct manipulation manner is the continuous zoom. Zooming and panning offer provocative possibilities for accessing information in hierarchical structures. Originally proposed by Ken Perlin (PERLIN & FOX), the Pad++ interface (BEDERSON & HOLLAN) allows users to control an infinitely scalable surface with a three-button mouse. This interface is especially effective for timelines, complex diagrams, and highly structured documents. RENNISON has applied zooming and panning in an electronic text environment and LIEBERMAN has demonstrated the effectiveness of zooming for geographic data.

Although these interfaces adopt different widgets, they share the common goal of enhancing users' abilities to combine analytical and browsing strategies for information seeking, view databases at aggregate and detailed levels according to specific attributes, and generally interact with the data in exploratory ways. The advantages of increased interactivity in a query environment were demonstrated by KOENEMANN & BELKIN. The interfaces emerging for today's Web environment tend to maximize interactivity. Although query and result subprocesses of the information-seeking process have finally become more closely integrated, much work remains to integrate problem definition and information manipulation and usage subprocesses. HENDRY & HARPER's Sketchtrieve system aims to go beyond information exploration to support information processing through tools for comparing documents and allowing annotations on documents and links among documents. Certainly much more progress must be made if interfaces for information seeking are to support the entire process, let alone the process embedded in larger work or play settings.

Directions

The Web in many ways stymied the advance of user interface research for a few years by providing a minimalist platform that did not maintain state, did not support multiple windows or sophisticated menuing, and limited user interactions to selections (clicking on links) and simple form fill-ins. The overwhelming advantage of such a simple platform soon became apparent. The subsequent improvements as HTML was enriched and Java applets and applications evolved have allowed user interface research and development advances to find applications in the Web environment. Search engines have evolved from simple forms-based interfaces that returned long lists of ranked Web pages to interfaces that provide fixed-entry categories (e.g., Yahoo!); give users many options for formulations (e.g., limiting by sources, fields, data types, and variants); provide results viewing options; and support relevance feedback (SHNEIDERMAN ET AL.). As the Web infrastructure continues to develop, the user interface techniques created for stand-alone environments will continue to migrate to Web interfaces.

New challenges for interface designers are emerging as Web interface designs for push technology (targeted channels of advertising or specialized services automatically sent to users) compete with designs for pull technology (users selecting what appears). An excellent interface design from the perspective of the intermediary service that uses pay-for-performance techniques to get user attention may be extremely annoying to users who do not wish to have their various browser clients affected. Filtering alternatives that will inevitably emerge offer new interface design challenges for giving users multiple alternatives and ways to manage those alternatives. Interfaces for the Web will differ by task/business just as much as they do by user preference; for example, government sites and search engine sites may want interfaces that encourage short sessions and quick exits, while sales and entertainment services will want interfaces that maintain user attention. In all cases, a design guideline that is gaining consensus is to minimize mouse clicks and quickly bring relevant information to the user. Design prototypes for the Library of Congress National Digital Library Project (MARCHIONINI ET AL., 1998) used compressed layouts to flatten hierarchies and minimize mouse clicks. Although this puts more words on a screen, it avoids potentially disorienting jumps and provides a better overview of the site. Likewise, corporate intranet designs will continue to minimize form to accommodate function in work environments. These information-rich designs will not be effective for entertainment or news applications that depend heavily on design novelty and continually changing content to attract users. The age-old tradeoffs of form and function today challenge interface designers as tensions grow among various stakeholders and movement continues toward universal access and more Web-based applications.

Perhaps the greatest research challenges are to develop alternative interfaces that meet the needs of wide-ranging sets of users, and models and mechanisms for optimally mapping interfaces to problem situations. In addition to the obvious work needed on user behavior, information scientists must reconceptualize their view of information systems as distinct entities in order to see them as elements embedded in a larger user-information milieu. Information systems might be considered to be more like geographic information systems (GISs) that store spatial data that may then be flexibly manifested according to user needs. In a GIS, the map displayed is a thematic view of the underlying data and may be easily changed according to the needs of the user (LAURINI & THOMPSON). Increasingly, web pages will be generated on the fly from back-end database stores and customized not only to user queries but also to user profiles and contexts. Additionally, user interfaces that support information seeking must allow users to view information according to their needs. To do so requires rich and well-documented data (the various representations for information) as well as the user control mechanisms for defining which view best meets the need. Extensible markup language (XML) provides potential for client-side customized views of generic data.

The information-seeking interface should be made part of the user's larger work environment so that interfaces support brainstorming, problem definition before the search, and information manipulation, usage, and communication after the search. Today's Web browser interfaces that integrate Web access, communication, and editing are a clear step in this direction. The Microsoft OS/browser issue currently receiving U.S. Department of Justice attention is largely about such issues.

Finally, new models of IR are needed that consider users as individuals so that the same query posed by two different people actually returns different and differently ranked documents (e.g., LOSEE proposed using Gray codes for this purpose); that are information-oriented (object) rather than document-oriented; and that support interoperation across databases (including merging of results). Such IR models will help interface designers to create more personalized and interactive experiences for information seekers.

CONCLUSION

User interfaces that support information seeking have benefited from the parallel developments of research on the information-seeking process and human-computer interaction, which in turn have been strongly driven by technology development. Interface design has become more user-centered and continues to serve the needs of larger portions of the population in approaching the goal of universal access. In addition to the variety implied by universal access, interface design has begun to take the user's context into account to establish a balance among user needs, organizational setting and task, and system capabilities.

Information systems and interfaces have caused information science research to elucidate more precise models of information-seeking strategies. Although early developments focused on query specification and subsequent development provided informal browsing support, the trend is toward more mature interfaces that support ranges of information-seeking strategies with direct manipulation and highly visual control mechanisms. Today's interface research aims to support user searches for and examination of multimedia information at various levels of granularity. These interfaces increasingly provide different coordinated multimodal input and output devices.

User interface research in the late 1990s points toward ubiquitous access to information objects. Most importantly, this access is embedded in the larger information activities of life and customizable to individual preferences and abilities.

BIBLIOGRAPHY

AHLBERG, CHRISTOPHER; WILLIAMSON, CHRISTOPHER; SHNEIDERMAN, BEN. 1992. Dynamic Queries for Information Exploration: An Implementation and Evaluation. In: Bauersfeld, Penny; Bennett, John; Lynch, Gene, eds. CHI '92: Proceedings of the Association for Computing Machinery Special Interest Group on Computer-Human Interaction (ACM/SIGCHI) Conference on Human Factors in Computing Systems; 1992 May 3-7; Monterey, CA. New York, NY: ACM; 1992. 619-626. ISBN: 0-201-53344-X.

ARMS, WILLIAM Y.; BLANCHI, CHRISTOPHE; OVERLY, EDWARD A. 1997. An Architecture for Information in Digital Libraries. D-Lib Magazine. 1997 February. ISSN: 1082-9873. Available WWW: http://www.dlib.org/dlib/february97/cnri/02arms1.html.

ARONS, BARRY. 1993. SpeechSkimmer: Interactively Skimming Recorded Speech. In: UIST '93: Proceedings of the Association for Computing Machinery (ACM) 6th Annual Symposium on User Interface Software and Technology; 1993 November 3-5; Atlanta, GA. New York, NY: ACM; 1993. 187-195. ISBN: 0-89791-628-X.

BAECKER, RONALD M.; GRUDIN, JONATHAN; BUXTON, WILLIAM A.S.; GREENBERG, S. 1995. A Historical and Intellectual Perspective. In: Baecker, Ronald, ed. Readings in Human-Computer Interaction: Toward the Year 2000. 2nd edition. San Francisco, CA: Morgan Kaufmann; 1995. 35-48. ISBN: 1-55860-246-1.

BASS, LEN; KASABACH, CHRIS; MARTIN, RICHARD; SIEWIOREK, DAN; SMAILAGIC, ASIM; STIVORIC, JOHN. 1997. The Design of a Wearable

Computer. In: Pemberton, Steve, ed. CHI '97: Proceedings of the Association for Computing Machinery Special Interest Group on Computer-Human Interaction (ACM/SIGCHI) Conference on Human Factors in Computing Systems; 1997 March 22-27; Atlanta, GA. New York, NY: ACM; 1997. 139-146. ISBN: 0-201-32229-3.

BATES, MARCIA. 1979a. Idea Tactics. Journal of the American Society for Information Science. 1979 September; 30(5): 280-289. ISSN: 0002-8231.

BATES, MARCIA. 1979b. Information Search Tactics. Journal of the American Society for Information Science. 1979 July; 30(4): 205-214. ISSN: 0002-8231.

BATES, MARCIA. 1989. The Design of Browsing and Berrypicking Techniques for the Online Search Interface. Online Review. 1989 October; 13(5): 407-424. ISSN: 0309-314X.

BATES, MARCIA. 1990. Where Should the Person Stop and the Information Search Interface Start? Information Processing & Management. 1990; 26(5): 575-591. ISSN: 0306-4573.

BEDERSON, BENJAMIN; HOLLAN, JAMES. 1994. Pad++: A Zooming Graphical Interface for Exploring Alternative Interface Physics. In: UIST '94: Proceedings of the Association for Computing Machinery (ACM) 7th Annual Symposium on User Interface Software and Technology; 1994 November 2-4; Marina del Rey, CA. New York, NY: ACM; 1994. 17-26. ISBN: 0-89791-657-3.

BEHESHTI, JAMSHID. 1997. The Evolving OPAC. Cataloging & Classification Quarterly. 1997; 24(1/2): 163-185. ISSN: 0163-9374.

BEHESHTI, JAMSHID; LARGE, VALERIE; BIALEK, MARY. 1996. PACE: A Browsable Graphical Interface. Information Technology and Libraries. 1996 December; 15(4): 231-240. ISSN: 0730-9295.

BELKIN, NICHOLAS J. 1980. Anomalous States of Knowledge as a Basis for Information Retrieval. Canadian Journal of Information Science. 1980 May; 5: 133-143. ISSN: 0380-9218; CODEN: CJISDE.

BELKIN, NICHOLAS J. 1996. Intelligent Information Retrieval: Whose Intelligence? In: Krause, Jürgen; Herfurth, Matthias; Marx, Jutta, eds. ISI '96: Hearausforderungen an die Informationswirtschaft: Informationsverdichtung, Informationsbewertung und Datenvisualisierung. Konstanz, Germany: University of Konstanz; 1996. 25-31. ISBN: 3-87940-506-7.

BENNETT, JOHN. 1972. The User Interface in Interactive Systems. In: Cuadra, Carlos; Luke, Ann W., eds. Annual Review of Information Science and Technology: Volume 7. Washington, DC: American Society for Information Science; 1972. 159-196. ISBN: 0-87715-206-3.

BESSER, HOWARD. 1990. Visual Access to Visual Images: The UC Berkeley Image Database Project. Library Trends. 1990 Spring; 38(4): 787-798. ISSN: 0024-2594.

BORCHERS, JAN. 1997. WorldBeat: Designing a Baton-Based Interface for an Interactive Music Exhibit. In: Pemberton, Steve, ed. CHI '97: Proceedings of the Association for Computing Machinery Special Interest Group on Computer-Human Interaction (ACM/SIGCHI) Conference on Human Factors in Computing Systems; 1997 March 22-27; Atlanta, GA. New York, NY: ACM; 1997. 131-138. ISBN: 0-201-32229-3.

BORGMAN, CHRISTINE L. 1984. Psychological Research in Human-Computer Interaction. In: Williams, Martha E., ed. Annual Review of Information Science and Technology: Volume 19. White Plains, NY: Knowledge Industry Publications, Inc. for the American Society for Information Science; 1984. ISSN: 0066-4200; ISBN: 0-86729-093-5; CODEN: ARISBC.

BORGMAN, CHRISTINE L. 1986. Why Are Online Catalogs Hard to Use? Lessons Learned from Information-Retrieval Studies. Journal of the American Society for Information Science. 1986 November; 37(6): 387-400. ISSN: 0002-8231.

BORGMAN, CHRISTINE L. 1996. Why Are Online Catalogs *Still* Hard to Use? Journal of the American Society for Information Science. 1996 July; 47(7): 493-503. ISSN: 0002-8231.

BORGMAN, CHRISTINE L.; HIRSH, SANDRA G.; WALTER, VIRGINIA A.; GALLAGHER, ANDREA. 1995. Children's Searching Behavior on Browsing and Keyword Online Catalogs: The Science Library Catalog Project. Journal of the American Society for Information Science. 1995 October; 46(9): 663-684. ISSN: 0002-8231.

BROOKS, FREDERICK P. 1975. The Mythical Man-Month: Essays on Software Engineering. Reading, MA: Addison-Wesley; 1975. 322p. ISBN: 0-201-83595-9.

BUSEY, PAULA; DOERR, TOM. 1993. Kid's Catalog: An Information Retrieval System for Children. Journal of Youth Services in Libraries. 1993 Fall; 7(1): 77-84. ISSN: 0894-2498.

CARD, STUART K.; MORAN, THOMAS P.; NEWELL, ALLEN. 1983. The Psychology of Human-Computer Interaction. Hillsdale, NJ: Lawrence Erlbaum Associates; 1983. 469p. ISBN: 0-89859-243-7.

CARD, STUART K.; ROBERTSON, GEORGE G.; MACKINLAY, JOCK D. 1991. The Information Visualizer, an Information Workspace. In: Robertson, Scott P.; Olson, Gary M.; Olson, Judith S., eds. CHI '91: Proceedings of the Association for Computing Machinery Special Interest Group on Computer-Human Interaction (ACM/SIGCHI) Conference on Human Factors in Computing Systems; 1991 April 28-May 2; New Orleans, LA. New York, NY: ACM; 1991. 181-188. ISBN: 0-201-51278-5.

CARD, STUART K.; ROBERTSON, GEORGE G.; YORK, WILLIAM. 1996. The WebBook and the Web Forager: An Information Workspace for the World-Wide Web. In: Tauber, Michael, ed. CHI '96: Proceedings of the Association for Computing Machinery Special Interest Group on Computer-Human Interaction (ACM/SIGCHI) Conference on Human Factors in Computing Systems; 1996 April 13-18; Vancouver, Canada. New York, NY: ACM; 1996. 111-117. ISBN: 0-201-94687-4.

CARROLL, JOHN M.; ROSSON, MARY BETH. 1987. Paradox of the Active User. In: Carroll, John M., ed. Interfacing Thought: Cognitive Aspects of Human-Computer Interaction. Cambridge, MA: MIT Press; 1987. 80-111. ISBN: 0-262-03125-6.

CARROLL, JOHN M.; ROSSON, MARY BETH. 1992. Getting Around the Task-Artifact Cycle: How to Make Claims and Design by Scenario. ACM Transactions on Information Systems. 1992 April; 10(2): 181-212. ISSN: 0734-2047.

CHANG, SHAN-JU; RICE, RONALD E. 1993. Browsing: A Multidimensional Framework. In: Williams, Martha E., ed. Annual Review of Information Science and Technology: Volume 28. Medford, NJ: Learned Information, Inc. for the American Society for Information Science; 1993. 231-276. ISSN: 0066-4200; ISBN: 0-938734-75-X; CODEN: ARISBC.

CHEN, HSINCHUN; HOUSTON, ANDREA L.; SEWELL, ROBIN R.; SCHATZ, BRUCE R. 1998. Internet Browsing and Searching: User Evaluations of Category Map and Concept Space Techniques. Journal of the American Society for Information Science. 1998 May 15; 49(7): 582-603. ISSN: 0002-8231.

CHUAH, MEI; ROTH, STEVEN; KOLOJEJCHICK, JOHN; MATTIS, JOE; JUAREZ, OCTAVIO. 1995. SageBook: Searching Data-Graphics by Content. In: Katz, Irvin; Mack, Robert; Marks, Linn, eds. CHI '95: Proceedings of the Association for Computing Machinery Special Interest Group on Computer-Human Interaction (ACM/SIGCHI) Conference on Human Factors in Computing Systems; 1995 May 7-11; Denver, CO. New York, NY: ACM; 1995. 338-345. ISBN: 0-201-84705-1.

CUTTING, DOUGLASS R.; KARGER, DAVID R.; PEDERSEN, JAN O.; TUKEY, JOHN W. 1992. Scatter/Gather: A Cluster-Based Approach to Browsing Large Document Collections. In: Belkin, Nicholas; Ingwersen, Peter; Pejtersen, Annelise Mark, eds. SIGIR '92: Proceedings of the Association for Computing Machinery Special Interest Group on Information Retrieval (ACM/SIGIR) 15th Annual International Conference on Research and Development in Information Retrieval; 1992 June 21-24; Copenhagen, Denmark. New York, NY: ACM; 1992. 318-329. ISBN: 0-89791-523-2.

DALRYMPLE, PRUDENCE W.; RODERER, NANCY K. 1994. Database Access Systems. In: Williams, Martha E., ed. Annual Review of Information Science and Technology: Volume 29. Medford, NJ: Learned Information, Inc. for the American Society for Information Science; 1994. 137-178. ISSN: 0066-4200; ISBN: 0-938734-91-1; CODEN: ARISBC.

DAVIS, RUTH M. 1966. Man-Machine Communication. In: Cuadra, Carlos A., ed. Annual Review of Information Science and Technology: Volume 1. New York, NY: Interscience Publishers; 1966. 221-254. LC: 66-25096.

DERVIN, BRENDA. 1977. Useful Theory for Librarianship: Communication, Not Information. Drexel Library Quarterly. 1977 July; 13(3): 16-32. ISSN: 0012-6160.

DILLON, ANDREW; WATSON, CHARLES. 1996. User Analysis in HCI: The Historical Lessons from Individual Differences Research. International Journal of Human-Computer Studies. 1996; 45: 619-637. ISSN: 1071-5819.

DOAN, KHOA; PLAISANT, CATHERINE; SHNEIDERMAN, BEN; BRUNS, TOM. 1997. Query Previews for Networked Information Systems: A Case Study with NASA Environmental Data. SIGMOD Record. 1997 March; 26(1): 75-81. ISSN: 0163-5808.

DOSZKOCS, TAMAS E. 1983. CITE NLM: Natural-Language Searching in an Online Catalog. Information Technology and Libraries. 1983 December; 2(4): 364-380. ISSN: 0730-9295.

DRUIN, ALLISON; SOLOMON, CYNTHIA. 1996. Designing Multimedia Environments for Children. 2nd edition. New York, NY: John Wiley & Sons; 1996. 263p. ISBN: 0-471-11688-2.

DUGGAN, MARY KAY. 1992. Access to Sound and Image Databases. In: Stone, Susan; Buckland, Michael, eds. Studies in Multimedia: State-of-the-Art Solutions in Multimedia and Hypertext. Medford, NJ: Learned Information, Inc.; 1992. 83-97. ISBN: 0-938734-59-8.

DUMAIS, SUSAN; LANDAUER, THOMAS K. 1984. Psychological Investigations of Natural Language Terminology for Command & Query Languages. In: Badre, Albert; Shneiderman, Ben, eds. Directions in Human-Computer Interaction. Norwood, NJ: Ablex; 1984. 95-109. ISBN: 0-89391-144-5.

ENGELBART, DOUGLAS. 1963. A Conceptual Framework for the Augmentation of Man's Intellect. In: Howerton, Paul; Weeks, D., eds. Vistas in Information Handling: Volume 1. Washington, DC: Spartan Books; 1963. 1-29. OCLC: 2502347.

FELS, SIDNEY; HINTON, GEOFFREY. 1995. Glove-TalkII: An Adaptive Gesture-to-Formant Interface. In: Katz, Irvin; Mack, Robert; Marks, Linn, eds. CHI '95: Proceedings of the Association for Computing Machinery Special Interest Group on Computer-Human Interaction (ACM/SIGCHI) Conference on Human Factors in Computing Systems; 1995 May 7-11; Denver, CO. New York, NY: ACM; 1995. 456-463. ISBN: 0-201-84705-1.

FERNSTROM, MIKAEL; BANNON, LIAM. 1997. Sonic Browsing. In: People and Computers XII: Proceedings of HCI '97; 1997 August; Bristol, England. London, England: Springer, in collaboration with the British Computer Society; 1997. 117-131. ISBN: 3-540-76172-1.

FISHKIN, KEN; STONE, MAUREEN. 1995. Enhanced Dynamic Queries via Movable Filters. In: Katz, Irvin; Mack, Robert; Marks, Linn, eds. CHI '95: Proceedings of the Association for Computing Machinery Special Interest Group on Computer-Human Interaction (ACM/SIGCHI) Conference on Human Factors in Computing Systems; 1995 May 7-11; Denver, CO. New York, NY: ACM; 1995. 415-420. ISBN: 0-201-84705-1.

FOX, EDWARD A.; HIX, DEBORAH; NOWELL, LUCY; BRUENI, DENNIS; WAKE, WILLIAM; HEATH, LENWOOD; RAO, DURGESH. 1993. Users, User Interfaces, and Objects: Envision, a Digital Library. Journal of the American Society for Information Science. 1993 September; 44(8): 480-491. ISSN: 0002-8231; CODEN: AISJB6.

FURNAS, GEORGE W. 1986. Generalized Fisheye Views. In: Mantei, Marilyn; Orbeton, Peter, eds. CHI '86: Proceedings of the Association for Computing Machinery Special Interest Group on Computer-Human Interaction (ACM/SIGCHI) Conference on Human Factors in Computing Systems; 1986 April 13-17; Boston, MA. New York, NY: ACM; 1986. 16-23. ISBN: 0-89791-180-6.

GECHMAN, MARVIN C. 1972. Generation and Use of Machine-Readable Bibliographic Data Bases. In: Cuadra, Carlos; Luke, Ann W., eds. Annual Review of Information Science and Technology: Volume 7. Washington, DC: American Society for Information Science; 1972. 323-378. ISBN: 0-87715-206-3; CODEN: ARISBC.

GOLOVCHINSKY, GENE; CHIGNELL, MARK. 1997. The Newspaper as an Information Exploration Metaphor. Information Processing & Management. 1997 September; 33(5): 663-683. ISSN: 0306-4573; CODEN: IPMADK.

GOMEZ, LOUIS M.; LOCHBAUM, CAROL C.; LANDAUER, THOMAS K. 1990. All the Right Words: Finding What You Want as a Function of Richness of Indexing Vocabulary. Journal of the American Society for Information Science. 1990 December; 41(8): 547-559. ISSN: 0002-8231; CODEN: AISJB6.

GRAHAM, EVAN; MACKENZIE, CHRISTINE. 1996. Physical versus Virtual Pointing. In: Tauber, Michael, ed. CHI '96: Proceedings of the Association for Computing Machinery Special Interest Group on Computer-Human Interaction (ACM/SIGCHI) Conference on Human Factors in Computing Systems; 1996 April 13-18; Vancouver, Canada. New York, NY: ACM; 1996. 292-299. ISBN: 0-201-94687-4.

GUPTA, AMARANTH; SANTINI, SIMONE; JAIN, RAMESH. 1997. In Search of Information in Visual Media. Communications of the ACM. 1997 December; 40(12): 35-42. ISSN: 0001-0782.

HAWKINS, DONALD T. 1981. Online Information Retrieval Systems. In: Williams, Martha E., ed. Annual Review of Information Science and Technology: Volume 16. White Plains, NY: Knowledge Industry Publications, Inc. for the American Society for Information Science; 1981. 171-208. ISSN: 0066-4200; ISBN: 0-914236-90-3; CODEN: ARISBC.

HEARST, MARTI. 1997. TextTiling: Segmenting Text into Multi-Paragraph Subtopic Passages. Computational Linguistics. 1997 March; 23(1): 33-64. ISSN: 0891-2017.

HENDRY, DAVID; HARPER, DAVID. 1997. An Informal Information-Seeking Environment. Journal of the American Society for Information Science. 1997 November; 48(11): 1036-1048. ISSN: 0002-8231; CODEN: AISJB6.

HILDRETH, CHARLES R. 1982. Online Public Access Catalogs: The User Interface. Dublin, OH: Online Computer Library Center; 1982. 263p. ISBN: 0-933418-34-5.

HILDRETH, CHARLES R. 1984. Pursuing the Ideal: Generations of Online Catalogs. In: Aveney, Brian; Butler, Brett, eds. Online Catalogs, Online Reference: Converging Trends: Proceedings of a Library and Information Technology Association Preconference Institute; 1983 June 23-24; Los Angeles, CA. Chicago, IL: American Library Association; 1984. 31-56. ISBN: 0-8389-3308-4.

HILDRETH, CHARLES R. 1985. Online Public Access Catalogs. In: Williams, Martha E., ed. Annual Review of Information Science and Technology: Volume 20. White Plains, NY: Knowledge Industry Publications, Inc. for the American Society for Information Science; 1985. 233-285. ISSN: 0066-4200; ISBN: 0-86729-175-3; CODEN: ARISBC.

HIX, DEBORAH; HARTSON, H. REX. 1993. Developing User Interfaces: Ensuring Usability through Product & Process. New York, NY: John Wiley; 1993. 381p. ISBN: 0-471-57813-4.

HJERPPE, ROLAND. 1989. HYPERCAT at LIBLAB in Sweden: A Progress Report. In: Hildreth, Charles R., ed. The Online Catalogue: Developments and Directions. London, England: The Library Association; 1989. 177-209. ISBN: 0-85365-708-4.

HOLT, BONNIE; WEISS, KEN; NIBLACK, WAYNE; FLICKNER, MYRON; PETKOVIC, DRAGUTIN. 1997. The QBIC Project in the Department of

Art and Art History at UC Davis. In: Schwartz, Candy; Rorvig, Mark, eds. ASIS '97: Proceedings of the American Society for Information Science (ASIS) 60th Annual Meeting: Volume 34; 1997 November 1-6; Washington, DC. Medford, NJ: Information Today, Inc. for ASIS; 1997. 189-195. ISSN: 0044-7870; ISBN: 1-57387-048-X.

INGWERSEN, PETER. 1996. Cognitive Perspectives of Information Retrieval Interaction: Elements of a Cognitive IR Theory. Journal of Documentation. 1996 March; 52(1): 3-50. ISSN: 0022-0418.

JACOB, ROBERT; LEGGETT, JOHN; MYERS, BRAD; PAUSCH, RANDY. 1993. Interaction Styles and Input/Output Devices. Behaviour and Information Technology. 1993 March-April; 12(2): 69-79. ISSN: 0144-929X.

JANKE, RICHARD V. 1983. BRS/After Dark: The Birth of an Online Self-Service. Online. 1983 September; 7(5): 12-29. ISSN: 0146-5422.

JOHN, BONNIE E.; KIERAS, DAVID E. 1996a. The GOMS Family of User Interface Analysis Techniques: Comparison and Contrast. ACM Transactions on Computer-Human Interaction. 1996 December; 3(4): 320-351. ISSN: 1073-0516.

JOHN, BONNIE E.; KIERAS, DAVID E. 1996b. Using GOMS for User Interface Design and Evaluation: Which Technique? ACM Transactions on Computer-Human Interaction. 1996 December; 3(4): 287-319. ISSN: 1073-0516.

KASKE, NEAL K. 1984. Studies of Online Catalogs. In: Aveney, Brian; Butler, Brett, eds. Online Catalogs, Online Reference: Converging Trends: Proceedings of a Library and Information Technology Association Preconference Institute; 1983 June 23-24; Los Angeles, CA. Chicago, IL: American Library Association; 1984. 20-30. ISBN: 0-8389-3308-4.

KEHOE, CYNTHIA. A. 1985. Interfaces and Expert Systems for Online Retrieval. Online Review. 1985 December; 9(6): 489-505. ISSN: 0309-314X.

KLINE, RICHARD L.; GLINERT, EPHRAIM. 1995. Improving GUI Accessibility for People with Low Vision. In: Katz, Irvin; Mack, Robert; Marks, Linn, eds. CHI '95: Proceedings of the Association for Computing Machinery Special Interest Group on Computer-Human Interaction (ACM/SIGCHI) Conference on Human Factors in Computing Systems; 1995 May 7-11; Denver, CO. New York, NY: ACM; 1995. 114-121. ISBN: 0-201-84705-1.

KOENEMANN, JÜRGEN; BELKIN, NICHOLAS J. 1996. A Case for Interaction: A Study of Interactive Information Retrieval Behavior and Effectiveness. In: Tauber, Michael, ed. CHI '96: Proceedings of the Association for Computing Machinery Special Interest Group on Computer-Human Interaction (ACM/SIGCHI) Conference on Human Factors in Computing Systems; 1996 April 13-18; Vancouver, BC. New York, NY: ACM; 1996. 205-212. ISBN: 0-201-94687-4.

KOMLODI, ANITA; MARCHIONINI, GARY. 1998. Key Frame Preview Techniques for Video Browsing. In: Proceedings of the 3rd International Conference on Digital Libraries; 1998 June 23-26; Pittsburgh, PA. New York, NY: ACM; 1998. ISBN: 0-89791-965-3.

KORFHAGE, ROBERT. 1997. Information Storage and Retrieval. New York, NY: John Wiley; 1997. 349p. ISBN: 0-471-14338-3.

KUHLTHAU, CAROL COLLIER. 1988. Longitudinal Case Studies of the Information Search Process of Users in Libraries. Library and Information Science Research. 1988 July-September; 10(3): 257-304. ISSN: 0740-8188.

KURTENBACH, GORDON; BUXTON, WILLIAM. 1991. Issues in Combining Marking and Direct Manipulation Techniques. In: UIST '91: Proceedings of the Association for Computing Machinery (ACM) 4th Annual Symposium on User Interface Software and Technology; 1991 November 11-13; Hilton Head, SC. New York, NY: ACM; 1991. 137-144. ISBN: 0-89791-451-1.

LARSON, RAY R. 1991. The Decline of Subject Searching: Long-Term Trends and Patterns of Index Use in an Online Catalog. Journal of the American Society for Information Science. 1991; 42(3): 197-215. ISSN: 0002-8231.

LARSON, RAY R.; MCDONOUGH, JEROME; O'LEARY, PAUL; KUNTZ, LUCY; MOON, RALPH. 1996. Cheshire II. Designing a Next-Generation Online Catalog. Journal of the American Society for Information Science. 1996 July; 47(7): 555-567. ISSN: 0002-8231; CODEN: AISJB6.

LAURINI, ROBERT; THOMPSON, DEREK. 1992. Fundamentals of Spatial Information Systems. 2nd edition. London, England: Academic Press; 1992. 680p. ISBN: 0-12-438380-7.

LICKLIDER, J.C.R. 1968. Man-Computer Communication. In: Cuadra, Carlos, ed. Annual Review of Information Science and Technology: Volume 3. Chicago, IL: Encyclopaedia Britannica, Inc.; 1968. 201-240. LC: 66-25096.

LIEBERMAN, HENRY. 1994. Powers of Ten Thousand: Navigating in Large Information Spaces. In: UIST '94: Proceedings of the Association for Computing Machinery (ACM) 7th Annual Symposium on User Interface Software and Technology; 1994 November 2-4; Marina del Rey, CA. New York, NY: ACM; 1994. 15-16. ISBN: 0-89791-657-3.

LIN, XIA. 1995. Searching and Browsing on Map Displays. In: Kinney, Tom, ed. ASIS '95: Proceedings of the American Society for Information Science (ASIS) 58th Annual Meeting: Volume 32; 1995 October 9-12; Chicago, IL. Medford, NJ: Information Today, Inc. for ASIS; 1995. 13-18. ISSN: 0044-7870; ISBN: 1-57387-017-X.

LOSEE, ROBERT. 1997. Browsing Document Collections: Automatically Organizing Digital Libraries and Hypermedia Using the Gray Code. Information Processing & Management. 1997 March; 33(2): 175-192. ISSN: 0306-4573; CODEN: IPMADK.

LUHN, HANS PETER. 1957. A Statistical Approach to Mechanized Encoding and Searching of Literary Information. IBM Journal of Research and Development. 1957 October; 1(4): 309-317. ISSN: 0018-8646.

MAES, PATTIE. 1995. Modeling Adaptive Autonomous Agents. In: Langton, Christopher G., ed. Artificial Life: An Overview. Cambridge, MA: MIT Press; 1995. 135-162. ISBN: 0-262-62112-6.

MARCHIONINI, GARY. 1992. Interfaces for End-User Information Seeking. Journal of the American Society for Information Science. 1992 March; 43(2): 156-163. ISSN: 0002-8231; CODEN: AISJB6.

MARCHIONINI, GARY. 1995. Information Seeking in Electronic Environments. New York, NY: Cambridge University Press; 1995. 224p. ISBN: 0-521-44372-5.

MARCHIONINI, GARY; ASHLEY, MARYLE; KORZENDORFER, LOIS. 1993. ACCESS at the Library of Congress. In: Shneiderman, Ben, ed. Sparks of

Innovation in Human-Computer Interaction. Norwood, NJ: Ablex; 1993. 251-258. ISBN: 1-56750-078-1.

MARCHIONINI, GARY; PLAISANT, CATHERINE; KOMLODI, ANITA. 1998. Interfaces and Tools for the Library of Congress National Digital Library Program. Information Processing & Management. 1998; 34(5): 535-556. ISSN: 0306-4573.

MARCUS, RICHARD S. 1983. An Experimental Comparison of the Effectiveness of Computers and Humans as Search Intermediaries. Journal of the American Society for Information Science. 1983 November; 34(6): 381-404. ISSN: 0002-8231; CODEN: AISJB6.

MARCUS, RICHARD S.; BENENFELD, ALAN R.; KUGEL, PETER. 1971. The User Interface for the Intrex Retrieval System. In: Walker, Donald, ed. Interactive Bibliographic Search: The User/Computer Interface. Montvale, NJ: AFIPS Press; 1971. 159-201. LC: 70182192.

MARTIN, THOMAS H. 1973. The User Interface in Interactive Systems. In: Cuadra, Carlos A.; Luke, Ann W., eds. Annual Review of Information Science and Technology: Volume 8. Washington, DC: American Society for Information Science; 1973. 203-217. ISBN: 0-87715-208-X; CODEN: ARISBC.

MEADOW, CHARLES T.; CERNY, BARBARA A.; BORGMAN, CHRISTINE L.; CASE, DONALD O. 1989. Online Access to Knowledge: System Design. Journal of the American Society for Information Science. 1989 March; 40(2): 86-98. ISSN: 0002-8231; CODEN: AISJB6.

MEREU, STEPHEN; KAZMAN, RICK. 1996. Audio-Enhanced 3D Interfaces for Visually Impaired Users. In: Tauber, Michael, ed. CHI '96: Proceedings of the Association for Computing Machinery Special Interest Group on Computer-Human Interaction (ACM/SIGCHI) Conference on Human Factors in Computing Systems; 1996 April 13-18; Vancouver, Canada. New York, NY: ACM; 1996. 221-227. ISBN: 0-201-94687-4.

MILLS, R.G. 1967. Man-Machine Communication and Problem Solving. In: Cuadra, Carlos A., ed. Annual Review of Information Science and Technology: Volume 2. New York, NY: Interscience Publishers; 1967. 223-254. LC: 66-25096.

MISCHO, WILLIAM H.; LEE, JOUNGHYOUN. 1987. End-User Searching of Bibliographic Databases. In: Williams, Martha E., ed. Annual Review of Information Science and Technology: Volume 22. Amsterdam, The Netherlands: Elsevier Science Publishers B. V. for the American Society for Information Science; 1987. 227-263. ISSN: 0066-4200; ISBN: 0-444-70302-0; CODEN: ARISBC.

MITEV, NATHALIE NADIA. 1989. Human-Computer Interaction and Online Catalogues. In: OPACS and Beyond: Joint Meeting of the British Library, DBMIST, and OCLC; 1988 August 17-18; Dublin, OH. Dublin, OH: Online Computer Library Center; 1989. 95-102. ISBN: 1-55653-070-6.

MITEV, NATHALIE NADIA; VENNER, GILLIAN M.; WALKER, STEPHEN. 1985. Designing an Online Public Access Catalogue: Okapi, a Catalogue on a Local Area Network. London, England: British Library; 1985. 254p. ISBN: 0-7123-3058-5.

MOSTAFA, JAVED. 1994. Digital Image Representation and Access. In: Williams, Martha E., ed. Annual Review of Information Science and Technology: Volume 29. Medford, NJ: Information Today, Inc. for the American Society for Information Science; 1994. 91-135. ISSN: 0066-4200; ISBN: 0-938734-91-1.

MOSTAFA, JAVED; DILLON, ANDREW. 1996. Design and Evaluation of a User Interface Supporting Multiple Image Query Models. In: Hardin, Steve, ed. ASIS '96: Proceedings of the American Society for Information Science (ASIS) 59th Annual Meeting; 1996 October 21-24; Baltimore, MD. Medford, NJ: Information Today, Inc. for ASIS; 1996. 52-57. ISSN: 0044-7870; ISBN: 1-57387-037-4.

MUKHERJEA, SOUGATA; FOLEY, JAMES; HUDSON, SCOTT. 1995. Visualizing Complex Hypermedia Networks through Multiple Hierarchical Views. In: Katz, Irvin; Mack, Robert; Marks, Linn, eds. CHI '95: Proceedings of the Association for Computing Machinery Special Interest Group on Computer-Human Interaction (ACM/SIGCHI) Conference on Human Factors in Computing Systems; 1995 May 7-11; Denver, CO. New York, NY: ACM; 1995. 331-337. ISBN: 0-201-84705-1.

NARDI, BONNIE A. 1996. Studying Context: A Comparison of Activity Theory, Situated Action Models, and Distributed Cognition. In: Nardi, Bonnie A., ed. Context and Consciousness. Cambridge, MA: MIT Press; 1996. 69-102. ISBN: 0-262-14058-6.

NATION, DAVID A.; PLAISANT, CATHERINE; MARCHIONINI, GARY; KOMLODI, ANITA. 1997. Visualizing Websites Using a Hierarchical Table of Contents Browser: WebTOC. In: Proceedings of the 3rd Conference on Human Factors and the Web; 1997 June 12; Denver, CO. Available WWW: http://www.uswest.com/web-conference/proceedings/nation.html.

NEWBY, GREGORY B. 1993. Virtual Reality. In: Williams, Martha E., ed. Annual Review of Information Science and Technology: Volume 28. Medford, NJ: Learned Information, Inc. for the American Society for Information Science; 1993. 187-230. ISSN: 0066-4200; ISBN: 0-938734-75-X; CODEN: ARISBC.

NEWLIN, BARBARA B. 1985. In-Search: The Design and Evolution of an End User Interface to DIALOG. In: Williams, Martha E.; Hogan, Thomas H., eds. National Online Meeting Proceedings 1985; 1985 April 30-May 2; New York, NY. Medford, NJ: Learned Information, Inc.; 1985. 313-320. ISBN: 0-938734-09-1.

NIELSEN, JAKOB. 1993. Usability Engineering. Boston, MA: Academic Press Professional; 1993. 362p. ISBN: 0-12-518406-9.

NISHIYAMA, HARUHIKO; KIN, SUMI; YOKOYAMA, TERUO; MATSUSHITA, YUTAKA. 1994. An Image Retrieval System Considering Subjective Perception. In: Adelson, Beth; Dumais, Susan; Olson, Judith, eds. CHI '94: Proceedings of the Association for Computing Machinery Special Interest Group on Computer-Human Interaction (ACM/SIGCHI) Conference on Human Factors in Computing Systems; 1994 April 24-28; Boston, MA. New York, NY: ACM; 1994. 30-36. ISBN: 0-201-76557-8.

NORMAN, DONALD A. 1988. The Psychology of Everyday Things. New York, NY: Basic Books; 1988. 257p. ISBN: 0-465-06709-3.

OARD, DOUGLAS W. 1997. Speech-Based Information Retrieval for Digital Libraries. College Park, MD: University of Maryland at College Park; 1997 March. Available WWW: http://www.clis.umd.edu/dlrg/filter/papers/speech/paper.html.

OARD, DOUGLAS W.; DIEKEMA, ANNE R. 1998. Cross-Language Information Retrieval. In: Williams, Martha E., ed. Annual Review of Information Science and Technology: Volume 33. Medford, NJ: Information Today, Inc. for the American Society for Information Science; 1998. 223-256. ISSN: 0066-4200; ISBN: 1-57387-065-X.

OGOZALEK, VIRGINIA. 1994. A Comparison of the Use of Text and Multimedia Interfaces to Provide Information to the Elderly. In: Adelson, Beth; Dumais, Susan; Olson, Judith, eds. CHI '94: Proceedings of the Association for Computing Machinery Special Interest Group on Computer-Human Interaction (ACM/SIGCHI) Conference on Human Factors in Computing Systems; 1994 April 24-28; Boston, MA. New York, NY: ACM; 1994. 65-71. ISBN: 0-201-76557-8.

PEJTERSEN, ANNELISE MARK. 1993. A New Approach to Design of Document Retrieval and Indexing Systems for OPAC Users. In: Raitt, David I.; Jeapes, Ben, eds. Online Information 93: Proceedings of the 17th International Online Information Meeting; 1993 December 7-9; London, England. Oxford, England: Learned Information (Europe) Ltd.; 1993. 273-290. ISBN: 0-904933-85-7.

PERLIN, KEN; FOX, DAVID. 1993. Pad: An Alternative Approach to the Computer Interface. In: Proceedings of the Association for Computing Machinery (ACM) 20th Annual SIGGRAPH Conference; 1993 August 1-6; Anaheim, CA. New York, NY: ACM; 1993. 57-64. ISBN:0-89791-601-8.

PETAJAN, ERIC; BISCHOFF, BRADFORD; BODOFF, DAVID; BROOKE, N. MICHAEL. 1988. An Improved Automatic Lipreading System to Enhance Speech Recognition. In: Soloway, Elliot; Frye, Douglas; Sheppard, Sylvia B., eds. CHI '88: Proceedings of the Association for Computing Machinery Special Interest Group on Computer-Human Interaction (ACM/SIGCHI) Conference on Human Factors in Computing Systems; 1988 May 15-19; Washington, DC. New York, NY: ACM; 1988. 19-25. ISBN: 0-201-14237-6.

PIROLLI, PETER; CARD, STUART K. 1998. Information Foraging Models of Browsers for Very Large Document Spaces. In: Catarci, T.; Costabile, M.F.; Santucci, G.; Tarantino, L., eds. Proceedings of the Working Conference on Advanced Visual Interfaces: AVI '98; 1998 May 24-27; L'Aquila, Italy. New York, NY: ACM; 1998. 83-93. Available from: ACM, P.O. Box 12114, Church Street Station, New York, NY 10257.

PLAISANT, CATHERINE; MILASH, BRETT; ROSE, ANNE; WIDOFF, SETH; SHNEIDERMAN, BEN. 1996. LifeLines: Visualizing Personal Histories. In: Tauber, Michael, ed. CHI '96: Proceedings of the Association for Computing Machinery Special Interest Group on Computer-Human Interaction (ACM/SIGCHI) Conference on Human Factors in Computing Systems; 1996 April 13-18; Vancouver, Canada. New York, NY: ACM; 1996. 221-227, color plate 518. ISBN: 0-201-94687-4.

POTTER, RICHARD; WELDON, LINDA; SHNEIDERMAN, BEN. 1988. Improving the Accuracy of Touch Screens: An Experimental Evaluation of Three Strategies. In: Soloway, Elliot; Frye, Douglas; Sheppard, Sylvia B., eds. CHI '88: Proceedings of the Association for Computing Machinery Special Interest Group on Computer-Human Interaction (ACM/SIGCHI) Conference on Human Factors in Computing Systems; 1988 May 15-19; Washington, DC. New York, NY: ACM; 1988. 27-32. ISBN: 0-201-14237-6.

RAMAN, T.V. 1996. Emacspeak—A Speech Interface. In: Tauber, Michael, ed. CHI '96: Proceedings of the Association for Computing Machinery Special Interest Group on Computer-Human Interaction (ACM/SIGCHI) Conference on Human Factors in Computing Systems; 1996 April 13-18; Vancouver, Canada. New York, NY: ACM; 1996. 66-71. ISBN: 0-201-94687-4.

RENNISON, EARL. 1994. Galaxy of News: An Approach to Visualizing and Understanding Expansive News Landscapes. In: UIST '94: Proceedings of the Association for Computing Machinery (ACM) 7th Annual Symposium on User Interface Software and Technology; 1994 November 2-4; Marina del Rey, CA. New York, NY: ACM; 1994. 3-12. ISBN: 0-89791-657-3.

RESNICK, PAUL; VIRZI, ROBERT. 1995. Relief from the Audio Interface Blues: Expanding the Spectrum of Menu, List, and Form Styles. ACM Transcations on Computer-Human Interaction. 1995 June; 2(2): 145-176. ISSN: 1073-0516.

RHYNE, JAMES R.; WOLF, CATHERINE G. 1993. Recognition-Based User Interfaces. In: Hartson, Rex; Hix, Deborah, eds. Advances in Human-Computer Interaction: Volume 4. New York, NY: Ablex; 1993. 191-250. ISSN: 0748-8602; ISBN: 0-89391-934-9.

ROBERTSON, STEPHEN E. 1997. Overview of the Okapi Projects. Journal of Documentation. 1997 January; 53(1): 3-7. ISSN: 0022-0418.

RORVIG, MARK E. 1993. A Method for Automatically Abstracting Visual Documents. Journal of the American Society for Information Science. 1993 January; 44(1): 40-56. ISSN: 0002-8231; CODEN: AISJB6.

ROSE, ANNE; DING, WEI; MARCHIONINI, GARY; BEALE, JOSEPHUS; NOLET, VICTOR. 1998. Building an Electronic Learning Community: From Design to Implementation. In: Karat, Clare-Marie; Lund, Arnold; Coutaz, Joelle; Karat, John, eds. CHI '98: Proceedings of the Association for Computing Machinery Special Interest Group on Computer-Human Interaction (ACM/SIGCHI) Conference on Human Factors in Computing Systems; 1998 April 18-23; Los Angeles, CA. New York, NY: ACM; 1998. 203-210. ISBN: 0-201-30987-4.

SAARI, DAVID S.; FOSTER, GEORGE A. 1989. Head-to-Head Evaluation of the Pro-Cite and Sci-Mate Bibliographic Database Management Systems. Database. 1989 February; 12(1): 22-38. ISSN: 0162-4104.

SALTON, GERARD; MCGILL, MICHAEL J. 1983. Introduction to Modern Information Retrieval. New York, NY: McGraw-Hill; 1983. 448p. ISBN: 0-07-054484-0.

SARACEVIC, TEFKO. 1996. Modeling Interaction in Information Retrieval (IR): A Review and Proposal. In: Hardin, Steve, ed. ASIS '96: Proceedings of the American Society for Information Science (ASIS) 59th Annual Meeting; 1996 October 21-24; Baltimore, MD. Medford, NJ: Information Today, Inc. for ASIS; 1996. 3-9. ISSN: 0044-7870; ISBN: 1-57387-037-4.

SAVIDIS, ANTHONY; STEPHANIDIS, CONSTANTINE. 1995. Improving GUI Accessibility for People with Low Vision. In: Katz, Irvin; Mack, Robert; Marks, Linn, eds. CHI '95: Proceedings of the Association for Computing Machinery Special Interest Group on Computer-Human Interaction (ACM/SIGCHI) Conference on Human Factors in Computing Systems; 1995 May 7-11; Denver, CO. New York, NY: ACM; 1995. 106-113. ISBN: 0-201-84705-1.

SCHMANDT, CHRISTOPHER. 1994. Voice Communication with Computers: Conversational Systems. New York, NY: Van Nostrand Reinhold; 1994. 319p. ISBN: 0-442-23935-1.

SHACKEL, BRIAN. 1959. Ergonomics for a Computer. Design. 1959; 120: 36-39. ISSN: 0011-9245.

SHACKEL, BRIAN. 1997. Human-Computer Interaction—Whence and Whither? Journal of the American Society for Information Science. 1997 January; 48(11): 970-986. ISSN: 0002-8231; CODEN: AISJB6.

SHAW, DEBORA. 1991. The Human-Computer Interface for Information Retrieval. In: Williams, Martha E., ed. Annual Review of Information Science and Technology: Volume 26. Medford, NJ: Learned Information, Inc. for the American Society for Information Science; 1991. 155-195. ISSN: 0066-4200; ISBN: 0-938734-55-5; CODEN: ARISBC.

SHERIDAN, PÁRAIC; BALLERINI, JEAN PAUL. 1996. Experiments in Multilingual Information Retrieval Using the SPIDER System. In: Frei, Hans-Peter; Harman, Donna; Schäuble, Peter; Wilkinson, Ross, eds. SIGIR '96: Proceedings of the Association for Computing Machinery Special Interest Group on Information Retrieval (ACM/SIGIR) 19th Annual International Conference on Research and Development in Information Retrieval; 1996 August 18-22; Zurich, Switzerland. New York, NY: ACM; 1996. 58-65. ISBN: 3-89191-999-9 (Hartung-Gorre); ISBN: 0-89791-792-8 (ACM).

SHIPMAN, FRANK; MARSHALL, CATHERINE; MORAN, THOMAS P. 1995. Finding and Using Implicit Structure in Human-Organized Spatial Layouts of Information. In: Katz, Irvin; Mack, Robert; Marks, Linn, eds. CHI '95: Proceedings of the the Association for Computing Machinery Special Interest Group on Computer-Human Interaction (ACM/SIGCHI) Conference on Human Factors in Computing Systems; 1995 May 7-11; Denver, CO. New York, NY: ACM; 1995. 346-353. ISBN: 0-201-84705-1.

SHNEIDERMAN, BEN. 1998a. Codex, Memex, Genex: The Pursuit of Transformational Technologies. International Journal of Human-Computer Interaction. 1998; 10(2): 87-106. ISSN: 1044-7318.

SHNEIDERMAN. BEN. 1998b. Designing the User Interface: Strategies for Effective Human-Computer Interaction. 3rd edition. Reading, MA: Addison-Wesley; 1998. 639p. ISBN: 0-201-69497-2.

SHNEIDERMAN, BEN; BYRD, DON; CROFT, W. BRUCE. 1997. Clarifying Search: A User-Interface Framework for Text Searches. D-Lib Magazine. 1997 January. ISSN: 1082-9873. Available WWW: http://www.dlib.org/dlib/january97/retrieval/01shneiderman.html.

SPINK, AMANDA; LOSEE, ROBERT M. 1996. Feedback in Information Retrieval. In: Williams, Martha E., ed. Annual Review of Information Science and Technology: Volume 31. Medford, NJ: Information Today, Inc. for the American Society for Information Science; 1996. 33-78. ISSN: 0066-4200; ISBN: 1-57387-033-1.

SPRING, MICHAEL. 1992. "Being There," or Models for Virtual Reality. In: Stone, Susan; Buckland, Michael, eds. Studies in Multimedia: State-of-the-Art Solutions in Multimedia and Hypertext. Medford, NJ: Learned Information, Inc.; 1992. 237-253. ISBN: 0-938734-59-8.

SUMMIT, ROGER. 1971. DIALOG and the User: An Evaluation of the User Interface with a Major Online Retrieval System. In: Walker, Donald E., ed. Interactive Bibliographic Search: The User/Computer Interface. Montvale, NJ: AFIPS Press; 1971. 83-94. LC: 70182192.

SUTHERLAND, IVAN. 1963. Sketchpad: A Man-Machine Graphical Communication System. In: Spring Joint Computer Conference; 1963 May; Detroit, MI. Washington, DC: Spartan Books; 1963. 329-346. OCLC: 35419465.

SUTHERLAND, IVAN. 1968. A Head-Mounted Three Dimensional Display. In: Fall Joint Computer Conference; 1968 December 9-11; San Francisco, CA. Washington, DC: Thompson Books; 1968. 757-764. OCLC: 35419608.

TALBERT, NANCY. 1998. William Wulf on the Many Faces of Innovation: Interviewed by Nancy Talbert. Computer. 1998 January; 31(1): 37-38. ISSN: 0018-9162.

TAYLOR, ROBERT S. 1962. The Process of Asking Questions. American Documentation. 1962 October; 13(4): 391-397. ISSN: 0002-8231.

TURNER, JAMES. 1995. Comparing User-Assigned Terms with Indexer-Assigned Terms for Storage and Retrieval of Moving Images: Research Results. In: Kinney, Tom, ed. ASIS '95: Proceedings of the American Society for Information Science (ASIS) 58th Annual Meeting; 1995 October 9-12; Chicago, IL. Medford, NJ: Information Today, Inc. for ASIS; 1995. 9-12. ISSN: 0044-7870; ISBN: 1-57387-017-X.

TURTLE, HOWARD P.; PENNIMAN, W. DAVID; HICKEY, THOMAS. 1981. Data Entry/Display Devices for Interactive Information Retrieval. In: Williams, Martha E., ed. Annual Review of Information Science and Technology: Volume 16. White Plains, NY: Knowledge Industry Publications, Inc. for the American Society for Information Science; 1981. 55-84. ISSN: 0066-4200; ISBN: 0-914236-90-3; CODEN: ARISBC.

TWIDALE, MICHAEL B.; NICHOLS, DAVID M. 1998. Computer Supported Cooperative Work in the Information Search and Retrieval Process. In: Williams, Martha E., ed. Annual Review of Information Science and Technology: Volume 33. Medford, NJ: Information Today, Inc. for the American Society for Information Science; 1998. 259-319. ISSN: 0066-4200; ISBN: 1-57387-065-X.

VICKERY, B. C.; VICKERY, ALINA. 1993. Online Search Interface Design. Journal of Documentation. 1993 June; 49(2): 103-187. ISSN: 0022-0418.

VIGIL, PETER J. 1983. The Psychology of Online Searching. Journal of the American Society for Information Science. 1983; 34(4): 281-287. ISSN: 0002-8231.

WACTLAR, HOWARD D.; KANADE, TAKEO; SMITH, MICHAEL A.; STEVENS, SCOTT M. 1996. Intelligent Access to Digital Video: Informedia Project. Computer. 1996 May; 29(5): 46-52. ISSN: 0018-9162.

WALKER, DONALD, ed. 1971. Interactive Bibliographic Search: The User/ Computer Interface. Montvale, NJ: AFIPS Press; 1971. 468p. LC: 70182192.

WALKER, JANET; SPROULL, LEE; SUBRAMANI, R. 1994. Using a Human Face in an Interface. In: Adelson, Beth; Dumais, Susan; Olson, Judith, eds. CHI '94: Proceedings of the Association for Computing Machinery Special Interest Group on Computer-Human Interaction (ACM/SIGCHI) Conference on Human Factors in Computing Systems; 1994 April 24-28; Boston, MA. New York, NY: ACM; 1994. 85-91. ISBN: 0-201-76557-8.

WEISER, MARK. 1991. The Computer for the 21st Century. Scientific American. 1991 September; 265(3): 94-104. ISSN: 0036-8733.

WILENSKY, ROBERT. 1996. Toward Work-Centered Digital Information Services. Computer. 1996 May; 29(5): 37-43. ISSN: 0018-9162.

WILLIAMS, JAMES G.; SOCHATS, KENNETH M.; MORSE, EMILE. 1995. Visualization. In: Williams, Martha E., ed. Annual Review of Information Science and Technology: Volume 30. Medford, NJ: Learned Information, Inc. for the American Society for Information Science; 1995. 161-207. ISSN: 0066-4200; ISBN: 1-57387-019-6; CODEN: ARISBC.

WILLIAMS, MARTHA E. 1974. Generation and Use of Machine-Readable Bibliographic Data Bases. In: Cuadra, Carlos A.; Luke, Ann W.; Harris, Jessica L., eds. Annual Review of Information Science and Technology: Volume 9. Washington, DC: American Society for Information Science; 1974. 221-284. ISBN: 0-87715-209-8; CODEN: ARISBC.

WILLIAMSON, CHRISTOPHER; SHNEIDERMAN, BEN. 1992. The Dynamic HomeFinder: Evaluating Dynamic Queries in a Real-Estate Information Exploration System. In: Bauersfeld, Penny; Bennett, John; Lynch, Gene, eds. CHI '92: Proceedings of the Association for Computing Machinery Special Interest Group on Computer-Human Interaction (ACM/SIGCHI) Conference on Human Factors in Computing Systems; 1992 May 3-7; Monterey, CA. New York, NY: ACM; 1992. 338-346. ISBN: 0-201-53344-X.

WORDEN, AILEEN; WALKER, NEFF; BHARAT, KRISHNA; HUDSON, SCOTT. 1997. Making Computers Easier for Older Adults to Use: Area Cursors and Sticky Icons. In: Pemberton, Steve, ed. CHI '97: Proceedings of the Association for Computing Machinery Special Interest Group on Computer-Human Interaction (ACM/SIGCHI) Conference on Human Factors in Computing Systems; 1997 March 22-27; Atlanta, GA. New York, NY: ACM; 1997. 266-271. ISBN: 0-201-32229-3.

YAMAASHI, KIMIYA; KAWAMATA, YUKIHIRO; TANI, MASAYKI; MATSUMOTO, HIDEKAZU. 1995. User-Centered Video: Transmitting Video Images Based on the User's Interest. In: Katz, Irvin; Mack, Robert; Marks, Linn, eds. CHI '95: Proceedings of the Association for Computing Machinery Special Interest Group on Computer-Human Interaction (ACM/SIGCHI) Conference on Human Factors in Computing Systems; 1995 May 7-11; Denver, CO. New York, NY: ACM; 1995. 325-330. ISBN: 0-201-84705-1.

YANKELOVICH, NICOLE; LEVOW, GINA-ANNE; MARX, MATT. 1995. Designing SpeechActs: Issues in Speech User Interfaces. In: Katz, Irvin; Mack, Robert; Marks, Linn, eds. CHI '95: Proceedings of the Association for Computing Machinery Special Interest Group on Computer-Human Interaction (ACM/SIGCHI) Conference on Human Factors in Computing Systems; 1995 May 7-11; Denver, CO. New York, NY: ACM; 1995. 369-376. ISBN: 0-201-84705-1.

4

Sociocognitive Perspectives on Representation

**ELIN K. JACOB and
DEBORA SHAW
Indiana University, Bloomington**

INTRODUCTION

This review discusses research dealing with the cognitive aspects of formal systems of knowledge representation. The objective is to focus attention on the need to expand the parameters of cognitive research in information science so as to encompass the development, application, and use of such systems. Accordingly, this chapter both complements and extends previous *ARIST* chapters on cognitive research (ALLEN, 1991) and the user-centered perspective (SUGAR).

SHERA (1965a) observes that effective retrieval depends on congruence between the cognitive organization imposed on knowledge by the individual and the representational structure imposed on documents by the indexer. ALLEN (1996a) points out, however, that emphasizing the individual introduces unnecessary multiplicity and complexity into the design of retrieval systems. Because individual knowledge develops within a particular social environment, a more meaningful approach is to identify shared patterns of representation that characterize a knowledge domain or discourse community (ALLEN, 1996b; SHERA, 1965a). And, because representation is predominantly linguistic, the development of truly effective systems of retrieval must also include a thorough appreciation of how language is used in the social processes of communicating knowledge (BLAIR, 1990; SHERA, 1965a).

Work in the area of information retrieval (IR) has dominated research undertaken from the cognitive viewpoint. This research has made significant contributions to a more comprehensive understanding of the retrieval process and has been instrumental in shifting the focus from the system per se to the interaction between the user and the system. It is important, however, to extend current efforts to encompass

Annual Review of Information Science and Technology (ARIST), Volume 33, 1998
Martha E. Williams, Editor
Published for the American Society for Information Science (ASIS)
By Information Today, Inc., Medford, NJ

the interaction between the user and the representational structure on which effective document retrieval depends. More importantly, research from the cognitive perspective should eschew the unique and the idiosyncratic and focus instead on the social foundations of knowledge. Such efforts to identify shared patterns of cognitive organization will provide the basis for further improving retrieval systems. This chapter outlines the origins and the theoretical foundations of the cognitive viewpoint; it assesses the strengths and weaknesses of the cognitive viewpoint; it describes recent efforts to shift the focus from representation as an individual cognitive phenomenon to the social origins of representation within discourse communities; and it reviews research that exemplifies a sociocognitive approach to investigation of processes of representation.

COGNITION

The term cognition is inherently nebulous. In his discussion of the nature of human thought and intellect, GUILFORD defines cognition as that which "provides discovery, comprehension, or understanding, in other words, the awareness of information," where information refers to "that which the individual discriminates" (p. 10). He identifies cognition as one of five distinct operations performed by the intellect: (1) cognition, (2) memory, (3) divergent production, (4) convergent production, and (5) evaluation. In current usage, however, cognition is generally employed to refer to all of the faculties or functions of the brain that perceive, record, process, and/or manipulate information to produce intelligent behavior (LYCAN). In this broader sense, cognition is viewed as the superordinate processing faculty subsuming the other, more specific operations of intellect identified by Guilford.

Behavioral psychology has rejected as unscientific the notion that intelligent behavior can be explained by internal mechanisms and has adopted a theoretical framework of stimulus and response: that is, the individual is presumed to be a tabula rasa whose behavior can be explained by reference to the observable stimuli and responses that constitute the individual's learning history. Cognitive psychology, on the other hand, assumes that there exist certain internal faculties or cognitive mechanisms that are shared by all humans and perhaps by other animals; that these several faculties participate in the activities of information processing, including perception, thought, planning, action, memory, and learning; and that the products of these information processing activities can be observed, described, and ultimately generalized to predict intelligent behavior. In his introduction to cognitive psychology written for cognitive scientists, BARSALOU points out that, because there is no direct physiological evidence to support the existence of these internal mechanisms, cognitive psychologists posit internal cognitive constructs that represent their theoretical understanding of how the brain functions as an information processing system. Such internal constructs do not attempt to describe the physiological activities of the brain. Rather, they are intended to represent the psychologist's current understanding of how individuals process information. As Barsalou observes, to the extent that cognitive constructs do correspond to actual cognitive processes occurring in the brain, psychologists should be able to use them to predict human behavior. And, by extension, to the extent that these constructs contribute to the general understanding of how humans actually process information, researchers in information science should be able to apply this knowledge in the design and development of more effective systems of representation.

Cognition and Information Science

When the cognitive approach is understood as focusing on how individuals process information, the range of potential research topics in information science is quite broad. In 1993, the Research Committee of the American Society for Information Science (ASIS) published an analysis of research reported in *ARIST*, 1989-1991 (SHAW & FOUCHEREAUX). Statements of research need culled from these three volumes were analyzed, synthesized, and reformulated as 41 separate questions clustered in five main areas of information research: (1) automated systems, (2) economics, (3) indexing, (4) information retrieval, and (5) information seeking. Cognitive processing is specifically identified as a primary focus for research involving automated systems, indexing and classification of materials, and information retrieval; but even a cursory review of the remaining questions indicates an underlying need for greater understanding of the implications of human cognitive processing and for investigation of the role, or roles, of cognitive functions within the more formalized processes that constitute the domain of information science.

To date, cognitive research in information science has tended to focus almost exclusively on the interaction between the user and the system. Whether this interaction involves mediation by a human (the librarian) or by a computer interface, much of the empirical research carried out from the cognitive viewpoint has centered on the individual user and has avoided (or ignored) the broader social context of information processing. Research adopting the cognitive viewpoint has emphasized the development of interfaces or intelligent intermediaries designed to facilitate interaction between the user and the system so as to retrieve a set of relevant documents. Like a physician who treats the surface symptoms without investigating their underlying causes, such palliative research efforts (DILLON) seek to remedy a problematic retrieval situation by focusing on the last and most obvious component of a complex system that begins with the processes of representation and organization.

With a few significant exceptions, there has been little consideration and even less empirical investigation of the cognitive processes involved in the development and application of representational languages or the cognitive processes of indexing, abstracting, and classification. More striking still is the apparent assumption that cognitive processing occurs only at selected points along the knowledge production chain. For example, BELKIN (1984) identifies 17 different cognitive models (or "states of knowledge") that affect the retrieval process. The models he lists are those of the author, the knowledge resource, the intermediary, and the user. While he does state that the cognitive models of those who constructed the knowledge resource are relevant in an adaptive retrieval system, he fails to acknowledge the central role of the cognitive models formed by the developer(s) of a representational language or by the indexers or classifiers who subsequently apply that language to create the surrogates upon which effective retrieval depends.

No one would seriously contest the statement that effective retrieval is the supervening goal of the information professional. SHERA (1965b) observes that retrieval is "the focal point" of a theory of library and information science and "the end toward which all our efforts are directed" (p. 136). But he cautions that the ultimate success of these efforts depends on development of a theoretical structure that encompasses both:

1. An understanding of language and the communication process itself and its role in the transmission of knowledge; and

2. A comprehension of human thought patterns so expressed that patterns of recourse to recorded knowledge can be derived from them (SHERA, 1965a, p. 56).

Shera argues that optimal levels of retrieval can be achieved only when information professionals develop and implement representational systems that establish congruence between the cognitive organization imposed on knowledge by the individual and the conceptual organization imposed on documents by the information specialist. Congruence between these two structures of organization must constitute the central component in any effective process of retrieval. Furthermore, the development of effective systems of retrieval depends on the identification of patterns of cognitive organization shared among individuals and on analysis of the influence of language and of the communication process itself on the transmission of knowledge. Building on the theoretical foundation prescribed by Shera, the need to provide for effective retrieval leads us to four fundamental research questions:

1. How does language influence the individual's cognitive representation and organization of information?
2. What effect does the need to communicate have on the individual's symbolic representation and/or cognitive organization of information?
3. What patterns or structures of cognitive organization are shared by individuals or by groups of individuals?
4. How can retrieval mechanisms be designed to facilitate, augment, or mimic these natural patterns of cognitive organization?

Shera's arguments and the research questions derived from them not only point to the applicability and potential utility of cognitive research in information science, but also provide a framework for future cognitive research. They underscore the importance of investigating the influence of language and communication on the organization of knowledge at the individual level and, more importantly, at the social level. And they suggest that the ultimate utility of cognitive research can be realized only by expanding its range to encompass all of the activities that comprise a retrieval system: generation, acquisition, representation, organization, mediation, and retrieval. Following Shera's argument, it is imperative that cognitive investigation address the nature of shared knowledge structures and the role of language in the communication process as well as the impact of cognitive structures on the development, organization, and maintenance of representational languages and the subsequent activities of indexing, abstracting, and classification.

The Cognitive Viewpoint

Much of the work that has been carried out under the rubric of the cognitive viewpoint is closely identified with research in information retrieval (IR). Working within the theoretical framework employed by MASTERMAN, ELLIS (1992a; 1992b) applies KUHN's criteria to identify the two research paradigms—or "quasi-paradigms" (ELLIS, 1992b, p. 57)—that currently function in IR: the physical paradigm and the cognitive paradigm. Ellis points out that the physical paradigm was introduced through the model of information retrieval adopted by Cyril Cleverdon in the Cranfield experiments of the 1950s. Although these experiments were intended to assess indexing languages, their design was framed by the analogy Cleverdon drew between retrieval systems and mechanical systems in aeronautical engineering. Ellis argues that, because retrieval systems were viewed as analogous to mechanical systems, the assumptions and methodologies of the research paradigm in engineering could be imported to support research on retrieval. By adopting the engineering paradigm, the Cranfield tests not only established IR research as empirically grounded, but also provided the methodological exemplar on which future research—and the physical paradigm itself—was based. HARTER & HERT provide a comprehensive overview of the historical development of IR research.

The cognitive paradigm currently provides the dominant alternative to the physical paradigm in information science research. ELLIS (1992b) points out that, in contrast to the physical paradigm, which is supported by the model of the Cranfield experiments, the cognitive paradigm is not grounded by any particular experimental model or research achievement, inside or outside information science, that can serve as an exemplar for further cognitive research. Rather, the assumptions driving the cognitive paradigm in information science are apparently derived from a statement made by Marc de Mey at the International Workshop on the Cognitive Viewpoint held at the University of Ghent in 1977:

> The central point of the cognitive view is that any *processing of information*, whether perceptual or symbolic, is *mediated* by a system of categories or concepts which, for the information-processing device, are a *model* of his *world* (DE MEY, 1977, pp. xvi-xvii; see also DE MEY, 1980, p. 48; 1982, p. 4).

The frequency with which this single passage is cited is highly indicative of its centrality to research ostensibly carried out under the cognitive paradigm. (See, for example; BELKIN, 1990, p. 11; DANIELS, p. 273; ELLIS, 1992a, p. 175; 1992b, p. 52; FROHMANN, 1992b, p. 374; INGWERSEN, 1982, p. 168; 1984a, pp. 466-467; 1984b, p. 328; 1992a, pp. 121-122; 1992b, pp. 16, 18, 30; 1993, p. 60; 1994, p. 25; 1996, p. 5.)

Taken at face value, the significance of de Mey's statement lies in the proposed shift in research orientation away from the physical system per se and toward the central role of "prerequisite knowledge" (DE MEY, 1982, p. 15) that constitutes the perceiver's world view or mental model. This reorientation draws attention from the object/signal and focuses it, instead, on the subject/receiver; on the knowledge embodied in the subject's "model of his world" which he invokes to interpret a signal so as to find meaning that is "congruent with" his prerequisite knowledge (DE MEY, 1977, p. xxiii).

DE MEY (1980) contends, however, that widespread adoption of the cognitive view has actually precipitated two shifts in focus. The first shift is in accord with de Mey's original statement in that it emphasizes the organizing activities of the individual who, when encountering an object or message, discovers meaning on the basis of prerequisite knowledge. The second shift identified by de Mey emphasizes the social nature of these organizing activities and directs attention from "clearly delineated [information] units handled in isolation" (p. 54) to information processing handled in terms of the world models embedded in language. Thus, while de Mey's first shift can be said to direct attention toward the world view or mental model of the individual, the second shift broadens the arena of cognitive research by focusing attention on the role of social interaction in generating shared models of the world and on the "common cognitive processes in individuals functioning within certain patterns of social organization" (DE MEY, 1982, p. xvi).

It can be argued that information science has not yet realized either of the cognitive shifts de Mey outlined. Although there has been a vocal redirection of attention from a system-based orientation to what is currently identified as the user-centered perspective, much research in information science continues to emphasize the mechanical perspective. Cognitive research has too often focused narrowly on the individual user. It attempts, for example, to analyze interaction between librarian and user in order to replicate the mediating activity of the librarian through the design of user-friendly interfaces that incorporate models of the cognitive state of the user. Attempts to provide the system with a model of the user's world view tend to mask the fact that a retrieval system is no more than a communication tool intended to bring the query representations of the user into accord with the document representations of the indexer, or, in full-text systems, with those of the author. Advocates of the cognitive viewpoint in IR have generally attempted to model the individual user and to establish the system as an intelligent partner in the communication process. Such efforts tend to divert attention from the seminal function performed by representational structures. More importantly, they have engendered criticisms that, although frequently deserved, are too often generalized to condemn all efforts to understand how human cognitive functions relate to the retrieval process.

By emphasizing the system and the role of the system interface in the interaction between system and user, the lingering shadow of the physical paradigm has limited widespread adoption of the cognitive viewpoint in investigations of knowledge representation and organization. FROHMANN (1992b, p. 380) suggests that the tendency of cognitive research to treat all processing devices as alike loses the distinction between human and machine. By subsuming human cognitive processes within the framework of the technological processes of signal generation, transmission, and reception, Frohmann argues, the cogni-

tive viewpoint adopts the limited perspective of a mechanistic instru-
mentality. It is possible, however, to posit an alternative interpretation
and to suggest that this tendency to equate the functions of the ma-
chine/system with the human cognitive process is a tacit expression of
the anthropomorphic role assumed for the system by the cognitive
viewpoint. Thus the fundamental assumptions which, according to
INGWERSEN (1992b), are characteristic of the cognitive viewpoint
underscore the anthropomorphic tendencies of much of this research:
(1) computers and processing devices are treated "*as if* they are humans"; (2) each processing device is independent and consists of "its
own 'system of categories and concepts'"; (3) each event in which a
processing device participates is mediated by "his/its actual knowledge structures, expectations, goals, etc."; and (4) these knowledge
structures are the product of "*individual cognition* in a *social context*" (p.
17). Whether one subscribes to the mechanistic or the anthropomorphic
reading of the relationship between human user and retrieval system
embedded in the cognitive viewpoint is, however, irrelevant. Either
interpretation leaves the cognitive viewpoint open to charges of
cognitivism.

Cognitivism, Mentalism, and Subjective Individualism

Information science in general supports the design of access systems
that respond to the idiosyncratic language and world view of the
individual searcher. Indeed, the general perception of research undertaken from the cognitive viewpoint is that it follows (or should follow)
MOLHOLT's injunction to look to "new technologies, including artificial intelligence ... [as] a means to design systems that can respond to
users as individuals rather than as classes" (p. 108). BROOKS argues
that research on expert systems was instrumental in directing attention
away from traditional algorithmic approaches and toward a more heuristic approach that focuses on the user and on human-computer interaction. Whether the cognitive viewpoint is more heavily indebted to the
legacy of artificial intelligence or the influence of expert system research is not important. The significance of much of the research currently undertaken by proponents of the cognitive viewpoint is the
emphasis on the individual's interaction with the physical system.
Thus, while Ingwersen himself acknowledges the cognitive contribution of the indexer (HARBO ET AL.) and the influence of "collective
cognitive mechanisms... [on] the structure of classification and indexing systems" (INGWERSEN, 1982, p. 169), the cognitive viewpoint has
evolved into a subjective approach intended to "investigate the variety
of *individual* world models and knowledge structures that underly [sic]
the surface structures of the variables of interaction" (INGWERSEN,

1992b, p. 18. Emphasis added). The inherent subjectivity of the cognitive viewpoint in IR is its Achilles heel and has exposed cognitive research in general to charges that it is redolent of cognitivism, mentalism (FROHMANN, 1990; 1992a; 1992b), methodological individualism (HJØRLAND, 1997; HJØRLAND & ALBRECHTSEN), and subjective idealism (HJØRLAND, 1992).

Cognitivism, as described by SEARLE (1984), embodies the strong AI perspective that "'the brain is just a digital computer and the mind is just a computer program'" (quoted in INGWERSEN, 1992b, pp. 19-20). INGWERSEN (1992b) defends the cognitive viewpoint from charges of cognitivism by emphasizing the human aspect of cognitive research in information science. He argues that the cognitive viewpoint in IR does not advocate research into human cognitive processes in order to develop computer systems that will replace those activities; rather, it endeavors to identify the prerequisite knowledge that the user brings to human-computer interaction in order to simulate human cognitive processing and thereby "to provide each individual user with that context which satisfies him by yielding desired information" (p. 23). Thus the argument presented by Ingwersen attempts to avoid charges of cognitivism by emphasizing the cognitive viewpoint's focus on the individual user so as to simulate—but not to duplicate—human cognitive processing.

Unfortunately, this argument simply opens the cognitive viewpoint to the charges of mentalism and individualism leveled by FROHMANN (1990; 1992a; 1992b) and HJØRLAND (HJØRLAND, 1992; 1997; HJØRLAND & ALBRECHTSEN). FROHMANN (1992b) points out that "Knowledge of users' internal realities—their 'internal programmes', 'sense-making processes', 'images', 'world models', or 'cognitive maps'— is the whole point of the 'paradigm shift from system to user' ushered in by the cognitive viewpoint" (p. 379). Accordingly, he finds the cognitive viewpoint to be reductionist in nature, imposing "a discourse of *interiors*" (p. 374) within which the complexities of real-world context and practice become little more than external triggers determining the individual's construction of internalized representations. This focus on interiors and the resulting opposition of internal and external states supports introduction of a radical individualism that is captured, for Frohmann, in DERVIN's contention that "sense" cannot be imposed from without but that "each individual must make his own sense" (p. 28). Inherent in the cognitive viewpoint is the assumption that "crucial differences" are situated within the individual in the particular world view that he or she has constructed. For FROHMANN (1992b), this extreme individualism represents what he facetiously identifies as one of the most "significant" contributions of the cognitive viewpoint: "The erasure of the social" (p. 376).

Like Frohmann, HJØRLAND (1992) attacks the cognitive viewpoint for its inherent subjectivity, which he equates with subjective idealism. Idealism, according to Hjørland, is characterized by the view that consciousness is primary and that the reality of the material world is, in consequence, a mental construct. Subjective idealism implies that reality is not externally determined but is generated internally by the mental processes of each individual mind. HJØRLAND (1997) contends that proponents of the cognitive viewpoint do not consciously adopt an idealistic stance. Rather, when cognitive researchers assume that the content of the system is a given and focus on the subjective knowledge structures of the individual searcher or mediator, "they inadvertently fall into idealistic modes of thought" (p. 61). Such inadvertent adherence to subjective idealism within IR has given primacy to the computer interface and the ability of the system to reflect the individual's "subjective perception of knowledge" (p. 62). In representation theory, Hjørland argues, subjective idealism has engendered an extremist or mentalist interpretation of aboutness that assumes each document is an independent knowledge source to be indexed according to "the user's level of presupposition" (p. 62) rather than on the basis of the document's own contribution to the relevant domain of knowledge. Similar arguments regarding aboutness are also advanced by ALBRECHTSEN (1993) and WEINBERG.

Closely aligned to subjective idealism is what HJØRLAND (1997) calls the "mentalistic pitfall" of methodological individualism. The primary assumption supporting methodological individualism is that knowledge exists as subjective mental states within the individual. Hjørland argues that, although more traditional research approaches in information science, such as bibliometrics and citation analysis, focus on collective structures, the basic assumption of methodological individualism both authorizes and supports research activities that isolate the individual from the social, cultural, and historical influences that contribute to cognitive development. Thus what Hjørland finds most problematic in the cognitive viewpoint is precisely what FROHMANN (1992b) characterizes as "erasure of the social" (p. 376): the exclusion of the sociocultural environment(s) in which the individual participates. HJØRLAND (1997) admits, however, that this research does have a role in information science and that it can contribute to a thorough understanding of the processes of knowledge generation, representation, organization, and retrieval:

> It is of relevance to describe information processes on the individual level, on the machine level, on the level of "thought and discourse communities," and on the cultural-sociological level. However, it is of vital importance to know how these levels are connected (p. 120).

Hjørland advocates the adoption of "a methodological collectivistic point of view" (p. 118) that incorporates psychological investigation of the individual within a broader sociocultural and historical perspective, grounding the internal/individual within the external/environment and thereby integrating the various levels of investigation to achieve truly effective systems of representation and retrieval.

The Sociocognitive Perspective

The emphasis on user-friendly systems and intelligent interfaces that characterizes the system orientation of current cognitive research has become firmly entrenched as the cognitive viewpoint in information science. Much of the work identified as emanating from the cognitive viewpoint has attempted, as BELKIN (1984) observes, to find "clues for improving at least the intermediary component of the information interaction" (p. 128). Unfortunately, such efforts neglect the central role of representational languages in facilitating effective communication between the author/indexer and the searcher/intermediary. More importantly, they have diverted attention from alternative research approaches that address the cognitive role of language and the nature of shared knowledge structures. As both Frohmann and Hjørland indicate, emphasis on the idiosyncratic nature of individual knowledge structures has taken the individual out of context by removing from consideration the influences of the social, cultural, and historical milieu. A potentially more productive approach would be to construct a theoretical and methodological framework that includes the broader social context(s) that influence cognitive processing. Ideally, such a framework would incorporate both de Mey's second cognitive shift—recognition of the social nature of organizing activities and the importance of shared models—and Shera's insistence on the primacy of language, on the importance of the communication process and on the identification of fundamental patterns of human thought.

Albrechtsen and Hjørland (ALBRECHTSEN & HJØRLAND; HJØRLAND, 1997; HJØRLAND & ALBRECHTSEN) suggest that the most fruitful alternative to the mentalism and subjectivity of much cognitive research is to reorient the unit of study from the level of the individual to the level of social, disciplinary, or knowledge communities. HJØRLAND & ALBRECHTSEN contend that knowledge is adaptive and is formed through "a dialectical relationship between a community and its members . . . mediated by language and influenced by the history of the specific [domain]" (p. 407).

The sociocognitive perspective espoused by Albrechtsen and Hjørland is closely related to activity theory, which provides a pragmatic framework for the study of human cognition and behavior. Activity theory is generally identified with the work of Wertsch, Lave, and others in anthropology and is based in large part on the work of the Russian psychologists L.S. Vygotsky and A.N. Leontiev and the writings of the American philosophers C.S. Peirce, John Dewey, and George Herbert Mead, as well as the Russian literary theorist Mikhail Bakhtin. Drawing extensively on the work of SARVIMÄKI, ALBRECHTSEN & HJØRLAND set out the basic assumptions informing activity theory: that the individual lives within a world that is at once physically, socially, and subjectively constructed and that the very activity of living and acting in this world constitutes knowledge. Because knowledge is constructed through and embedded within acting, it provides an internal determinant for subsequent actions, which in turn modify the individual's internal knowledge. In this way, the individual-as-actor constructs internal knowledge of facts, values, and procedures through ongoing interaction between his internalized knowledge and his participation in the external world. Knowledge is thus both explicit in that it can be communicated through language and implicit, or tacit, in that it can be embedded within particular activities.

In an effort to integrate the cognitive viewpoint in a more sociological or sociocultural approach to research, the sociocognitive perspective shifts attention from individual knowledge structures to discourse domains to: knowledge-producing, knowledge-sharing, and knowledge-consuming communities. Activity theory provides a theoretical framework for the sociocognitive perspective and supports the contention of HJØRLAND & ALBRECHTSEN that discourse domains and knowledge communities are the appropriate unit of study in information science. The notion of "discourse domain" covers a wide range of social institutions including, for example, traditional disciplines, trades, professions, and religions. Furthermore, a discourse domain is not an autonomous entity but a social construct comprised of individuals who exhibit their own individual knowledge structures, biases, and cognitive styles. Within the boundaries of a domain, however, there is continual interaction "between domain structures and individual knowledge, an interaction between the individual and the social level" (HJØRLAND & ALBRECHTSEN, p. 409). From this perspective, the individual's internal knowledge structures are shaped through participation in socially grounded domain(s) and are viewed as constructed adaptations to the externally generated influences of the domain(s).

The arguments advanced by Hjørland and Albrechtsen are not unique. Relevant work in information science, particularly in IR, both amplifies and extends the sociocognitive perspective. Although the contributions of BLAIR (1990; 1992), BRIER (1992; 1996), and FROEHLICH, like those of Hjørland and Albrechtsen, are primarily theoretical, they do support the initiation of research programs undertaken from the sociocognitive perspective.

Working within the post-modern framework of antifoundationalist philosophy, FROEHLICH argues that, while there can be no absolute knowledge, this assumption does not rule out the possibility of knowledge per se. Because the individual is "born into a history and a culture that gives us a set of distinctions and interpretations about what it means to be" (p. 308), these sociocultural and historical constructs constitute a set of "shared meanings ... that reside in and behind language ... in a set of practices" (p. 309). Froehlich contends that the function of these shared meanings can be captured in the Aristotelian notion of *phronesis*, or practical knowledge about living and doing. He suggests that, because knowledge must be defined in terms of its social, cultural, and historical environment, "the ideal objective of information science is a *phronesis* about *phronesis*, practical wisdom about what stands for practical wisdom . . . [and] knowledge in that domain" (p. 309). Froehlich rejects the notion of an epistemic community proposed by HOLZNER & MARX and suggests in its stead the designation "axiological community," arguing that "shared values (including cognitive ones) are the basic condition for the formation of a community and bind members together, both at the conscious and unconscious level, in choice and in practices" (p. 310). While Froehlich's arguments support the theoretical framework advanced by Hjørland and Albrechtsen, his most important contribution to the sociocognitive perspective may be the cautionary injunction that neither the individual nor the social institution (neither the axiological community nor the discourse domain) should be accorded primacy: "'Each is constituted in and through recurrent practices. The notion of human "action" presupposes that of "institution" and vice versa'" (GIDDENS; quoted in FROEHLICH, p. 310).

Support for the sociocognitive perspective is also provided by BRIER (1992; 1996), whose own approach is grounded in the union of cybernetics and semiotics he identifies as *cybersemiotics*. He contends that embedded in natural language are "general principles that guide cognition and retrieval of information by the human mind" (BRIER, 1996, p. 24). He argues that the information processing approach has adopted "a structural-syntactical understanding of language and knowledge as cognitive information structures . . . common for all cognitive systems, including computers" (p. 29). This emphasis on the structural and syntactic aspects of cognition ignores the social, cultural, and historical dimensions of communication in which the meaning of a word is grounded:

> The meaning of words is created by language's cultural-historical background and the social communicative praxis between people, who again have their own subjective historical access to the sign's meanings. We are never in full agreement as to all of a word's or concept's meanings. But

through developed customs we can agree on a meaning in situations we have experienced together (BRIER, 1996, p. 35).

Thus Brier contends that the major issues in information science are not technical but sociolinguistic and cluster around the central problem of communication: "how meaning is generated, represented and controlled in written media in different social contexts" (p. 35) and, presumably, over time. Defining communication as "a shared actualization of meaning that is able to inform at least one of the participants" (p. 33), he observes that in order to understand the meaning of a word in communication it is necessary first to understand both its use by the author and its use within a particular knowledge domain. But he concludes that it is not sufficient simply to understand the word in the context of a particular knowledge domain: one must also understand its meaning for a group of searchers and the way it is used in the retrieval process itself. He suggests that it is precisely this broad level of understanding of both the semiotic and the sociolinguistic knowledge informing language and communication that provides the theoretical foundation for the domain-analysis approach advocated by Hjørland and Albrechtsen.

BRIER's (1996) argument draws on WITTGENSTEIN's notions of language games and forms of life and is thus related to the work of BLAIR (1990), who has argued the relevance of Wittgenstein's philosophy of language for IR research. Although Blair's work is ostensibly directed toward the IR community, it has significance for the entire process of document representation, organization, and retrieval; and, in the immediate context, it provides a well-articulated philosophical foundation for sociocognitive research addressing representation theory. Blair sets the stage for his approach to Wittgenstein by pointing out that the effectiveness of document retrieval depends on the nature and quality of the document representations available to the system. Because the process of document representation is linguistic in nature, "the problem of describing documents for retrieval is, first and foremost, a problem of how language is used" (p. 122). In contrast to Brier's cybersemiotic approach, Blair contends that semiotics can offer "suggestions and adumbrations, but few hard 'facts' or reliable methods" (p. 123). The fundamental orientation of semiotic theory is, in his opinion, too mentalistic and does not contribute to an effective understanding of meaning in representation. He suggests that analysis of actual patterns of language use offers a more pragmatic approach to the problem of meaning: "Instead of concerning ourselves with *definitive* uses of expressions, we can recognize this endless regression of meaning/signification and concentrate on elucidating *conventional* uses of expressions" (p. 137).

BLAIR (1990) points out that the very fact that a particular linguistic term may have an unlimited number of possible definitions or interpretations places two significant constraints on representation. (1) There can be no one representation of a text that is inherently complete. (2) The basis for assessing the utility of a representation must be one of appropriateness rather than of correctness: because a representation can be neither correct nor incorrect, it must be judged as to how appropriate it is within a specific domain or for a particular task. In this manner, he shifts attention away from the meanings of words and to their functions in communication as the basis for his implementational or "tools-and-jobs" (p. 141) approach to language, in which words are used as tools to perform particular activities or tasks. He concludes that the effective use/implementation of these words-as-tools depends "not just on the tool's inherent physical qualities, but also on the skill and background of the person who uses the tool and the task at hand to be accomplished" (p. 139).

The parallel that Blair draws between words and tools helps to clarify WITTGENSTEIN's notion that words are used in language games, the various activities in which words-as-tools are employed to accomplish specific tasks. Language games are associated with forms of life, "the everyday human activities which make up our lives in a social sense" (BLAIR, 1990, p. 148). Participation in a language game requires both familiarity with the form of life/activity and knowledge of how to use/implement the words/tools appropriately to accomplish the task at hand. In this way, the language game (or, more broadly, the form of life with which a particular language game is associated) provides constraints that determine the effective use of words. Blair argues that language is understood through participation in the forms of life: "the intensely human activities which make up our 'natural history'" (p. 154). Because the appropriate use of a word is both shaped by and learned from participation in the language game(s), the meaning of a word can be understood only through its appropriate use in a particular situation or institution: "Our language, then, is inextricably caught up in the things that we do, and we must understand how we participate in these activities before we can understand how language is used in them" (p. 205).

Blair's contention that words and their associated meanings must be understood in the context of their use in the activities or institutions in which a language game is played supports and extends the arguments of both FROEHLICH and BRIER (1992; 1996) and echoes the assumptions of activity theory as outlined by ALBRECHTSEN & HJØRLAND. More importantly, BLAIR (1990; 1992) argues persuasively that, because effective retrieval depends on the linguistic process of representation, development of effective systems of retrieval depends on a thorough understanding of how language is used in human institutions and activities; in the knowledge domains and discourse communities that collectively constitute the sociocultural setting of a document collection. Blair's insistence on the fundamental importance of representation as the basis for effective retrieval shifts the focus of cognitive research from the individual user and the interface to the heart of the retrieval problem: how language is used to communicate in various social activities. His argument provides strong support for the sociocognitive perspective by emphasizing the socially constructed nature of language and, because "language [is] not the *product* of thought, but the *vehicle* of thought" (BLAIR, 1992, p. 205), the socially constructed nature of cognition itself.

REPRESENTATION

BLAIR (1990) argues persuasively that language is the foundation on which representation rests. But what exactly is representation? More specifically, how does representation serve the purposes of information science? Obviously, the term "representation" is used to refer both to the process or activity of representing and to the object(s) produced by an instance of that activity. The process of representing seeks to establish systematic correspondence between the target domain and the modeling domain and to capture or "re-present," through the medium of the modeling domain, the object, data, or information in the target domain. BARSALOU observes that, to the extent that this re-presentation corresponds to, or models, the object, data, or information in the target domain, the two can be thought of as representationally equivalent. The product of the modeling process is thus a surrogate in that it stands for, or takes the place of, the corresponding object, data, or information in the target domain. DE MEY (1992) suggests that cognitive science is the "science of representation" (p. xiii) and that its "core problem . . . [is] to render different (kinds of) representations in such a way that they can be combined" (p. xxii). Given the assumption of the cognitive viewpoint that "*processing* of information . . . is *mediated* by a system of categories or concepts which, for the information-processing device, are a *model* of his *world*" (DE MEY, 1977, pp. xvi-xvii), the core problem of cognitive research in information science might be restated in the form of a question: How are the conceptual structures that model the domain of the user as information processor to be brought into correspondence with the conceptual structures that model the domain of the retrieval system?

Unfortunately, the problem of representation in information science is not as simple as this question suggests. BLAIR (1990) points out that effective document retrieval depends on the linguistic representations used to describe documents "and the problem of describing documents for retrieval is, first and foremost, a problem of how language is used" (p. 122). Within the framework for representation outlined above, Blair's argument implies at least two distinct but overlapping areas of correspondence: (1) correspondence between the content of the document as the target domain and the modeling mechanism of the indexing language; and (2) correspondence between the meaning of a word (how it is actually used in a language game or form of life) as the target domain and the modeling mechanism of the indexing language. Thus the problem of representation in document retrieval involves more than simply providing for communication between the generator of a document and the information seeker (BELKIN, 1977; PAISLEY & PARKER). Rather, it is a far more complex process that seeks to establish correspondence between the modeling domain of the indexing language and multiple target domains. Target domains include the knowledge structure of the document's author; the knowledge represented in the document itself; the structure of knowledge in the discourse domain to which the document belongs; and the individual's understanding, as indexer or as searcher, of a word's meaning in both the language game of the relevant domain and the language game of the retrieval system itself.

The very complexity of the representational process is, perhaps, one of the primary reasons that researchers have simply accepted the representational structure as given and turned, instead, to development of auxiliary devices intended to circumvent the problems of traditional representational languages. Thus the inception of BELKIN's (1977) anomalous states of knowledge (ASK) model can be traced, at least in part, to his recognition that "traditional classification and indexing languages seem not to be designed as good representations of either [need or text], but rather as available, convenient intermediate languages" that are "bound to fail" (p. 189). Although his proposal to identify the searcher's information need and then to represent the content of the text in equivalent terms has not yet produced a viable system, it is instructive, nonetheless, to follow Belkin's lead and look at the problem of representation from a different perspective.

DE MEY's (1980; see also DE MEY, 1977; 1982) model of the development of information processing theory offers just such a productive framework for reconsideration of the problems of effective representation. This model identifies four distinct stages[1] in the evolution of information processing theory: (1) Monadic: characterized by template

---

[1]De Mey's four stages of information processing are an extension of the three levels (monadic, structural, and epistemic) proposed by MICHIE. According to DE MEY (1982), use of the term contextual for the third level was proposed by B. Raphael "who presented the same distinction in a lecture at an ASI on 'Artificial Intelligence and Heuristic Programming', Menaggio, Italy, August 1970" (p. 261 n3). De Mey also indicates that support for the distinction between contextual and cognitive is found in WINOGRAD.

matching in pattern recognition and by translation in communication, in the monadic stage signals are considered as "standard representations" to be matched against "canonical forms" (DE MEY, 1980, pp. 49, 50). (2) Structural: characterized by feature analysis in pattern recognition and by syntax in communication, the structural stage is dominated by the assumption "that there is some set of universal grammatical categories which has, in each language, specific syntactic mechanisms to express those categories" (p. 52). (3) Contextual: characterized by analysis of the structural organization in pattern recognition and by social or cultural conventions in communication, the contextual stage is dominated by the notion that meaning is determined by immediate context (e.g., "I" is indexical in that its reference is determined by the speaker). (4) Cognitive: characterized by "analysis by synthesis" (p. 51) in pattern recognition and by "ubiquitous knowledge" (p. 54) in communication, the cognitive stage assumes that context is provided by the individual as "the knowledge he invokes ... to look for and to detect very selectively those structural characteristics and those contextual elements which yield an interpretation of the message that is congruent with that knowledge" (p. 54).

The four stages outlined by DE MEY (1980) provide a useful structure for consideration of current approaches to systematic representation.[2] The "standard representations" of de Mey's monadic stage can be likened to systems of physical representations in information science such as cataloging records or bibliographic entries. These representations rely on canonical formats to represent the physical characteristics of the document (e.g., author, title, publisher, date of publication, volume number). Because these representations are constructed according to a prescribed structure, the linguistic content of any particular field need not be meaningful for the purpose of retrieval. Rather, the representations rely on the physical format itself to support known-item searching. BLAIR (1990) refers to physical representations as "context descriptions" (p. 155) because they indicate the physical context in which the document currently exists. He points out that they provide greater determinacy than do representations of a document's subject content. And he concludes (BLAIR, 1990; 1992) that the utility

---

[2]It is interesting that INGWERSEN (1992b) has adapted DE MEY's (1982) four stages as a framework for outlining the development of information retrieval systems: "*In IR* (e.g. text representation) one might suggest: 1) one book = one assigned class or index term, or single extraction from the text, 2) keyword phrases, morpho-syntactic term extraction, clustering, 3) semantic values combined with request modelling [sic], 4) really adaptive, knowledge-based systems, pragmatic systems. The stages 1) and 2) represent the present level of traditional, system-driven IR research which, in conjunction with more user-oriented IR, attempts to catch at stage 3). . . . So far, stage 3) has *not* been reached completely and stage 4) cannot be reached in computerized systems, except by direct support from humans" (pp. 22-23).

of physical representations would be enhanced by representation of the document's performative act (its genre or format) based on a taxonomy of illocutionary acts such as that proposed by AUSTIN or by SEARLE (1969).

DE MEY's (1980) structural stage assumes a set of standardized or universal categories that can be likened to the conceptual representations provided by so-called universal systems of organization. Traditional indexing languages, including classification schemes, precoordinate subject heading systems, and postcoordinate controlled vocabularies, generally assume that knowledge can be enumerated as a set of universally applicable classes or concept labels whose meanings are defined either by the structural relationships determined by the scheme's overall organizational structure or through the use of a syndetic reference structure. Faceted classifications are generally viewed as avoiding the pitfalls of their more enumerative cousins; but faceted classification schemes rely on enumeration (analysis) of the possible variables (foci) of a set of characteristics (facets), which are then joined (synthesized) in a standardized sequence (citation order) to represent the subject content of a document. From this perspective, it is apparent that traditional indexing languages, including faceted classification schemes, depend on internal and external structural relationships in order to establish correspondence with the target domain. It is interesting, too, as BEGHTOL (1995) points out, that Ranganathan himself referred to facets as standard units before his adoption of the more specific term in 1944.

Because DE MEY's (1980) contextual stage assumes that meaning is determined by immediate context, it can be likened to the contextual representations provided by abstracts. Although abstracts frequently adhere to general dictates regarding the type of content to be included (e.g., methodology, results), these document representations are not constrained by a controlled vocabulary, as are conceptual representations, or by the standardized format of physical representations. Rather, they attempt to establish the intellectual context in which the knowledge content of the document is presented. The importance of context in constraining meaningful interpretation of subject descriptors is addressed by BLAIR (1990). More specifically, SWIFT ET AL. (1979) point to the need to replace what they call "objectivist" systems of representation with systems "based on the notion of describing and organizing documents in terms of the dimensions on which [individual] perspectives differ" (p. 218). To this end, they recommend the construction of several title-like paraphrases or mini-abstracts, each of which would represent the content of the document from a different point of view.

A system of integrative or sociocognitive representations corresponds to DE MEY's (1980) cognitive stage and reflects the importance of "ubiquitous knowledge" (p. 54). Representation at this level recognizes

that individuals disambiguate or interpret the meaning of representations by integrating the representations in the context of the cognitive
expectations associated with the internal knowledge structures that
each of them brings to the process of interpretation. The context provided by the individual is, as BLAIR (1990; 1992) points out, the product
of participation in a language game, and is therefore shared by other
participants in that language game. Unlike the three previous levels of
representation, integrative or sociocognitive representations do not impose a canonical format, a relational structure, or a list of preferred
contents. Rather, the notion of integrative representations implies the
adoption of a sociocognitive perspective in the development, implementation, and ongoing maintenance of systems of physical, conceptual, and contextual representations. Within this framework, then, integrative systems of representation expand on existing representational
approaches by integrating into the representational language the knowledge structures characteristic of domain participants. While rudimentary examples of such systems may exist in the highly specialized
indexing and abstracting services tied to specific industries or organizations (e.g., the POWERLINK textbase described by WARD), most systems tend to reflect a single, well-defined point of view, thus limiting
both their effectiveness and their ultimate utility.

The theoretical grounding of sociocognitive representation in
WITTGENSTEIN's notion of language games (and forms of life) points
to the need for analysis of the knowledge structures embedded in
individual discourse domains, as advocated by HJØRLAND &
ALBRECHTSEN. Wilson's work on Project INISS (WILSON; WILSON
& STREATFIELD) can be viewed as one of the first examples of empirical research that takes a sociocognitive approach. Adopting the methodology of structured observation, WILSON studied information behavior and use in social services departments. Although his research
emphasized organizational communication and information provision,
his conclusion that "social workers have a 'unitary' concept of information . . . [as] anything that bears upon a problem, whatever its origins"
(p. 211) seems to indicate that an appropriate representational structure
in this domain would be constructed around the problems actually
confronted by social workers.

In a similar vein, SWIFT ET AL. (1977; 1979) investigated the representational needs of social scientists. They conclude that, to provide
effective access for members of this discourse community, information
scientists should adopt a "multi-modal" or "difference" model of representation. This approach would use multiple representational structures to represent the range of orientations (e.g., theoretical content,
empirical situation, data collection, and analysis) that social science
researchers adopt when searching a document database. BUCHANAN
ET AL. conducted similar research on the representational needs of the

interdisciplinary community of environmental researchers and proposed both a standard format and a metalanguage that, in tandem, would provide "a common frame of reference [and] mediate between independent structures and vocabularies" (p. 287).

TIBBO reports on a content analysis of 120 abstracts drawn from the chemical, psychological, and historical literature. Comparison of her findings with the content categories recommended in the ANSI/NISO standards indicates that, while more than 90% of the sentences from chemistry and psychology could be identified with the categories in the suggested model, fewer than 40% of the sentences in the historical literature could be matched to categories in the model. She concludes that use of a single abstracting standard is not appropriate: "the uniformity of results within each set and across the history samples indicates the potential desirability of standardization for surrogates within a particular subject literature" (p. 51). She points out that discipline-based approaches to surrogation will require research that focuses not on the documents themselves but on the nature of intellectual discourse within a discipline and on specific discipline-oriented behaviors of document producers and users.

Other significant research studies focusing on representational or organizational approach(es) characteristic of a particular domain or sociocultural group include those by CASE and KWAŚNIK (1989a; 1989b). Kwaśnik describes an investigation of the organization of personal documents in the offices of eight academics and concludes that physical characteristics and intended use are important contextual characteristics that influence the organization of document spaces. In a similar vein, Case reports on the cognitive categories and metaphors used by 20 historians to organize materials in their private offices. He found consensus on four main variables that influence the historian's organization of a personal document collection: (1) spatial configuration or features of the office; (2) physical format of the documents in the collection; (3) grouping by broad historical topics, subject areas, or chronological period; and (4) treatment (e.g., autobiography), purpose (e.g., textbook), or quality. Case concludes that, because the cognitive processes of historians are grounded in the physical world, representational systems should include "richer contextual cues" such as format, treatment, and purpose. The findings of Kwaśnik and Case provide insight on specific, domain-based contextual cues that can enhance existing systems of representation; and they indicate the need for further research leading to the identification of patterns of sociocognitive representations that are characteristic of other discourse domains and knowledge communities.

Another research approach adopting a sociocognitive perspective is exemplified by the work of WANTING (1984; 1986), who investigated the nature of questions asked by children in Danish libraries. She concludes that children's requests for books are generally concrete and often visual in nature, frequently representing either the actual physical characteristics of the requested document or a conceptualization of thematic content based on visual associations. Her research included investigation of representations based on the children's age and gender. PEJTERSEN carried out similar research on communication between children and librarians. The findings of these studies have been influential in shaping the representational structure for children's materials developed for the Danish multimedia project Database 2001 (ALBRECHTSEN, 1997; ALBRECHTSEN & JACOB).

In contrast to the empirical research carried out by CASE, KWAŚNIK (1989a; 1989b), PEJTERSEN, and WANTING (1984; 1986), SUTTON draws on anecdotal information and the accepted heuristics of legal practice to construct base-level theoretical models of attorney behavior and cognitive processing. He uses these models to identify the dynamics involved in the evolution of attorneys' legal expertise as they interact with primary and secondary literature. Sutton concludes that the LEXIS and WESTLAW retrieval systems fail to account for the dynamic nature of attorneys' cognitive models of core legal issues and recommends adoption of a representational structure "based on legal schema of increasing complexity" (p. 199) that would provide more meaningful representation. Although Sutton's cognitive and behavioral models are theoretical, his work demonstrates the potential applicability of the sociocognitive approach and sets the stage for future empirical research that can evaluate the relevance of these models for the design of more effective document representation in legal databases.

STAM proposes a representational model or typology that takes into account the intellectual needs and thought processes of art historians. Unfortunately, the empirical and/or disciplinary foundations of her model are not made explicit. In contrast, GARBER & GRUNES used work-flow study and task analysis to describe the search behavior of art directors and to develop a model interface to support searching image sets. They conclude that the success of such a system depends on the representational structure and on establishment of explicit relationships between concepts and terms. In an excellent article on image indexing that emphasizes the role of indexing in providing useful groupings of items (or references to items), LAYNE suggests four general categories of document attributes that should provide the basis for representation in image indexing. (1) Biographical attributes are the fixed characteristics of the target item such as creator and title. (2) Subject attributes include what the image is, what it is of, and what it is about. (3) Exemplified attributes refer to the specific form of the item such as sculpture, video, or novel. (4) Relationship attributes identify related materials.

NEELAMEGHAN reports on the development of MEDIS, a database of medical case histories intended to support research and education. He states that selection and organization of data elements in MEDIS was carried out in close consultation with specialists who were also users of the system and that "grouping of fields and the organization among coordinate fields appear to conform to the principles of helpful sequence of the general theory of knowledge classification" (p. 95). However, because the organization of the MEDIS database parallels the structure of the hospital's case sheets, the actual contribution of the medical specialists is unclear. Based on the information provided, it is not possible to evaluate the validity of his claim that the specialists' organization of the data conforms to classificatory principles of helpful sequence. This is, nonetheless, an important area for future research undertaken from the sociocognitive perspective and could prove highly relevant to the development and implementation of integrative representational systems.

Many of the principles governing traditional representational structures have been based on a theoretical foundation and have not been subjected to empirical evaluation. OLSON (1994; 1996) examined the assumption of universality as a necessary prerequisite for knowledge organization in the *Dewey Decimal Classification* (DDC) and the *Universal Decimal Classification* (UDC). She concludes that the activities of naming and organizing knowledge legitimate a particular world view and necessarily embed both the historical context and the contemporary context or world view in which the organizing activity occurs. FROHMANN (1994b) analyzed the epistemological basis of DDC and concludes that it does not reflect an objective reality that exists independently of the classification system. Rather, DDC constructs its own reality as the product of "a negotiated social process located firmly in its cultural, political and economic context" (p. 110). More importantly, he argues that recognition of the social, political, and/or disciplinary base upon which a knowledge structure is constructed effectively removes questions about adequacy of representation: because the reality represented by a system of knowledge organization is itself the product of that system, there exists a one-to-one correspondence between the internal reality of the structure and the external reality it represents.

Developing a pragmatic understanding of the social, historical, and disciplinary functions of representational systems in general and of classification schemes in particular is an important aspect of the sociocognitive approach to integrative representation. JACOB (1994a) reviews the role of traditional classificatory structures in the establishment and maintenance of disciplinary boundaries. STAR & RUHLEDER (see also BISHOP & STAR) investigated the notion of infrastructure as a relational concept embedded in practice. Infrastructure occurs at the point where "the tension between *local and global is resolved*. That is, an infrastructure occurs when local practices are afforded by a larger-scale technology, which can be used in a natural, ready-to-hand fashion" (p. 114). Although this analysis is based on the development and implementation of technological tools, the underlying connection between technological infrastructures and classification schemes affords new insights into the role of classification schemes in contributing to the knowledge structures of a particular social, professional, or disciplinary group. In a similar vein, STAR and STAR & GRIESEMER investigated the role of boundary objects as representational structures that facilitate communication between members of heterogeneous discourse communities. Boundary objects are "plastic enough to adapt to local needs and constraints of the several parties employing them, yet robust enough to maintain a common identity across sites" (STAR, pp. 46-47). A boundary object thus serves as an intermediary representation that facilitates correspondence between two or more target domains. Star identifies different types of boundary objects, including repositories, platonic objects, coincident boundaries, and standardized forms. The MARC format is an example of a standardized boundary object in that it facilitates sharing of the information among libraries while allowing a particular library to use only those MARC record fields that are supported by its database.

Through their work with the developers of the *Nursing Interventions Classification* (NIC) (MCCLOSKEY & BULECHEK, 1994; 1996; 1998), Bowker and his associates (BOWKER; BOWKER ET AL.; TIMMERMANS ET AL.) have contributed significantly to current appreciation of the pragmatic functions of representational structures in specific domains. As BOWKER observes, NIC is an attempt to make visible the invisible work performed by nurses. Its objective is not only to demarcate the practical boundaries of the profession but also to make those boundaries explicit for other professional groups that participate in the broader domain of health care and to legitimize nursing practitioners by enumerating activities that are viewed in the nursing community as having been taken for granted. In particular, TIMMERMANS ET AL. analyze the activity of classification building and conclude that it is a simultaneous process of constructing similarities and establishing differences that must accommodate three primary challenges: (1) to provide for correspondence or comparability across points of use; (2) to make visible the constituent entities, tasks, or characteristics; and (3) to establish an appropriate level of control that effectively eliminates confusion and forestalls breakdowns in communication. In a related paper, JACOB & ALBRECHTSEN review the role of dialog in the construction, or reconstruction, of three very different representational languages: NIC; *Diagnostic and Statistical Manual of Mental Disorders*, fourth edition

(AMERICAN PSYCHIATRIC ASSOCIATION); and the *HIV/AIDS and HIV/AIDS-Related Terminology* of HUBER & GILLASPY. They conclude that the effectiveness of a representational scheme depends, in large part, on critical assessment of the sociopolitical and ideological intentions underlying the contributing dialogs.

Categorization

Categorization is the cognitive process of dividing the world of experience into groups of entities, or categories, to construct order out of the physical and social world(s) in which the individual participates. JACOB (1992; 1994b) points out that, without recourse to the cognitive process of categorization, the experience of any one entity would be unique: each separate entity encountered by the individual—each blade of grass or drop of rain—would require unique labeling and storage in human memory along with its own particular set of defining characteristics. MARKMAN states that categorization is the fundamental cognitive mechanism that simplifies the individual's interaction with the environment: it not only facilitates the efficient storage and retrieval of information, but also reduces demands on human memory. Recognition of similarities leads to the creation of new knowledge: by grouping entities according to observed similarities, the individual generalizes from past experiences to form concepts about the environment that can then be extended to new encounters. Without recourse to the cognitive process of categorization, behavior based on learning, or on the generalization of acquired information, would be impossible. It is not surprising, then, that categories are generally thought of as the building blocks of cognition.

Categorization disdains both the unique and the universal. As MEDIN observes, "the only case in which categorization would not be useful is where all individuals are treated alike" (p. 1469). ZERUBAVEL, in his exhaustive analysis of the social implications of categories and category formation, illustrates the ubiquity of categorization. He points out that categorization is not simply an individual cognitive process but a socially and culturally determined process of constructing reality. More importantly, Zerubavel demonstrates how the process of categorization, or of lumping together objects or people by ignoring individual uniqueness, is simultaneously a process of division: a process of drawing fine lines to split the world of experience into islands of meaning that are treated "as if they were discrete, totally detached from their surroundings" (p. 5).

There are obvious similarities between the cognitive process of categorization and the formal processes of indexing (JACOB, 1992; PARSONS & WAND; THOMPSON & THOMPSON). GREEN (1992b) recommends that information specialists draw from cognitive psychology research in determining the most appropriate level of representation and points to the notion of basic-level categories proposed by BROWN and subsequently expanded by ROSCH (MERVIS & ROSCH; ROSCH, 1977; ROSCH ET AL.). Rosch contends that within a hierarchical structure there is a basic level of inclusiveness, such as that represented by BROWN's notion of common names, at which category labels are of greatest utility. The basic-level category is the "most cognitively efficient" (MERVIS & ROSCH, p. 92) because it carries the greatest amount of information about category members; that is, the basic-level category maximizes characteristics common to all members of one category while minimizing characteristics that overlap with other categories. GREEN (1992b) addresses several potential problems associated with basic-level indexing (e.g., identification of the basic-level category based on searcher expertise, problems of congruence with the more specific knowledge of expert searchers, and excessively high recall without discrimination). She concludes that, in combination with other indexing strategies such as the use of indexing frames, indexing at the basic level could support more effective retrieval.

In information science, only a handful of studies have looked at categorization empirically. As discussed previously, CASE reports on the criteria used by historians to organize disciplinary materials. Using observation and verbal reporting techniques, KWAŚNIK (1989a; 1989b) reports on a study of the effects of immediate surroundings and document content on the categorization process. Her purpose was to identify salient dimensions and underlying patterns of the categorization process. She concludes that the influence of context (defined here as individual, situational, and physical) is "so pronounced that any description of personal classification that does not take the context into account seems to be severely limited" (KWAŚNIK, 1989b, p. 146).

One of the earliest empirical studies of categorization in information science was reported by EVANS in 1982. Following ROSCH's (1975) methodology for priming of natural semantic categories, Evans evaluated Rosch's notion that the category prototype provides the "cognitive reference point" for a naturally occurring category. Based on her findings, Evans concludes that there are multiple access points to a category and that patterns of similarity relations within the set of category members determine the particular reference point that is most useful. In a related study of document categorization and subsequent retrieval, A.J. CAÑAS ET AL. (1985) used an experimental methodology to investigate the criteria individuals employ to facilitate retrieval from an unstructured document collection. They asked subjects to create a system of categories for an initial set of 50 proverbs. Over four separate sessions, the original structure was modified as a total of 200 proverbs were categorized. Retrieval tasks were performed on the collection at each session. The researchers conclude that three criteria in the categorization process contribute to retrieval effectiveness: (1) indexing on intended meaning; (2) creation of a shallow, two-level hierarchy; and (3) maintenance of a relatively small number of proverbs per category. In an experimental study of category structure, JACOB (1994b) investigated the effects of immediate context on the individual's cognitive organization of category members during communication. Her findings indicate that, while participants in a linguistic community appear to share a general level of representational structure based on context-independent information, the more that individuals rely on personalized, context-dependent information, the more variable are their resulting cognitive structures.

Although the results of empirical research focusing on the categorization process seem to hold potential for the development of effective indexing languages and organizational structures, more immediate applications can be seen in their contribution to the conceptual organization presented to the user by a system interface. For example, BORGMAN ET AL. investigated how children categorized scientific concepts presented in the Project Seed database. The results of this research were then used to construct an interface intended to provide "a consistent conceptual framework, based on the knowledge held by the children [that] should be more effective than some externally-derived model" (p. 86).

Mental Models

The term "mental model" is both ambiguous and imprecise, as ALLEN (1991) demonstrates. In an extensive review of the literature on mental models in human-computer interaction and information science, TURNER & BÉLANGER identify a multiplicity of overlapping terms and concepts that are used to describe both the cognitive modeling process and its products. In an attempt to bring order out of confusion, and drawing heavily on the earlier formulation of NORMAN, Turner and Bélanger outline four types of model: (1) the design model, or designer's model of the system; (2) the user model, or designer's model of the system user; (3) the user's model of the system; and (4) the conceptual model devised to explain the system to the user. Unfortunately, this typology of mental models is constructed within and limited by the perspective of computer system design and does not account for the more pervasive role performed by mental models in the cognitive processing of individuals.

As it is used here, "mental model" refers to the internal cognitive structures that the individual constructs, explicitly or implicitly, to represent a particular target domain, be it an event, an activity, an object, or a subject area. In this sense, mental models are the conceptual frameworks that individuals form, based on experience and formal knowledge acquisition, which allow them not only to predict the results of explicit behaviors but also to interpret and understand their environment. As DREYFUS & DREYFUS point out, "we human beings proceed from the past into the future with our past experience always going before us organizing the way the next events show up for us" (p. 88). It is this past experience which gives shape to the individual's mental models and provides a set of context-dependent expectations that can be drawn on to make sense of the world.

Within this broader interpretation, then, mental models is a cognitive construct that subsumes the notions of scripts (SCHANK & ABELSON), schemata (RUMELHART, 1980; 1983), and frames (MINSKY). It is, in fact, congruent with DE MEY's (1982) notion of a world view in that it is an internalized organizational structure that represents the individual's understanding of how the world works. Individuals have many such mental models or internal knowledge structures that are constantly being formed, modified, and re-formed as they interact with the world around them. J.J. CAÑAS ET AL. (1994) investigated the generation of mental models by two groups of novice programmers. Their findings indicate that, although the groups represented programming concepts differently, actual performance on the programming task was independent of the mental model induced by the learning conditions. They conclude that, in the early stages of learning, a mental model of the immediate task is necessary, but the explicit nature of the model may not have a perceptible impact on performance. Their findings support NORMAN's contention that it is not necessary for mental models to be accurate; it is necessary only that they be functional.

DIMITROFF reaches a similar conclusion in her study of the relationship between mental models of a retrieval system and search outcomes. She observes that there was a distinct relationship between completeness of a mental model and search success: searchers who lacked a working mental model of the system were generally unsuccessful. Although subject access was not within the scope of her study, she indicates the need for further research to investigate whether the critical element in the interaction between searchers and retrieval systems is the searcher's model of the system or of specific components of the system, such as the representational structure. KUHLTHAU ET AL. emphasize the centrality of the individual's model of the search process and suggest that expectations embedded in the models may limit the individual's access to information. But HOPPE & SCHIELE argue that information seeking is frequently embedded in the context of a higher-level task or domain that provides the searching process with an external structure. PITTS's findings appear to support the argument of HOPPE & SCHIELE. Pitts concludes that, although the students in her study relied on prior knowledge of the search process to solve problems, this knowledge "was never accessed in isolation . . . [S]tudents always used their information-seeking-and-use knowledge in conjunction with a subject matter . . . [or] knowledge domain" (p. 182).

PAYNE observes that investigation of mental models emphasizes the use of knowledge structures; and he argues that "a lot of explanatory work can be done by a description of what people know and believe, and how this affects their behaviour, without regard to the design of their mental machinery" (p. 4). Although this argument may forestall criticism of cognitivism in mental-model research, it does not address potential attacks of mentalism, subjective idealism, or methodological individualism such as those leveled against the cognitive viewpoint by FROHMANN (1990; 1992a; 1992b) and HJØRLAND (HJØRLAND, 1992; 1997; HJØRLAND & ALBRECHTSEN). Research by TIJSSEN points to a more objective approach to mental-model research that holds potential for the analysis and representation of knowledge domains. He reports on the use of multidimensional scaling techniques to generate a conceptual map of a knowledge domain based on the mental models of 14 domain experts in the field of neural networks. These representations of the domain structure were used to construct an "aggregate knowledge structure" or "'common' mental map" (p. 115). Tijssen contends that macro-level mappings of a domain based on bibliographic data are artificial representations. In contrast, domain mappings based on the mental models of domain experts reflect shared external influences such as "communal notions and cultural perceptions" that experts use "to construct a socially determined mental repertoires [sic] which can act as a mediating device for communication with others" (p. 116). Tijssen concludes that the use of multidimensional scaling generates "a *meso-level* account of expert knowledge structures ... [that] represents the communality across individual (*micro level*) opinions" (p. 118).

Sociocognitive Approaches to Indexing

WELLISCH describes indexing as the act of pointing to. As such, indexing is the superordinate process that subsumes more specific forms of pointing to, including postcoordinate indexing, precoordinate indexing, subject heading assignment, and classification. Indexing is both a process of representation through the systematic assignment of surrogates (descriptors or category labels) that model, or point to, the intellectual content of a group of documents and a process of categorization (grouping like things together to create order). JACOB (1992) points out that the terms categorization and classification are frequently used as synonyms and argues that this erroneous conflation of the two terms may reflect the simple fact that both are mechanisms for establishing order. There is, nonetheless, a fundamental distinction between these two processes in the way in which order is effected. The process of formal classification entails systematic arrangement of documents within a hierarchical structure of mutually exclusive and non-overlapping categories or classes. It is the most rigorous application of indexing in that it mandates that a document can be a member of one, and only one, class. In contrast, less rigorous processes of categorization provide for the generation of groups or categories of documents whose members bear some immediate similarity in the immediate context. That this context, and thus the membership of the category may vary is the basis for the flexibility exemplified in cognitive categorization and, to a more limited extent, in both postcoordinate and precoordinate indexing. BLAIR (1990) makes a similar distinction between indexing and classification and concludes that:

> Since document indexing is often called document 'classification', we could speculate that indexing theorists may have confused the more objective processes of scientific classification/description with the description of documents. Scientific taxonomies are built around *observable* differences between members of categories. These differences, though often subtle, must be objectively verifiable (p. 163).

Based on these arguments, the term indexing will be used in the following discussion to refer to the general process of document representation, and reference will be made to specific forms or products of indexing only when necessary.

The definition of indexing as an ostensive act of pointing to masks the cognitive nature of the indexing process by emphasizing the physical product of the process (the actual "pointers") over the intellectual activities involved. JONES (1990) observes that the literature is sparse on extraction of concepts from a text, or what he identifies as the "core activity" of indexing (p. 114). Rather, the focus has been on the physical format of indexes or, as JONES (1983) says in an earlier paper, on "the mechanics of alphabetization, cross-indexing and the form of name, subject or 'idea'" (p. 1). BAKEWELL's 1993 review of indexing research reflects this preoccupation with physical format in the subheadings used to structure the review: "Evaluation of indexes, Length of indexes, Alphabetization, Presentation of indexes, PRECIS, and User reactions." The final section does address the need for assessment of user perceptions of various indexes, but even here the emphasis is on evaluation of physical styles of indexing. In a similar vein, FIDEL's article on user-centered indexing provides a succinct overview of the foundational literature on indexing and outlines the practical issues involved in development of an indexing policy, but it, too, focuses narrowly on the product. Indeed, much valuable research contributes to the construction of more effective interfaces by investigating user interaction with the physical characteristics of indexes (see, for example, BISHOP ET AL.; DIODATO, 1994a, 1994b; JÖRGENSEN & LIDDY; LIDDY & JÖRGENSEN). The research discussed here, however, will necessarily focus on the cognitive activities involved in the indexing process itself.

The fact that the activity of indexing has received relatively little attention from information scientists may be a result of its inherent invisibility. Indexing is an intellectual process that involves the cognitive activities of text comprehension and document representation. As noted previously, the purpose of representation is to establish systematic correspondence between two or more domains. For the purposes of document retrieval, it involves, at a minimum, both correspondence between the intellectual content of the document as the target domain and the modeling mechanism of the indexing language and correspondence between what a word means (how it is actually used in a language game) as the target domain and the modeling mechanism of the indexing language. Investigation of the cognitive aspects of indexing indicates three primary areas of indexing activity: (1) text comprehension, or identification of the intellectual content of a document; (2) text generation, or translation of the intellectual content into the vocabulary of the indexing language; and (3) the representational or order-creating properties of the indexing language itself.

FARROW (1991) argues persuasively that the processes of text comprehension and text generation are closely related and that indexer-generated representations are subject to constraints that are inherent in the retrieval systems for which they are generated. More specifically, he claims that the product of the representational process (a set of descriptors, a classification label, or an abstract) and the indexing language employed necessarily influence the indexer's cognitive analysis of a document's intellectual content. For this reason, it is important to understand how the structure of the information system affects the interaction between document analysis, content representation, and retrieval. And, because indexing is primarily a process of categorization, it is instructive to consider how the activity of the indexer and the structure of the modeling domain (the indexing language) constrain category formation and membership.

Because an indexing language consists of the complete set of possible representations that can serve as surrogates for documents in a collection, it prescribes not only what entities or concepts can be represented but also the precise form of those representations. The representational structures generated by the various types of indexing languages can be understood as points on a continuum, progressing from natural language at one end to traditional classification schemes at the other and ordered by increasing constraints on the nature and composition of the resulting categories. Free-text searching with natural language is the simple act of pattern matching and entails no external controls. Category formation is carried out by the searcher, who selects one or more terms as the basis for category membership. The product is a set of documents whose membership in the category is determined by the presence of a given string of alphanumeric characters and not by any inherent similarity of subject content. Uniterm indexing is a refinement on this process in that the indexer selects as descriptors one or more natural-language terms appearing in the text. Here, too, the searcher determines the set of terms to be used as the criteria for category membership; but category membership is limited by the indexer who identifies the terms he or she considers most indicative of the text's conceptual content. The set of retrieved documents that meet the searcher's category definition is thus constrained by, or filtered through, the indexer. Because matching is limited to selected natural-language terms, there is no assurance that the terms from potentially relevant texts will match the terms used by the searcher or that matching terms will actually refer to the intended concept. Obviously, then, the searcher's and the indexer's approaches to ordering documents that are based on natural language do not constitute representational systems because they do not establish systematic correspondence between the target domain and the modeling domain of an indexing language.

The introduction of controlled vocabulary provides indexing with a systematic representational structure. Ideally, a controlled vocabulary establishes a unique surrogate term or phrase for each concept and ensures that each surrogate will refer to only one concept. In a postcoordinate system, the searcher can define the most appropriate search category and establish the parameters of category membership by selecting a term or set of terms from the indexing language. However, the searcher is necessarily constrained in the formulation of a search category by the indexing language, which enumerates the concepts that can be represented, and by the search engine, which establishes the combinatorial capabilities of the system. Category membership is limited by the indexer, who determines the intellectual content of the document(s) and assigns the corresponding surrogate(s) or representation(s) from the indexing language.

The searcher's formulation of a search category is more tightly constrained in precoordinate indexing systems in that the indexing language enumerates the set of available categories. Because categories are established by the indexing language, the searcher does not have the ability, as with postcoordinate indexing, to define a category but must select the pre-existing category or categories that most closely approximate his or her purpose. In precoordinate systems using subject headings, the tyranny of the indexing language is frequently mitigated, however, by the possibility that more than one predefined category will be assigned to a given work. Category membership is nonetheless limited by the indexer's activities of content analysis and category assignment. The influence of the indexer is paramount, however, in the case of traditional classification schemes as typically applied in libraries and other information environments: not only are the categories predetermined, but the indexer working with a classificatory indexing language must select the one category or single class that best represents the work in its entirety.

The nature of the indexing language is obviously a strong determinant in the ordering of a document collection because it constrains not only which concepts can be represented and how, but also, and more importantly, whether the representations can be combined to reflect the searcher's immediate task adequately. It is the indexer, however, who ultimately controls the category membership by selecting and assigning the descriptors that provide the basis for the grouping (and any subsequent regrouping) of documents by subject content.

When the representational tools—the modeling domains—of information science are approached from the perspective of constraints imposed on the system by the composition of the indexing language, by the intended product, and by the indexer's activities of analysis and translation, the research emphasis must shift from concern with the physical format of the final product (the interface) to a realization of the centrality of the sociocognitive foundations of the indexing language and, more importantly, of the cognitive activities of the indexer. To this end, BEGHTOL (1986) explores the implications of VAN DIJK's (1979; 1980a; 1980b) theories of aboutness and text linguistics and constructs a theoretical model of the cognitive processes involved in classification. An important aspect of Beghtol's argument is van Dijk's distinction between conceptual, top-down processing and perceptual, bottom-up processing in text comprehension. Conceptual processing involves conventional knowledge of the world that is not contained in the text but is provided by the reader. Perceptual processing, in contrast, relies on knowledge presented in the text which, through the process of summarization, generates a statement of the topic of discourse. Beghtol focuses specifically on intertextuality in classification schemes: on the notion that the perceived subject of a document is influenced by its assignment within the class structure as well as its relationship to other documents in the same or hierarchically related classes. However, her arguments regarding intertextuality are relevant to all forms of systematic representation with an indexing language.

FROHMANN (1990) criticizes the mentalism inherent in any attempt to identify cognitive rules that underlie text comprehension and/or the practice of indexing: "Since following a rule is a practice and practices are necessarily public, . . . the identity of the practice of a rule (or system of rules) depends upon its role in social life" (p. 92). FARROW (1991) also expresses concern that reliance on rule-based structures may be problematic when applied to a task such as indexing that does not involve close reading. Based on the work of VAN DIJK & KINTSCH, Farrow generates a model of text comprehension that places greater emphasis on the identification of strategies rather than rules and that prioritizes conceptual processing over perceptual processing. Drawing on research that investigates the relationship between reading speed and reading comprehension, he likens the initial task of the indexer to rapid reading and to the indexer's cognitive ability to infer connections between the portions of text actually sampled. He also cites research indicating that identification of the overall meaning or intent of a passage is primarily conceptual, or top-down, while reading is goal-directed as it is in indexing. His conclusion that indexers must have specialized subject knowledge pertinent to the texts being indexed points to the need for empirical investigation of the impact of subject expertise on the indexing process. Perceptual processing, on the other hand, involves scanning of the text for visual cues that identify relevant information and points to research addressing not only the cues used by indexers but also, and more importantly, the role of the indexer's knowledge of the discourse structure(s) exemplified by texts in various domains.

FARROW (1991) develops separate models for the processes of text comprehension and text production, but cautions that the two models must merge in practice. In a later paper, FARROW (1995) expands on his original formulation and identifies three separate task models that constitute the indexing process: (1) text reduction, (2) text comprehension, and (3) text production. Although he concedes that his models are theoretical and their pragmatic relevance for indexing rests on "analogy and anecdote" (p. 247), some empirical work has been initiated in this area that, if it does not draw directly on the text-based approach of Beghtol and Farrow, does begin to address some of the questions raised by their models.

BERTRAND & CELLIER investigate the effects of indexing expertise on the work of novice and expert indexers. They theorized that three aspects of indexer expertise would affect both the indexing process and its products: (1) familiarity with the indexing language; (2) knowledge of the subject domain; and (3) experience with the indexing task. To test their hypothesis, the researchers had 20 individuals generate lists of indexing terms for four books under four different experimental conditions. They made audiovisual recordings of the indexing activities of eight of these individuals. Analysis of indexing protocols indicated specific strategies used by expert indexers, but not by novices, in the identification of concepts and in the subsequent translation of concepts into the indexing language. In a related paper, BERTRAND ET AL. analyzed the impact of criteria used to identify indexable concepts and concluded that the style of text processing adopted by novice indexers is generally bottom-up in that it is influenced by textual cues, while experts more frequently rely on top-down processing influenced by prior knowledge.

BERTRAND & CELLIER suggest that indexing may also be affected by external constraints imposed by recognition of the needs of potential users and advocate further research along this line. This conclusion is supported by previous research undertaken by IIVONEN. She reports on interindexer consistency in a study of ten librarians from five academic and five special library environments. Indexers were asked to assign descriptors for ten different works under four separate experimental conditions. Although Iivonen does not indicate how the process of indexing may have differed for librarians from different types of libraries, she does suggest, based on indexer self-reports, that the focus or objective of the indexing process was affected by institutional constraints: by the specific environment of the indexer's home institution, its clients and its "economic, technological and legal-political environment as well as the socio-cultural context" (p. 259). She identifies six primary causes of inconsistency, including indexer anticipation of how patrons would request texts and the influence of the indexing language used by indexers in their working environment.

Two papers by a group of Canadian researchers (BERTRAND-GASTALDY ET AL.; DAVID ET AL.) report on complementary attempts to explain how indexers select descriptors and why their products may differ for the same document. The paper by BERTRAND-GASTALDY ET AL. describes the textual analysis of 833 indexing records prepared by seven indexers to determine congruence between terms assigned as descriptors and occurrence of the term in the title or abstract. This study is very traditional both in its data collection and analysis and in its expressed objective to provide an empirical grounding for automatic indexing algorithms. However, when the researchers compare differences in the indexing products of the two most prolific indexers in their study, the questions they pose indicate several potentially productive lines of research.

In contrast, the paper by DAVID ET AL. adopts a more cognitive perspective in its investigation of the problem of interindexer consistency. In addition to analysis of the indexing product, the researchers used three methodological approaches in their investigation: (1) concurrent verbal reporting or think-aloud protocols, (2) retrospective verbalization by the subject, and (3) interviewing focused on peer evaluation. Working from the initial assumptions that indexing is a problem-solving activity and that lack of consistency across indexers may result from individual variation in the indexer's model of the solution, they concluded that variation in assigned descriptors is a result of differences in individual models of what constitutes good indexing. This study is important not only for its application of nontraditional methodologies to investigation of interindexer consistency, but also for the implications of the findings for the education and training of future indexers.

Although lack of interindexer consistency is generally considered problematic, DAVID ET AL. point out that the indexers in their study "are to a large extent in agreement with respect to certain central concepts contained in the document, while they differ dramatically in the attribution of secondary notions" (p. 51). MANN reviews problems of interindexer consistency from the perspective of subject cataloging. He argues that GREGOR & MANDEL's claim that "the average likelihood that any two people will use the same term for a concept or a book is ten to 20 percent" (p. 46) has potentially serious consequences in that it minimizes the need for catalogers to discriminate between available subject headings. Mann provides a thorough review and analysis of the research literature on which this claim is based and concludes that "many of the studies to which [Gregor and Mandel] appeal indicate that problems of inconsistent vocabulary choice appear not when subject headings and vocabulary control mechanisms are present—rather, such problems arise precisely when control mechanisms are absent" (p. 40). His interpretation of the research literature is supported by JONES (1983) in an article not cited by Mann. Jones summarizes observations from a series of indexing workshops where participants used an ad hoc approach to indexing texts. He points out that "specification of an artificial language, even an imaginary one, appears to divert the indexer away from behaviour which closely corresponds with textual frequencies" (p. 8). Given the findings of David et al., the retrospective analysis of Mann, and the observations of Jones, there is an immediate need for rethinking the problem of interindexer consistency and for redirecting research in this area to address perceived lack of consistency as one aspect of a task-based or problem-solving approach.

FROHMANN (1990) and BLAIR (1990) point out that the literature on indexing tends to focus on assignment of subject descriptors from the indexing language and generally ignores the initial process of identifying the document's intellectual content. ALBRECHTSEN (1993) argues that the concept of aboutness, as introduced by FAIRTHORNE in 1969 and subsequently expanded on by MARON in 1977, HUTCHINS in 1978, and BEGHTOL in 1986, has frequently been seen as justification for attempts "to avoid the difficulties of addressing the concept of 'subject' proper" (ALBRECHTSEN, 1993, p. 220) and that the vagueness surrounding the concept of subject was simply transferred to the notion of aboutness. ALBRECHTSEN (1993) points out that "the concept of 'subject' still constitutes a pioneering area of study for research" (p. 223) and distinguishes between three approaches to the conceptualization of subject: (1) the simplistic approach, (2) the content-oriented approach, and (3) the requirements-oriented approach. She argues for a requirements-oriented or sociocognitive approach to representation and urges investigation into methods for generalizing domain-specific subject aspects across multiple domains. In her discussion of image representation, LAYNE also describes three approaches to the notion of subject: what the item is of specifically, what it is of generically, and what it is about. Although her approach to subject attributes is grounded in a discussion of image indexing, it has significance for content representation in all media.

Another approach to indexing and representation that attempts to circumvent the inherent messiness of subject identification is the notion of cognitive universals. In her multidisciplinary overview of theoretical and empirical research on universals, IYER points out that the search for cognitive universals, or "for things that are universally true about the human mind" (p. 178), has led some theorists to posit underlying cognitive structures, or deep structures, that can account for differences in observed behavior across individuals. FARRADANE's (1980a; 1980b) system of relational indexing, for example, is predicated on the developmental stages of cognition proposed by Piaget. Working from the assumption that these stages are universal in nature and constrain how individuals can represent concepts, Farradane proposes a system of nine role indicators intended to capture all possible relationships that might exist between any two or more terms.

More recent attempts to extend current indexing practices through the investigation of universal cognitive structures have focused on language use and communication. Drawing on the notion of illocutionary acts as proposed by AUSTIN and SEARLE (1969), BLAIR (1992) states that documents exhibit characteristics external to the subject content of the text and that representation of these characteristics can enhance retrieval. Blair suggests that "documents, like language in general, can be used to perform certain types of acts, and that it might be useful to use a performative taxonomy [of illocutionary acts] to represent documents for retrieval" (p. 202). GREEN (1992a; 1995a; 1995b) takes a slightly different approach to the search for universal cognitive structures. She points out that the semantic content of most indexing languages currently takes into account only paradigmatic or category relationships between conceptual units and ignores the syntagmatic relationships between conceptual elements that, in combination, generate higher-order conceptual constructs. GREEN (1995b) contends that, because "conceptual syntagmatic structures are not ontological structures in the world so much as they are perceptual structures of the human mind" (p. 381), syntagmatic representations can be used to express any semantic relationship. There is, she claims, a finite number of such conceptual structures in any natural language and their utility as representational mechanisms can be increased through metaphorical extension. She also suggests that use of frame-based indexing to represent these syntagmatic relationships will result in increased discrimination in document retrieval.

Sociocognitive Approaches to Abstracting

The representational process of abstracting has received even less attention than the process of indexing using a controlled vocabulary. MOLINA proposes a theoretical model of the general abstracting process that attempts to account for both the textual and the documentary aspects of abstracting. Although her four-step model does not appear to differ significantly from previous models proposed by CREMMINS or BORKO & BERNIER, it is explicitly grounded in a linguistic and cognitive approach to text analysis. ENDRES-NIGGEMEYER develops a naturalistic or conceptual model of the abstracting process by combining the model proposed by KINTSCH & VAN DIJK of text comprehension with the model proposed by HAYES & FLOWER of text production. The model Endres-Niggemeyer presents is based on empirical observation intended to identify "how expert abstractors organize their working process, which intellectual tools (standard strategies) they use, and how [sic] successful natural working contexts (steps, moves) look like" (p. 181). Using a thinking-aloud protocol, she recorded 36 abstracting processes of six expert abstractors and identified 453 abstracting strategies. These strategies are grouped into four general classes: (1) metacognitive skills involved in self-monitoring; (2) control skills involved in organizing the intellectual process; (3) general intellectual skills such as reading, writing, and thinking; and (4) genuine abstracting expertise. Taken together, these skills comprise "the intellectual toolbox" (p. 183) used by the expert abstractor. The plethora of abstracting strategies is daunting, but the study finds that general abstracting expertise combines processes of information acquisition with strategies for concept presentation.

CONCLUSION

SHERA (1965a) points out that the development of effective systems of retrieval will depend on investigation of the cognitive patterns of representation shared by communities of system users. He and BLAIR (1990) argue persuasively for research into the sociocognitive linguistic and communication practices that affect representation and ultimately determine the utility of retrieval systems. ELLIS (1992a; 1992b) observes, however, that the cognitive viewpoint lacks an exemplar or empirical model: a set of research assumptions and experimental standards that both define the problem area and provide benchmarks for analysis, evaluation, and cumulation of results. His comments apply equally to what has been sketched here as the sociocognitive approach. Indeed, there is no one methodological approach that can serve as an exemplar for sociocognitive research by investigating either the activity of indexing or the conceptual organization embedded in the linguistic practices of a knowledge domain. Rather, the sociocognitive perspective must be understood as providing a theoretical framework that identifies the focal objective of such research without prescribing precise methodological strategies. The lack of a single paradigmatic exemplar should not be viewed as a limitation, however, but as an opportunity for information scientists to draw from a wide range of methodological approaches as they build a coherent body of accepted knowledge. The very flexibility of problem definition and research design accorded the researcher by the lack of a single dominating exemplar supports application of a variety of research methods as knowledge cumulates through the replication or falsification of earlier findings.

The research identified here as exemplifying the sociocognitive perspective encompasses a wide range of potential methodological approaches. For example, in the investigation of interindexer consistency, DAVID ET AL. used concurrent verbal reporting, retrospective verbalization, and interviewing, while BERTRAND & CELLIER combined protocol analysis with quantitative evaluation of indexing products. HJØRLAND & ALBRECHTSEN describe several lines of possible research that support a domain-analytic approach and advocate the integration of historical and sociocultural analyses of knowledge communities with more traditional approaches such as bibliometrics and citation analysis. TIJSSEN, on the other hand, concludes that the application of multidimensional scaling to map experts' models of a knowledge domain can identify the conceptual structure of that domain more accurately and with greater systematicity than is possible through either interviewing domain experts or content-analyzing review articles. When combined with the flexibility of problem definition, this plethora of potential methodological approaches will make the sociocognitive per-

perspective a powerful tool in investigation of cognitive processes and physical systems of representation.

Although FIDEL's comment that "studying information seeking and searching behavior is necessary for user-centered indexing" (p. 576) appears to shift attention away from the processes and systems of representation and to the activity of searching, its importance for the sociocognitive perspective is readily apparent when the statement is interpreted in light of FROHMANN's (1990) critique on the mentalist approach to indexing:

> Rules of indexing are rules of text representation for the purpose of text retrieval. But text retrieval designates a set of particular social practices. Consequently, the construction of indexing rules institutes or facilitates particular kinds of retrieval practices and depends, therefore, upon a preliminary understanding of the social practices constituting text retrieval in the actual, historically real social world (p. 97).

Frohmann points out that rules of indexing must be understood as accepted standards for correctness that are embedded in social practice. As such, they serve both as justification for existing practice and as tools for instruction. Any attempt to define standards of representation must be undertaken, therefore, from a sociocognitive perspective that does not isolate the cognitive activities of either the searcher or the expert indexer, but takes into account the range of social dimensions that underlie all aspects of document retrieval. This is supported by the research of DAVID ET AL., which provides a unique example of how the social perceptions of the indexer contribute to and shape the cognitive activity of indexing. Just as important, however, are the potential educational benefits that may accrue from such investigations. Thus, for example, by investigating not only the cognitive process(es) involved in representational activities but also the impact of the indexer's mental model of a good representation on the final product, it may be possible to provide future indexers with effective, domain-based pragmatic frameworks that will enhance consistency of representation in individual knowledge communities.

Representation is not an independent and self-fulfilling exercise. Rather, it is an integral component of the overall process of document acquisition, organization, storage, and retrieval. Ultimately, sociocognitive research in information science will support the supervening goal of efficient and effective retrieval by facilitating the development of representational languages and organizational structures that reflect the needs of specific language games or of specific knowledge domains or linguistic communities. To effect this goal, it will be necessary to investigate the linguistic, communicative, and organizational aspects of representation from a multiplicity of sociocognitive perspectives and within the full range of discourse domains and knowledge communities.

BIBLIOGRAPHY

ALBRECHTSEN, HANNE. 1993. Subject Analysis and Indexing: From Automated Indexing to Domain Analysis. The Indexer. 1993 October; 18(4): 219-224. ISSN: 0019-4131; CODEN: IDXRA5.

ALBRECHTSEN, HANNE. 1997. Database 2001: Design af en Multimedie Web Katalog på Ballerup Bibliotekerne. Copenhagen, Denmark: Royal School of Librarianship; 1997. (In Danish. English title: Database 2001: The Design of a Multimedia Web Catalog in Ballerup Public Library.) The Royal School of Librarianship, Copenhagen, Denmark.

ALBRECHTSEN, HANNE; HJØRLAND, BIRGER. 1997. Information Seeking and Knowledge Organization: The Presentation of a New Book. Knowledge Organization. 1997; 24(3): 136-144. ISSN: 0943-7444; CODEN: KNOREM.

ALBRECHTSEN, HANNE; JACOB, ELIN K. 1998. Classification Systems as Boundary Objects in Diverse Information Ecologies. In: Efthimiadis, Efthimis N., ed. Advances in Classification Research: Volume 8: Proceedings of the 8th ASIS SIG/CR Classification Research Workshop; 1997 November 2; Washington, DC. Medford, NJ: Information Today, Inc. for the American Society for Information Science; 1998. ISBN: 1-57387-061-7.

ALLEN, BRYCE L. 1991. Cognitive Research in Information Science: Implications for Design. In: Williams, Martha E., ed. Annual Review of Information Science and Technology: Volume 26. Medford, NJ: Learned Information, Inc. for the American Society for Information Science; 1991. 3-37. ISSN: 0066-4200; ISBN: 0-938734-55-5; CODEN: ARISBC.

ALLEN, BRYCE L. 1996a. From Research to Design: A User-Centered Approach. In: Ingwersen, Peter; Pors, Niels Ole, eds. CoLIS 2: 2nd International Conference on Conceptions of Library and Information Science: Integration in Perspective; 1996 October 13-16; Copenhagen, Denmark. Copenhagen, Denmark: Royal School of Librarianship; 1996. 45-59. ISBN: 87-7415-260-2.

ALLEN, BRYCE L. 1996b. Information Tasks: Toward a User-Centered Approach to Information Systems. San Diego, CA: Academic Press; 1996. 308p. ISBN: 0-12-051040-5.

AMERICAN PSYCHIATRIC ASSOCIATION. 1994. Diagnostic and Statistical Manual of Mental Disorders. 4th edition. Washington, DC: American Psychiatric Association; 1994. 886p. ISBN: 0-89042-061-0; ISBN: 0-89042-062-9 (paper).

AUSTIN, JOHN L. 1962. How to Do Things with Words. Oxford, England: Oxford University Press; 1962. 166p. OCLC: 3087197.

BAKEWELL, KEN G.B. 1993. Research in Indexing: More Needed? The Indexer. 1993 April; 18(3): 147-151. ISSN: 0019-4131; CODEN: IDXRA5.

BARSALOU, LAWRENCE W. 1992. Cognitive Psychology: An Overview for Cognitive Scientists. Hillsdale, NJ: Lawrence Erlbaum; 1992. 410p. ISBN: 0-8058-0691-1.

BEGHTOL, CLARE. 1986. Bibliographic Classification Theory and Text Linguistics: Aboutness Analysis, Intertextuality and the Cognitive Act of Classifying Documents. Journal of Documentation. 1986 June; 42(2): 83-113. ISSN: 0022-0418; CODEN: JDOCAS.

BEGHTOL, CLARE. 1995. "Facets" as Interdisciplinary Undiscovered Public Knowledge: S.R. Ranganathan in India and L. Guttman in Israel. Journal of Documentation. 1995 September; 51(3): 194-224. ISSN: 0022-0418; CODEN: JDOCAS.

BELKIN, NICHOLAS J. 1977. Internal Knowledge and External Information. In: de Mey, Marc; Pinxten, Rik; Poriau, M.; Vandamme, Fernand, eds. CC77: International Workshop on the Cognitive Viewpoint; 1977 March 24-26; Ghent, Belgium. Ghent, Belgium: University of Ghent; 1977. 187-194. OCLC: 6906871.

BELKIN, NICHOLAS J. 1984. Cognitive Models and Information Transfer. Social Science Information Studies. 1984 April/July; 4(2/3): 111-129. ISSN: 0143-6236; CODEN: SOSSD3.

BELKIN, NICHOLAS J. 1990. The Cognitive Viewpoint in Information Science. Journal of Information Science. 1990; 16(1): 11-15. ISSN: 0165-5515; CODEN: JISCDI.

BERTRAND, ANNICK; CELLIER, JEAN-MARIE. 1995. Psychological Approach to Indexing: Effects of the Operator's Expertise upon Indexing Behaviour. Journal of Information Science. 1995; 21(6): 459-472. ISSN: 0165-5515.

BERTRAND, ANNICK; CELLIER, JEAN-MARIE; GIROUX, LUC. 1996. Expertise and Strategies for the Identification of the Main Ideas in Document Indexing. Applied Cognitive Psychology. 1996; 10: 419-433. ISSN: 0888-4080.

BERTRAND-GASTALDY, SUZANNE; LANTEIGNE, DIANE; GIROUX, LUC; DAVID, CLAIRE. 1995. Convergent Theories: Using a Multidisciplinary Approach to Explain Indexing Results. In: Kinney, Tom, ed. Forging New Partnerships in Information: Converging Technologies: Proceedings of the American Society for Information Science (ASIS) 58th Annual Meeting: Volume 32; 1995 October 9-12; Chicago, IL. Medford, NJ: Information Today, Inc. for ASIS; 1995. 56-60. ISSN: 0044-7870; ISBN: 1-57387-017-X; CODEN: PAISDQ.

BISHOP, ANN PETERSON; LIDDY, ELIZABETH D.; SETTEL, BARBARA. 1991. Index Quality Study, Part I: Qualitative Description of Back-of-the-Book Indexes. In: Indexing Tradition and Innovation: Proceedings of the 22nd Annual Conference of the American Society of Indexers; 1990 June 27; Chicago, IL. Medford, NJ: Learned Information, Inc.; 1991. 15-51. ISBN: 0-936547-13-8.

BISHOP, ANN PETERSON; STAR, SUSAN LEIGH. 1996. Social Informatics of Digital Library Use and Infrastructure. In: Williams, Martha E., ed. Annual Review of Information Science and Technology: Volume 31. Medford, NJ: Learned Information, Inc. for the American Society for Information

Science; 1996. 301-401. ISSN: 0066-4200; ISBN: 1-57387-033-1; CODEN: ARISBC.

BLAIR, DAVID C. 1990. Language and Representation in Information Retrieval. Amsterdam, The Netherlands: Elsevier Science; 1990. 335p. ISBN: 0-444-88437-8.

BLAIR, DAVID C. 1992. Information Retrieval and the Philosophy of Language. The Computer Journal. 1992; 35(3): 200-207. ISSN: 0010-4620.

BORGMAN, CHRISTINE L.; CHIGNELL, MARK H.; VALDEZ, FELIX. 1989. Designing an Information Retrieval Interface Based on Children's Categorization of Knowledge: A Pilot Study. In: Katzer, Jeffrey; Newby, Gregory B., eds. ASIS '89: Proceedings of the American Society for Information Science (ASIS) 52nd Annual Meeting: Volume 26; 1989 October 30-November 2; Washington, DC. Medford, NJ: Learned Information, Inc. for ASIS; 1989. 81-87. ISSN: 0044-7870; ISBN: 0-938734-40-7.

BORKO, HAROLD; BERNIER, CHARLES L. 1975. Abstracting Concepts and Methods. San Diego, CA: Academic Press; 1975. 250p. ISBN: 0-12-118650-4.

BOWKER, GEOFFREY C. 1998. Lest We Remember: Organizational Forgetting and the Production of Knowledge. Accounting, Management and Information Technologies. (In press). ISSN: 0959-8022.

BOWKER, GEOFFREY C.; TIMMERMANS, STEFAN; STAR, SUSAN LEIGH. 1995. Infrastructure and Organizational Transformation: Classifying Nurses' Work. In: Orlikowski, Wanda; Walsham, Geoff; Jones, Matthew; DeGross, Janice, eds. Information Technology and Changes in Organizational Work. London, England: Chapman and Hall; 1995. 344-379. ISBN: 0-412-64010-4.

BRIER, SØREN. 1992. A Philosophy of Science Perspective: On the Idea of a Unifying Information Science. In: Vakkari, Pertti; Cronin, Blaise, eds. Conceptions of Library and Information Science: Historical, Empirical and Theoretical Perspectives: Proceedings of the International Conference Held for the Celebration of the 20th Anniversary of the Department of Information Studies, University of Tampere; 1991 August 26-28; University of Tampere, Finland. London, England: Taylor Graham; 1992. 97-108. ISBN: 0-947568-52-2.

BRIER, SØREN. 1996. Cybersemiotics: A New Paradigm in Analyzing the Problems of Knowledge Organization and Document Retrieval in Information Science. In: Ingwersen, Peter; Pors, Niels Ole, eds. CoLIS 2: 2nd International Conference on Conceptions of Library and Information Science: Integration in Perspective; 1996 October 13-16; Copenhagen, Denmark. Copenhagen, Denmark: Royal School of Librarianship; 1996. 23-43. ISBN: 87-7415-260-2.

BROOKS, HELEN M. 1987. Expert Systems and Intelligent Information Retrieval. Information Processing and Management. 1987; 23(4): 367-382. ISSN: 0306-4573; CODEN: IPMADK.

BROWN, ROGER. 1958. How Shall a Thing Be Called? Psychological Review. 1958 January; 65(1): 14-21. ISSN: 0033-295X; CODEN: PSRVAX.

BUCHANAN, J.M.; ROBINS, P.C.; WYATT, B.K. 1979. Perspectives on a Polluted World: Tools and Procedures for Information Management. In:

MacCafferty, Maxine; Gray, Kathleen, eds. The Analysis of Meaning: Informatics 5: Proceedings of a Conference Held by the Aslib Informatics Group and the British Computer Society Information Retrieval Specialist Group; 1979 March 26-28; Queen's College, Oxford, England. London, England: Aslib; 1979. 280-289. ISBN: 0-85142-125-3.

CAÑAS, ALBERTO J.; SAFAYENI, FRANK R.; CONRATH, DAVID W. 1985. A Conceptual Model and Experiments on How People Classify and Retrieve Documents. In: SIGIR '85: Proceedings of the Association for Computing Machinery Special Interest Group on Information Retrieval (ACM/SIGIR) 8th Annual International Conference on Research and Development in Information Retrieval; 1985 June 5-7; Montreal, Quebec. New York, NY: ACM; 1985. 282-287. ISBN: 0-89791-159-8.

CAÑAS, JOSÉ JUAN; BAJO, MARIA TERESA; GONZALVO, PILAR. 1994. Mental Models and Computer Programming. International Journal of Human-Computer Studies. 1994; 40: 795-811. ISSN: 1071-5819.

CASE, DONALD O. 1991. Conceptual Organization and Retrieval of Text by Historians: The Role of Memory and Metaphor. Journal of the American Society for Information Science. 1991; 42(9): 657-668. ISSN: 0002-8231; CODEN: AISJB6.

CREMMINS, EDWARD T. 1982. The Art of Abstracting. Philadelphia, PA: ISI Press; 1982. 150p. ISBN: 0-89495-015-0.

DANIELS, PENNY J. 1986. Cognitive Models in Information Retrieval: An Evaluative Review. Journal of Documentation. 1986 December; 42(4): 272-304. ISSN: 0022-0418; CODEN: JDOCAS.

DAVID, CLAIRE; GIROUX, LUC; BERTRAND-GASTALDY, SUZANNE; LANTEIGNE, DIANE. 1995. Indexing as Problem Solving: A Cognitive Approach to Consistency. In: Kinney, Tom, ed. Forging New Partnerships in Information: Converging Technologies: Proceedings of the American Society for Information Science (ASIS) 58th Annual Meeting: Volume 32; 1995 October 9-12; Chicago, IL. Medford, NJ: Information Today, Inc. for ASIS; 1995. 49-55. ISSN: 0044-7870; ISBN: 1-57387-017-X; CODEN: PAISDQ.

DE MEY, MARC. 1977. The Cognitive Viewpoint: Its Development and Its Scope. In: de Mey, Marc; Pinxten, Rik; Poriau, M.; Vandamme, Fernand, eds. CC77: International Workshop on the Cognitive Viewpoint; 1977 March 24-26; Ghent, Belgium. Ghent, Belgium: University of Ghent; 1977. xvi-xxxi. OCLC: 6906871.

DE MEY, MARC. 1980. The Relevance of the Cognitive Paradigm for Information Science. In: Harbo, Ole; Kajberg, Leif, eds. Theory and Application of Information Research: Proceedings of the 2nd International Research Forum on Information Science; 1977 August 3-6; Copenhagen, Denmark, Royal School of Librarianship. London, England: Mansell; 1980. 48-61. ISBN: 0-7201-1513-2.

DE MEY, MARC. 1982. The Cognitive Paradigm: An Integrated Understanding of Scientific Development. Dordrecht, The Netherlands: D. Reidel Publishing Co.; 1982. 314p. ISBN: 90-277-1382-0.

DE MEY, MARC. 1984. Cognitive Science and Science Dynamics: Philosophical and Epistemological Issues for Information Science. Social Science

Information Studies. 1984 April/July; 4(2/3): 97-110. ISSN: 0143-6236; CODEN: SOSSD3.

DE MEY, MARC. 1992. Introduction to the 1992 Edition: Has the Cognitive Revolution Already Begun? In: The Cognitive Paradigm: An Integrated Understanding of Scientific Development. 2nd edition. Chicago, IL: University of Chicago Press; 1992. xi-xxiv. ISBN: 0-226-14259-0.

DERVIN, BRENDA. 1977. Useful Theory for Librarianship: Communication, Not Information. Drexel Library Quarterly. 1977; 13(3): 16-32. ISSN: 0012-6160.

DILLON, ANDREW. 1994. Designing Usable Electronic Text: Ergonomic Aspects of Human Information Usage. Bristol, PA: Taylor and Francis; 1994. 195p. ISBN: 0-7484-0112-1.

DIMITROFF, ALEXANDRA. 1992. Mental Models Theory and Search Outcome in a Bibliographic Retrieval System. Library & Information Science Research. 1992; 14: 141-156. ISSN: 0740-8188; CODEN: LISRDH.

DIODATO, VIRGIL P. 1994a. Duplicate Entries Versus Cross-References in Back-of-Book Indexes. The Indexer. 1994 October; 19(2): 83-87. ISSN: 0019-4131; CODEN: IDXRA5.

DIODATO, VIRGIL P. 1994b. User Preferences for Features in Back-of-Book Indexes. Journal of the American Society for Information Science. 1994 August; 45(7): 529-536. ISSN: 0002-8231; CODEN: AISJB6.

DREYFUS, HUBERT L.; DREYFUS, STUART E. 1986. Mind over Machine: The Power of Human Intuition and Expertise in the Era of the Computer. New York, NY: The Free Press; 1986. 231p. ISBN: 0-02-908061-4.

ELLIS, DAVID. 1992a. Paradigms and Proto-Paradigms in Information Retrieval Research. In: Vakkari, Pertti; Cronin, Blaise, eds. Conceptions of Library and Information Science: Historical, Empirical and Theoretical Perspectives: Proceedings of the International Conference Held for the Celebration of the 20th Anniversary of the Department of Information Studies, University of Tampere; 1991 August 26-28; University of Tampere, Finland. London, England: Taylor Graham; 1992. 165-186. ISBN: 0-947568-52-2.

ELLIS, DAVID. 1992b. The Physical and Cognitive Paradigms in Information Retrieval Research. Journal of Documentation. 1992 March; 48(1): 45-64. ISSN: 0022-0418; CODEN: JDOCAS.

ENDRES-NIGGEMEYER, BRIGITTE. 1994. A Naturalistic Model of Abstracting. In: Albrechtsen, Hanne; Oernager, Susanne, eds. Knowledge Organization and Quality Management: Proceedings of the 3rd International ISKO Conference; 1994 June 20-24; Copenhagen, Denmark. Frankfurt/Main, Germany: Indeks Verlag; 1994. 181-187. (Advances in Knowledge Organization: Volume 4). ISSN: 0938-5495; ISBN: 3-88672-023-3.

EVANS, NANCY J. 1982. Human Processing of Natural Categories. In: Petrarca, Anthony E.; Taylor, Celianna I.; Kohn, Robert S., eds. Proceedings of the American Society for Information Science (ASIS) 45th Annual Meeting: Volume 19; 1982 October 17-21; Columbus, OH. White Plains, NY: Knowledge Industry Publications, Inc. for ASIS; 1982. 80-83. ISSN: 0044-7870; ISBN: 0-86729-038-2; CODEN: PAISDQ.

FAIRTHORNE, ROBERT A. 1969. Content Analysis, Specification and Control. In: Cuadra, Carlos, ed. Annual Review of Information Science and Technology: Volume 4. Chicago, IL: Encyclopaedia Britannica, Inc.; 1969. 73-109. ISBN: 0-85229-147-7.

FARRADANE, JASON E.L. 1980a. Relational Indexing: Part I. Journal of Information Science. 1980; 1(5): 267-276. ISSN: 0165-5515.

FARRADANE, JASON E.L. 1980b. Relational Indexing: Part II. Journal of Information Science. 1980; 1(6): 313-324. ISSN: 0165-5515.

FARROW, JOHN F. 1991. A Cognitive Process Model of Document Indexing. Journal of Documentation. 1991 June; 47(2): 149-166. ISSN: 0022-0418; CODEN: JDOCAS.

FARROW, JOHN F. 1995. All in the Mind: Concept Analysis in Indexing. The Indexer. 1995 October; 19(4): 243-247. ISSN: 0019-4131; CODEN: IDXRA5.

FIDEL, RAYA. 1994. User-Centered Indexing. Journal of the American Society for Information Science. 1994; 45(8): 572-576. ISSN: 0002-8231; CODEN: AISJB6.

FROEHLICH, THOMAS J. 1989. The Foundations of Information Science in Social Epistemology. In: Hoervel, Lee W.; Milutirinovic, Veljko, eds. Proceedings of the 22nd Annual Hawaii International Conference on System Sciences: Volume 4; 1989 January 3-6; Kailua Kona, Hawaii. Los Alamitos, CA: IEEE Computer Society Press; 1989. 306-314. ISBN: 0-8186-1914-7.

FROHMANN, BERND. 1990. Rules of Indexing: A Critique of Mentalism in Information Retrieval Theory. Journal of Documentation. 1990 June; 46(2): 81-101. ISSN: 0022-0418; CODEN: JDOCAS.

FROHMANN, BERND. 1992a. Knowledge and Power in Library and Information Science: Toward a Discourse Analysis of the Cognitive Viewpoint. In: Vakkari, Pertti; Cronin, Blaise, eds. Conceptions of Library and Information Science: Historical, Empirical and Theoretical Perspectives: Proceedings of the International Conference Held for the Celebration of the 20th Anniversary of the Department of Information Studies, University of Tampere; 1991 August 26-28; University of Tampere, Finland. London, England: Taylor Graham; 1992. 135-147. ISBN: 0-947568-52-2.

FROHMANN, BERND. 1992b. The Power of Images: A Discourse Analysis of the Cognitive Viewpoint. Journal of Documentation. 1992 December; 48(4): 365-386. ISSN: 0022-0418; CODEN: JDOCAS.

FROHMANN, BERND. 1994a. Discourse Analysis as a Research Method in Library and Information Science. Library & Information Science Research. 1994; 16: 119-138. ISSN: 0740-8188; CODEN: LISRDH.

FROHMANN, BERND. 1994b. The Social Construction of Knowledge Organization: The Case of Melvil Dewey. In: Albrechtsen, Hanne; Oernager, Susanne, eds. Knowledge Organization and Quality Management: Proceedings of the 3rd International ISKO Conference; 1994 June 20-24; Copenhagen, Denmark. Frankfurt/Main, Germany: Indeks Verlag; 1994. 109-117. (Advances in Knowledge Organization: Volume 4). ISSN: 0938-5495; ISBN: 3-88672-023-3.

GARBER, SHARON R.; GRUNES, MITCH B. 1992. The Art of Search: A Study of Art Directors. In: Bauersfeld, Penny; Bennett, John; Lynch, Gene, eds. CHI '92: Proceedings of the Association for Computing Machinery Special

Interest Group on Computer-Human Interaction (ACM/SIGCHI) Conference on Human Factors in Computing Systems; 1992 May 3-7; Monterey, CA. New York, NY: ACM; 1992. 157-162. ISBN: 0-89791-514-3; ISBN: 0-89791-513-5 (paper).

GIDDENS, ANTHONY. 1982. Profiles and Critiques in Social Theory. Berkeley, CA: University of California Press; 1982. 239p. ISBN: 0-520-04933-0; ISBN: 0-520-04964-0 (paper).

GREEN, REBECCA. 1992a. The Expression of Syntagmatic Relationships in Indexing: Are Frame-Based Index Languages the Answer? In: Williamson, Nancy J.; Hudon, Michèle, eds. Classification Research for Knowledge Representation and Organization: Proceedings of the 5th International Study Conference on Classification Research; 1991 June 24-28; Toronto, Canada. Amsterdam, The Netherlands: Elsevier; 1992. 79-88. ISBN: 0-444-89343-1.

GREEN, REBECCA. 1992b. Insights into Classification from the Cognitive Sciences: Ramifications for Index Languages. In: Williamson, Nancy J.; Hudon, Michèle, eds. Classification Research for Knowledge Representation and Organization: Proceedings of the 5th International Study Conference on Classification Research; 1991 June 24-28; Toronto, Canada. Amsterdam, The Netherlands: Elsevier; 1992. 215-222. ISBN: 0-444-89343-1.

GREEN, REBECCA. 1995a. The Expression of Conceptual Syntagmatic Relationships: A Comparative Survey. Journal of Documentation. 1995 December; 51(4): 315-338. ISSN: 0022-0418; CODEN: JDOCAS.

GREEN, REBECCA. 1995b. Syntagmatic Relationships in Index Languages: A Reassessment. Library Quarterly. 1995 October; 65(4): 365-385. ISSN: 0024-2519.

GREGOR, DOROTHY; MANDEL, CAROL. 1991. Cataloging Must Change! Library Journal. 1991 April 1; 116(6): 42-47. ISSN: 0363-0277.

GUILFORD, JAY PAUL. 1960. Basic Conceptual Problems in the Psychology of Thinking. Annals of the New York Academy of Sciences. 1960 December; 91(1): 6-21. ISSN: 0077-8923.

HARBO, OLE; INGWERSEN, PETER; TIMMERMANN, POVL. 1977. Cognitive Processes in Information Storage and Retrieval. In: de Mey, Marc; Pinxten, Rik; Poriau, M.; Vandamme, Fernand, eds. CC77: International Workshop on the Cognitive Viewpoint; 1977 March 24-26; Ghent, Belgium. Ghent, Belgium: University of Ghent; 1977. 214-218. OCLC: 6906871.

HARTER, STEPHEN P.; HERT, CAROL A. 1997. Evaluation of Information Retrieval Systems: Approaches, Issues, and Methods. In: Williams, Martha E., ed. Annual Review of Information Science and Technology: Volume 32. Medford, NJ: Information Today, Inc. for the American Society for Information Science; 1997. 3-94. ISSN: 0066-4200; ISBN: 1-57387-047-1; CODEN: ARISBC.

HAYES, JOHN R.; FLOWER, LINDA S. 1980. Identifying the Organization of Writing Processes. In: Gregg, Lee W.; Steinberg, Erwin R., eds. Cognitive Processes in Writing. Hillsdale, NJ: Erlbaum; 1980. 3-30. ISBN: 0-89859-032-9.

HJØRLAND, BIRGER. 1992. The Concept of "Subject" in Information Science. Journal of Documentation. 1992 June; 48(2): 172-200. ISSN: 0022-0418; CODEN: JDOCAS.

HJØRLAND, BIRGER. 1997. Information Seeking and Subject Representation: An Activity-Theoretical Approach to Information Science. Westport, CT: Greenwood Press; 1997. 213p. ISBN: 0-313-29893-9.

HJØRLAND, BIRGER; ALBRECHTSEN, HANNE. 1995. Toward a New Horizon in Information Science: Domain Analysis. Journal of the American Society for Information Science. 1995; 46(6): 400-425. ISSN: 0002-8231; CODEN: AISJB6.

HOLZNER, BURKHART; MARX, JOHN H. 1979. Knowledge Application: The Knowledge System in Society. Boston, MA: Allyn and Bacon; 1979. 388p. ISBN: 0-205-06516-3.

HOPPE, H. ULRICH; SCHIELE, FRANZ. 1992. Towards Task Models for Embedded Information Retrieval. In: Bauersfeld, Penny; Bennett, John; Lynch, Gene, eds. CHI '92: Proceedings of the Association for Computing Machinery Special Interest Group on Computer-Human Interaction (ACM/ SIGCHI) Conference on Human Factors in Computing Systems; 1992 May 3-7; Monterey, CA. New York, NY: ACM; 1992. 173-180. ISBN: 0-89791-514-3; ISBN: 0-89791-513-5 (paper).

HUBER, JEFFREY T.; GILLASPY, MARY L. 1996. HIV/AIDS and HIV/AIDS-Related Terminology: A Means of Organizing the Body of Knowledge. New York, NY: Haworth Press; 1996. 107p. ISBN: 1-5602-4970-6; ISBN: 1-5602-3871-2.

HUTCHINS, WILLIAM J. 1978. The Concept of "Aboutness" in Subject Indexing. Aslib Proceedings. 1978 May; 30(5): 172-181. ISSN: 0001-253X.

IIVONEN, MIRJA. 1990. The Impact of the Indexing Environment on Interindexer Consistency. In: Fugmann, Robert, ed. Tools for Knowledge Organization and the Human Interface: Proceedings of the 1st International ISKO-Conference; 1990 August 14-17; Darmstadt, Germany. Frankfurt/Main, Germany: Indeks Verlag; 1990. 259-261. (Advances in Knowledge Organization: Volume 1). ISSN: 0938-5495; ISBN: 3-88672-020-9.

INGWERSEN, PETER. 1982. Search Procedures in the Library: Analysed from the Cognitive Point of View. Journal of Documentation. 1982 September; 38(3): 165-191. ISSN: 0022-0418; CODEN: JDOCAS.

INGWERSEN, PETER. 1984a. A Cognitive View of Three Selected Online Search Facilities. Online Review. 1984 October; 8(5): 465-492. ISSN: 0309-314X.

INGWERSEN, PETER. 1984b. Online Man-Machine Interaction Facilities: A Cognitive View. In: Dietschmann, Hans J., ed. Representation and Exchange of Knowledge as a Basis of Information Processes: Proceedings of the 5th International Research Forum in Information Science (IRFIS 5); 1983 September 5-7; Heidelberg, F.R.G. Amsterdam, The Netherlands: North-Holland; 1984. 325-358. ISBN: 0-444-87563-8.

INGWERSEN, PETER. 1992a. Information and Information Science in Context. Libri. 1992; 42(2): 99-135. ISSN: 0024-2667.

INGWERSEN, PETER. 1992b. Information Retrieval Interaction. London, England: Taylor Graham; 1992. 246p. ISBN: 0-947568-54-9.

INGWERSEN, PETER. 1993. The Cognitive Viewpoint in IR. Journal of Documentation. 1993 March; 49(1): 60-63. ISSN: 0022-0418; CODEN: JDOCAS.

INGWERSEN, PETER. 1994. The Cognitive Perspective in Information Retrieval. International Forum on Information and Documentation. 1994 April; 19(2): 25-32. ISSN: 0304-9701; CODEN: IFIDD7.

INGWERSEN, PETER. 1996. Cognitive Perspectives of Information Retrieval Interaction: Elements of a Cognitive IR Theory. Journal of Documentation. 1996 March; 52(1): 3-50. ISSN: 0022-0418; CODEN: JDOCAS.

IYER, HEMALATA. 1995. Classificatory Structures: Concepts, Relations and Representation. Frankfurt/Main, Germany: Indeks Verlag; 1995. 230p. (Textbooks for Knowledge Organization: Volume 2). ISBN: 3-88672-501-4.

JACOB, ELIN K. 1992. Classification and Categorization : Drawing the Line. In: Kwaśnik, Barbara H.; Fidel, Raya, eds. Advances in Classification Research: Volume 2. Medford, NJ: Learned Information, Inc. for the American Society for Information Science; 1992. 67-83. ISBN: 0-938734-67-9.

JACOB, ELIN K. 1994a. Classification and Crossdisciplinary Communication : Breaching the Boundaries Imposed by Classificatory Structure. In: Albrechtsen, Hanne; Oernager, Susanne, eds. Knowledge Organization and Quality Management: Proceedings of the 3rd International ISKO Conference; 1994 June 20-24; Copenhagen, Denmark. Frankfurt/Main, Germany: Indeks Verlag; 1994. 101-108. (Advances in Knowledge Organization: Volume 4). ISBN: 3-88672-023-3.

JACOB, ELIN K. 1994b. Sharing Concepts: Communicative Constraints on the Structure of Categories. Chapel Hill, NC: University of North Carolina at Chapel Hill; 1994. 236p. (Ph.D. dissertation). Available from: UMI, Ann Arbor, MI. (UMI order no. AAC 9430838).

JACOB, ELIN K.; ALBRECHTSEN, HANNE. 1997. Constructing Reality: The Role of Dialogue in the Development of Classificatory Structures. In: Proceedings of the 6th International Study Conference on Classification Research; 1997 June 16-18; London, England. The Hague, The Netherlands: International Federation for Information and Documentation; 1997. ISBN: 92-660-0716-1.

JONES, KEVIN P. 1983. How Do We Index? A Report of Some Aslib Informatics Group Activity. Journal of Documentation. 1983 March; 39(1): 1-23. ISSN: 0022-0418; CODEN: JDOCAS.

JONES, KEVIN P. 1990. Natural-Language Processing and Automatic Indexing: A Reply. The Indexer. 1990 October; 17(2): 114-115. ISSN: 0019-4131; CODEN: IDXRA5.

JÖRGENSEN, CORINNE L.; LIDDY, ELIZABETH D. 1996. Information Access or Information Anxiety: An Exploratory Evaluation of Book Index Features. The Indexer. 1996 October; 20(2): 64-68. ISSN: 0019-4131; CODEN: IDXRA5.

KINTSCH, WALTER; VAN DIJK, TEUN ADRIANUS. 1983. Strategies of Discourse Comprehension. Orlando, FL: Academic Press; 1983. 418p. ISBN: 0-12-712050-5.

KUHLTHAU, CAROL COLLIER; TUROCK, BETTY J.; BELVIN, ROBERT J. 1988. Facilitating Information Seeking through Cognitive Models of the Search Process. In: Borgman, Christine L.; Pai, Edward Y. H., eds. ASIS '88: Proceedings of the American Society for Information Science (ASIS) 51st Annual Meeting: Volume 25; 1988 October 23-27; Atlanta, GA. Medford, NJ: Learned Information, Inc. for ASIS; 1988. 70-75. ISSN: 0044-7870; ISBN: 0-938734-29-6.

KUHN, THOMAS S. 1970. The Structure of Scientific Revolutions. 2nd edition, enlarged. Chicago, IL: University of Chicago Press; 1970. 210p. ISBN: 0-226-45803-2 (cloth); 0-226-45804-0 (paper).

KWAŚNIK, BARBARA H. 1989a. How a Personal Document's Intended Use or Purpose Affects Its Classification in an Office. In: Belkin, Nicholas J.; van Rijsbergen, C. J., eds. SIGIR '89: Proceedings of the Association for Computing Machinery Special Interest Group on Information Retrieval (ACM/ SIGIR) 12th Annual International Conference on Research and Development in Information Retrieval; 1989 June 25-28; Cambridge, MA. New York, NY: ACM; 1989. 207-210. ISBN: 0-89791-321-3.

KWAŚNIK, BARBARA H. 1989b. The Influence of Context on Classificatory Behavior. New Brunswick, NJ: Rutgers State University of New Jersey; 1989. 250p. (Ph.D. dissertation). Available from: UMI, Ann Arbor, MI. (UMI order no. AAC 9008910).

LAYNE, SARA SHATFORD. 1994. Some Issues in the Indexing of Images. Journal of the American Society for Information Science. 1994; 45(8): 583-588. ISSN: 0002-8231; CODEN: AISJB6.

LIDDY, ELIZABETH D.; JÖRGENSEN, CORINNE L. 1993. Reality Check! Book Index Characteristics That Facilitate Information Access. In: Mulvany, Nancy C., ed. Indexing, Providing Access to Information: Looking Back, Looking Ahead: Proceedings of the 25th Annual Meeting of the American Society of Indexers; 1993 May 20-22; Alexandria, VA. Port Aransas, TX: American Society of Indexers; 1993. 125-138. ISBN: 0-936547-19-7.

LYCAN, WILLIAM G. 1990. Ontology from Behaviorism to Functionalism: Introduction. In: Lycan, William G., ed. Mind and Cognition: A Reader. Cambridge, MA: Basil Blackwell; 1990. 3-13. ISBN: 0-631-16763-3 (paper); ISBN: 0-631-16076-0.

MANN, THOMAS. 1997. "Cataloging Must Change!" and Indexer Consistency Studies: Misreading the Evidence at Our Peril. Cataloging & Classification Quarterly. 1997; 23(3/4): 3-45. ISSN: 0163-9374.

MARKMAN, ELLEN M. 1989. Categorization and Naming in Children: Problems of Induction. Cambridge, MA: MIT Press; 1989. 250p. ISBN: 0-262-13239-7.

MARON, M.E. 1977. On Indexing, Retrieval and the Meaning of About. Journal of the American Society for Information Science. 1977 January; 28(1): 38-43. ISSN: 0002-8231; CODEN: AISJB6.

MASTERMAN, MARGARET M. 1970. The Nature of Paradigm. In: Lakatos, Imre; Musgrave, Alan, eds. Criticism and the Growth of Knowledge. Cambridge, England: Cambridge University Press; 1970. 59-91. ISBN: 0-521-07826-1.

MCCLOSKEY, JOANNE COMI; BULECHEK, GLORIA M. 1994. Standardizing the Language for Nursing Treatments: An Overview of the Issues. Nursing Outlook. 1994 March/April; 42(2): 56-63. ISSN: 0029-6554.

MCCLOSKEY, JOANNE COMI; BULECHEK, GLORIA M. 1996. Nursing Interventions Classification (NIC): Iowa Intervention Project. 2nd edition. St. Louis, MO: Mosby; 1996. 739p. ISBN: 0-8151-6302-9.

MCCLOSKEY, JOANNE COMI; BULECHEK, GLORIA M. 1998. Nursing Interventions Classification (NIC): Development and Use. In: Schwartz, Ray, ed. Advances in Classification Research: Volume 6: Proceedings of the 6th ASIS SIG/CR Classification Research Workshop; 1995 October 8; Chicago, IL. Medford, NJ: Information Today, Inc. for the American Society for Information Science; 1998. 79-98. ISBN: 1-57387-046-3.

MEDIN, DOUGLAS L. 1989. Concepts and Conceptual Structure. American Psychologist. 1989 December; 44(12): 1469-1481. ISSN: 0003-066X.

MERVIS, CAROLYN B.; ROSCH, ELEANOR. 1981. Categorization of Natural Objects. Annual Review of Psychology. 1981; 32: 89-115. ISSN: 0066-4308.

MICHIE, DONALD. 1974. On Machine Intelligence. Edinburgh, Scotland: Edinburgh University Press; 1974. 199p. ISBN: 0-470-60150-7.

MINSKY, MARVIN. 1975. A Framework for Representing Knowledge. In: Winston, Patrick H., ed. The Psychology of Computer Vision. New York, NY: McGraw-Hill; 1975. 211-277. ISBN: 0-07-071048-1.

MOLHOLT, PAT. 1988. Research Issues in Information Access. In: Mathews, Anne J., ed. Rethinking the Library in the Information Age: Volume II: Issues in Library Research: Proposals for the 1990s. Washington, DC: Prepared for the Office of Library Programs by the U. S. Department of Education; 1988. 93-113. OCLC: 18820533.

MOLINA, MARIA PINTO. 1995. Documentary Abstracting: Toward a Methodological Model. Journal of the American Society for Information Science. 1995; 46(3): 225-234. ISSN: 0002-8231; CODEN: AISJB6.

NEELAMEGHAN, ARASHANAPALAI. 1991. Concept Categorization and Knowledge Organization in Specialized Databases: A Case Study. International Classification. 1991; 18(2): 92-97. ISSN: 0340-0050.

NORMAN, DONALD A. 1983. Some Observations on Mental Models. In: Gentner, Dedre; Stevens, Albert L., eds. Mental Models. Hillsdale, NJ: Lawrence Erlbaum; 1983. 7-14. ISBN: 0-89859-242-9.

OLSON, HOPE. 1994. Universal Models: A History of the Organization of Knowledge. In: Albrechtsen, Hanne; Oernager, Susanne, eds. Knowledge Organization and Quality Management: Proceedings of the 3rd International ISKO Conference; 1994 June 20-24; Copenhagen, Denmark. Frankfurt/Main, Germany: Indeks Verlag; 1994. 72-80. (Advances in Knowledge Organization: Volume 4). ISSN: 0938-5495; ISBN: 3-88672-023-3.

OLSON, HOPE. 1996. Dewey Thinks Therefore He Is: The Epistemic Stance of Dewey and UDC. In: Green, Rebecca, ed. Knowledge Organization and Change: Proceedings of the 4th International ISKO Conference; 1996 July 15-18; Washington, DC. Frankfurt/Main, Germany: Indeks Verlag; 1996. 302-312. (Advances in Knowledge Organization: Volume 5). ISSN: 0938-5495; ISBN: 3-88672-024-1.

PAISLEY, WILLIAM J.; PARKER, EDWIN B. 1965. Information Retrieval as a Receiver-Controlled Communication System. In: Heilprin, Laurence B.; Markuson, Barbara E.; Goodman, Frederick L., eds. Proceedings of the Symposium on Education for Information Science; 1965 Septermber 7-10; Warrenton, VA. Washington, DC: Spartan Books; 1965. 23-31. LC: 65-28375.

PARSONS, JEFFREY; WAND, YAIR. 1997. Choosing Classes in Conceptual Modeling. Communications of the ACM. 1997 June; 40(6): 63-69. ISSN: 0001-0782.

PAYNE, STEPHEN J. 1991. A Descriptive Study of Mental Models. Behaviour & Information Technology. 1991; 10(1): 3-21. ISSN: 0144-929X.

PEJTERSEN, ANNELISE MARK. 1994. A New Approach to Design of Document Retrieval and Indexing Systems for OPAC Users. In: Raitt, David I.; Jeapes, Ben, eds. Online Information 93: Proceedings of the 17th International Online Information Meeting; 1993 December 7-9; London, England. Oxford, England: Learned Information; 1994. 273-290. ISBN: 0-904933-85-7.

PITTS, JUDY M. 1995. Mental Models of Information: The 1993-94 AASL/ Highsmith Research Award Study. McGregor, Joy H.; Stripling, Barbara K., eds. School Library Media Quarterly. 1995 Spring; 23(3): 177-184. ISSN: 0278-4823.

ROSCH, ELEANOR. 1975. Cognitive Representations of Semantic Categories. Journal of Experimental Psychology: General. 1975; 104: 192-233. ISSN: 0096-3445.

ROSCH, ELEANOR. 1977. Classification of Real-World Objects: Origins and Representations in Cognition. In: Johnson-Laird, Philip Nicholas; Wason, Peter Cathcart, eds. Thinking: Readings in Cognitive Science. Cambridge, England: Cambridge University Press; 1977. 212-222. ISBN: 0-521-21756-3; ISBN: 0-521-29267-0 (paper).

ROSCH, ELEANOR; MERVIS, CAROLYN B.; GRAY, WAYNE; JOHNSON, DAVID; BOYES-BRAEM, PENNY. 1976. Basic Objects in Natural Categories. Cognitive Psychology. 1976 July; 8(3): 382-439. ISSN: 0010-0285.

RUMELHART, DAVID E. 1980. Schemata: The Building Blocks of Cognition. In: Spiro, Rand J.; Bruce, Bertram C.; Brewer, William F., eds. Theoretical Issues in Reading Comprehension: Volume 1. Hillsdale, NJ: Lawrence Erlbaum; 1980. 33-58. ISBN: 0-89859-036-1.

RUMELHART, DAVID E. 1983. Schemata and the Cognitive System. In: Gentner, Dedre; Stevens, Albert L., eds. Mental Models. Hillsdale, NJ: Lawrence Erlbaum; 1983. 161-188. ISBN: 0-89859-242-9.

SARVIMÄKI, ANNELI. 1988. Knowledge in Interactive Practice Disciplines: An Analysis of Knowledge in Education and Health Care. Helsinki, Finland: University of Helsinki; 1988. 276p. ISBN: 95-14-54787-X.

SCHANK, ROGER; ABELSON, ROBERT P. 1977. Scripts, Plans, Goals, and Understanding: An Inquiry into Human Knowledge Structures. Hillsdale, NJ: Lawrence Erlbaum; 1977. 203p. ISBN: 0-470-99033-3.

SEARLE, JOHN. 1969. Speech Acts: An Essay in the Philosophy of Language. Cambridge, England: Cambridge University Press; 1969. 203p. ISBN: 0-521-07184-4.

SEARLE, JOHN. 1984. Minds, Brains and Science. Cambridge, MA: Harvard University Press; 1984. 107p. ISBN: 0-674-57631-4; ISBN: 0-674-57633-0 (paper).

SHAW, DEBORA; FOUCHEREAUX, KAREN. 1993. Research Needs in Information Science. Bulletin of the American Society for Information Science. 1993 February/March; 19(3): 25. ISSN: 0095-4403; CODEN: BASICR.

SHERA, JESSE H. 1965a. Putting Knowledge to Work. In: Shera, Jesse H., ed. Libraries and the Organization of Knowledge. Hamden, CT: Archon Books; 1965. 51-62. OCLC: 574302. Also available in part in: Special Libraries. 1956 September; 47: 322-326. ISSN: 0038-6723.

SHERA, JESSE H. 1965b. What Lies Ahead in Classification. In: Shera, Jesse H., ed. Libraries and the Organization of Knowledge. Hamden, CT: Archon Books; 1965. 129-142. OCLC: 574302.

STAM, DEIRDRE C. 1991. What *About* the Mona Lisa? Making Bibliographic Databases More Useful to Art Historians by Classifying Documents According to the Aspect of Art Object(s) under Consideration. Art Documentation. 1991 Fall; 10(3): 127-130. ISSN: 0730-7187.

STAR, SUSAN LEIGH. 1989. The Structure of Ill-Structured Solutions: Heterogeneous Problem-Solving, Boundary Objects and Distributed Artificial Intelligence. In: Huhns, Michael N.; Gasser, Leslie G., eds. Distributed Artificial Intelligence 2. Menlo Park, CA: Morgan Kaufmann; 1989. 37-54. ISBN: 0-273-08810-6 (paper).

STAR, SUSAN LEIGH; GRIESEMER, JAMES R. 1989. Institutional Ecology, "Translations" and Boundary Objects: Amateurs and Professionals in Berkeley's Museum of Vertebrate Zoology, 1907-1939. Social Studies of Science. 1989; 19(3): 387-420. ISSN: 0306-3127.

STAR, SUSAN LEIGH; RUHLEDER, KAREN. 1996. Steps Toward an Ecology of Infrastructure: Design and Access for Large Information Spaces. Information Systems Research. 1996 March; 7(1): 111-134. ISSN: 1047-7047.

SUGAR, WILLIAM. 1995. User-Centered Perspective of Information Retrieval Research and Analysis Methods. In: Williams, Martha E., ed. Annual Review of Information Science and Technology: Volume 30. Medford, NJ: Information Today, Inc. for the American Society for Information Science; 1995. 77-109. ISSN: 0066-4200; ISBN: 1-57387-019-6; CODEN: ARISBC.

SUTTON, STUART A. 1994. The Role of Attorney Mental Models of Law in Case Relevance Determinations: An Exploratory Analysis. Journal of the American Society for Information Science. 1994 April; 45(3): 186-200. ISSN: 0002-8231; CODEN: AISJB6.

SWIFT, DONALD F.; WINN, VIOLA A.; BRAMER, DAWN A. 1977. A Multi-Modal Approach to Indexing and Classification. International Classification. 1977; 4(2): 90-94. ISSN: 0340-0050.

SWIFT, DONALD F.; WINN, VIOLA A.; BRAMER, DAWN A. 1979. A Sociological Approach to the Design of Information Systems. Journal of the American Society for Information Science. 1979 July; 30(4): 215-223. ISSN: 0002-8231; CODEN: AISJB6.

TESSIER, JUDITH A. 1992. Hypertext Linking as a Model of Expert Indexing. In: Kwaśnik, Barbara H.; Fidel, Raya, eds. Advances in Classification Research: Volume 2: Proceedings of the 2nd ASIS SIG/CR Classification

Research Workshop; 1991 October 27; Washington, DC. Medford, NJ: Learned Information, Inc.; 1992. 171-178. ISBN: 0-938734-67-9.

THOMPSON, BILL; THOMPSON, BEV. 1991. Overturning the Category Bucket. Byte. 1991 January; 16(1): 249-255. ISSN: 0360-5280.

TIBBO, HELEN R. 1992. Abstracting across the Disciplines: A Content Analysis of Abstracts from the Natural Sciences, the Social Sciences, and the Humanities with Implications for Abstracting Standards and Online Information Retrieval. Library & Information Science Research. 1992; 14: 31-56. ISSN: 0740-8188; CODEN: LISRDH.

TIJSSEN, R. J. W. 1993. A Scientometric Cognitive Study of Neural Network Research: Expert Mental Maps Versus Bibliometric Maps. Scientometrics. 1993; 28(1): 111-136. ISSN: 0138-9130.

TIMMERMANS, STEFAN; BOWKER, GEOFFREY C.; STAR, SUSAN LEIGH. 1998. The Architecture of Difference: Visibility, Control, and Comparability in Building a Nursing Interventions Classification. In: Berg, Marc; Mol, Annemarie, eds. Differences in Medicine. Durham, NC: Duke University Press; 1998. 202-225. ISBN: 0-8223-2162-9; ISBN: 0-8223-2174-2 (paper).

TURNER, JAMES M.; BÉLANGER, FRANÇOIS PAPIK. 1996. Escaping from Babel: Improving the Terminology of Mental Models in the Literature of Human-Computer Interaction. Canadian Journal of Information and Library Science. 1996 September-December; 21(3/4): 35-58. ISSN: 1195-096X.

VAN DIJK, TEUN ADRIANUS. 1979. Relevance Assignment in Discourse Comprehension. Discourse Processes. 1979; 2: 113-126. ISSN: 0163-853X.

VAN DIJK, TEUN ADRIANUS. 1980a. Macrostructures: An Interdisciplinary Study of Global Structures in Discourse, Interaction, and Cognition. Hillsdale, NJ: Lawrence Erlbaum; 1980. 317p. ISBN: 0-89859-039-6.

VAN DIJK, TEUN ADRIANUS. 1980b. Text and Context: Explorations in the Semantics and Pragmatics of Discourse. London, England: Longman; 1980. 216p. ISBN: 0-582-55085-8.

VAN DIJK, TEUN ADRIANUS; KINTSCH, WALTER. 1983. Strategies of Discourse Comprehension. New York, NY: Academic Press; 1983. 418p. ISBN: 0-12-712050-5.

WANTING, BIRGIT. 1984. How Do Children Ask Questions in Children's Libraries? Concepts of Visual and Auditory Perception and Language Expression. Social Science Information Studies. 1984 April/July; 4(2/3): 217-234. ISSN: 0143-6236; CODEN: SOSSD3.

WANTING, BIRGIT. 1986. Some Results from an Investigation in Danish Libraries. Scandinavian Public Library Quarterly. 1986; 19(3): 96-99. ISSN: 0036-5602.

WARD, MARTIN L. 1996. The Future of the Human Indexer. Journal of Librarianship and Information Science. 1996 December; 28(4): 217-225. ISSN: 0961-0006.

WEINBERG, BELLA HASS. 1988. Why Indexing Fails the Researcher. The Indexer. 1988 April; 16(1): 3-6. ISSN: 0019-4131; CODEN: IDXRA5.

WELLISCH, HANS H. 1995. Indexing from A to Z. 2nd edition, revised and enlarged. New York, NY: H.W. Wilson; 1995. 569p. ISBN: 0-8242-0882-X.

WILSON, THOMAS D. 1980. Information System Design Implications of Research into the Information Behaviour of Social Workers and Social Administrators. In: Harbo, Ole; Kajberg, Leif, eds. Theory and Application of Information Research: Proceedings of the 2nd International Research Forum on Information Science; 1977 August 3; Copenhagen, Denmark. London, England: Mansell; 1980. 198-213. ISBN: 0-7201-1513-2.

WILSON, THOMAS D.; STREATFIELD, DAVID R. 1977. Information Needs in Local Authority Social Services Departments: An Interim Report on Project INISS. Journal of Documentation. 1977; 33: 277-293. ISSN: 0022-0418; CODEN: JDOCAS.

WINOGRAD, TERRY. 1977. On Some Contested Suppositions of Generative Linguistics about the Scientific Study of Language. Cognition. 1977 June; 5(2): 151-179. ISSN: 0010-0277; CODEN: CGTNAU.

WITTGENSTEIN, LUDWIG. 1953. Philosophical Investigations. New York, NY: Macmillan; 1953. 232p. OCLC: 371912.

ZERUBAVEL, EVIATAR. 1991. The Fine Line: Making Distinctions in Every-day Life. Chicago, IL: University of Chicago Press; 1991. 205p. ISBN: 0-226-98159-2.

5 Metadata

SHERRY L. VELLUCCI
St. John's University

INTRODUCTION

As the Internet becomes an accepted source of electronic information, librarians and information specialists strive to improve methods for the description, organization, and retrieval of remotely accessed digitized objects. They are not alone in this endeavor, because creators, providers, and users of electronic resources in the academic, public, and commercial sectors also are concerned with managing this vast body of information. Each group has approached the problem of organization and access from its own frame of reference. VELLUCCI (1997) notes that it is important for these groups to recognize each other's contributions so that together they might provide a flexible structure for the organization and access of Internet resources. The strength of the structure is its ability to layer and exchange descriptive data from a wide variety of creators in a loosely coupled system of organization. The information used for this description and resource management is called metadata, a term that transcends boundaries among various stakeholders in the Internet arena and provides a common vocabulary to describe a variety of data structures. The stakeholders interested in metadata are diverse and include the computer scientists and engineers who develop Internet search engines and create standards for Internet documents, the scholars in specific disciplines who develop Internet texts and image documents and databases, the librarians and archivists who organize and provide access to electronic resources, and the general Internet users who want to improve web site retrieval.

Annual Review of Information Science and Technology (ARIST), Volume 33, 1998
Martha E. Williams, Editor
Published for the American Society for Information Science (ASIS)
By Information Today, Inc., Medford, NJ

Scope and Limitations

This review complements the 1996 *ARIST* chapter, "Cataloging and Classifying Information Resources on the Internet," by WOODWARD. Woodward covers the early literature on metadata from 1990 through part of 1996; this review covers metadata literature between mid-1996 and the beginning of 1998. Earlier documents are cited only when they are considered source material on a particular topic. Although Woodward compares traditional library cataloging with alternative methods of organization that use some early metadata structures, her review emphasizes approaches to organization and retrieval that employ classification schemes and subject terms; coverage of metadata structures is only a small portion of her topic. The focus of this literature review is specifically on the development and application of metadata standards used by the library and information science communities to describe, retrieve, and manage information in the digital environment. The large amount of literature on this topic and the number of existing metadata schemes required that boundaries be set for this review. Metadata schemes outside the purview of the library and information science communities, or those that are not widely used in the United States and other English-speaking countries, are not included here. Several topics closely associated with metadata, especially in the areas of identifiers, filters, content rating, digital signatures, digital libraries, preservation, and intellectual property rights, are also excluded.

Networked electronic information is often transitory, without the quality control or stability provided by the familiar peer-review and print publication process. For this reason, printed versions of electronic documents are cited when available; but like many of the documents that metadata seeks to manage, the current and relevant literature on this topic is frequently available only in electronic form via the Internet. Thus, the author selected documents that appear in established electronic journals, or those published under the auspices of an official organization. When this was not possible, the status and reputation of the document's author were considered determining factors for inclusion in this review.

Related Works

Articles and project reviews. In addition to the 1996 *ARIST* review by Woodward, several other metadata review articles and metadata project reviews have appeared in recent years. LANGE & WINKLER approach their review from a strong library cataloging point of view, comparing the pros and cons of traditional library cataloging with the newer metadata structures. They include background and history information for the early efforts of cataloging electronic resources, examine several general metadata structures, and provide an overview of digital libraries. They limit treatment of specialized metadata to the Text Encoding Initiative (TEI) header, the Encoded Archival Description (EAD), and the Federal Geographic Data Committee (FGDC) standards.

The United Kingdom is an especially strong supporter of projects that describe, compare, and evaluate metadata sets. An excellent article by HEERY (1996) systematically compares five metadata formats (IAFA/ Whois++, MARC, Text Encoding Initiative Headers, Dublin Core, and Uniform Resource Characteristics) in a preliminary report for the Resource Organisation and Discovery in Subject-Based Services (ROADS) project. Writing from the perspective of bibliographic control requirements, Heery establishes "a comparative context in which to discuss the IAFA (Internet Anonymous Ftp Archive) template which is being used in [the ROADS] project" (p. 345). She prefaces the evaluation by discussing the unique characteristics of network resources that must be considered when developing metadata standards. Particularly important is an awareness that remotely accessed objects with dynamic locations, fluid content, and many possible mirrored locations present unique problems for descriptive metadata. Heery's review is especially valuable because she evaluates each of the five metadata sets using identical criteria: constituency, ease of creation, content, associated Internet protocols, and progress toward international standard status.

A more extensive review of metadata by DEMPSEY & HEERY (1997) was prepared for the Development of a European Service for Information on Research and Education (DESIRE) Project, in order to assess the implications of using particular metadata schemes. An introductory section creates a typology of three metadata categories: (1) unstructured data, automatically extracted from resources and indexed for searching; (2) basic structured data that supports field searching of discrete objects; and (3) highly structured rich formats for location, discovery, and description of specialized, domain-specific discrete objects or collections. The second part of this review, which is one of the most comprehensive comparisons of metadata structures to date, includes details of 22 metadata formats and provides in-depth evaluation using the criteria earlier defined by HEERY (1996).

Another extensive project report, prepared for the Arts and Humanities Data Service (AHDS) and the UK Office for Library and Information Networking (UKOLN) by MILLER & GREENSTEIN, evaluates metadata in terms of their ability to enable resource discovery across domains and examines one specific metadata set, the Dublin Core. Miller and Greenstein adopt a different structural approach in this report. Rather than comparing many different metadata structures, they evaluate the metadata needs of many different arts and humanities communities. They examine a wide variety of media perspectives, including archaeological excavation and survey data, databases, digital images and image banks, electronic texts, digital and nondigital film and video, geospatial data, linguistic corpora, multimedia objects, and sound recordings. The report covers six domains: (1) archaeological and spatial data, (2) film and video, (3) historical data, (4) music, (5) texts, and (6) visual arts, museum, and cultural heritage information. For each domain, the authors assess how the Dublin Core meets the domain-specific requirements, recommend alterations of the Dublin Core to meet the requirements, and provide examples of how a core metadata set can be implemented for a range of information resources within that domain.

Metadata bibliographies and resource directories. A number of organizations maintain Web sites that organize and link to a variety of Web resources related to metadata. Most extensive is the Metadata Resources site of the INTERNATIONAL FEDERATION OF LIBRARY ASSOCIATIONS AND INSTITUTIONS. This extensive site covers 19 metadata schemes and includes links to articles, projects, and resources associated with specific schemes. Background documents and links to metadata authoring tools are also provided, along with annotations describing many of the resources.

Several metadata resource sites are maintained by government agencies and technology centers around the world. Especially noteworthy are the U.S. ENVIRONMENTAL PROTECTION AGENCY and the WORLD WIDE WEB CONSORTIUM (W3C) (1998a) sites in the United States, the UKOLN site in Great Britain (DAY & POWELL), and the Resource Discovery Unit site in Australia (DISTRIBUTED SYSTEMS TECHNOLOGY CENTRE). In addition to listing their own projects and initiatives, these sites connect to resources for many different metadata schemes, provide bibliographies of metadata publications and presentations, link to software tools for handling metadata, list crosswalk sites that map between various types of metadata, and provide other useful features such as glossaries of metadata terminology.

BAILEY's Scholarly Electronic Publishing Bibliography, which presents more than 600 articles, books, electronic documents, and other sources that are useful in understanding scholarly electronic publishing, contains an extensive section on "Cataloging, Classification, and Metadata." This bibliography covers both print and electronic resources, with live links to sources available on the Internet.

DEFINING AND CATEGORIZING METADATA

In their metadata review article, LANGE & WINKLER trace the history of the term metadata back to the 1960s, but note that the term began to appear more frequently in the literature on database management systems (DBMSs) in the 1980s. PHILLIPS, in a discussion of metadata for electronic records management, says the term is used to describe the information required to document the characteristics of information contained in databases. In the DBMS domain, which assumes that the computer is the milieu for both the data being described and the descriptive data itself, metadata is defined simply as data about data. This has become the fundamental definition upon which other definitions are built, and while the term metadata does not exclude non-electronic data, it is applied most often to data in electronic form.

The parallel world of library cataloging, with its centuries-old history of describing non-electronic objects by means of a detailed and established set of descriptive rules, traditionally uses the terms bibliographic data or cataloging data for this surrogate information. When information organization methods from library science and information science converged in the electronic environment, the term metadata, which already had the connotation of describing electronic data, became commonly used in both disciplines. The rudimentary definition, however, caused some in the library cataloging community to balk at the term on the basis that data about data, or metadata, is merely cataloging or bibliographic data by another name. In a conference paper that examines the development of geospatial metadata within the framework of traditional cataloging practice, LARSGAARD views it as ironic that cataloging information had to be called by a different term before the noncataloging community would deal with it. A somewhat more positive view is presented by CAPLAN (1995) in one of the early and most often cited articles on metadata. Caplan points out that an advantage of using the term metadata is that it is a neutral term with no pejorative meaning associated with it, while the traditional term catalog record carries negative connotations for many outside the library cataloging environment.

Other definitions of metadata provide more detail. For example, the WORLD WIDE WEB CONSORTIUM (1998a), the organization responsible for developing Web standards, defines metadata as "machine understandable information about Web objects," and includes a qualifying statement that metadata might be extended to apply to other electronic resources as they are developed in the future. In their metadata project review, DEMPSEY & HEERY (1997) define metadata as "data which describes attributes of a resource," or "data associated with objects which relieves their potential users of having to have full advance knowledge of their existence or characteristics." The latter definition, although awkwardly worded, incorporates the concept of metadata as a surrogate for the resource being described, and in that respect equates metadata with other types of document surrogates such as catalog records or index entries. In contrast, DANIEL & LAGOZE

(1997a, 1997b) emphasize that metadata can be data in their own right and that limiting it to a surrogate definition would be inaccurate. NG ET AL. (p. 341) introduce the functional concepts of relatedness, retrieval, and use into their operational definition of metadata as "data which characterizes source data, describes their relationships, and supports its discovery and effective use."

This review incorporates components of each of these definitions. Metadata is defined here as data that describe attributes of a resource, characterize its relationships, support its discovery and effective use, and exist in an electronic environment. Metadata usually consist of a set of data elements where each element describes an attribute of the resource, its management, or use. Figure 1 shows an example of normal data for an online article. Figure 2 shows an example of Dublin Core metadata for the same article.

Categories and Functions of Metadata

Many creators of metadata interpret the data-about-data definition within the narrow parameters of the cataloging community, that is, data that describe what the object is and provide access to the object. This concept of metadata as a basic resource descriptor that facilitates identification and retrieval is certainly a primary aspect; however, in the networked information infrastructure, other types of metadata are needed to serve different functions. A technical report that describes a new architecture for aggregating sets of metadata (LAGOZE, 1996; LAGOZE ET AL.) provides an excellent overview of six additional metadata types required for a variety of applications beyond the more narrow context of resource identification and description. These metadata categories expand on the functions of identification, description, and retrieval and thus extend into the areas of resource management and use. They include (1) terms and conditions data, (2) administrative data, (3) content ratings data, (4) provenance data, (5) linkage or relationship data, and (6) structural data. DEMPSEY (1996a) characterizes an additional type of metadata that can be used to describe community resources, including metadata about people, organizations, courses, research departments, and other objects. This last metadata category appears to be similar to the type of information provided by the MARC Community Information Format (LIBRARY OF CONGRESS. NETWORK DEVELOPMENT, 1993).

The extent to which any particular metadata set incorporates these data categories varies depending on the needs of the community responsible for its development and the age of the data format, that is, whether the metadata format is newly developed or based upon an existing structure. For example, the MARC record currently provides

VELLUCCI, SHERRY L. 1997. Options for Organizing Electronic Resources: The
Coexistence of Metadata. Bulletin of the American Society for Information Science.
1997 October/November; 24(1). ISSN: 0095-4403. Available WWW:
http://www.asis.org/Bulletin/Oct-97/vellucci.htm.

Figure 1. Normal Citation Data for Online Journal Article

```
<HTML>
<HEAD>
<TITLE></TITLE>
<META NAME="DC.Title" CONTENT="Options for Organizing Electronic Resources">
<META NAME="DC.Title.Alternative" CONTENT="The Coexistence of Metadata">
<META NAME="DC.Creator.PersonalName" CONTENT="Vellucci, Sherry L.">
<META NAME="DC.Creator.PersonalName.Address"
CONTENT="velluccs@stjohns.edu">
<META NAME="DC.Subject" SCHEME="LCSH" CONTENT="Metadata">
<META NAME="DC.Subject" SCHEME="LCSH" CONTENT="Cataloging of computer
network resources">
<META NAME="DC.Subject" SCHEME="LCSH" CONTENT="World Wide Web
(Information retrieval system)">
<META NAME="DC.Subject" SCHEME="DDC" CONTENT="005.721">
<META NAME="DC.Subject" SCHEME="LCC" CONTENT="QA76.9">
<META NAME="DC.Description" CONTENT="Article discusses organizing Internet
resources in library, scholarly, and Internet communities and the need to layer, exchange,
and translate data among various metadata formats.">
<META NAME="DC.Publisher" CONTENT="American Society for Information
Science">
<META NAME="DC.Publisher.Address" CONTENT="asis@asis.org">
<META NAME="DC.Date" SCHEME="ISO8601" CONTENT="1997-10">
<META NAME="DC.Type" CONTENT="Text.Article">
<META NAME="DC.Format" SCHEME="IMT" CONTENT="text/html">
<META NAME="DC.Identifier"
CONTENT="http://www.asis.org/Bulletin/Oct-97/vellucci.htm">
<META NAME="DC.Source" SCHEME="ISSN" CONTENT="0095-4403">
<META NAME="DC.Language" SCHEME="ISO639-1" CONTENT="en">
<META NAME="DC.Relation" CONTENT="Bulletin of the American Society for
Information Science, vol. 24, no. 1, October/November 1997">
<META NAME="DC.Rights" SCHEME="URL"
CONTENT="http://www.asis.org/policies/web-policy.html">
<META NAME="DC.Date.X-MetadataLastModified" SCHEME="ISO8601"
CONTENT="1998-10-03">
<LINK REL=SCHEMA.dc HREF="http://purl.org/metadata/dublin_core_elements">
</HEAD>
```

Figure 2. Metadata for Online Journal Article

for some of these data in both descriptive and nondescriptive fields, but because of its long history, the existing MARC format is less flexible than some of the new metadata structures and does not provide a logical conceptual structure for these data. LAGOZE ET AL. predict that the range of metadata categories needed to describe and manage electronic resources will continue to expand as users become more sophisticated in the use and control of networked information resources.

DEMPSEY & HEERY (1998) focus on the important role of metadata in resource discovery and retrieval. The authors give examples of metadata use by information seeking consumers and stress the need to define the relationships among objects in order to improve resource discovery. In a discussion of trends, they note the increasing use of metadata by Internet search engines and address the growing interest, by product developers such as Apple Computer, Netscape, and Microsoft, in metadata for resource retrieval.

The primary functions of metadata, therefore, are to facilitate the identification, location, retrieval, manipulation, and use of digitized objects in the networked electronic environment. Exactly which types of metadata are necessary to achieve these objectives and which data structure is optimal for storing, manipulating, and exchanging metadata are still to be determined and will vary depending on the user community.

Metadata Models

Three persistent questions relate to the creation and use of metadata: Who will provide it? What will be the level of description (often referred to as granularity)? Where will it reside? In their report on the second Metadata Workshop, HAKALA ET AL. note that when the metadata are contained inside documents, they are usually provided by the author. Schemes for metadata creation by authors and other nonspecialists must be simple, short, and easy to understand and use. Hakala et al. note that specialist catalogers will provide metadata for only a small percentage of the total electronic resources, concentrating on high-quality and durable documents. VELLUCCI (1996; 1997) discusses the pros and cons of basic self-generated descriptions from Internet search engines versus the detailed metadata provided by catalogers, archivists, and scholars in MARC records and TEI headers, and stresses the need for a way to mediate between these extremes. One answer is a basic metadata set embedded in documents that can be converted into a variety of metadata structures and expanded as needed.

CROMWELL-KESSLER summarizes the problem of granularity in her discussion of Dublin Core implementation when she observes that "aggregates of images or texts might be described as collections, as single entities, or as both. Determining the appropriate level of description and distinguishing between levels of description to insure intelligible assessment of search results can be problematic." Both Cromwell-Kessler and DANIEL & LAGOZE (1997a; 1997b) suggest fuller development of relationship metadata as one solution to this problem.

WEIBEL (1997) discusses three models for the creation and use of metadata: (1) the embedded model, where metadata are formulated by the creator of the electronic document and reside in the resource being described using the HTML META tag; (2) the third-party metadata model, where an agency creates, collects, and manages separate metadata records that refer to resources, but are not actually embedded in the resources; and (3) the view-filter model, where a distinct agency manages many metadata records, from a variety of sources using different structures, and maps these variant metadata descriptive sets into a common set such as the Dublin Core. In Weibel's embedded model, the metadata are integral to the resource, require no additional organizational system, and can be "harvested" by Web indexing agencies. The third-party model requires an organizational system to use the metadata and is exemplified by bibliographic records in a library catalog. This second model may link the separate metadata records to their electronic resource using the HTML HREF tag and the Uniform Resource Locator (URL) address. Weibel's view-filter model provides users with a single query model and facilitates a cross-disciplinary network infrastructure. Examples of each of these models can be found in the real metadata environment.

METADATA ELEMENT SETS

Metadata did not develop linearly. As each community that created or provided access to networked electronic resources developed its own methods to organize electronic information, parallel and independent metadata schemes gradually emerged. According to YOUNGER (p. 465), "each of these schemes is constructed from an understanding of specific domains, information resource needs, and unique requirements for describing document-like objects and was developed by experts closely associated with the field." Some of these structures, such as the MARC format and the Dublin Core Metadata Element Set, are general in nature and are designed to accommodate descriptive information about electronic resources in a wide variety of disciplines. Other metadata schemes, such as the Government Information Locator Service (GILS) and the Federal Geographic Data Committee (FGDC) Geospatial Metadata, are more specialized and apply to digital information in a specific discipline or domain.

Early Metadata: The Internet Community

The Internet Engineering Task Force (IETF) is one of the major international groups concerned with the architecture and operation of the Internet. The technical work of the IETF is conducted by working groups. Several early metadata structures were proposed or developed by IETF working groups, including RFC 1807 (LASHER & COHEN), a proposal that defines a format for the exchange of bibliographic descriptions of technical reports via electronic mail. Another metadata structure, the IAFA/ Whois++ templates, had wider applicability, and, therefore, appealed to a wider audience. File transfer protocol (ftp) was an early method used to access files of information via the Internet. The Internet Anonymous Ftp Archive (IAFA) working group of the IETF designed templates to facilitate effective access to ftp file information by describing the contents and services available from a particular ftp archive (HEERY, 1996). Template formats were created to describe a variety of resources, including images, documents, sound, services (such as listservs and databases), and software packages. Originally designed to help ftp site administrators organize and describe the files in their archives, IAFA templates were expanded to a metadata format that is simple enough to be generated by the wide variety of individuals and organizations responsible for both Web resources and ftp archives (HEERY, 1996).

IAFA template records are simple ASCII text with data elements defined as attribute/value pairs, and are used in a flat file structure that allows only limited relationship linkage. PALOWITCH & HOROWITZ list 27 suggested data elements in the record structure. The template includes both bibliographic data and record-management information, which allows system administrators to track and maintain information on rapidly changing resources. In addition, clusters of information are maintained about individuals and organizations (name, address, etc.), which can be used like authority data for a variety of purposes.

The directory service software Whois++ was developed to search IAFA templates across multiple databases. Because the ROADS project incorporated the IAFA/Whois++ templates into its software, several projects in the United Kingdom (UK) now use this metadata structure, including the Social Science Information Gateway (SOSIG) and the Organising Medical Information Gateway (OMNI) (HEERY, 1996). Heery notes that at present the IAFA template attribute sets and record structures do not fit well with those used by the Z39.50 Web interface protocol.

MARC as Metadata: The Library Community

When the library community decided to add bibliographic records for Internet resources to their local online public access catalogs (OPACs), they applied traditional cataloging techniques to the description of electronic resources using the *Anglo-American Cataloguing Rules (AACR) (AMERICAN LIBRARY ASSOCIATION)* and the USMARC format. JUL, the driving force behind the Online Computer Library Center's (OCLC) InterCat project (see below), cites many benefits of using traditional cataloging for Internet resources:

> Catalogers represent a highly trained workforce, with practitioners distributed across library types, subject areas and geographic locations. Moreover, this distributed workforce is linked through common standards, practices and systems that can be applied immediately to the problems of providing improved description and access for Internet resources. USMARC format bibliographic records can be readily exchanged among library systems, which means that the work of one cataloger can be distributed and subsequently incorporated into an infinite number of OPACs (p. 7).

At the same time, Jul also recognizes certain disadvantages of traditional cataloging practice, noting that it is labor-intensive and requires highly specialized skills.

As an electronic record structure designed to contain descriptive data, the MARC record is one of the earliest metadata structures. Several authors (DILLON & JUL; VELLUCCI, 1996; WOODWARD) discuss the initial days of cataloging electronic resources using the MARC format. All emphasize the importance of the MARC 856 field, which allowed the MARC format to become a serious contender as a metadata structure for Internet resource description. This relatively new MARC field contains resource location information, such as the Uniform Resource Locator (URL), and permits direct hypertext linking between the MARC record and the electronic resource. The Machine-Readable Bibliographic Information (MARBI) Committee, which maintains the USMARC format, developed detailed guidelines explaining the data content and use of the 856 field (LIBRARY OF CONGRESS. NETWORK DEVELOPMENT, 1997c). Both OCLC and the Library of Congress now publish guidelines to assist in cataloging electronic resources (LIBRARY OF CONGRESS. CATALOGING POLICY AND SUPPORT OFFICE; OLSON).

Projects using MARC as metadata. One of the earliest cataloging projects to use the MARC record to describe Internet resources was the InterCat project sponsored by OCLC. Several articles (DILLON & JUL; JUL; WOODWARD) provide background details of this two-phase project. The first phase examined the feasibility of applying traditional cataloging techniques to Internet resources. According to JUL, this phase had the two major results mentioned above: development of the MARC 856 field and publication of a cataloging manual for describing Internet resources (OLSON). The second phase of the InterCat project saw the expansion of the Web-based InterCat Catalog through the voluntary participation of librarians worldwide who selected and cataloged Internet resources. This proof-of-concept database "demonstrated the union of catalog searching with its host of functions—keyword and phrase searching, selected index searching and Boolean operations— with direct Web access to the Internet resources" (JUL, p. 6). The InterCat catalog continues to grow as MARC cataloging for electronic resources is integrated into the daily routine of many libraries.

MORGAN describes another early project—albeit an informal, local endeavor rather than a nationally funded project—that used MARC-based records to create a Web catalog. After addressing some of the broader issues involved with cataloging Internet resources, Morgan explains the evolution of the Alcuin Catalog of Internet resources. Originally called the Alex Catalog and designed for Gopher links using a simple dBase IV database, the project was later expanded to include the newly developed hypertext transfer protocol (HTTP) of the World Wide Web. Morgan describes this evolution from the Gopher link database to a Web browser front-end catalog based on the MARC record.

MARC-based literature. The InterCat project served to raise the consciousness of library catalogers regarding the organization of Internet resources and MARC as a home for metadata, and a body of literature soon began to evolve. Several articles discuss the more practical considerations of developing policies and procedures for cataloging Internet resources (BEALL; JOHNS; NEUMEISTER; SUN). BEALL's brief article focuses on the issues of cataloging Web sites that consist primarily of links to other Internet resources, sites which he suggests should be thought of as a modern form of bibliography. In addition to describing the main types and characteristics of these sites, Beall discusses questions of granularity and subject access.

The articles on cataloging Internet resources by JOHNS and NEUMEISTER complement each other in that Johns presents the administrative viewpoint, while Neumeister presents the practitioner viewpoint. Both authors describe their participation in the OCLC InterCat Project. Johns adopts a question-and-answer format to discuss administrative issues that must be addressed before beginning an Internet resources cataloging project. She then discusses the administrative process of decision making, planning, and implementation for her library's participation in the InterCat Project. Neumeister addresses the more pragmatic side of the project, including issues of seriality, OPAC record and holdings display, and multiple versions of documents in electronic and paper form.

SUN examines the problems involved in MARC cataloging for remotely accessed Chinese electronic serials. These include the use of vernacular character sets, the need for Chinese system software, parallel access points in both romanized and vernacular character sets, and the complexity of Chinese name authority control.

Other authors contributed to the discussion in a more theoretical way, evaluating the pros and cons of MARC-based cataloging and comparing it with other developing metadata schemes. These comparisons frequently refer to the more popular metadata schemes such as the Text Encoding Initiative (TEI) Header and the Dublin Core metadata element set (BRUGGER; GAYNOR; HILLMAN; JENG; PALOWITCH & HOROWITZ; VELLUCCI, 1996, 1997; YOUNGER). Two project reports cited earlier in this review by DEMPSEY & HEERY (1997) and HEERY (1996) include detailed discussions of MARC as metadata.

SGML-Based Metadata:
Scholarly, Archival, and Museum Communities

Just as the MARC format currently provides the encoded record structure for most library OPACs, markup languages form the encoded structure for many Internet documents. But unlike MARC, where the bibliographic record is separate from the document it describes, markup languages can be used to encode both the descriptive data and the object being described. This allows metadata to be imbedded within the document itself. Currently, the most common markup language used for metadata is Standard Generalized Markup Language (SGML).

The term document type definition (DTD) refers to implementations of SGML. Widely used as a nonproprietary standard for text encoding, SGML supports the definition of various data element sets for specific types of documents (LIBRARY OF CONGRESS. NETWORK DEVELOPMENT, 1997d). GAYNOR explains that DTDs "define types of documents and their structures by stating what elements are required in a particular type, and what elements may be present in the document. The structure of a document can be marked up and checked against a DTD . . . to ensure that it is valid and that it conforms to the structure of the document type defined by the DTD" (p. A). Probably the best-known DTD is Hypertext Markup Language (HTML), the markup language of the World Wide Web.

MARC Document Type Definition (MARC DTD). A document type definition was developed recently for the MARC format to create an SGML DTD that supports the conversion of cataloging data back and forth between the MARC data structure and SGML without loss of data. The underlying structure for this conversion from one metadata format to another is called a crosswalk. The Network Development and MARC Standards Office at the Library of Congress provides a detailed discussion of the background and development of the MARC DTD, including its design principles and considerations, its attributes and naming conventions, and issues involved in converting data from MARC to SGML (LIBRARY OF CONGRESS. NETWORK DEVELOPMENT, 1997d). GAYNOR notes that the new MARC DTD is designed for use in a library online catalog that employs SGML as its underlying record format, and is the first step toward a Web-based catalog that is both Z39.50-compliant and SGML-aware.

Text Encoding Initiative (TEI) headers. One of the earliest metadata schemes to use SGML developed in the international scholarly communities of literature and linguistics as a means of embedding descriptive data in SGML-encoded text. The TEI developed guidelines for the preparation and interchange of electronic texts in the broadest sense, including both textual and nontextual resources in electronic form (SPERBERG-MCQUEEN & BURNARD). The descriptive documentation for each TEI-encoded document can be embedded in the TEI-conformant text it describes, or it can be maintained in a separate file and point to the electronic text. Called the TEI header, this required documentation provides information about the text, its source, its encoding practices, and its revision history.

GIORDANO provides an excellent detailed overview of the form and function of the TEI header. He explains that the TEI header describes both bibliographic and nonbibliographic information, and supports the identification, retrieval, and machine-analysis of encoded text. He describes and presents marked-up examples of the four functional header components: (1) file description, (2) encoding description, (3) profile description, and (4) revision description. The file description portion is modeled on the *Anglo-American Cataloguing Rules (AACR)* and International Standard Bibliographic Description (ISBD) standards for cataloging, and is somewhat analogous with the title page of a book. Giordano says the TEI header can vary greatly in size and complexity depending on the nature of the project and the amount of information that encoders wish to attach to the text. The final section of Giordano's article discusses the pros and cons involved with the use of the TEI header to support document retrieval and analysis.

In her review of various metadata formats, HEERY (1996) provides another, more succinct, overview of the TEI header. After a brief background discussion on the development of the TEI project, she describes three operational settings for use of the TEI header. (1) As part of TEI-conformant text, it can be used by researchers in textual analysis and as a means of bibliographic control. (2) As an independent header, it can be used in catalogs or databases to refer to remote TEI-encoded texts. (3)

As an independent header, it also can be used in catalogs or databases to describe networked resources that are not themselves TEI-encoded. Heery says that it is only in this last capacity that the TEI header fits her broad context for metadata that can be applied to any electronic resource. In describing the content designation of the TEI header, Heery emphasizes the flexibility of the TEI guidelines, which allow for both structured and unstructured data. She notes that many of the structured data elements prescribed by the Guidelines are based on *AACR* and ISBD, thus allowing a certain level of interoperability between TEI header information and MARC records.

VELLUCCI (1996) also addresses interoperability, noting that several groups within the library community are examining possibilities for the automatic conversion of TEI header information into a MARC record. She discusses the *tei2marc* computer conversion program, developed at the University of Virginia, that reads the data from a TEI header and converts them, field by field, into a MARC record format. PALOWITCH & HOROWITZ discuss problems with conversion between TEI headers and MARC records. They explain that the flexible TEI headers do not require structured data or authority-controlled headings, and that often there is not one-to-one mapping between a TEI header tag and a specific MARC field. Vellucci speculates that as it becomes more prevalent, this process of data conversion between TEI headers, MARC records, or any other metadata format may become the copy cataloging of tomorrow.

More than 60 electronic text projects use the TEI Guidelines for full-text markup (TEXT ENCODING INITIATIVE). However, although several articles discuss the content and use of TEI headers in theoretical terms, few projects discuss the specific use of the TEI header in the retrieval process (as opposed to the entire text markup). DUNLOP does focus on use of the TEI header in the British National Corpus project, and also brings another perspective to the discussion: description at the corpus or collection level. As project manager, Dunlop uses TEI headers in three capacities: (1) to describe a corpus, (2) to describe an individual text, and (3) as a free-standing bibliographic record. He offers detailed discussion of the four TEI header components, suggests ways to use the corpus (i.e., collective) header for information that is common to many texts in the collection, and touches on such issues as automatic generation of headers in a relational database structure. Because Dunlop writes for readers already familiar with SGML and TEI encoding terminology, readers unfamiliar with the details of the TEI application of SGML coding might be confused by many of the cryptic tag references.

Another project description that discusses the use of TEI metadata is presented by GARTNER. Gartner describes the Bodleian Library's first digital imaging project: a collection of printed ephemera images covering motoring and transportation from the library's John Johnson Collection. Gartner explains briefly the process of database creation using TEI metadata linked to scanned images, and provides an example of database retrieval results that presents an image of the document with its associated bibliographic data. This article would be more helpful to others contemplating such a project if the author had provided greater depth and detail in his project description.

In a comparison of the USMARC format and the TEI Header, BRUGGER uses the access points defined by the Stanford Digital Libraries Project Information Bus as the basis for comparison. She concludes that although the USMARC format provides a useful level of detail and precision, the TEI Header presents more possibilities as a metadata system for the future. She says the TEI Header has two advantages over USMARC: it uses the same verbal tagging to encode both the document and the header (the surrogate), and it embeds the surrogate data in the document it describes. Brugger cautions readers to "pay attention to what the creators and users of digital libraries say they want us to provide for them, and that we do not close ourselves off to a radical re-thinking of USMARC" (p. 72).

PALOWITCH & HOROWITZ state that a new metadata structure should be part of a larger network architecture, and therefore more generally applicable than the current SGML-encoded TEI header on which the new metadata structure would be based. Their metadata vision includes the best features of the IAFA templates, the TEI header, and the MARC record, and creates a metadata standard potentially acceptable to all Internet communities. Additionally, they see the need for a network authority-control server to maintain and distribute authority records for all known Uniform Resource Locators (URLs).

Encoded Archival Description (EAD) metadata. Another SGML DTD was developed more recently for the archival community, to respond to the increasing role of networks in accessing information and a desire to expand on the data provided in the MARC record. A cooperative project based at the University of California, Berkeley investigated the feasibility of developing a nonproprietary encoding standard for machine-readable finding aids (THIBODEAU ET AL.). Two years of development resulted in a new SGML standard: the Encoded Archival Description (EAD) DTD. Although the term finding aid usually includes inventories, registers, indexes, and other documents created for archives, libraries, museums, and manuscript repositories to support the use of their holdings, the EAD standard was designed primarily for inventories and registers. Finding aids typically describe a unique collection, its intellectual organization, and its components.

According to THIBODEAU ET AL., the functional requirements for the new EAD standard include "1) the ability to present extensive and interrelated descriptive information found in archival finding aids; 2) the ability to preserve the hierarchical relationships existing between levels of description; 3) the ability to represent descriptive information that is inherited by one hierarchical level from another; 4) the ability to move within a hierarchical information structure; and 5) support for element-specific indexing and retrieval." SGML was selected as the markup language because it accommodates these complex formatting and navigation requirements better than the less sophisticated HTML.

The newly developed EAD DTD consists of two segments: the header segment, which was modeled on the TEI header and consists of information about the finding aid itself, and a segment that describes a body of archival material (the actual finding aid) (THIBODEAU ET AL.). In a detailed comparison of three SGML metadata formats—TEI, EAD, and Computer Interchange of Museum Information (CIMI)—BURNARD & LIGHT note that the components of the EAD header differ slightly from those of the TEI header. The authors also explain that the finding-aid segment may include two types of information: hierarchical information that describes a unit of records or papers and their components, and adjunct information that facilitates use of the described unit. The EAD is considered pure metadata because the finding aids themselves are metadata. In this sense, the EAD header, which describes the finding aid, can be considered meta-metadata.

The EAD DTD standard is currently maintained by the Library of Congress, in partnership with the Society of American Archivists (LIBRARY OF CONGRESS. NETWORK DEVELOPMENT, 1997b). One of the early implementations of the EAD standard was by the Library of Congress when it made the registers of its archival collections available via the World Wide Web (DAVIS-BROWN & WILLIAMSON). The EAD Web home page provides a list of links to archival projects with EAD finding aids. It includes the collaborative American Heritage Virtual Archive and the Berkeley Finding Aid Project, along with finding-aid projects of many individual universities and museums. In an article that discusses one such project, the Digital Scriptorium at Duke University, HENSEN describes the need for this newly developed metadata standard when he states that "digital information as it exists on the Internet today requires more navigational, contextual, and descriptive data than is currently provided in traditional card catalogs or their more modern electronic equivalent." Hensen discusses the merits of the EAD metadata structure in a seamless online environment in which a scholar can launch a search for archival material in an online catalog, follow dynamic links from that catalog into ever more detailed layers of description, and ultimately access digital images in the collection.

One current drawback to the use of EAD finding aids (or any SGML-encoded document) is that they require an SGML-aware search engine for document retrieval and can be viewed only with an SGML viewer such as Panorama, unless the SGML encoding is converted to HTML so that it can be read by current Web browsers. Fred: The SGML Grammar Builder is an ongoing research project at OCLC to study the manipulation of encoded text. Some repositories are experimenting with the use of Fred to translate their EAD SGML finding aids on the fly into HTML files for distribution over the Web (LIBRARY OF CONGRESS. NETWORK DEVELOPMENT, 1997b).

Two recent issues of *The American Archivist* (DOOLEY, 1997a; 1997b) are devoted entirely to the EAD. These issues contain two categories of papers: conceptual essays describing the context in which EAD exists as a watershed development in archival automation, and implementation case studies offering a variety of approaches to use of these new metadata. The conceptual category consists of articles written by active participants in the development of EAD. The authors include Steven deRose (the value of SGML as a tool for structuring, navigating, and controlling information), Michael Fox (critical management issues involved with implementation of EAD), Steven Hensen (EAD as a key element in a seamless web of online tools for description of and access to archival materials), Kris Kiesling (the process to develop EAD as an official archival standard and the development and management of EAD documentation), Daniel Pitti (early development of the EAD DTD at UC Berkeley), and Janice Ruth (overview of the structure of EAD). Six articles describing implementation case studies are by Nicole Bouche (Yale University), Elizabeth Dow (University of Vermont), Dennis Meissner (Minnesota Historical Society), Anne Mitchell and Mary Lacy (Library of Congress), Leslie Morris (Harvard University), and David Seaman (University of Virginia).

Domain-Specific Metadata

Metadata that are developed within and for a specific discipline are often referred to as domain-specific metadata. In some cases, a specific syntactic structure is prescribed for the data. In other cases, the metadata structure is designed to be syntax-independent.

Computer Interchange of Museum Information (CIMI DTD) and other visual metadata. The international Consortium for the Computer Interchange of Museum Information (CIMI) adopted SGML as an interchange format in 1994, and has been experimenting with it in various projects (BURNARD & LIGHT). As part of Project CHIO (Cultural Heritage Information Online), CIMI developed an SGML DTD for exhibition catalogs. This is the first DTD in a comprehensive set of DTDs to be developed for each genre of museum information (DEMPSEY & HEERY, 1997). Burnard and Light explain that this domain-specific application of the generic TEI framework uses the standard TEI header to encode core metadata about each document. Particular emphasis is placed on bibliographic information and information about conditions of access. The authors explain that the CIMI DTD introduces metadata concepts that apply within the document itself. Notable among these concepts are the ability to define primary and secondary access points, to define topics that can apply to the entire document or only sections of it and, for advanced retrieval purposes, to define a context for a specific topic.

In their comparison of the three SGML metadata schemes, BURNARD & LIGHT observe that the TEI is the most general (i.e., least prescriptive), in that it is intended to accommodate the widest variety of documents, while both the EAD and the CIMI metadata records are more prescriptive, in that they are intended for use with specific kinds of documents. The detailed comparison by Burnard and Light includes discussion of the linking systems used by the schemes, the user community, control agency, expression of metadata, metadata concepts supported, rules for formulation of content, extensibility, future development, and relationships to other schemes (Dublin Core and MARC).

The Visual Arts Data Service (VADS), one component of the Arts and Humanities Data Service (AHDS), produced a domain-specific review of standards for visual arts, museum, and cultural heritage information (GILL ET AL.). The CIMI DTD is among the dozen standards for visual materials described in the review, which contains a table of the 35 basic access points defined for the CIMI DTD. Other metadata standards primarily define core records that are not SGML-based. These include the Dublin Core; IAFA Templates; the Art Information Task Force's Categories for the Description of Works of Art; the Visual Arts Network for the Exchange of Cultural Knowledge (Van Eyck); the Visual Resources Association (VRA) Core Record; the Documentation Committee of the International Council of Museums (CIDOC) standards; SPECTRUM: The UK Museum Documentation Standard; and the Scottish Cultural Resources Access Network (SCRAN) Data Standards. The review provides a basic description of each visual metadata standard, lists its basic data elements, and includes links to other Web sites that provide fuller descriptions of each standard.

Government Information Locator Service (GILS). GILS is designed as a metadata system to document government information, and is treated here as domain-specific metadata. The origins of GILS and its metadata component are well documented (ADAMS & THIBODEAU; ANDREWS & DUHON; MOEN). Mandated by U.S. law, GILS was implemented to help the public identify, locate, access, and acquire government information distributed by a wide range of agencies, and to reduce duplication of information by different government agencies. MOEN describes in detail the distributed client/server structure designed to operate with the Z39.50 Internet retrieval protocol. Each GILS server is a machine-readable database that contains locator records describing federal information resources. Locator records consist of numerous metadata elements that identify, describe, and provide access to information for a particular resource. Moen provides a description of the registered GILS core element metadata set. Guidelines for applying the core data are available from several other sources (CANADA, 1996a; U. S. NATIONAL ARCHIVES).

CHRISTIAN describes the expansion of GILS into the global information infrastructure, where the acronym has changed to mean Global Information Locator Service. He explains that one advantage of GILS for the international arena is that it references registered semantic data elements rather than a specific syntactic structure. This affords GILS an interoperability that is not tied to any one format for structured metadata. Thus, GILS can support the interoperable search of many different metadata structures such as MARC, SGML, or Dublin Core, to name a few. GILS is already implemented in Japan, Canada, and Australia, and Christian says there is now consensus among the G7 countries to employ GILS as infrastructure for a Global Environmental Locator Service. The Canadian government currently provides guidelines for creating GILS records in an SGML environment (CANADA, 1996b), while a recent report from Australia indicates that the Dublin Core is being explored as the possible structure for the Australian Government Locator Service (AUSTRALIAN GOVERNMENT LOCATOR SERVICE WORKING GROUP).

Geospatial Metadata. Developed by the Federal Geographic Data Committee, the Content Standards for Digital Geospatial Metadata (CSDGM) is often referred to as the FGDC standard (FEDERAL GEOGRAPHIC DATA COMMITTEE). Under executive order of the U.S. government, federal agencies began using FGDC standards to document new geospatial data in 1995, providing the metadata to the public through the National Geospatial Data Clearinghouse (DEMPSEY & HEERY, 1997). An early article by ALLEN sets the context for discussion of the FGDC metadata standard by providing an overview of the committee's evolution and its place and function in the National Information Infrastructure and the National Spatial Data Infrastructure. Allen explains that this metadata standard "is intended to help prospective users determine what data already exist, the quality of the data, conditions for accessing the data, and what might be required to process the data" (ALLEN, p. 12). To this end, all metadata for digital geospatial data will be centrally maintained by the National Geospatial Data Clearinghouse.

The FGDC standard was developed to provide common terminology and definitions for the documentation of digital geospatial data. It establishes the names of simple and compound data elements, defines them, and establishes information about the values to be provided for them (FEDERAL GEOGRAPHIC DATA COMMITTEE). One weakness of the FGDC standard, according to T.R. SMITH (1996a), is that it does not accommodate description of analog spatial materials as well as it does digital objects. He also views the lack of a formally defined FGDC metadata syntactic structure as a drawback because it results in a variety of structural implementations that make the import and export of FGDC metadata more difficult.

DOMARATZ also describes the development of the National Spatial Data Infrastructure and the National Geospatial Data Clearinghouse, but expands the purely geographic context by explaining that needs for spatial data exist in a variety of socioeconomic and demographic communities. Domaratz's emphasis is on finding and retrieving data. He explains the role of geospatial metadata in this process and suggests that the data producer is the best source for creating metadata. He describes seven informational characteristics of spatial metadata: (1) identification information, (2) data quality information, (3) spatial data organization information, (4) spatial reference information, (5) entity/attribute information, (6) distribution information, and (7) metadata reference information. Domaratz envisions the future as a dynamic environment where the entire community will contribute, share, integrate, and use spatial data for varying units of space, time, and thematic detail.

The collection of conference papers in which the Domaratz article appears (L.C. SMITH & GLUCK) also covers in depth several other aspects of geospatial metadata. LARSGAARD describes the strengths and weaknesses of using USMARC and the *Anglo-American Cataloguing Rules (AACR)* to catalog planetospatial data in digital form. Planetospatial data are similar to cartographic data but encompass more than maps. Larsgaard defines planetospatial data as narrower than spatial data, which encompass measurement of any type of object in space, and broader than geospatial data in that they are not limited to data about the earth. Her discussion addresses briefly the problems associated with multilevel description, subject headings, bounding coordinates, and time. Larsgaard argues for *AACR* rule revision to focus more on content rather than carrier format. MOEN addresses the use of Government Information Locator Service (GILS) metadata records for discovering, identifying, and accessing spatial data that are created, collected, or held by government agencies. With an emphasis on retrieval, Moen discusses the primary metadata elements that characterize spatial data selection (attributes, time, and user task) and explains how these elements can be used to search for and retrieve spatial data. The real strength of this paper, however, is in its clear and concise general explanation of the GILS, its data element set, and the GILS retrieval process, which is based on the Z39.50 information retrieval protocol.

The Alexandria Project (FREW ET AL.; T.R. SMITH, 1996a, 1996b) was designed to explore problems related to a distributed library for geographically referenced information. The ALEXANDRIA DIGITAL LIBRARY (ADL) is the centerpiece of the project. The ADL collection includes a variety of geospatial data coupled with its metadata, as well as stand-alone metadata for a variety of geographic reference sources. T.R. SMITH (1996a) describes the implementation of the ADL catalog using metadata that combines features of USMARC for structure and FGDC metadata for spatial content.

Cooperative Efforts: The Dublin Core Element Set

NG ET AL. suggest that the task of developing standards for metadata at the document level must be a cooperative effort among system designers, who traditionally develop standards for network interoperability, and data providers, bibliographic information specialists, and electronic text-encoding specialists. The recent literature on metadata indicates that this is happening. Although independent groups are developing metadata for their own constituencies, collaborative international projects are also underway to define and test standards for metadata content and architectures that will allow the necessary interoperability of data in the networked environment.

The Dublin Core metadata scheme (DUBLIN CORE METADATA), named for the site of the first Metadata Workshop held in Dublin, Ohio, is maintained by OCLC and developed in an international, interdisciplinary environment through the collaboration of various Internet stakeholders. Originally conceived for author-generated description of Web resources, the Dublin Core metadata effort has expanded to include the interests of libraries and other communities concerned with resource description. According to the report of the first Metadata Conference, the scheme was conceived with six guiding principles: (1) intrinsicality, (2) extensibility, (3) syntax-independence, (4) optionality, (5) repeatability, and (6) modifiability (WEIBEL ET AL., 1995). The number of descriptive data elements has increased from 13 to the current 15 elements. Weibel, the central figure behind the development of the Dublin Core, views the scheme as a lowest common denominator for resource description. He does not see it as a replacement for richer description models, but rather as a set of elements that can be used by anyone for simple resource description. This simplicity and flexibility coupled with a stable environment (OCLC) for continued development makes the Dublin Core the major metadata focal point today (CROMWELL-KESSLER & ERWAY).

Dublin Core literature. An excellent introduction to the growing body of literature on the Dublin Core is provided by THIELE. His review categorizes the literature into five clusters: (1) proceedings and reports from various workshops; (2) crosswalks and mapping Dublin Core to other metadata systems; (3) relationship of standards organizations to Dublin Core; (4) digital library and metadata projects; and (5) miscellaneous articles. Thiele says most of the literature has been descriptive in nature and suggests that future research should take a more empirical approach to the behavioral, technical, and sociological aspects of Dublin Core metadata.

The content and structure of the Dublin Core data element set were developed through a series of workshops that began in 1995 (CAPLAN, 1997; DUBLIN CORE METADATA; MILLER & GILL; WEIBEL ET AL., 1995, 1997; WEIBEL & HAKALA; WEIBEL & MILLER). THIELE provides a brief description of the contributions and refinements made by each of the five workshops held to date, including expansion from 13 to 15 elements, additional support of networked nontextual resources, and the development of formalized qualifiers and syntactical expressions related to HTML. A variety of support documents and discussion papers describes Dublin Core refinements and extensions (BAKER; BECKETT; CROMWELL-KESSLER; DUBLIN CORE METADATA; GUENTHER; KNIGHT & HAMILTON; E.J. MILLER, 1996; RESEARCH LIBRARIES GROUP; SPERBERG-MCQUEEN; WEIBEL, 1996). Several articles and Web sites discuss interoperability issues involved with mapping Dublin Core elements to other metadata schemes (CAPLAN & GUENTHER; CROMWELL-KESSLER & ERWAY; LIBRARY OF CONGRESS. NETWORK DEVELOPMENT, 1997e), and providing crosswalk details (DAY, 1997b; LIBRARY OF CONGRESS. NETWORK DEVELOPMENT, 1997a; E.J. MILLER, 1997).

Dublin Core projects and applications. As momentum grew in support of the Dublin Core metadata element set, its potential for a variety of general and domain-specific resource descriptions was evaluated (DEMPSEY & HEERY, 1997; HEERY, 1996; MILLER & GREENSTEIN), and projects implementing the Dublin Core were undertaken. The Dublin Core Web site (DUBLIN CORE METADATA) provides an extensive list of more than 40 projects arranged by country with links and brief descriptions of each project.

In addition to these projects, several authors discuss possible implementations of the Dublin Core and tools designed to generate Dublin Core records. P. MILLER provides examples of Dublin Core applications using HTML and discusses use of the <LINK> tag for clarifying ambiguities. SUTTON & OH explain their efforts to expand on the basic Dublin Core element set to include domain-specific metadata useful in the description and retrieval of educational resources. POWELL describes three models for managing metadata across a Web site and describes tools such as Server Side Include (SSI) scripts and DC-dot to embed Dublin Core metadata into Web pages. GODBY & MILLER describe the Spectrum Cataloging Markup Language (SCML), a tool that can extract data from structured records, implement extensions to the Dublin Core element set, and generate Dublin Core records. KNIGHT (1997b) examines the possibility of incorporating Dublin Core elements into Apple Computer's Metadata Content Format (MCF), and its use with Apple metadata tools such as HotSauce. In another article, KNIGHT (1997a) describes how a metadata convertor module written in Perl can be used to extract Dublin Core metadata embedded in HTML documents and convert it into a skeleton MARC record. Finally, CRIDDLE describes the possible use of Dublin Core metadata for a public libraries initiative in the United Kingdom, while DAY (1997a) suggests how metadata such as the Dublin Core can be extended to provide information in the area of digital preservation.

Cooperative Efforts: Metadata Architecture

Early in the development of the Dublin Core element set, questions arose about the usefulness of such a simple, unstructured metadata core, the type and extent of metadata that should be included, and the relationship of Dublin Core metadata to other metadata schemes under development (LAGOZE, 1996; LAGOZE ET AL.). According to LAGOZE (1996), workshop attendees at the second metadata meeting held in Warwick, England, concluded that progress lay in the formulation of a higher-level context for the Dublin Core, which "should define how the Core can be combined with other sets of metadata in a manner that addresses the individual integrity, distinct audiences, and separate realms of responsibility of these distinct metadata sets." The meeting resulted in the conceptualization of what is called the Warwick Framework.

The Warwick Framework. The Warwick Framework is a container architecture for aggregating multiple sets of metadata; it allows lowest-common-denominator descriptions such as Dublin Core to exist alongside complex descriptions such as MARC, and enables access to each or all metadata packages. THIELE notes that much of the theoretical structure of the Warwick Framework is based on the concept of the distributed digital object as theorized by KAHN & WILENSKY. While several workshop reports are available that describe the development and structure of the Warwick Framework (DEMPSEY & WEIBEL; HAKALA

ET AL.; LAGOZE, 1996; LAGOZE ET AL.), LAGOZE ET AL. provide the most detailed and extensive explanation. The authors set the context for development of the new architecture with a discussion of the functions, creators, users, and structural models of metadata. They define the two fundamental components of the Framework: the packages, or typed metadata sets, and the container, or unit for aggregating the metadata sets. They explain in detail the types of metadata packages and types and operations of containers. Several unresolved issues for the Warwick Framework are addressed in the report. These include semantic interaction of overlapping sets, type registry for metadata packages, syntax for data encoding at the container level, efficient operation of the distributed architecture, and protocols for repository access. Framework implementation models that extend beyond the existing Web infrastructure are described in detail, including HTML, MIME, SGML, and Distributed Object environments.

DANIEL & LAGOZE (1997a; 1997b) generalize the Warwick Framework concept to allow containers to hold or reference any type of digital resource—not just metadata—both inside and outside the container. The authors recognize the need to express explicitly the relationships between networked resources, and to allow those relationships to be dynamically downloadable and executable. In these two insightful papers, Daniel and Lagoze describe the development of an extension to the Warwick Framework called Distributed Active Relationships (DARs). DARs operate within the context of a Warwick Framework Catalog, which provides the mechanism for expressing relationships between the packages in a Warwick Framework container. Two possible implementations of the DAR framework are offered, one that uses the Flexible and Extensible Digital Object Repository Architecture (FEDORA) and a second that employs the Resource Description Framework (RDF).

Resource Description Framework (RDF). The Resource Description Framework is the latest architecture and is currently under development (WORLD WIDE WEB CONSORTIUM, 1998b). Like the Warwick Framework, the RDF provides an infrastructure to support automated processing of metadata across the Internet and allows for content description and relationship expression of a particular Web site, Web page, or digital library. It serves as a data model for representing metadata and a possible syntax for expressing and transporting the metadata in a way that maximizes the interoperability of independently developed Web servers and clients (WORLD WIDE WEB CONSORTIUM, 1998a). Unlike the Warwick Framework, RDF is restricted to the use of eXtensible Markup Language (XML) for encoding the metadata, although the basic data model is syntax-independent. The full RDF specification is available online (WORLD WIDE WEB CONSORTIUM, 1998c).

In her basic overview of the RDF architecture, HEERY (1998) explains that the RDF data model represents the properties of a resource and the values of those properties. The data model, which influences the way properties are described, makes the structure of the descriptions explicit. While this means that the RDF works well describing Web resources, Heery questions its ability to accommodate legacy data, that is, older data such as MARC, that is not based on such a data model. In spite of her wait-and-see attitude, Heery recognizes that the RDF has potential significance as an architectural framework for the Dublin Core community. The UKOLN Metadata Resources site (DAY & POWELL) provides several examples of Dublin Core data encoded in RDF.

CONCLUSIONS

This chapter covers many diverse metadata schemes that describe a wide variety of networked resources. There is no doubt that individual user communities will continue to develop and enhance domain-specific metadata. The cataloging community will expand its work with MARC metadata and experiment with ways of using other metadata schemes both in and beyond existing OPACS. Other information communities, such as text scholars, art and museum curators, and government agencies will work to improve the cross-domain search capabilities of domain-specific data. As DEMPSEY & HEERY (1998) predict, the wider Internet community will proceed with its own vision of resource description and retrieval by using metadata to refine search engines. Metadata will become an integral organizing component of the Web and various aspects of desktop applications. The difference between the current scenario and the early days of isolated metadata development, however, is the collective level of awareness and the realization that interoperability is critical for the development of all future systems. This is exemplified in the efforts to develop the Dublin Core, the Warwick Framework, and the Resource Description Framework. Almost all metadata efforts now occur on an international stage and are applied on an international basis. Increasingly, metadata will be used in an integrated multilevel networked environment. But unlike the hesitant developers of library catalogs who were constrained by the structural limitations of the MARC record and vast quantities of legacy data, metadata developers are free to experiment with new architectures that fully utilize the two things that computers do well: connectivity and computation (DANIEL & LAGOZE, 1997a, 1997b). This area of metadata research will see a great deal of activity in the future.

Several authors (CROMWELL-KESSLER; DANIEL & LAGOZE, 1997a, 1997b; DEMPSEY & HEERY, 1998) predict that there will be more emphasis in the future on improving the ways in which metadata systems express relationships and link related data. CROMWELL-KESSLER speculates that the RDF, when implemented, may offer solutions to the relationship problem, as this framework is better able to handle one-to-one relationship links between sets of metadata describing a single entity. Both metadata content and structure must be examined for ways to identify and provide different levels of description that respond meaningfully to user queries. Metadata must be able to clarify issues of surrogacy and to provide context to distinguish between data used as data and data used as metadata. This will become increasingly important if issues of granularity, surrogacy, multiple versions, and cross-domain descriptions are to be resolved.

In addition to these concerns, researchers will continue to develop tools for the automatic extraction, generation, and conversion of descriptive metadata, while metadata structures will be extended to include many of the other metadata categories discussed by LAGOZE ET AL. There is no doubt that evolving architectural structures such as the Distributed Active Relationships (DARs) described by DANIEL & LAGOZE (1997a, 1997b) eventually will be commonplace. The new structures will require a broader application of data registries in order to develop into truly efficient retrieval systems. These issues begin to press the boundaries of this review, however, and must be left for future chapters on metadata.

BIBLIOGRAPHY

ADAMS, MARGARET O'NEILL; THIBODEAU, SHARON GIBBS. 1996. The Government Information Locator Service: Origins and Potential. Journal of Government Information. 1996; 23(4): 453-462. ISSN: 1352-0237.

ALEXANDRIA DIGITAL LIBRARY. 1997. Alexandria Digital Library Home Page. 1997. Available WWW: http://alexandria.sdc.ucsb.edu/.

ALLEN, ROBERT S. 1995. An Overview of the Federal Geographic Data Committee, National Spatial Data Infrastructure, National Geospatial Data Clearinghouse, and the Digital Geospatial Metadata Standard: What Will It Mean for Tomorrow's Libraries? Bulletin of the Special Libraries Association Geography and Map Division. 1995 June; 180: 2-28. ISSN: 0036-1607.

AMERICAN LIBRARY ASSOCIATION. 1988. Anglo-American Cataloguing Rules. 2nd edition; 1988 revision. Chicago, IL: American Library Association; 1988. 677p. (Prepared by the Joint Steering Committee for Revision of AACR; Gorman, Michael; Winkler, Paul W., eds.). ISBN: 0-8389-3346-7; LC: 88-19349.

ANDREWS, JUDY; DUHON, LUCY. 1997. GILS, Government Information Locator Service: Blending Old and New to Access US Governmental Information. Serials Librarian. 1997; 31(1/2): 327-333. ISSN: 0361-526X.

ARMS, WILLIAM Y.; BLANCHI, CHRISTOPHE; OVERLY, EDWARD A. 1997. An Architecture for Information in Digital Libraries. D-Lib Magazine.

1997 February. ISSN: 1082-9873. Available WWW: http://www.dlib.org/dlib/february97/cnri/02arms1.html.

AUSTRALIAN GOVERNMENT LOCATOR SERVICE WORKING GROUP. 1997. Australian Government Locator Service Implementation Plan. 1997 December. Available WWW: http://www.aa.gov.au/AA_WWW/AGLSfinal.html.

BAILEY, CHARLES W., JR. 1998. Scholarly Electronic Publishing Bibliography. Version 21. 1998 September 18. Available WWW: http://info.lib.uh.edu/sepb/sepb.html.

BAKER, THOMAS. 1997. Metadata Semantics Shared across Languages: Dublin Cores in Languages Other Than English. 1997. Available WWW: http://www.cs.ait.ac.th/~tbaker/Cores.html.

BEALL, JEFFREY. 1997. Cataloging World Wide Web Sites Consisting Mainly of Links. Journal of Internet Cataloging. 1997; 1(1): 83-92. ISSN: 1091-1367.

BECKETT, DAVE. 1996. Proposed Encodings for Dublin Core Metadata. Draft V0.4. 1996 December 3. Available WWW: http://www.cs.ukc.ac.uk/people/staff/djb1/research/metadata.

BRUGGER, JUDITH M. 1996. Cataloging for Digital Libraries. Cataloging & Classification Quarterly. 1996; 22(3/4): 59-73. ISSN: 0163-9374.

BULLETIN OF THE AMERICAN SOCIETY FOR INFORMATION SCIENCE. 1997. Organizing Internet Resources: Metadata and the Web. Bulletin of the American Society for Information Science. 1997 October/November; 24(1): 29p. (Entire issue on title topic). ISSN: 0095-4403; CODEN: BASICR.

BURNARD, LOU; LIGHT, RICHARD. 1996. Three SGML Metadata Formats: TEI, EAD, and CIMI: A Study for BIBLINK Work Package 1.1. 1996 December. Available WWW: http://hosted.ukoln.ac.uk/biblink/wp1/sgml/.

CANADA. 1996a. The Canadian Government Information Locator Service Guidelines for the Preparation of GILS Records. 1996. Available WWW: http://gils.gc.ca/gils/guide_e.html.

CANADA. 1996b. Creating GILS Records in an SGML Environment. 1996. Available WWW: http://gils.gc.ca/gils/creatingg_e.html.

CAPLAN, PRISCILLA L. 1995. You Call It Corn, We Call It Syntax-Independent Metadata for Document-Like Objects. The Public-Access Computer Systems Review. 1995; 6(4): 19-23. ISSN: 1048-6542. Also available WWW: http://info.lib.uh.edu/pr/v6/n4/capl6n4.html.

CAPLAN, PRISCILLA L. 1997. To Hel(sinki) and Back for the Dublin Core. The Public-Access Computer Systems Review. 1997; 8(4): 26-30. ISSN: 1048-6542. Also available WWW: http://info.lib.uh.edu/pr/v8/n4/capl8n4.html.

CAPLAN, PRISCILLA L.; GUENTHER, REBECCA. 1996. Metadata for Internet Resources: The Dublin Core Metadata Elements Set and Its Mapping to USMARC. Cataloging & Classification Quarterly. 1996; 22(3/4): 43-58. ISSN: 0163-9374.

CHRISTIAN, ELIOT J. 1996. GILS: What Is It? Where's It Going? D-Lib Magazine. 1996 December. ISSN: 1082-9873. Available WWW: http://www.dlib.org/dlib/december96/12christian.html.

CRIDDLE, SALLY. 1997. Public Libraries Corner: A Public Library Metadata Initiative. Ariadne: The Web Version. 1997 September; 11. ISSN: 1361-

3200.   Available   WWW: http://www.ariadne.ac.uk/issue11/public-
   libraries/.
CROMWELL-KESSLER, WILLY. 1997. Dublin Core Metadata in the RLG
   Information Landscape. D-Lib Magazine. 1997 December. ISSN: 1082-
   9873.   Available WWW: http://www.dlib.org/dlib/december97/
   12cromwell-kessler.html.
CROMWELL-KESSLER, WILLY; ERWAY, RICKY. 1997. Metadata Summit:
   Organized by the Research Libraries Group, Mountain View, California:
   Meeting Report. 1997 July. Available WWW: http://www.rlg.org/
   meta9707.html.
DANIEL, RON, JR.; LAGOZE, CARL. 1997a. Distributed Active Relationships
   in the Warwick Framework. In: Proceedings of the 2nd IEEE Metadata
   Conference; 1997 September 16-17; Silver Spring, MD. Available WWW:
   http://computer.org/conferen/proceed/meta97/papers/rdaniel/
   rdaniel.pdf.
DANIEL, RON, JR.; LAGOZE, CARL. 1997b. Extending the Warwick Framework: From Metadata Containers to Active Digital Objects. D-Lib Magazine. 1997 November. ISSN: 1082-9873. Available WWW: http://
   www.dlib.org/dlib/november97/daniel/11daniel.html.
DAVIS-BROWN, BETH; WILLIAMSON, DAVID. 1996. Cataloging at the
   Library of Congress in the Digital Age. Cataloging & Classification Quarterly. 1996; 22(3/4): 171-196. ISSN: 0163-9374.
DAY, MICHAEL. 1997a. Extending Metadata for Digital Preservation. Ariadne:
   The Web Version. 1997 May; 9. ISSN: 1361-3200. Available WWW: http:/
   /www.ariadne.ac.uk/issue9/metadata/.
DAY, MICHAEL. 1997b.   Metadata: Mapping between Metadata Formats.
   1997 December 22. Available WWW: http://www.ukoln.ac.uk/metadata/
   interoperability/.
DAY, MICHAEL; POWELL, ANDY. 1998. Metadata. UK Office for Library
   and Information Networking (UKOLN). 1998. Available WWW: http://
   www.ukoln.ac.uk/metadata/.
DEMPSEY, LORCAN. 1996a. Meta Detectors. Ariadne: The Web Version.
   1996 May; 3. ISSN: 1361-3200. Available WWW: http://
   www.ariadne.ac.uk/issue3/metadata/.
DEMPSEY, LORCAN. 1996b. ROADS to Desire: Some UK and Other Euro-
   pean Metadata and Resource Discovery Projects. D-Lib Magazine. 1996
   July/August. ISSN: 1082-9873. Available WWW: http://www.dlib.org/
   dlib/july96/07dempsey.html.
DEMPSEY, LORCAN; HEERY, RACHEL. 1997. A Review of Metadata: A
   Survey of Current Resource Description Formats. Work Package 3 of
   Telematics for Research Project DESIRE (RE 1004). 1997 May 15. Available
   WWW: http://www.ukoln.ac.uk/metadata/desire/overview/.
DEMPSEY, LORCAN; HEERY, RACHEL. 1998. Metadata: A Current View of
   Practice and Issues. Journal of Documentation. 1998 March; 54(2): 145-172.
   ISSN: 0022-0418; CODEN: JDOCAS.
DEMPSEY, LORCAN; WEIBEL, STUART L. 1996. The Warwick Metadata
   Workshop: A Framework for the Deployment of Resource Description.
   1996. Available WWW: http://www.oclc.org/oclc/research/publications/
   review96/warwick.htm.

DESAI, BIPIN C. 1997. Supporting Discovery in Virtual Libraries. Journal of the American Society for Information Science. 1997 March; 48(3): 190-204. ISSN: 0002-8231.

DILLON, MARTIN; JUL, ERIK. 1996. Cataloging Internet Resources: The Convergence of Libraries and Internet Resources. Cataloging & Classification Quarterly. 1996; 22(3/4): 197-238. ISSN: 0163-9374.

DISTRIBUTED SYSTEMS TECHNOLOGY CENTRE. 1998. Resource Discovery Unit. 1998. Available WWW: http://www.dstc.edu.au/RDU/.

DOMARATZ, MICHAEL. 1996. Finding and Accessing Spatial Data in the National Spatial Data Infrastructure. In: Smith, Linda C.; Gluck, Myke, eds. Geographic Information Systems and Libraries: Patrons, Maps, and Spatial Information: Papers Presented at the 1995 Clinic on Library Applications of Data Processing, Graduate School of Library and Information Science, University of Illinois at Urbana-Champaign; 1995 April 10-12; Urbana, IL. Champaign, IL: University of Illinois, Graduate School of Library and Information Science; 1996. 31-40. ISBN: 0-87845-097-1.

DOOLEY, JACKIE M., ed. 1997a. Encoded Archival Description. Part 1: Context and Theory. The American Archivist. 1997 Summer; 60(3): 264-366. (Entire issue on title topic). ISSN: 0360-9081.

DOOLEY, JACKIE M., ed. 1997b. Encoded Archival Description. Part 2: Case Studies. The American Archivist. 1997 Fall; 60(4): 367-496. (Entire issue on title topic). ISSN: 0360-9081.

DUBLIN CORE METADATA. 1997. Dublin Core Metadata. 1997 November 2. Available WWW: http://purl.oclc.org/metadata/dublin_core/main.html.

DUNLOP, DOMINIC. 1995. Practical Considerations in the Use of TEI Headers in a Large Corpus. Computers and the Humanities. 1995; 29(1): 85-98. ISSN: 0010-4817.

FEDERAL GEOGRAPHIC DATA COMMITTEE. 1998. Content Standard for Digital Geospatial Metadata. 1998. Available WWW: http://www.fgdc.gov/metadata/contstan.html.

FREW, JAMES; FREESTON, MICHAEL; KEMP, RANDALL B.; SIMPSON, JASON; SMITH, TERENCE R.; WELLS, ALEX; ZHENG, QI. 1996. The Alexandria Digital Library Testbed. D-Lib Magazine. 1996 July/August. ISSN: 1082-9873. Available WWW: http://www.dlib.org/dlib/july96/alexandria/07frew.html.

GARTNER, RICHARD. 1997. Digitising the Bodleian Revisited: Linking Word and Image. Audiovisual Librarian: Multimedia Information. 1997 February; 23(1): 47-50. ISSN: 0302-3451.

GAYNOR, EDWARD. 1996. From MARC to Markup: SGML and Online Library Systems. ALCTS Newsletter. 1996; 7(2): A-D. (Insert: From Catalog to Gateway: Briefings from the Cataloging Form and Function Committee (CFFC); no. 7). ISSN: 1047-949X. Also available WWW: http://www.lib.virginia.edu/speccol/scdc/articles/alcts_brief.html.

GILL, TONY; GROUT, CATHERINE; SMITH, LOUISE. 1997. Visual Arts, Museums, & Cultural Heritage Information Standards: A Domain-Specific Review of Relevant Standards for Networked Information Discovery. 1997 March 20. Available WWW: http://vads.ahds.ac.uk/standards.html.

GIORDANO, RICHARD. 1995. The TEI Header and the Documentation of Electronic Texts. Computers and the Humanities. 1995; 29(1): 75-84. ISSN: 0010-4817.

GODBY, C. JEAN; MILLER, ERIC J. 1997. A Metalanguage for Describing Internet Resources. The Annual Review of OCLC Research 1996. Dublin, OH: OCLC; 1997. 45-49. ISSN: 0894-198X. Also available WWW: http://www.purl.org/oclc/review1996.

GUENTHER, REBECCA. 1997. Dublin Core Qualifiers/Substructure: A Proposal. 1997 October 15. Available WWW: http://www.loc.gov/marc/dcqualif.html.

HAKALA, JUHA; HUSBY, OLE; KOCH, TRAUGOTT. 1996. Warwick Framework and Dublin Core Set Provide a Comprehensive Infrastructure for Network Resource Description: Report from the Metadata Workshop II, Warwick, UK, April 1-3, 1996. 1996 June 10. Available WWW: http://www.nordinfo.helsinki.fi/nordnytt/nnytt2_96/nn_2_9.htm.

HEERY, RACHEL. 1996. Review of Metadata Formats. Program. 1996; 30(4): 345-373. ISSN: 0033-0337. Also available as a pre-publication draft WWW: http://www.ukoln.ac.uk/metadata/review.html.

HEERY, RACHEL. 1998. What Is . . . RDF? Ariadne: The Web Version. 1998 March; 14. ISSN: 1361-3200. Available WWW: http://www.ariadne.ac.uk/issue14/what-is/.

HENSEN, STEVEN L. 1997. Primary Sources, Research, and the Internet: The Digital Scriptorium at Duke. First Monday. 1997 September 1; 2(9). LC: sn97-36844. Available WWW: http://www.firstmonday.dk/issues/issue2_9/hensen/.

HILLMAN, DIANE I. 1996. "Parallel Universes" or Meaningful Relationships: Envisioning a Future for the OPAC and the Net. Cataloging & Classification Quarterly. 1996; 22(3/4): 97-103. ISSN: 0163-9374.

INTERNATIONAL FEDERATION OF LIBRARY ASSOCIATIONS AND INSTITUTIONS. 1998. Digital Libraries: Metadata Resources. 1998 March 26. Available WWW: http://www.nlc-bnc.ca/ifla/II/metadata.htm.

JENG, LING HWEY. 1996. A Converging Vision of Cataloging in the Electronic World. Information Technology and Libraries. 1996 December; 15(4): 222-230. ISSN: 0730-9295.

JOHNS, CECILY. 1997. Cataloging Internet Resources: An Administrative View. Journal of Internet Cataloging. 1997; 1(1): 17-23. ISSN: 1091-1367.

JUL, ERIK. 1997. Cataloging Internet Resources: Survey and Prospectus. Bulletin of the American Society for Information Science. 1997 October/November; 24(1): 6-9. ISSN: 0095-4403; CODEN: BASICR

KAHN, ROBERT; WILENSKY, ROBERT. 1995. A Framework for Distributed Digital Object Services. 1995 May 13. Available WWW: http://www.cnri.reston.va.us/cstr/arch/k-w.html.

KNIGHT, JON. 1997a. Making a MARC with Dublin Core. Ariadne: The Web Version. 1997 March; 8. ISSN: 1361-3200. Available WWW: http://www.ariadne.ac.uk/issue8/marc/.

KNIGHT, JON. 1997b. Will Dublin Form the Apple Core? Ariadne: The Web Version. 1997 January; 7. ISSN: 1361-3200. Available WWW: http://www.ariadne.ac.uk/issue7/mcf/.

KNIGHT, JON; HAMILTON, MARTIN. 1997. Dublin Core Qualifiers. Draft
    Document. 1997. ROADS. Available WWW: http://www.roads.lut.ac.uk/
    Metadata/DC-Qualifiers.html.
LAGOZE, CARL. 1996. The Warwick Framework: A Container Architecture
    for Diverse Sets of Metadata. D-Lib Magazine. 1996 July/August. ISSN:
    1082-9873. Available WWW: http://www.dlib.org/dlib/july96/lagoze/
    07lagoze.html.
LAGOZE, CARL. 1997. From Static to Dynamic Surrogates: Resource Discov-
    ery in the Digital Age. D-Lib Magazine. 1997 June. ISSN: 1082-9873.
    Available WWW: http://www.dlib.org/dlib/june97/06lagoze.html.
LAGOZE, CARL; LYNCH, CLIFFORD A.; DANIEL, RON, JR. 1996. The
    Warwick Framework: A Container Architecture for Aggregating Sets of
    Metadata. 1996 July 12. Available WWW: http://cs-tr.cs.cornell.edu:80/
    Dienst/Repository/2.0/Body/ncstrl.cornell%2fTR96-1593/html.
LANGE, HOLLEY R.; WINKLER, B. JEAN. 1997. Taming the Internet: Metadata,
    a Work in Progress. In: Godden, Irene, ed. Advances in Librarianship:
    Volume 21. San Diego, CA: Academic Press; 1997. 47-72. ISSN: 0065-2830.
LARSGAARD, MARY LYNETTE. 1996. Cataloging Planetospatial Data in
    Digital Form: Old Wine, New Bottles—New Wine, Old Bottles. In: Smith,
    Linda C.; Gluck, Myke, eds. Geographic Information Systems and Librar-
    ies: Patrons, Maps, and Spatial Information: Papers Presented at the 1995
    Clinic on Library Applications of Data Processing, Graduate School of
    Library and Information Science, University of Illinois at Urbana-
    Champaign; 1995 April 10-12; Urbana, IL. Champaign, IL: University of
    Illinois, Graduate School of Library and Information Science; 1996. 17-30.
    ISBN: 0-87845-097-1.
LASHER, R.; COHEN, D. 1995. RFC1807: A Format for Bibliographic Records.
    1995 June. Available WWW: http://www.cis.ohio-state.edu/htbin/rfc/
    rfc1807.html.
LIBRARY OF CONGRESS. CATALOGING POLICY AND SUPPORT OFFICE
    (CPSO). 1997. Draft Interim Guidelines for Cataloging Electronic Re-
    sources. 1997. Available WWW: http://lcweb.loc.gov/catdir/cpso/
    elec_res.html.
LIBRARY OF CONGRESS. NETWORK DEVELOPMENT AND MARC STAN-
    DARDS OFFICE. 1993. USMARC Format for Community Information:
    Including Guidelines for Content Designation. Washington, DC: Catalog-
    ing Distribution Service; 1993. 1 volume. ISBN: 0-84440-779-8; LC: 92-45199.
LIBRARY OF CONGRESS. NETWORK DEVELOPMENT AND MARC STAN-
    DARDS OFFICE. 1997a. Dublin Core/MARC/GILS Crosswalk. 1997
    April 7. Available WWW: http://lcweb.loc.gov/marc/dccross.html.
LIBRARY OF CONGRESS. NETWORK DEVELOPMENT AND MARC STAN-
    DARDS OFFICE. 1997b. The Encoded Archival Description Document
    Type Definition. Available WWW: http://lcweb.loc.gov/ead/.
LIBRARY OF CONGRESS. NETWORK DEVELOPMENT AND MARC STAN-
    DARDS OFFICE. 1997c. Guidelines for the Use of Field 856. Revised 1997
    August. Available WWW: http://lcweb.loc.gov/marc/856guide.html.
LIBRARY OF CONGRESS. NETWORK DEVELOPMENT AND MARC STAN-
    DARDS OFFICE. 1997d. MARC DTDs: Document Type Definitions:

Background and Development. 1997 February 21. Available WWW: http://lcweb.loc.gov/marc/marcdtd/marcdtdback.html.

LIBRARY OF CONGRESS. NETWORK DEVELOPMENT AND MARC STANDARDS OFFICE. 1997e. Metadata, Dublin Core and USMARC: A Review of Current Efforts. (MARBI Discussion Paper no. 99). 1997 January 21. Available WWW: http://lcweb.loc.gov/marc/marbi/dp/dp99.html.

LYONS, PATRICE A. 1997/1998. Managing Access to Digital Information: Some Basic Terminology Issues. Bulletin of the American Society for Information Science. 1997/1998 December/January; 24(2): 21-24. ISSN: 0095-4403; CODEN: BASICR.

MILLER, ERIC J. 1996. An Approach for Packaging Dublin Core Metadata in HTML 2.0. 1996. Available WWW: http://www.oclc.org:5046/~emiller/publications/metadata/minimal.html.

MILLER, ERIC J. 1997. Monticello Electronic Library: Dublin Core Element Set Crosswalk. 1997. Available WWW: http://www.oclc.org:5046/~emiller/DC/crosswalk.html.

MILLER, PAUL. 1996. Metadata for the Masses. Ariadne: The Web Version. 1996 September; 5. ISSN: 1361-3200. Available WWW: http://www.ariadne.ac.uk/issue5/metadata-masses/.

MILLER, PAUL; GILL, TONY. 1997. Down Under with the Dublin Core. Ariadne: The Web Version. 1997 March; 8. ISSN: 1361-3200. Available WWW: http://www.ariadne.ac.uk/issue8/canberra-metadata/intro.html.

MILLER, PAUL; GREENSTEIN, DANIEL. 1997. Discovering Online Resources across the Humanities: A Practical Implementation of the Dublin Core. 1997. Arts and Humanities Data Service (AHDS) and UK Office for Library and Information Networking (UKOLN). Available WWW: http://ahds.ac.uk/public/metadata/discovery.html.

MOEN, WILLIAM E. 1996. The Government Information Locator Service: Discovering, Identifying, and Accessing Spatial Data. In: Smith, Linda C.; Gluck, Myke, eds. Geographic Information Systems and Libraries: Patrons, Maps, and Spatial Information: Papers Presented at the 1995 Clinic on Library Applications of Data Processing, Graduate School of Library and Information Science, University of Illinois at Urbana-Champaign; 1995 April 10-12; Urbana, IL. Champaign, IL: University of Illinois, Graduate School of Library and Information Science; 1996. 41-67. ISBN: 0-87845-097-1.

MORGAN, ERIC LEASE. 1996. Possible Solutions for Incorporating Digital Information Mediums into Traditional Library Cataloging Services. Cataloging & Classification Quarterly. 1996; 22(3/4): 143-170. ISSN: 0163-9374.

NEUMEISTER, SUSAN M. 1997. Cataloging Internet Resources: A Practitioner's Viewpoint. Journal of Internet Cataloging. 1997; 1(1): 25-45. ISSN: 1091-1367.

NG, KWONG BOR; PARK, SOYEON; BURNETT, KATHLEEN. 1997. Control or Management: A Comparison of the Two Approaches for Establishing Metadata Schemes in the Digital Environment. In: Schwartz, Candy; Rorvig, Mark, eds. Digital Collections: Implications for Users, Funders, Developers, and Maintainers: Proceedings of the American Society for Information Science (ASIS) 60th Annual Meeting: Volume 34; 1997 November 1-6; Washington, DC. Medford, NJ: Information Today, Inc. for

ASIS; 1997. 337-346. ISSN: 0044-7870; ISBN: 1-57387-048-X; LC: 64-8303; CODEN: PAISDQ.

OLSON, NANCY B., ed. 1997. Cataloging Internet Resources: A Manual and Practical Guide. 2nd edition. Dublin, OH: OCLC; 1997. 55p. ISBN: 1-55653-236-9. Also available WWW: http://www.purl.org/oclc/cataloging-internet.

PALOWITCH, CASEY; HOROWITZ, LISA. 1996. Meta-Information Structures for Networked Information Resources. Cataloging & Classification Quarterly. 1996; 22(3/4): 127-141. ISSN: 0163-9374.

PHILLIPS, JOHN T. 1995. Metadata: Information about Electronic Records. ARMA Records Management Quarterly. 1995 October; 29(4): 52-57. ISSN: 0191-1503.

POWELL, ANDY. 1997. Dublin Core Management. Ariadne: The Web Version. 1997 July; 10. ISSN: 1361-3200. Available WWW: http://www.ariadne.ac.uk/issue10/dublin/.

RESEARCH LIBRARIES GROUP. 1997. Guidelines for Extending the Use of Dublin Core Elements to Create a Generic Application Integrating All Kinds of Information Resources. Draft. 1997 October 1. Available WWW: http://www.rlg.org/metawg.html.

SMITH, LINDA C.; GLUCK, MYKE, eds. 1996. Geographic Information Systems and Libraries: Patrons, Maps, and Spatial Information: Papers Presented at the 1995 Clinic on Library Applications of Data Processing, Graduate School of Library and Information Science, University of Illinois at Urbana-Champaign; 1995 April 10-12; Urbana, IL. Champaign, IL: University of Illinois, Graduate School of Library and Information Science; 1996. 240p. ISSN: 0069-4789; ISBN: 0-87845-097-1.

SMITH, TERENCE R. 1996a. A Digital Library for Geographically Referenced Materials. Computer. 1996 May; 29(5): 54-60. ISSN: 0018-9162. Also available WWW: http://computer.org/computer/dli/r50054/r50054.htm.

SMITH, TERENCE R. 1996b. The Meta-Information Environment of Digital Libraries. D-Lib Magazine. 1996 July/August. ISSN: 1082-9873. Available WWW: http://www.dlib.org/dlib/july96/new/07smith.html.

SPERBERG-MCQUEEN, C. M. 1996. On Information Factoring in Dublin Metadata Records. 1996 April 17. Available WWW: http://www.uic.edu/~cmsmcq/tech/metadata.factoring.html.

SPERBERG-MCQUEEN, C. M.; BURNARD, LOU. 1994. Guidelines for Electronic Text Encoding and Interchange. Chicago, IL; Oxford, England: Text Encoding Initiative; 1994. Also available WWW: http://etext.virginia.edu/TEI.html.

SUN, DAJIN. 1997. Issues in Cataloging Chinese Electronic Journals. Journal of Internet Cataloging. 1997; 1(1): 65-82. ISSN: 1091-1367.

SUTTON, STUART A.; OH, SAM G. 1997. GEM: Using Metadata to Enhance Internet Retrieval by K-12 Teachers. Bulletin of the American Society for Information Science. 1997 October/November; 24(1): 21-24. ISSN: 0095-4403.

TEXT ENCODING INITIATIVE. 1998. Text Encoding Initiative Home Page. 1998 April 1. Available WWW: http://www.uic.edu:80/orgs/tei/.

THIBODEAU, SHARON G.; PITTI, DANIEL V.; BARRY, RANDALL K. 1996. Development of the Encoded Archival Description Document Type Definition. 1996 August. Available WWW: http://lcweb.loc.gov/ead/eadback.html.

THIELE, HAROLD. 1998. The Dublin Core and Warwick Framework: A Review of the Literature, March 1995-September 1997. D-Lib Magazine. 1998 January. ISSN: 1082-9873. Available WWW: http://www.dlib.org/dlib/january98/01thiele.html.

TRAVICA, BOB. 1997. Organizational Aspects of the Virtual/Digital Library: A Survey of Academic Libraries. In: Schwartz, Candy; Rorvig, Mark, eds. Digital Collections: Implications for Users, Funders, Developers, and Maintainers: Proceedings of the American Society for Information Science (ASIS) 60th Annual Meeting: Volume 34; 1997 November 1-6; Washington, DC. Medford, NJ: Information Today, Inc. for ASIS; 1997. 149-161. ISSN: 0044-7870; ISBN: 1-57387-048-X; LC: 64-8303; CODEN: PAISDQ.

U.S. ENVIRONMENTAL PROTECTION AGENCY. 1998. EPA Scientific Metadata Standards Project. 1998. Available WWW: http://www.lbl.gov/~olken/epa.html.

U. S. GEOLOGICAL SURVEY. 1997. GILS (Global Information Locator Service/Government Information Locator Service) Home Page. 1997. Available WWW: http://www.usgs.gov/public/gils/.

U. S. NATIONAL ARCHIVES AND RECORDS ADMINISTRATION. 1995. Guidelines for the Preparation of GILS Core Entries. 1995. Available WWW: http://www.dtic.mil/gils/documents/naradoc/.

VELLUCCI, SHERRY L. 1996. Herding Cats: Options for Organizing Electronic Resources. Internet Reference Services Quarterly. 1996; 1(4): 9-30. ISSN: 1087-5301.

VELLUCCI, SHERRY L. 1997. Options for Organizing Electronic Resources: The Coexistence of Metadata. Bulletin of the American Society for Information Science. 1997 October/November; 24(1): 14-17. ISSN: 0095-4403.

WEIBEL, STUART L. 1996. A Proposed Convention for Embedding Metadata in HTML. 1996 June 2. Available WWW: http://www.oclc.org/~weibel/html-meta.html.

WEIBEL, STUART L. 1997. The Dublin Core: A Simple Content Description Model for Electronic Resources. Bulletin of the American Society for Information Science. 1997 October/November; 24(1): 9-11. ISSN: 0095-4403.

WEIBEL, STUART L.; GODBY, C. JEAN; MILLER, ERIC J.; DANIEL, RON, JR. 1995. OCLC/NCSA Metadata Workshop Report. Available WWW: http://www.oclc.org:5046/conferences/metadata/dublin_core_report.html.

WEIBEL, STUART L.; HAKALA, JUHA. 1998. DC-5: The Helsinki Metadata Workshop: A Report on the Workshop and Subsequent Developments. D-Lib Magazine. 1998 February. ISSN: 1082-9873. Available WWW: http://www.dlib.org/dlib/february98/02weibel.html.

WEIBEL, STUART L.; IANNELLA, RENATO; CATHRO, WARWICK. 1997. The 4th Dublin Core Metadata Workshop Report: DC-4, March 3-5, 1997, National Library of Australia, Canberra. D-Lib Magazine. 1997 June. ISSN: 1082-9873. Available WWW: http://www.dlib.org/dlib/june97/metadata/06weibel.html.

WEIBEL, STUART L.; MILLER, ERIC J. 1997. Image Description on the Internet: A Summary of the CNI/OCLC Image Metadata Workshop, September 24-25, 1996, Dublin OH. D-Lib Magazine. 1997 January. ISSN: 1082-9873. Available WWW: http://www.dlib.org/dlib/january97/oclc/ 01weibel.html.

WOODWARD, JEANNETTE. 1996. Cataloging and Classifying Information Resources on the Internet. In: Williams, Martha E., ed. Annual Review of Information Science and Technology: Volume 31. Medford, NJ: Information Today, Inc. for the American Society for Information Science (ASIS); 1996. 189-220. ISSN: 0066-4200; ISBN: 1-57387-033-1.

WORLD WIDE WEB CONSORTIUM (W3C). 1998a. Metadata and Resource Description. World Wide Web home page. 1998. Available WWW: http://www.w3.org/Metadata.

WORLD WIDE WEB CONSORTIUM (W3C). 1998b. Resource Description Framework (RDF). World Wide Web home page. Available WWW: http://www.w3.org/RDF/Overview.html.

WORLD WIDE WEB CONSORTIUM (W3C). 1998c. Resource Description Framework (RDF) Model and Syntax. W3C Working Draft 1998 October 8. Available WWW: http://www.w3.org/TR/WD-rdf-syntax/.

YOUNGER, JENNIFER A. 1997. Resources Description in the Digital Age. Library Trends. 1997 Winter; 45(3): 462-487. ISSN: 0024-2594.

6

Cross-Language Information Retrieval

DOUGLAS W. OARD
University of Maryland

ANNE R. DIEKEMA
Syracuse University

INTRODUCTION

This chapter reviews research and practice in cross-language information retrieval (CLIR) that seeks to support the process of finding documents written in one natural language (e.g., English or Portuguese) with automated systems that can accept queries expressed in other languages. With the globalization of the economy and the continued internationalization of the Internet, CLIR is becoming an increasingly important capability that facilitates the effective exchange of information. For retrospective retrieval, CLIR allows users to state queries in their native language and then retrieve documents in any supported language. This can simplify searching by multilingual users and, if translation resources are limited, can allow searchers to allocate those resources to the most promising documents. In selective dissemination applications, CLIR allows monolingual users to specify a profile using words from one language and then use that profile to identify promising documents in many languages. Adaptive filtering systems that seek to learn profiles automatically can use CLIR to process training documents that may not be in the same language as the documents that later must be selected.

This review uses the term documents fairly broadly, because CLIR can be applied to a variety of modalities including character-coded text, scanned images of printed pages, and recordings of human speech. Similarly, supporting the process of finding documents should be construed broadly as well, including both fully automated functions and capabilities that support productive human-system interaction. CLIR also appears in the literature as multilingual information retrieval (HULL

Annual Review of information Science and Technology (ARIST), Volume 33, 1998
Martha E. Williams, Editor
Published for the American Society for Information Science (ASIS)
By Information Today, Inc., Medford, NJ

& GREFENSTETTE), and as translingual information retrieval (CARBONELL ET AL.), but all work conforming to the definition stated above is described in this chapter as CLIR for consistency.

The first reported work on CLIR was the development in 1964 of the International Road Research Documentation system that used a controlled-vocabulary thesaurus with aligned indexing terms in English, French, and German (PIGUR). PEVZNER (1969; 1972) also implemented a Boolean exact-match text retrieval system, translating a Russian thesaurus into English. SALTON (1970; 1973) conducted some smaller studies, augmenting the SMART system with hand-constructed bilingual term lists. By the mid-1970s it had been established that systems built using these techniques could achieve performance across languages on a par with their within-language performance. Commercial acceptance soon followed, and by 1977 ILJON was able to identify four multilingual text retrieval systems operating in Europe. Standardization quickly emerged as an important issue. In 1978 the International Standardization Organization formally adopted ISO Standard 5964 on the construction of multilingual thesauri (INTERNATIONAL ORGANIZATION FOR STANDARDIZATION), and that standard has remained unmodified since 1985.

Multilingual thesauri do not, however, completely solve the CLIR problem. DUBOIS identified three factors that motivate the search for other techniques: cost, currency, and usability. First, indexing and maintenance costs limit the scalability of thesaurus-based systems, although some automated tools are able to assist with these tasks. Second, thesauri in production applications often lag somewhat behind the current use of terminology because new words enter human languages each year. Third, perhaps the most serious limitation of thesaurus-based techniques is that untrained users seem to have difficulty exploiting their capabilities. Searching free text is the obvious alternative to use of a controlled vocabulary, and LANDAUER & LITTMAN (1990; 1991) were the first to explore the potential for free-text CLIR. Extending an automatic technique for reducing the effect of vocabulary differences on retrieval effectiveness, they sought to partially overcome the systematic vocabulary differences that result from choosing a different language. RADWAN & FLUHR began work in 1991 on an alternative technique that was based on translating the queries using manually encoded translation knowledge. Although much progress has been made since that time, these two early explorations of broad-coverage free-text CLIR defined the two dominant themes that still guide research and practice: corpus-based and knowledge-based approaches.

Scope

This review brings together historical and contemporary research on automated techniques for cross-language retrieval of written and spoken text, both for retrospective retrieval and for selective dissemination. The review does not cover gestural languages such as American Sign Language, nor does it address language-independent techniques for recommending documents based either on ratings assigned by other users or on hypertext links. This is the first *ARIST* review of CLIR, but ERES in 1989 reviewed international information transfer and METOYER-DURAN in 1993 reviewed work on transfer of information across language barriers in a domestic context. Other surveys have addressed CLIR with more limited scope. PIGUR in 1979 described early work on CLIR, with particular emphasis on developments in the former Soviet Union. In 1990s, FLUHR provided an overview of modern approaches, and OARD (1997b) provided a more recent overview. JONES & JAMES reviewed the field with particular attention to cross-language speech retrieval, and OARD & DORR (1996) produced the most extensive survey to date.

Organization

The review begins with an examination of the literature on user needs for CLIR. The main part of the chapter then follows the retrieval system model shown in Figure 1, adapted from OARD (1997c). Each section highlights the unique requirements imposed on one or more stages of that model in cross-language retrieval applications. The matching stage is covered in somewhat greater detail, reflecting the treatment in the literature. Evaluation techniques are then described, and the review concludes with some observations regarding future research directions.

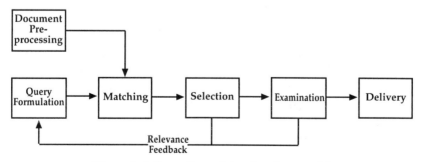

Figure 1. Information retrieval system model

USER NEEDS

MEADOWS cited a number of studies that together suggest that in the early 1970s about half of the world's scientific literature was published in English. WELLISCH observed that English-language secondary sources (e.g., indexing and abstracting services) add to this total. Several massive translation efforts also contribute to the availability of information in English. World Translations Index, for example, lists 269 journals for which cover-to-cover translations (mostly into English) of every issue are prepared, and hundreds more that are selectively translated on a regular basis (INTERNATIONAL TRANSLATIONS CENTRE). STUDEMAN reported that the U.S. Foreign Broadcast Information Service translated 200 million words in a single year from more than 3,500 publications in 55 languages. So English does serve, to some degree, as what WELLISCH (p. 149) called the "*lingua franca* of information retrieval tools."

Despite these efforts, much of the world's information is not available in English. HUTCHINS ET AL. found that about a third of the researchers at the University of Sheffield (United Kingdom) suspected that they had failed to learn of relevant work in a non-English-speaking country. It turned out that a similar proportion had in fact discovered foreign-language work that would have been more useful had it turned up earlier. MEADOWS found corroborating evidence for this problem on a larger scale, noting that researchers writing in English tend to overcite other work in English and to underuse foreign-language work, when compared to the linguistic distribution of scholarly writing in their field.

Discovering documents in a foreign language is, of course, only part of the problem. GOLDSTEIN found that between 20% and 45% of electrical engineers in Mexico encountered documents in unfamiliar languages at least once each month, and WOOD (1967) and ELLEN obtained similar results for a broad range of disciplines in the United Kingdom. WOOD (1974) offered some insight into the assistance that may be needed, reporting that more than half the researchers requesting full-text translations from the British Library felt that summary translations of the results along with translations of figure and table captions were sufficient to provide the information that they required.

The recent growth of the global Internet has focused increased attention on the need for information exchange across linguistic barriers. A 1997 study by the INTERNET SOCIETY & ALIS TECHNOLOGIES, for example, found that 12% of World Wide Web pages that were randomly selected contained material in one of 14 languages other than English. With more than 100 million Web pages already indexed by the largest Web search engines, this translates into an

Recorded speech poses an even greater challenge, both with respect to speed and accuracy. Speech typically lacks explicit boundary markers between words, so the problem resembles the segmentation problem in languages such as Chinese, and variations in pronunciation, speaking rate, and the fidelity of the recording make speech recognition vastly more complex. Speech recognition systems trained on manually prepared time-synchronized transcripts can produce useful indexing features, but the needed training material is available for only a limited set of languages, recognition accuracy degrades when presented with applications for which the training material was not representative, and present processing speeds limit the size of the collections that can be indexed. SHERIDAN ET AL. (1997) used overlapping three-phoneme sequences (phone trigrams) as indexing features for recorded German speech in an attempt to overcome these limitations. Their initial results were disappointing, but NG & ZUE found that phone trigrams can offer a viable alternative to word-based indexing for spoken documents in English.

QUERY FORMULATION

TAYLOR observed that users must compromise their information needs to match the perceived capabilities of available information systems when creating queries. Information retrieval systems seek to support this process by providing facilities for query specification and through incorporation of query refinement techniques such as relevance feedback. Users with little exposure to controlled-vocabulary searching, for example, often find that formulation of effective queries using a printed thesaurus is difficult. Such users might benefit from a query interface that depicts the available indexing terms and their relationships in their preferred language. LI ET AL. developed such a system for English and Japanese, using versions of the INSPEC thesaurus in each language. Although no user study results were reported for multilingual applications, SMITH & POLLITT performed a qualitative assessment of a monolingual version of the same system.

The fully automatic query translation techniques described in the next section can be viewed as one type of support for query formulation in free-text CLIR systems, but more interactive approaches have also been implemented. The QUILT system described by DAVIS & OGDEN (1997), for example, optionally displayed the Spanish translation of English query terms. Users who are able to read Spanish might thus be able to recognize erroneous translations, even if they lacked the fluency necessary to form effective queries without assistance. If so, they could then switch to a monolingual mode and enter the correct Spanish terms. YAMABANA ET AL. implemented a more sophisticated approach in which candidate translations of each term were displayed immediately, along with retranslations of each candidate back into the query language. Users unable to read the candidate translations could quickly skim the retranslations, and an alternate candidate could be chosen if necessary. An Internet demonstration of the READWARE system from Management Information Technologies, Inc. illustrated a further extension of this approach that could accommodate several languages simultaneously. READWARE depicted known senses of every query term using one near-synonym in the query language for each sense and allowed the user to designate the intended senses. For each selected word sense, a set of near-synonyms in English, German, and French was passed on to the matching stage as a multilingual query. Together these three approaches illustrate a range of options that provide alternative ways of balancing capability with interface complexity.

MATCHING

Matching Strategies

Broadly stated, information retrieval systems construct representations of the documents and the information need and then match those representations to identify documents that are most likely to satisfy the need. In what MALONE ET AL. called content-based techniques, the representations are constructed from terms (e.g., stems, words, phrases, or character n-grams) that appear in the documents and the queries. Techniques for matching representations constructed from different vocabularies thus form a central component of CLIR systems. FURNAS ET AL. observed that information retrieval systems suffer from a vocabulary problem that results in part from variability in word usage. CLIR is simply an extreme case of this problem in which the words are selected from nearly disjoint vocabularies. As shown in Figure 2, four general approaches to cross-language matching have emerged in CLIR: cognate matching, query translation, document translation, and interlingual techniques.

Cognate matching. Cognate matching essentially automates the process by which readers might try to guess the meaning of an unfamiliar term based on similarities in spelling or pronunciation. A simple version of cognate matching in which untranslatable terms are retained unchanged is often used in CLIR systems to match proper nouns and technical terminology (BALLESTEROS & CROFT, 1997; DAVIS & OGDEN, 1998; ELKATEB & FLUHR; GEY & CHEN; HULL & GREFENSTETTE; KRAAIJ & HIEMSTRA). DAVIS extended this technique using fuzzy matching to discover Spanish cognates for English words that did not appear in a bilingual dictionary. BUCKLEY ET AL.

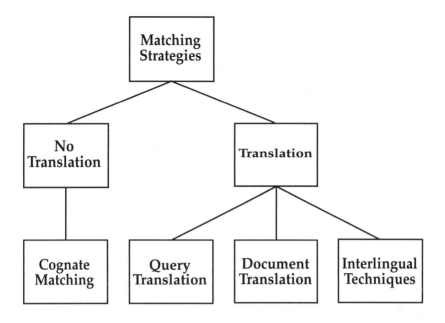

Figure 2. Matching strategies

(1998) applied a more sophisticated approach, creating equivalence classes for letter sequences with similar sounds (e.g., "c," "k," and "qu" share an equivalence class). Because the translation knowledge is embedded directly in the matching scheme, cognate matching can be used in isolation. Most often, however, cognate matching is combined with other cross-language matching approaches.

Query translation. Query translation is a more general strategy in which the query (or some internal representation of the query) is automatically converted into every supported language. Query translation is relatively efficient and can be done on the fly. The principal limitation of query translation is that queries are often short, and short queries provide little context for disambiguation. Homonymous words (those with more than one distinct meaning) produce undesirable matches even in monolingual retrieval (KROVETZ & CROFT). Translation ambiguity compounds this problem, potentially introducing additional terms that are themselves homonymous. For this reason, controlling translation ambiguity is a central issue in the design of effective query translation techniques. Phrases typically exhibit less translation ambiguity than single words, and the literature suggests that phrase recognition strategies can substantially improve retrieval effectiveness. BALLESTEROS & CROFT (1997) observed beneficial effects from manual translation of phrases identified through syntactic analysis, and both

RADWAN & FLUHR and KRAAIJ & HIEMSTRA explored techniques for automatically choosing an appropriate word order for phrases in which the constituent words had been translated separately. HULL & GREFENSTETTE investigated the effect of noncompositional phrases that cannot be reconstructed from translations of the constituent terms and found an additional benefit.

Document translation. Document translation is the opposite of query translation, automatically converting all of the documents (or their representations) into each supported query language. Documents typically provide more context than queries, so more effective strategies to limit the effect of translation ambiguity may be possible. Another potential advantage is that selected documents can be presented to the user for examination without on-demand translation (KRAAIJ). On the other hand, massive translation can be an expensive undertaking, and the costs are even greater if several query languages must be supported. As a result, relatively few experiments have compared document translation with query translation (OARD ET AL.), and ERBACH ET AL. suggested using document translation only for small collections in limited domains.

Interlingual techniques. Interlingual techniques convert both the query and the documents into a unified language-independent representation. Controlled-vocabulary techniques based on multilingual thesauri are the most common examples of this approach. Because each controlled-vocabulary term typically corresponds to exactly one concept, terms from any language can be used to index documents or to form queries. HLAVA ET AL. described a technique for partially automating the assignment of indexing terms to documents in several languages. Some fully automated interlingual techniques have also been implemented. Latent semantic indexing (BERRY & YOUNG; DUMAIS ET AL.; LANDAUER & LITTMAN, 1990; 1991; REHDER ET AL.) and the generalized vector space model (CARBONELL ET AL.) both use a document-aligned training corpus to learn a mapping from one or more languages into a language-neutral representation. Document and query representations from either language can be mapped into this space, allowing similarity measures to be computed both within and across languages.

Sources of Translation Knowledge

Each of the four matching approaches to CLIR depends on some form of translation knowledge. That knowledge may be encoded manually or extracted automatically from corpora, and CLIR techniques may exploit translation knowledge in more than one form. The literature typically refers to techniques using translation knowledge from manu-

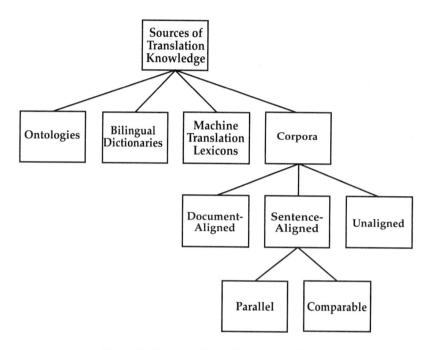

Figure 3. Sources of translation knowledge

ally encoded translation knowledge as knowledge-based approaches. Techniques using translation knowledge from corpora are referred to as corpus-based techniques. The correspondence rules used for cognate matching represent one form of manually encoded translation knowledge. As shown in Figure 3, three other manually encoded sources of translation knowledge have been applied to CLIR: ontologies, bilingual dictionaries, and machine translation lexicons. Three types of corpora have also been used: document-aligned corpora, sentence- and term-aligned corpora, and unaligned corpora. This section considers each of the six sources of translation knowledge in turn.

Ontologies. Ontologies are structures that encode domain knowledge by specifying relationships between concepts. Thesauri are ontologies that are designed specifically to support information retrieval. At present, multilingual thesauri are the dominant sources of translation knowledge in operational CLIR systems. Thesauri can support both controlled-vocabulary and free-text retrieval, providing insight into both hierarchical relationships (broader terms, narrower terms), synonymy, and more general associations (related terms). Such relationships can help experienced users define better queries by enhancing their understanding of the structure of knowledge for the topic being searched. The European Parliament's multilingual EUROVOC thesaurus is one example of a multilingual thesaurus. A common approach to create a multilingual thesaurus is to translate an existing monolingual thesaurus, and KALACHKINA provided algorithms to deal with terms that lack direct translations. SOERGEL, however, cautioned against merely translating an existing thesaurus because the expression of concepts in the original language will then dominate the conceptual structure. General-purpose ontologies such as WordNet (MILLER) are emerging as alternatives to traditional thesauri because their broader coverage permits use of sophisticated knowledge structures in broader domains than has heretofore been possible. By encoding additional relationships such as part-whole and kind-of, WordNet explicitly captures a broader range of structural knowledge than traditional thesauri. The EuroWordNet project is developing a multilingual ontology resembling WordNet with components in Dutch, English, Italian, and Spanish that are linked by an interlingual index. CLIR support is a specific design goal of the project. GILARRANZ ET AL. described how EuroWordNet might be used to support a query translation strategy. Other projects (e.g., GermaNet, described by HAMP & FELDWEG) are extending these ideas to other languages.

Bilingual dictionaries. Machine-readable bilingual dictionaries have been widely used to support query translation strategies (BALLESTEROS & CROFT, 1997; DAVIS; DAVIS & OGDEN, 1998; FLUHR ET AL.; GEY & CHEN; HULL & GREFENSTETTE; KRAAIJ & HIEMSTRA; KWOK; NGUYEN ET AL.; YAMABANA ET AL.). Bilingual dictionaries are typically designed for human use, so translations of individual terms are often augmented with examples showing how those terms could be used in context. It would be difficult to extract generalizations from those examples that could be used automatically, so machine-readable dictionaries are typically processed manually or automatically to reduce them to a bilingual term list, perhaps with additional information such as part of speech (e.g., noun or verb). In essence, dictionary-based translation consists of looking up each query term in the resulting bilingual term list and selecting the appropriate translation equivalents. The simplest way of using such a bilingual term list is to select every known translation for each term, and that approach is often used as a baseline in dictionary-based CLIR evaluations. Both RADWAN & FLUHR and DAVIS showed that limiting the translations to those with the same part of speech can improve retrieval effectiveness, and KRAAIJ & HIEMSTRA experimented with the use of preferred translations that were noted in their dictionary. OARD ET AL. demonstrated that in some cases arbitrarily choosing a single translation can be just as good (by the average precision measure), apparently because, on balance, as many queries are helped as are hurt. HULL explored the ability of structured queries to further limit translation ambiguity, implementing a weighted Boolean matching strategy that exploited the observation that correct translations are more likely to co-occur than incorrect translations. Dictionary-based CLIR can suffer from limited dictionary coverage, inaccuracies during automatic construction of the bilingual term list, and incorrect selection of the appropriate translation equivalents (BALLESTEROS & CROFT, 1997; FLUHR ET AL.; GAUSSIER ET AL.; HULL & GREFENSTETTE; NGUYEN ET AL.), but it is sufficiently efficient and effective to be useful in many applications.

Machine translation lexicons. Machine translation systems are becoming fairly widely available, although machine-readable dictionaries still cover a greater number of language pairs (KRAAIJ). Machine translation systems encode translation knowledge in a lexicon that contains the information needed for automatic analysis, translation, and generation of natural language. One goal of natural language analysis is to disambiguate terms in ways that can limit translation ambiguity, and the lexicon is often designed to provide information that is useful for this purpose. The most straightforward way to apply a machine translation lexicon to CLIR is to simply use the machine translation system to translate either the queries or the document collection. Queries are rarely provided as well-formed sentences, however, so the effectiveness of this approach may be limited in query translation applications (HULL & GREFENSTETTE; KRAAIJ). Machine translation systems necessarily choose a single preferred translation for each term, and ERBACH ET AL. observed that such a singular choice might adversely affect retrieval effectiveness. Examples of the use of machine translation for query and document translation can be found in OARD & HACKETT.

Document-aligned corpora. Document-aligned corpora are document collections in which useful relationships between sets of documents in different languages are known. Parallel corpora are made up of translation equivalent sets, each containing a document and one or more translations. Comparable collections, on the other hand, are typically separately authored but related by topical content. Aligned document sets in comparable corpora may contain one or more documents in each language (PETERS & PICCHI; SHERIDAN & BALLERINI). The basic strategy for using document-aligned corpora is to represent each term using the pattern of aligned sets in which that term occurs and then to construct language-neutral representations of documents in any supported language using the resulting term representations. Techniques from linear algebra are typically used to compute and manipulate these term representations. When the language of each document is known, each term is typically tagged with a language marker in order to avoid undesired conflation with different concepts in other languages.

CARBONELL ET AL. implemented one such technique, the General-ized Vector Space Model (GVSM), using a parallel corpus. Latent Semantic Indexing (LSI) extends this approach by conflating terms that have similar representations, often increasing recall without adversely affecting precision. Both parallel corpora (DUMAIS ET AL.; LANDAUER & LITTMAN, 1990; 1991) and comparable corpora (REHDER ET AL.) have been used with LSI. BERRY & YOUNG found that the effectiveness of LSI could be improved by using an aligned corpus of short passages rather than one formed from longer docu-ments. Although LSI is sometimes more effective than GVSM, compu-tation of the term conflation step is computationally intensive (CARBONELL ET AL.). SHERIDAN & BALLERINI and MATEEV ET AL. investigated an alternative approach, building a bilingual term list for query translation using term representations computed from a comparable corpus of news stories that was aligned using classifica-tion codes, publication dates, and cognates. They found the terms in each language that were most similar to each query term (using a vector similarity measure) and then used several of the most similar terms as the translated query. Although LSI uses more sophisticated techniques to conflate similar terms, the technique of Sheridan and Ballerini is more efficient.

Sentence- and term-aligned corpora. Comparable corpora can be aligned only to the document level, but many individual sentences in parallel corpora can be aligned automatically using dynamic programming techniques. DAVIS used a sentence-aligned parallel corpus directly to augment dictionary-based query translation without substantial im-provement over a simpler dictionary-based technique. OARD (1996; 1997a) used sentence alignments as a basis for aligning individual terms, but again found that knowledge-based techniques (in this case, machine translation) were more effective when the corpus-based tech-nique was required to extract translation knowledge from one collec-tion and then apply it to another. In those experiments, a set of sen-tence-aligned translations of United Nations documents was used as a source of translation knowledge, and a monolingual collection of Span-ish newswire articles was used for evaluation. CARBONELL ET AL. implemented a similar approach, evaluating retrieval effectiveness on a portion of the same corpus from which translation knowledge had been extracted. Under those conditions, the sentence-aligned corpus that was used to produce term alignments outperformed every other tech-nique they tried. OARD (1997a) saw a similar improvement when comparing the same-collection performance of LSI with the perfor-mance of the same algorithm when trained on a different collection. It thus appears that document- and sentence-aligned techniques may be most useful when the needed alignments are known within some portion of the same collection from which retrieval is desired. Although such a situation may exist in a few applications (e.g., if translations are being made routinely, but they are not available immediately), this factor is likely to somewhat circumscribe the utility of techniques based on document- and sentence-aligned corpora.

Unaligned corpora. A representative monolingual document collection is, of course, available in any application of CLIR to retrospective retrieval. Such collections are often assembled for filtering applications as well because they provide useful collection frequency statistics. When representative documents in more than one language are present in (or can be added to) such a collection, the collection itself can be used in conjunction with a bilingual term list as an additional source of translation knowledge even if a priori document alignments are not known. BALLESTEROS & CROFT (1997) applied fully automatic passage-level pseudo-relevance feedback using the query language portion of their unaligned corpus to refine the query representation. By augmenting the original query with terms appearing in top-ranked passages, monolingual pseudo-relevance feedback often improves recall without a significant adverse effect on precision. They then applied dictionary-based query translation to produce a version of the query in the desired language, followed by fully automatic passage-level pseudo-relevance feedback using the portion of the unaligned corpus containing documents in that language. When applied individually, each pseudo-relevance feedback step improved CLIR effectiveness, and the combination outperformed either step alone. KROVETZ & CROFT and SANDERSON showed that ranked retrieval techniques tend to reinforce the appropriate interpretation of words that admit more than one interpretation. Viewed in this light, the first pseudo-relevance feedback step serves to limit the adverse effect of translation ambiguity by including additional terms that are related to the original query terms. YAMABANA ET AL. sought to achieve the same result more directly. For each query term, they identified one related term in the unaligned corpus that often appeared in a sentence with the query term. They then selected the candidate that most often appeared in the same sentence as some possible translation of the related term. Yamabana et al. obtained some improvement in translation accuracy using this technique, but they did not evaluate the effect of that improvement on retrieval effectiveness. PICCHI & PETERS proposed a similar technique that exploits more context by considering the possible translations of groups of words surrounding each query term in the unaligned corpus. Although techniques based on unaligned corpora appear promising, SHERIDAN ET AL. (1997) failed to find any improvement when using languages and collections different from those used by BALLESTEROS & CROFT (1996; 1997). It thus appears the nature of the unaligned corpus and/or the way in which additional context-revealing terms are chosen can substantially affect the results.

SELECTION, EXAMINATION, AND DELIVERY

As MARCHIONINI observed, searching and browsing are complementary activities. Automated systems apply rather simple techniques to enormous volumes of information, while humans can effectively exploit quite sophisticated selection heuristics on fairly small sets. One important goal of the user interface is to expose the information on which users can base these decisions. Retrieval systems containing full text typically support two browsing strategies: selection of documents from a list of promising candidates identified by the system, and detailed examination of individual documents.

Support for selection presents unique challenges when the documents are written in an unfamiliar language. Monolingual selection interfaces typically present document titles along with some information about the source of the material and when it was produced. Occasionally some form of summary, such as the first few lines or some individual words automatically extracted from the document, are also presented. Conversion of names and dates using simple transliteration schemes is relatively straightforward, but title translation is more complex. Translation of titles using fully automatic machine translation is a possibility, but titles rarely consist of the well-formed linguistic expressions for which typical machine translation systems are optimized. KIKUI ET AL. reported that choosing the most common candidate translation (using a monolingual corpus) and then reordering the terms using some simple rules produced usable translations of English Web page titles into Japanese. RESNIK evaluated an alternative strategy for translating brief listings into English, displaying as many as three alternative translations when faced with translation ambiguity. Using a decision theoretic measure, they found that such translations were more effective than a naive Bayesian classifier, but not as effective as monolingual selection.

Support for examination poses an even greater challenge. Several companies market translation software that is compatible with popular Web browsers, and proxy translation servers are becoming available on the Internet. Typical machine translation systems are not yet fast enough to keep up with interactive selection and scrolling behavior, however, so interactive searching is inhibited to some extent when query translation is used. Approaches based on advance translation of every document avoid this problem, but the time and expense involved limit application of those techniques. Rapid word-by-word translation like that explored by KIKUI ET AL. and RESNIK could in principle be used with query translation, but the utility of such techniques for examining relatively long documents in a CLIR system has not yet been explored. Traditional abstracting services such as INSPEC have adopted a more parsimonious approach, manually preparing abstracts for every document in the supported query language (usually English) regardless of the abstracted documents' language. FRANZEN & KARLGREN proposed automating this process by translating brief extracts or summaries as an alternative to translating entire documents on demand, but research on cross-language summarization is just beginning.

The ultimate delivery of selected documents in a usable form may be a somewhat more tractable problem than support for interactive examination if adequate time for translation can be allowed when arranging for delivery. O'HAGAN provided an overview of the translation industry and observed that globally interconnected networks will make it possible to marshal worldwide translation resources on demand. Although fully automatic machine translation presently can produce high-quality translations only in very limited subject areas, O'Hagan suggested that a robust and responsive translation infrastructure could be built using machine-assisted human translation. The human effort required for translation will likely make delivery the most expensive component on a per-document basis, so it may be advisable to spend more effort on the recognition of the most promising documents using the query formulation, matching, selection, and examination stages.

EVALUATION

Experimental evaluation of CLIR systems poses unique challenges because the languages covered by the translation resources must match the languages covered by the evaluation resources. The situation is further complicated when alternative techniques that require different translation resources are compared. A CLIR test collection thus consists of a set of documents in one or more languages, a set of queries in a language or languages different from that of the documents, relevance judgments for each query-document pair, and translation resources such as dictionaries, bilingual corpora, or cognate matching rules.

LANDAUER & LITTMAN (1990) developed a simple evaluation technique known as mate finding for use with document-aligned corpora. Mate finding is a variation on known-item retrieval, a classic evaluation strategy in which the rank assigned to a unique item that is known to be relevant to the query is used as the measure of effectiveness. LANDAUER & LITTMAN (1990; 1991) partitioned an English-French parallel collection, extracting translation knowledge from one part and using the other part for evaluation. Each English document was then used as a query, and statistics describing the rank of the known French translation for each document were presented. CARBONELL ET AL. found that mate retrieval was less able to discriminate among fairly good techniques than more traditional strategies in which recall and precision were reported, but mate retrieval remains useful as a simple strategy for identifying promising CLIR techniques when more sophisticated evaluation resources are not available.

RADWAN & FLUHR used French translations of the 1,398 abstracts in the English Cranfield collection to compute precision-recall graphs and an average precision measure. DAVIS & DUNNING adopted an alternate strategy, manually translating Spanish topic descriptions into English and then using those topic descriptions to construct English queries to retrieve Spanish newswire articles from the Text REtrieval Conference (TREC) test collection. Manual translation of queries is now a widely used evaluation strategy because it permits existing test collections to be extended inexpensively to any language pair for which translation resources are available. Because manual translation requires the application of human judgment, evaluation collections constructed in this way exhibit some variability based on the terminology chosen by a particular translator. But if a standard set of translations is agreed on, such a strategy offers a meaningful basis for selecting between alternative CLIR techniques.

There are, however, some applications for which manual query translation would not produce an adequate test collection. Corpus-based techniques, for example, may not perform well on collections that differ markedly from the corpora on which they were trained. There presently is no widely accepted metric for reporting the similarity of two corpora, so same-corpus (i.e., best-case) evaluations are typically performed using a held-back portion of the corpus. CARBONELL ET AL. produced a test collection in this way by exhaustively performing 33,630 relevance judgments for a portion of a parallel collection of English and Spanish documents. This produced a test collection that was about the same size as the Cranfield collection used by RADWAN & FLUHR, but with the added characteristic that the remainder of the parallel corpus was available for the extraction of translation knowledge. SHERIDAN & BALLERINI also built a test collection from a document-aligned corpus, but they developed a genre-specific strategy for newswire articles. By constructing queries for unpredicted events and ending their search three days after the event (which produced a different collection size for each query), they cut down the number of relevance judgments considerably. Newswire stories are readily available in character-coded form, so this evaluation strategy may provide an economical alternative for many applications.

Evaluation of adaptive filtering techniques, which learn to select documents in one language based on user reactions to documents in other languages, imposes further requirements on an evaluation collection because a third partition of the evaluation collection may be needed. OARD (1997a) constructed such a collection using monolingual test collections in English and Spanish for which four topic descriptions were closely aligned, and a parallel corpus of English and Spanish documents for which no relevance judgments were needed. In addition to the adaptive filtering evaluation, some indication of the degree of similarity between one of the monolingual test collections and the parallel corpus was also obtained.

Relatively large document collections are needed to reflect accurately the performance of IR systems in large-scale applications, and the potential need to subdivide the collection two or three ways exacerbates the situation. Obtaining statistical significance often requires more queries for query translation experiments than for monolingual experiments on the same collection because uneven translation accuracy introduces an additional source of variation. Also, collections covering a wide range of languages and modalities will be needed to assess the effect of variations in morphology, word boundary marking, and recognition accuracy. At present, the TREC CLIR test collection described by MATEEV ET AL. and SCHÄUBLE & SHERIDAN is the most comprehensive step in that direction. Using an approach known as pooled relevance assessment, relevance judgments for over 140,000 newswire articles in each of three languages (English, French, and German) were developed by judging documents selected using several different retrieval techniques. The documents are not translations of each other, but they are drawn from the same genre and time frame. SHERIDAN ET AL. (1998) automatically identified some possible alignments between some of the French and German documents in the collection.

Some insight into the contribution of alternative translation techniques can be obtained by comparing CLIR results with the effectiveness of a similar monolingual technique on the same collection. Expressed as a percentage of monolingual effectiveness, reported values typically range from around 50% for unconstrained dictionary-based query translation to 75% or so for more sophisticated techniques. Direct comparisons are difficult, however, because (1) the monolingual reference technique is often different, (2) parameter variations can introduce additional variations even when the reference technique is nominally the same, (3) the effect of differing collections on relative effectiveness is not well-characterized, and (4) different effectiveness measures may have been used. HULL & GREFENSTETTE reported precision averaged over several fixed numbers of documents to characterize high-precision interactive searching, while BALLESTEROS & CROFT (1997) reported precision averaged over the full range of recall values. Relative performance figures can help identify particularly promising techniques, however, and then the most promising techniques can be subjected to a more rigorous side-by-side comparison.

RESEARCH DIRECTIONS

Nearly three decades of research on and practice of controlled-vocabulary techniques for CLIR and eight years of research on free-text techniques have produced a wide array of useful techniques, but more remains to be done. Existing research on user needs for CLIR, for example, addresses the deliberate dissemination of information well, but has not yet addressed the impact of ubiquitous networking and the resulting trend toward flattened organizational structures. Some issues, such as the impact of networked communications on the translation infrastructure supporting ultimate use of selected documents, have implications for both controlled-vocabulary and free-text CLIR. But free-text techniques are still relatively new, and it is there that many of the open research questions are to be found.

Important research issues are found in each stage of the model shown in Figure 1. The distinction between user-assisted and fully automatic query translation is rather sharply drawn at present, with users either being offered the opportunity to help resolve translation ambiguity for every term or for no terms. More sophisticated strategies might retain much of the benefit of user-assisted translation while avoiding unnecessary allocation of user effort and screen space to that task. Present document preprocessing systems are typically language-specific, often using hand-built components for tasks such as character set conversion, compound splitting, and stemming. The development of easily configured tools for such tasks would make the addition of different languages a far more tractable task. The matching stage has received a great deal of attention, but cognate matching has only recently been investigated carefully. Further work on additional language pairs and strategies for combining cognate matching with other techniques appear to be the natural next steps. The importance of selection, examination, and delivery for CLIR system design is now beginning to be recognized, but much remains to be done. It is not yet clear, for example, whether rapid translation of the entire text or automatic generation of translated summaries will provide the best support for examination, and resolving that issue may require the development of new evaluation techniques. Other evaluation issues also require attention. Perhaps most importantly, it will not be possible to characterize accurately the performance of document- and sentence-aligned corpus-based techniques in practical applications without some way to measure the degree of difference between the corpus from which the translation knowledge is extracted and the collection from which retrieval is desired.

As CLIR has matured, increasingly integrated approaches have been investigated. Dictionary-based query translation has been improved using unaligned corpora (BALLESTEROS & CROFT, 1996; 1997), and term-aligned corpora have been refined by seeding the alignments using a bilingual dictionary (YANG ET AL.). Fully automatic query translation techniques are being augmented with user-assisted query translation. This trend will likely continue, encompassing other components and techniques as productive interactions are discovered. GACHOT ET AL., for example, observed that closer coupling between machine translation and matching techniques might be helpful because additional linguistic information would be available. Ultimately, the distinctions that have been drawn in this chapter between separate components and different techniques may be as useful for explaining how they are coupled as for how they are different.

CONCLUSION

Controlled-vocabulary CLIR techniques are now widely deployed, and free-text systems for practical applications are beginning to appear. Although monolingual retrieval is still more effective for free text than CLIR, several useful CLIR techniques are known. Query translation, document translation, interlingual techniques, and cognate matching provide a range of alternatives that can be tailored to specific applications. Document preprocessing strategies have been developed for scanned page images and recorded speech, but character-coded text remains the most easily processed format. Interactive applications pose additional challenges because users may not have the language skills that are needed to select and examine documents in their original language. Additional opportunities are present as well, however, because the user can help refine translation knowledge that is extracted from dictionaries, bilingual corpora, or other sources. Evaluation poses additional challenges that the recent development of the TREC CLIR test collection has begun to address.

Many modern information systems support only a single language, but that limitation will likely become increasingly untenable in an era of ubiquitous global networks and vast international information flows. Cross-language information retrieval is one component of the technological infrastructure that will help make the World Wide Web a truly worldwide resource, and it will undoubtedly find widespread application in other parts of the information industry as well. Although much remains to be done, the techniques that have been developed and the ways in which they have been applied provide useful signposts for developers who wish to begin exploring the opportunities presented by cross-language information retrieval.

BIBLIOGRAPHY

ALLAN, JAMES; CALLAN, JAMES P.; CROFT, W. BRUCE; BALLESTEROS, LISA; BYRD, DON; SWAN, RUSSELL; XU, JINXI. 1998. INQUERY Does Battle with TREC-6. In: Proceedings of the 6th Text REtrieval Conference (TREC-6); 1997 November 19-21; National Institute of Standards and Technology (NIST), Gaithersburg, MD. Available WWW: http://trec.nist.gov/pubs/trec6/t6_proceedings.html.

ATA, B.M.A.; MOHD, T.; SEMBOK, T.; YUSOFF, M. 1995. SISDOM: A Multilingual Document Retrieval System. Asian Libraries. 1995; 4(3): 37-46. ISSN: 1017-6748.

AUSTIN, DEREK. 1977. Progress towards Standard Guidelines for the Construction of Multilingual Thesauri. In: 3rd European Congress on Information Systems and Networks: Volume 1; 1977 May 3-6; Luxembourg, Luxembourg. Munich, Germany: Verlag Dokumentation; 1977. 341-402. ISBN: 3-7940-5184-X.

BALLESTEROS, LISA; CROFT, W. BRUCE. 1996. Dictionary Methods for Cross-Lingual Information Retrieval. In: Wagner, R. R.; Thoma, H., eds. Proceedings of the 7th International DEXA Conference on Database and Expert Systems; 1996 September 9-13; Zurich, Switzerland. New York, NY: Springer; 1996. 791-801. (Lecture Notes in Computer Science no. 1134). ISBN: 3-540-61656-X.

BALLESTEROS, LISA; CROFT, W. BRUCE. 1997. Phrasal Translation and Query Expansion Techniques for Cross-Language Information Retrieval. In: SIGIR '97: Proceedings of the Association for Computing Machinery Special Interest Group on Information Retrieval (ACM/SIGIR) 20th Annual Conference on Research and Development in Information Retrieval; 1997 July 27-31; Philadelphia, PA. New York, NY: ACM; 1997. 84-91. ISBN: 0-89791-836-3.

BENKING, H.; KAMPFFMEYER, U. 1992. Harmonization of Environmental Meta-Information with a Thesaurus-Based Multi-Lingual and Multi-Medial Information System. In: Zygielbaum, Arthur, ed. Conference on Earth and Space Science Information Systems; 1992 February 10-13; Pasadena, CA. New York, NY: American Institute of Physics; 1992. 688-695. (AIP Conference Proceedings 283). ISBN: 1-56396-094-X.

BERRY, MICHAEL W.; YOUNG, PAUL G. 1995. Using Latent Semantic Indexing for Multilanguage Information Retrieval. Computers and the Humanities. 1995; 29(6): 413-429. ISSN: 0010-4817.

BLAKE, P. 1992. The MenUSE System for Multilingual Assisted Access to Online Databases, in the Context of Current EC Funded Projects. Online Review. 1992; 16(3): 139-146. ISSN: 0309-314X.

BUCKLEY, CHRIS; MITRA, MANDAR; WALZ, JANET; CARDIE, CLAIRE. 1998. Using Clustering and SuperConcepts within SMART: TREC 6. In: Proceedings of the 6th Text REtrieval Conference (TREC-6); 1997 November 19-21; National Institute of Standards and Technology (NIST), Gaithersburg, MD. Available WWW: http://trec.nist.gov/pubs/trec6/t6_proceedings.html.

BUCKLEY, CHRIS; SALTON, GERARD; ALLAN, JAMES; SINGHAL, AMIT. 1994. Automatic Query Expansion Using SMART: TREC 3. In: Harman, D.K., ed. Overview of the 3rd Text REtrieval Conference (TREC-3); 1994 November 2-4; National Institute of Standards and Technology (NIST), Gaithersburg, MD. Available WWW: http://trec.nist.gov/pubs/trec3/t3_proceedings.html.

CARBONELL, JAIME G.; YANG, YIMING; FREDERKING, ROBERT E.; BROWN, RALF D.; GENG, YIBING; LEE, DANNY. 1997. Translingual Information Retrieval: A Comparative Evaluation. In: Proceedings of the 15th International Joint Conference on Artificial Intelligence; 1997 August 23-29; Nagoya, Japan. San Francisco, CA: Morgan Kaufmann; 1997. 708-715. ISBN: 1-55860-480-4.

CHACHRA, VINOD. 1993. Subject Access in an Automated Multithesaurus and Multilingual Environment. In: McCallum, Sally; Ertel, Monica, eds. 2nd Satellite Meeting on Automated Systems for Access to Multilingual and Multiscript Library Materials; 1993 August 18-19; Madrid, Spain. Munich, Germany: Saur; 1993. 63-76. ISBN: 3-598-21797-8.

CHMIELEWSKA-GORCZYCA, EWA; STRUK, WACLAW. 1994. Translating Multilingual Thesauri. In: Stancikova, Pavla; Dahlberg, Ingetraut, eds. Proceedings of the 1st European Conference on Environmental Knowledge Organization and Information Management; 1994 September 14-16; Bratislava, Slovakia. Frankfurt, Germany: Indeks Verlag; 1994. 150-155. ISBN: 3-88672-600-2.

COOPER, DOUG. 1997. How to Read Less and Know More: Approximate OCR for Thai. In: Belkin, Nicholas J.; Narasimhalu, A. Desai; Willett, Peter, eds. SIGIR '97: Proceedings of the Association for Computing Machinery Special Interest Group on Information Retrieval (ACM/SIGIR) 20th Annual International Conference on Research and Development in Information Retrieval; 1997 July 27-31; Philadelphia, PA. New York, NY: ACM; 1997. 216-225. ISBN: 0-89791-836-3.

D'OLIER, JACQUES H. 1977. Multilingualism in Scientific and Technical Documentation. International Forum on Information and Documentation. 1977; 2(4): 20-24. ISSN: 0304-9706.

DAVIS, MARK W. 1997. New Experiments in Cross-Language Text Retrieval at NMSU 's Computing Research Lab. In: Proceedings of the 5th Text REtrieval Conference (TREC-5); 1996 November 20-22; National Institute of Standards and Technology (NIST), Gaithersburg, MD. Available WWW: http://trec.nist.gov/pubs/trec5/t5_proceedings.html.

DAVIS, MARK W.; DUNNING, T. 1995. A TREC Evaluation of Query Translation Methods for Multi-Lingual Text Retrieval. In: Proceedings of the 4th Text REtrieval Conference (TREC-4); 1995 November 1-3; National Institute of Standards and Technology (NIST), Gaithersburg, MD. Available WWW: http://trec.nist.gov/pubs/trec4/t4_proceedings.html.

DAVIS, MARK W.; OGDEN, WILLIAM C. 1997. Implementing Cross-Language Text Retrieval Systems for Large-Scale Text Collections and the World Wide Web. In: AAAI Spring Symposium on Cross-Language Text and Speech Retrieval; 1997 March 24-26; Palo Alto, CA. Available WWW: http://www.clis.umd.edu/dlrg/filter/sss/papers/.

DAVIS, MARK W.; OGDEN, WILLIAM C. 1998. Free Resources and Advanced Alignment for Cross-Language Text Retrieval. In: Proceedings of the 6th Text REtrieval Conference (TREC-6); 1997 November 19-21; National Institute of Standards and Technology (NIST), Gaithersburg, MD. Available WWW: http://trec.nist.gov/pubs/trec6/t6_proceedings.html.

DEFENSE ADVANCED RESEARCH PROJECTS AGENCY. 1996. TIPSTER Text Program, Phase II: Proceedings of a Workshop; 1996 May 6-8; Vienna, VA. San Francisco, CA: Morgan Kaufmann; 1996. 479p. ISBN: 1-5860-424-X.

DUBOIS, C.P.R. 1987. Free Text vs. Controlled Vocabulary: A Reassessment. Online Review. 1987; 11(4): 243-253. ISSN: 0309-314X.

DUCLOY, JACQUES. 1996. Tools and Techniques for Digital Libraries. ERCIM News. 1996 October; 27. Available WWW: http://www-ercim.inria.fr/publication/Ercim_News/enw27/ducloy.html.

DUMAIS, SUSAN T.; LETSCHE, TODD A.; LITTMAN, MICHAEL L.; LANDAUER, THOMAS K. 1997. Automatic Cross-Language Retrieval Using Latent Semantic Indexing. In: AAAI Spring Symposium on Cross-Language Text and Speech Retrieval; 1997 March 24-26; Palo Alto, CA. Available WWW: http://www.clis.umd.edu/dlrg/filter/sss/papers/.

ELKATEB, FAIZA; FLUHR, CHRISTIAN. 1998. EMIR at the CLIR Track of TREC 6. In: Proceedings of the 6th Text REtrieval Conference (TREC-6); 1997 November 19-21; Gaithersburg, MD. Gaithersburg, MD: National Institute of Standards and Technology; 1998. 395-402. (NIST Special Publication 500-240) OCLC: 40306269.

ELLEN, SANDRA R. 1979. Survey of Foreign Language Problems Facing the Research Worker. Interlending Review. 1979; 7(2): 31-41. ISSN: 0140-2773.

ERES, BETH KREVITT. 1989. International Information Issues. In: Williams, Martha E., ed. Annual Review of Information Science and Technology: Volume 24. Amsterdam, The Netherlands: Elsevier Science Publishers for the American Society for Information Science; 1989. 3-32. ISBN: 0-444-87418-6.

ERBACH, GREGOR; NEUMANN, GUNTER; USZKOREIT, HANS. 1997. MULINEX: Multilingual Indexing Navigation and Editing Extensions for the World-Wide Web. In: AAAI Spring Symposium on Cross-Language Text and Speech Retrieval; 1997 March 24-26; Palo Alto, CA. Available WWW: http://www.clis.umd.edu/dlrg/filter/sss/papers/.

EVANS, DAVID A.; HANDERSON, S.K.; MONARCH, I.A.; PEREIRO, J.; DELON, L.; HERSH, WILLIAM R. 1991. Mapping Vocabularies Using "Latent Semantics." Pittsburgh, PA: Carnegie Mellon University, Laboratory for Computational Linguistics; 1991. 15p. (CMU-LCL-91-1). OCLC: 28304719.

FLUHR, CHRISTIAN. 1995. Multilingual Information Retrieval. In: Cole, Ronald A.; Mariani, Joseph; Uszkoreit, Hans; Zaenen, Anne; Zue, Victor, eds. Survey of the State of the Art in Human Language Technology. Portland, OR: Center for Spoken Language Understanding, Oregon Graduate Institute; 1995. Available WWW: http://www.cse.ogi.edu/CSLU/HLTsurvey/ch8node7.html.

FLUHR, CHRISTIAN; RADWAN, KHALED. 1993. Fulltext Databases as Lexical Semantic Knowledge for Multilingual Interrogation and Machine Translation. In: Brezillon, Patrick; Stefanuk, Vadim, eds. Proceedings of the East-West Conference on Artificial Intelligence (EWAIC '93); 1993 September 7-9; Moscow, Russia. Moscow, Russia: Association for Artificial Intelligence of Russia, ICSTI; 1993. 124-128. OCLC: 30897332.

FLUHR, CHRISTIAN; SCHMIT, DOMINIQUE; ELKATEB, FAIZA; ORTET, PHILIPPE; GURTNER, KARINE. 1997. Multilingual Database and Crosslingual Interrogation in a Real Internet Application: Architecture and Problems of Implementation. In: AAAI Spring Symposium on Cross-Language Text and Speech Retrieval; 1997 March 24-26; Palo Alto, CA. Available WWW: http://www.clis.umd.edu/dlrg/filter/sss/papers/.

FRANZEN, KRISTOFER; KARLGREN, JUSSI. 1997. REPTILE—Retrieval Extraction Presentation and Translation Using Language Engineering. In: AAAI Spring Symposium on Cross-Language Text and Speech Retrieval; 1997 March 24-26; Palo Alto, CA. Available WWW: http://www.clis.umd.edu/dlrg/filter/sss/papers/.

FREDERKING, ROBERT E.; MITAMURA, TERUKO; NYBERG, ERIC; CARBONELL, JAIME G. 1997. Translingual Information Access. In: AAAI Spring Symposium on Cross-Language Text and Speech Retrieval; 1997 March 24-26; Palo Alto, CA. Available WWW: http://www.clis.umd.edu/dlrg/filter/sss/papers/.

FURNAS, GEORGE W.; LANDAUER, THOMAS K.; GOMEZ, L. M.; DUMAIS, SUSAN T. 1987. The Vocabulary Problem in Human-System Communication. Communications of the ACM. 1987; 30(11): 964-971. ISSN: 0001-0782.

GACHOT, DENIS A.; LANGE, ELKE; YANG, JIN. 1998. The SYSTRAN NLP Browser: An Application of Machine Translation Technology in Multilingual Information Retrieval. In: Grefenstette, Gregory, ed. Cross-Language Information Retrieval. Boston, MA: Kluwer Academic; 1998. ISBN: 0-7923-8122-X. Available WWW: http://www.rxrc.xerox.com/research/mltt/DMHead/CLIR/SIGIR96CLIR.html.

GAUSSIER, E.; GREFENSTETTE, GREGORY; HULL, DAVID A.; SCHULZE, B. MAXIMILLIAN. 1998. Xerox TREC-6 Site Report: Cross Language Text Retrieval. In: Proceedings of the 6th Text REtrieval Conference (TREC-6); 1997 November 19-21; National Institute of Standards and Technology (NIST), Gaithersburg, MD. Available WWW: http://trec.nist.gov/pubs/trec6/t6_proceedings.html.

GEY, F.C.; CHEN, A. 1998. Phrase Discovery for English and Cross-Language Retrieval at TREC 6. In: Proceedings of the 6th Text REtrieval Conference (TREC-6); 1997 November 19-21; National Institute of Standards and Technology (NIST), Gaithersburg, MD. Available WWW: http://trec.nist.gov/pubs/trec6/t6_proceedings.html.

GIBB, J.M.; PHILLIPS, E. 1977. Scientific and Technical Publishing in a Multilingual Society. In: 3rd European Congress on Information Systems and Networks; 1977 May 3-6; Luxembourg, Luxembourg: Munich, Germany: Verlag Dokumentation; 1977. 13-27. ISBN: 3-7940-5184-X.

GILARRANZ, JULIO; GONZALO, JULIO; VERDEJO, FELISA. 1997. An Approach to Conceptual Text Retrieval Using the EuroWordNet Multilingual Semantic Database. In: AAAI Spring Symposium on Cross-Language Text and Speech Retrieval; 1997 March 24-26; Palo Alto, CA. Available WWW: http://www.clis.umd.edu/dlrg/filter/sss/papers/.

GOLDSTEIN, EILEEN S. 1985. The Use of Technical Information by Engineers of the Electrical Sector of Mexico. Los Angeles, CA: University of California, Los Angeles; 1985. 412p. (Ph.D. dissertation). Available from: UMI, Ann Arbor, MI. (UMI order no. 8513113).

GONZALO, JULIO; VERDEJO, FELISA; PETERS, CAROL; CALZOLARI, NICOLETTA. 1998. Applying EuroWordNet to Cross-Language Text Retrieval. Computers and the Humanities. 1998; 32(2-3): 185-207. ISSN: 0010-4817.

GREFENSTETTE, GREGORY. 1995. Comparing Two Language Identification Schemes. In: Proceedings of the 3rd International Conference on the Statistical Analysis of Textual Data; 1995 December; Rome, Italy. Available WWW: http://www.rxrc.xerox.com/publis/mltt/jadt/jadt.html.

GREFENSTETTE, GREGORY, ed. 1998. Cross-Language Information Retrieval. Boston, MA: Kluwer Academic; 1998. 182p. ISBN: 0-7923-8122-X.

GUO, JIN. 1997. A Comparative Study on Sentence Tokenization Generation Schemes. 1997 January. Available WWW: http://sunzi.iss.nus.sg:1996/guojin/papers/.

HAMP, BIRGIT; FELDWEG, HELMUT. 1997. GermaNet—A Lexical-Semantic Net for German. Available WWW: http://www.sfs.nphil.uni-tuebingen.de/lsd/english.html.

HAYASHI, YOSHIHIKO; KIKUI, GEN'ICHIRO; SUSAKI, SEIJI. 1997. TITAN: A Cross-Linguistic Search Engine for the WWW. In: AAAI Spring Symposium on Cross-Language Text and Speech Retrieval; 1997 March 24-26; Palo Alto, CA. Available WWW: http://www.clis.umd.edu/dlrg/filter/sss/papers/.

HLAVA, MARJORIE M.K.; HAINEBACH, RICHARD; BELONOGOV, GEROLD; KUZNETSOV, BORIS. 1997. Cross-Language Retrieval—English/ Russian/ French. In: AAAI Spring Symposium on Cross-Language Text and Speech Retrieval; 1997 March 24-26; Palo Alto, CA. Available WWW: http://www.clis.umd.edu/dlrg/filter/sss/papers/.

HULL, DAVID A. 1997. Using Structured Queries for Disambiguation in Cross-Language Information Retrieval. In: AAAI Spring Symposium on Cross-Language Text and Speech Retrieval; 1997 March 24-26; Palo Alto, CA. Available WWW: http://www.clis.umd.edu/dlrg/filter/sss/papers.

HULL, DAVID A.; GREFENSTETTE, GREGORY. 1996. Querying across Languages: A Dictionary-Based Approach to Multilingual Information Retrieval. In: Frei, Hans-Peter; Harman, Donna K.; Schäuble, Peter; Wilkinson, Ross, eds. SIGIR '96: Proceedings of the Association for Computing Machinery Special Interest Group on Information Retrieval (ACM/SIGIR) 19th Annual International Conference on Research and Development in Information Retrieval; 1996 August 18-22; Zurich, Switzerland. New York, NY: ACM; 1996. 49-57. ISBN: 0-89791-792-8.

HUTCHINS, W.J.; PARGETER, LISBETH J.; SAUNDERS, W.L. 1971. The Language Barrier. Sheffield, UK: University of Sheffield Postgraduate School of Librarianship and Information Science; 1971. 306p. ISBN: 0-85426-009-9.

ILJON, ARIANE. 1977. Scientific and Technical Data Bases in a Multilingual Society. On-line Review. 1977; 1(2): 133-136. ISSN: 0309-314X.

INTERNATIONAL ORGANIZATION FOR STANDARDIZATION (ISO). 1985. Guidelines for the Establishment and Development of Multilingual Thesauri. Geneva, Switzerland: ISO; 1985. (ISO 5864:1985).

INTERNATIONAL TRANSLATIONS CENTRE. 1996. World Translations Index: Volume 10(9). Delft, The Netherlands: International Translations Centre; 1996. ISSN: 0259-8264.

INTERNET SOCIETY; ALIS TECHNOLOGIES. 1997. Web Languages Hit Parade. Available WWW: http://www.isoc.org:8080/palmares.en.html.

JONES, GARETH J.F.; JAMES, DAVID A. 1997. A Critical Review of State-of-the-Art Technologies for Cross-Language Speech Retrieval. In: AAAI Spring Symposium on Cross-Language Text and Speech Retrieval; 1997 March 24-26; Palo Alto, CA. Available WWW: http://www.clis.umd.edu/dlrg/filter/sss/papers/.

KALACHKINA, S.Y. 1987. Algorithmic Determination of Descriptor Equivalents in Different Natural Languages. Automatic Documentation and Mathematical Linguistics. 1987; 21(4): 21-29. (English translation from Russian). ISSN: 0005-1055.

KARATZOGLOU, M. 1997. Translib Edited Report. Patras, Greece: Knowledge S.A.; 1997. Available from: the author, NEO Patron—Athinon 37, Patras 264-41, Greece.

KIKUI, GEN'ICHIRO. 1996. Identifying the Coding System and Language of On-line Documents on the Internet. In: COLING-96: 16th International Conference on Computational Linguistics; 1996 August 5-9; Copenhagen, Denmark. Copenhagen, Denmark: Center for Sprogteknologi; 1996. 652-657. OCLC: 37576411.

KIKUI, GEN'ICHIRO; HAYASHI, YOSHIHIKO; SUZAKI, SEIJI. 1996. Cross-Lingual Information Retrieval on the WWW. In: Proceedings of the 1st Workshop on Multilinguality in Software Engineering: The AI Contribution (MULSAIC). European Coordinating Committee for Artificial Intelligence. Available WWW: http://www.iit.nrcps.ariadne-t.gr/~costass/muls3.html.

KRAAIJ, WESSEL. 1997. Multilingual Functionality in the TwentyOne Project. In: AAAI Spring Symposium on Cross-Language Text and Speech Retrieval; 1997 March 24-26; Palo Alto, CA. Available WWW: http://www.clis.umd.edu/dlrg/filter/sss/papers/.

KRAAIJ, WESSEL; HIEMSTRA, DJOERD. 1998. Cross Language Retrieval with the Twenty-One System. In: Proceedings of the 6th Text REtrieval Conference (TREC-6); 1997 November 19-21; National Institute of Standards and Technology (NIST), Gaithersburg, MD. Available WWW: http://trec.nist.gov/pubs/trec6/t6_procedings.html.

KROVETZ, ROBERT; CROFT, W. BRUCE. 1992. Lexical Ambiguity and Information Retrieval. ACM Transactions on Information Systems. 1992; 10(2): 115-141. ISSN: 1046-8188.

KWOK, K.L. 1997. Evaluation of an English-Chinese Cross-Lingual Retrieval Experiment. In: AAAI Spring Symposium on Cross-Language Text and Speech Retrieval; 1997 March 24-26; Palo Alto, CA. Available WWW: http://www.clis.umd.edu/dlrg/filter/sss/papers/.

LANDAUER, THOMAS K.; LITTMAN, MICHAEL L. 1990. Fully Automatic Cross-Language Document Retrieval Using Latent Semantic Indexing. In: Proceedings of the 6th Annual Conference of the UW Centre for the New Oxford English Dictionary and Text Research; 1990; Waterloo, Ontario. Waterloo, Ontario: UW Centre for the New OED and Text Research; 1990. 31-38. OCLC: 39490620. Available WWW: http://www.cs.duke.edu/~mlittman/docs/x-lang.ps.

LANDAUER, THOMAS K.; LITTMAN, MICHAEL L. 1991. A Statistical Method for Language-Independent Representation of the Topical Content of Text Segments. In: Proceedings of the 11th International Conference: Expert Systems and Their Applications: Volume 8; 1991 May 27-31; Avignon, France. Nanterre, France: EC2; 1991. 77-85. ISBN: 2-906899-63-1.

LEBOWITZ, ABRAHAM I.; ZWART, ROBERT P.; SCHMID, HELGA. 1991. Multilingual Indexing and Retrieval in Bibliographic Systems: The AGRIS Experience. Quarterly Bulletin of the International Association of Agricultural Information Specialists. 1991; 36(3): 187-192. ISSN: 0020-5966.

LEE, DAR-SHYANG; NOHL, CRAIG R.; BAIRD, HENRY S. 1996. Language Identification in Complex, Unoriented, and Degraded Document Images. In: IAPR 1996: Proceedings of the Workshop on Document Analysis Systems; 1996 October 14-16; Malvern, PA. 17-39.

LI, CHUNSHENG; POLLITT, A.S.; SMITH, MARK P. 1993. Multilingual MenUSE—A Japanese Front-End for Searching English Language Databases and Vice Versa. In: McEnery, Tony; Paice, C.D., eds. Proceedings of the BCS 14th Information Retrieval Colloquium; 1992 April 13-14; Lancaster, UK. New York, NY: Springer-Verlag; 1993. 14-37. ISBN: 3-540-19808-3.

LIN, CHUNG-HSIN; CHEN, HSINCHUN. 1996. An Automatic Indexing and Neural Network Approach to Concept Retrieval and Classification of Multilingual (Chinese-English) Documents. IEEE Transactions on Systems, Man, and Cybernetics. 1996; 26(1): 75-88. ISSN: 1083-4427.

LOGINOV, B.R.; V'YUGIN, V.V. 1989. Automated Maintenance of a Bilingual Medical Thesaurus on a Microcomputer. Automatic Documentation and Mathematical Linguistics. 1989; 23(2): 72-75. (English translation from Russian). ISSN: 0005-1055.

LOUKACHEVITCH, NATALIA V. 1997. Knowledge Representation for Multilingual Text Categorization. In: AAAI Spring Symposium on Cross-Language Text and Speech Retrieval; 1997 March 24-26; Palo Alto, CA. Available WWW: http://www.clis.umd.edu/dlrg/filter/sss/papers/.

MALONE, T.W.; GRANT, K.R.; TURBAK, F.A.; BROBST, S.A.; COHEN, M. D. 1987. Intelligent Information Sharing Systems. Communications of the ACM. 1987; 30(5): 390-402. ISSN: 0001-0782.

MARCHIONINI, GARY. 1995. Information Seeking in Electronic Environments. Cambridge, UK: Cambridge University Press; 1995. 224p. ISBN: 0-521-44372-5.

MATEEV, BOJIDAR; MUNTEANU, EUGEN; SHERIDAN, PÁRAIC; WECHSLER, MARTIN; SCHÄUBLE, PETER. 1998. ETH TREC-6: Routing, Chinese, Cross-Language and Spoken Document Retrieval. In: Proceedings of the 6th Text REtrieval Conference (TREC-6); 1997 November 19-21; National Institute of Standards and Technology (NIST),

Gaithersburg, MD. Available WWW: http://trec.nist.gov/pubs/trec6/
t6_proceedings.html.

MEADOWS, ARTHUR JACK. 1974. Communication in Science. London, UK:
Butterworths; 1974. 248p. ISBN: 0-408-70572-8.

METOYER-DURAN, CHERYL. 1993. Information Gatekeepers. In: Williams,
Martha E., ed. Annual Review of Information Science and Technology:
Volume 28. Medford, NJ: Learned Information, Inc. for the American
Society for Information Science; 1993. 111-150. ISBN: 0-938734-75-X.

MILLER, GEORGE A. 1990. WordNet: An On-line Lexical Database. International Journal of Lexicography. 1990; 3(4). (Special issue). ISSN: 0950-3846.

NELSON, P. 1991. Breaching the Language Barrier: Experimentation with Japanese to English Machine Translation. In: Raitt, David I., ed. Online Information 91: 15th International Online Information Meeting Proceedings;
1991 December 10-12; London, UK. Oxford, UK: Learned Information;
1991. 21-33. ISBN: 0-904933-79-2.

NEVILLE, H. H. 1970. Feasibility Study of a Scheme for Reconciling Thesauri
Covering a Common Subject. Journal of Documentation. 1970; 26(4): 313-
336. ISSN: 0022-0418.

NEVILLE, H. H. 1976. Alternatives to Conventional Multilingual Thesauri. In:
Horsnell, Verna, ed. Report of a Workshop on Multilingual Systems. London, UK: British Library; 1976. 10-12. (British Library Research and Development Report 5265). ISBN: 0-85350-137-8.

NG, K.; ZUE, V.W. 1998. Phonetic Recognition for Spoken Document Re-
trieval. In: Proceedings of the IEEE International Conference on Acoustics,
Speech, and Signal Processing: Volume I; 1998 May 12-15; Seattle, WA.
Piscataway, NJ: IEEE; 1998. 325-328. ISBN: 0-7803-4428-6.

NGUYEN, VAN BE HAI; WILKINSON, ROSS; ZOBEL, JUSTIN. 1997. Cross-
Language Retrieval in English and Vietnamese. In: AAAI Spring Symposium on Cross-Language Text and Speech Retrieval; 1997 March 24-26;
Palo Alto, CA. Available WWW: http://www.clis.umd.edu/dlrg/filter/
sss/papers/.

O'HAGAN, MINAKO. 1996. The Coming Industry of Teletranslation. Clevedon,
UK: Multilingual Matters; 1996. 120p. ISBN: 1-85359-326-5.

OARD, DOUGLAS W. 1996. Adaptive Vector Space Text Filtering for Monolingual and Cross-Language Applications. College Park, MD: University
of Maryland, College Park; 1996. 293p. (Ph.D. dissertation). Available
from: UMI, Ann Arbor, MI. (UMI order no. 9707650).

OARD, DOUGLAS W. 1997a. Adaptive Filtering of Multilingual Document
Streams. In: 5th RIAO Conference on Computer-Assisted Information
Searching on the Internet; 1997 June 25-27; Montreal, Canada. Paris,
France: CID; 1997. 233-254. ISBN: 2-905450-06-1.

OARD, DOUGLAS W. 1997b. Alternative Approaches for Cross-Language Text
Retrieval. In: AAAI Spring Symposium on Cross-Language Text and Speech
Retrieval; 1997 March 24-26; Palo Alto, CA. Available WWW: http://
www.clis.umd.edu/dlrg/filter/sss/papers/.

OARD, DOUGLAS W. 1997c. Serving Users in Many Languages: Cross-Language Information Retrieval for Digital Libraries. D-Lib Magazine. 1997
December. ISSN: 1082-9873. Available WWW: http://www.dlib.org/dlib/
december97/oard/12oard.html.

OARD, DOUGLAS W.; DORR, BONNIE J. 1996. A Survey of Multilingual Text Retrieval. College Park, MD: University of Maryland, Institute for Advanced Computer Studies; 1996. (CS-TR-3615). Available WWW: http://www.cs.umd.edu/TRs/authors/Douglas_W_Oard.html.

OARD, DOUGLAS W.; DORR, BONNIE J. 1998. Evaluating Cross-Language Text Filtering Effectiveness. In: Grefenstette, Gregory, ed. Cross-Language Information Retrieval. Boston, MA: Kluwer Academic; 1998. ISBN: 0-7923-8122-X. Available WWW: www.rxrc.xerox.com/research/mltt/DMHead/CLIR/SIGIR96CLIR.html.

OARD, DOUGLAS W.; DORR, BONNIE J.; HACKETT, PAUL G.; KATSOVA, MARIA. 1998. A Comparative Study of Knowledge-Based Approaches for Cross-Language Information Retrieval. College Park, MD: Institute for Advanced Computer Studies, University of Maryland; 1998. (CS-TR-3897). Available WWW: http://www.cs.umd.edu/TRs/authors/Douglas_W_Oard.html.

OARD, DOUGLAS W.; HACKETT, PAUL G. 1998. Document Translation for Cross-Language Text Retrieval at the University of Maryland. In: Proceedings of the 6th Text REtrieval Conference (TREC-6); 1997 November 19-21; National Institute of Standards and Technology (NIST), Gaithersburg, MD. Available WWW: http://trec.nist.gov/pubs/trec6/t6_proceedings.html.

OFFICE FOR OFFICIAL PUBLICATIONS OF THE EUROPEAN COMMUNITIES. 1995. Thesaurus EUROVOC. Volume 3: Multilingual Version. Luxembourg: Office for Official Publications of the European Communities; 1995. ISBN: 92-7786-375-7.

PASANEN-TUOMAINEN, IRMA. 1991. Analysis of Subject Searching in the TENTTU Books Database. IATUL Proceedings. 1992; 1: 72-77. ISSN: 0966-4769.

PASHCHENKO, N.A.; KALACHKINA, S.Y.; MATSAK, N.M.; PIGUR, V.A. 1982. Basic Principles for Creating Multilanguage Information Retrieval Thesauri (Experience with Implementing GOST 7.24-80). Automatic Documentation and Mathematical Linguistics. 1982; 16(3): 30-36. (English translation from Russian). ISSN: 0005-1055.

PELISSIER, D.; ARTUR, O. 1986. The Multilingual Evolution of PASCAL. In: 10th International Online Information Meeting; 1986 December 2-4; London, UK. Oxford, UK: Learned Information; 1986. 113-121. ISBN: 0-904933-57-1.

PETERS, CAROL; PICCHI, EUGENIO. 1997. Using Linguistic Tools and Resources in Cross-Language Retrieval. In: AAAI Spring Symposium on Cross-Language Text and Speech Retrieval; 1997 March 24-26; Palo Alto, CA. Available WWW: http://www.clis.umd.edu/dlrg/filter/sss/papers.

PEVZNER, B.R. 1969. Automatic Translation of English Text to the Language of the Pusto-Nepusto-2 System. Automatic Documentation and Mathematical Linguistics. 1969; 3(4): 40-48. (English translation from Russian). ISSN: 0005-1055.

PEVZNER, B.R. 1972. Comparative Evaluation of the Operation of the Russian and English Variants of the "Pusto-Nepusto-2" System. Automatic Documentation and Mathematical Linguistics. 1972; 6(2): 71-74. (English translation from Russian). ISSN: 0005-1055.

PICCHI, EUGENIO; PETERS, CAROL. 1998. Cross Language Information Retrieval: A System for Comparable Corpus Querying. In: Grefenstette, Gregory, ed. Cross-Language Information Retrieval. Boston, MA: Kluwer Academic; 1998. ISBN: 0-7923-8122-X. Available WWW: http://www.rxrc.xerox.com/research/mltt/DMHead/CLIR/SIGIR96CLIR.html.

PIGUR, V.A. 1979. Multilanguage Information-Retrieval Systems: Integration Levels and Language Support. Automatic Documentation and Mathematical Linguistics. 1979; 13(1): 36-46. (English translation from Russian). ISSN: 0005-1055.

PIONEER CONSULTING. 1997. Pioneer Forecast: International E-mail Growth. The Pioneer Report. 1997 August; 1: 3. Available WWW: http://www.pioneerconsulting.com.

POLLITT, A. STEVEN; ELLIS, GEOFFREY P. 1993. Multilingual Access to Document Databases. In: CAIS/ASCI '93: 21st Annual Conference, Canadian Association for Information Science; 1993 July 11-14; Antigonish, Canada. Toronto, Canada: CAIS/ASCI; 1993. 128-140. OCLC: 36339460.

POLLITT, A. STEVEN; ELLIS, GEOFFREY P.; SMITH, M.P.; GREGORY, M.R.; LI, C.S.; ZANGENBERG, H. 1993. A Common Query Interface for Multilingual Document Retrieval from Databases of the European Community Institutions. In: Raitt, David I.; Jeapes, Ben, eds. 17th International Online Information Meeting; 1993 December 7-9; London, UK. Oxford, UK: Learned Information, Ltd.; 1993. 47-61. ISBN: 0-904933-85-7.

RADWAN, KHALED. 1994. Vers l'Accés Multilingue en Langage Naturel aux Bases de Données Textuelles. Paris, France: Université de Paris-Sud, Centre d'Orsay; 1994. (Ph.D. dissertation).

RADWAN, KHALED; FLUHR, CHRISTIAN. 1995. Textual Database Lexicon Used as a Filter to Resolve Semantic Ambiguity Applications on Multilingual Information Retrieval. In: Proceedings of the 4th Annual Symposium on Document Analysis and Information Retrieval; 1995 April; Las Vegas, NV. Las Vegas, NV: Information Science Research Institute; 1995. 121-136.

READWARE. Available WWW: http://www.readware.com/webquery.htm.

REHDER, BOB; LITTMAN, MICHAEL L.; DUMAIS, SUSAN T.; LANDAUER, THOMAS K. 1998. Automatic 3-Language Cross-Language Information Retrieval with Latent Semantic Indexing. In: Proceedings of the 6th Text REtrieval Conference (TREC-6); 1997 November 19-21; National Institute of Standards and Technology (NIST), Gaithersburg, MD. Available WWW: http://trec.nist.gov/pubs/trec6/t6_proceedings.html.

RESNIK, PHILIP. 1997. Evaluating Multilingual Gisting of Web Pages. In: AAAI Spring Symposium on Cross-Language Text and Speech Retrieval; 1997 March 24-26; Palo Alto, CA. Available WWW: http://www.clis.umd.edu/dlrg/filter/sss/papers/.

RIDDLE, J.N. 1992. FBIS Requirements and Capabilities. In: 1st International Symposium on National Security and National Competitiveness; 1992 December 1-3; Tyson's Corner, VA. Falls Church, VA: Open Source Solutions (OSS); 1992. 264-271. OCLC: 28768071.

RIGBY, MALCOLM. 1981. Automation and the UDC, 1948-1980. 2nd edition. The Hague, The Netherlands: Federation Internationale de Documentation (FID); 1981. 160p. (FID publication 565). ISBN: 92-6600-565-7.

ROLLAND-THOMAS, PAUL; MERCURE, GERARD. 1989. Subject Access in a Bilingual Online Catalog. Cataloging and Classification Quarterly. 1989; 10(1/2): 141-163. ISSN: 0163-9374.

ROLLING, LOLL. 1976. Multilingual Systems: Survey of the European Scene. In: Horsnell, Verina, ed. Report of a Workshop on Multilingual Systems. London, UK: British Library; 1976. 4-5. (British Library Research and Development Report 5265). ISBN: 0-85350-137-8.

SALTON, GERARD. 1970. Automatic Processing of Foreign Language Documents. Journal of the American Society for Information Science. 1970; 21(3): 187-194. ISSN: 0002-8231.

SALTON, GERARD. 1973. Experiments in Multi-Lingual Information Retrieval. Information Processing Letters. 1973; 2(1): 6-11. ISSN: 0020-0190.

SANDERSON, MARK. 1994. Word Sense Disambiguation and Information Retrieval. In: Croft, W. Bruce; van Rijsbergen, C.J., eds. SIGIR '94: Proceedings of the Association for Computing Machinery Special Interest Group on Information Retrieval (ACM/SIGIR) 17th Annual International Conference on Research and Development in Information Retrieval; 1994 July 3-6; Dublin, Ireland. New York, NY: Springer-Verlag; 1994. 142-151. ISBN: 0-387-19887-X.

SCHÄUBLE, PETER; SHERIDAN, PÁRAIC. 1998. Cross-Language Information Retrieval (CLIR) Track Overview. In: Proceedings of the 6th Text REtrieval Conference (TREC-6); 1997 November 19-21; National Institute of Standards and Technology (NIST), Gaithersburg, MD. Available WWW: http://trec.nist.gov/pubs/trec6/t6_proceedings.html.

SEMTURS, FRIEDRICH. 1978. STAIRS/TLS —A System for "Free Text" and "Descriptor" Searching. In: Brenner, E.H., ed. The Information Age in Perspective: Proceedings of the American Society for Information Science (ASIS) 41st Annual Meeting: Volume 15; 1978 November 13-17; New York, NY. White Plains, NY: Knowledge Industry Publications, Inc. for ASIS; 1978. 295-298. ISSN: 0044-7870; ISBN: 0-914236-22-9.

SHERIDAN, PÁRAIC; BALLERINI, JEAN PAUL. 1996. Experiments in Multilingual Information Retrieval Using the SPIDER System. In: Frei, Hans-Peter; Harman, Donna K.; Schäuble, Peter; Wilkinson, Ross, eds. SIGIR '96: Proceedings of the Association for Computing Machinery Special Interest Group on Information Retrieval (ACM/SIGIR) 19th Annual International Conference on Research and Development in Information Retrieval; 1996 August 18-22; Zurich, Switzerland. New York, NY: ACM; 1996. 58-66. ISBN: 0-89791-792-8.

SHERIDAN, PÁRAIC; BALLERINI, JEAN PAUL; SCHÄUBLE, PETER. 1998. Building a Large Multilingual Test Collection from Comparable News Documents. In: Grefenstette, Gregory, ed. Cross Language Information Retrieval. Boston, MA: Kluwer Academic; 1998. ISBN: 0-7923-8122-X. Available WWW: http://www.rxrc.xerox.com/research/mltt/DMHead/CLIR/SIGIR96CLIR.html.

SHERIDAN, PÁRAIC; SCHÄUBLE, PETER. 1997. Cross-Language Information Retrieval in a Multilingual Legal Domain. In: Proceedings of the 1st

European Conference on Research and Advanced Technology for Digital Libraries; 1997 September 1-3; Pisa, Italy. Berlin, Germany: Springer; 1997. 253-268. ISBN: 3-540-63554-8.

SHERIDAN, PÁRAIC; WECHSLER, MARTIN; SCHÄUBLE, PETER. 1997. Cross-Language Speech Retrieval: Establishing a Baseline Performance. In: Belkin, N.J.; Narasimhalu, A. Desai; Willett, Peter, eds. SIGIR '97: Proceedings of the Association for Computing Machinery Special Interest Group on Information Retrieval (ACM/SIGIR) 20th Annual International Conference on Research and Development in Information Retrieval; 1997 July 27-31; Philadelphia, PA. New York, NY: ACM; 1997. 99-108. ISBN: 0-89791-836-3.

SMEATON, ALAN F.; SPITZ, A. LARRY. 1997. Using Character Shape Coding for Information Retrieval. In: Proceedings of the 4th International Conference on Document Analysis and Recognition, ICDAR'97; 1997 August 18-20; Ulm, Germany. Los Alamitos, CA: IEEE Computer Society; 1997. 974-978. ISBN: 0-8186-7898-4.

SMITH, MARK P.; POLLITT, A. STEVEN. 1993. An Evaluation of Concept Translation through Menu Navigation in the MenUSE Intermediary System. In: McEnery, Tony; Paice, C.D., eds. Proceedings of the BCS 14th Information Retrieval Colloquium; 1992 April 13-14; Lancaster, UK. London, UK: Springer-Verlag; 1993. 38-54. ISBN: 3-540-19808-3.

SOERGEL, DAGOBERT. 1997. Multilingual Thesauri in Cross-Language Text and Speech Retrieval. In: AAAI Spring Symposium on Cross-Language Text and Speech Retrieval; 1997 March 24-26; Palo Alto, CA. Available WWW: http://www.clis.umd.edu/dlrg/filter/sss/papers/.

STAMATATOS, E.; MICHOS, S.; PATELODIMOU, C.; FAKOTAKIS, N. 1997. TRANSLIB: An Advanced Tool for Supporting Multilingual Access to Library Catalogues. In: 2nd Workshop on Multilinguality in the Software Industry: The AI Contribution; 1997 August; Nagoya, Japan.

STEGENTRITT, ERWIN. 1994. German Analysis: Morpho-Syntax within the Framework of the Free-Text Retrieval Project E.M.I.R. Saarbrücken, Germany: AQ-Verlag; 1994. 97p. ISBN: 3-922441-63-7.

STUDEMAN, WILLIAM. 1992. Teaching the Giant to Dance: Contradictions and Opportunities in Open Source within the Intelligence Community. In: Proceedings of the 1st International Symposium on National Security and National Competitiveness: Volume 2; 1992 December 1-3; Tyson's Corner, VA. Falls Church, VA: Open Source Solutions; 1992. 82-92. OCLC: 28768071.

SUZUKI, M.; HASHIMOTO, K. 1996. Enhancing Source Text for WWW Distribution. In: Myaeng, S.H., ed. Proceedings of the Workshop on Information Retrieval with Oriental Languages; 1996 July 28-29; Taejon, Korea. Korea Research & Development Information Center; 1996. 51-56.

TAYLOR, ROBERT S. 1962. The Process of Asking Questions. American Documentation. 1962; 13(4): 391-396. ISSN: 0002-8231.

UNESCO. 1971. Guidelines for Establishment and Development of Multilingual Scientific and Technical Thesauri for Information Retrieval. Paris, France: Unesco; 1971. 20p. (SC/WS/501). OCLC: 5313118.

VOLODIN, K.I.; GUL'NITSKII, L.L.; MAKSAKOVA, R.N.; PARKHOMENKO, V.F.; POZHARISKII, I.F.; FEDOTOVA, L.V.; YAKOVLEVA, N.I. 1991. Bilingual Indexing of Geological Documents. Automatic Documentation and Mathematical Linguistics. 1991; 25(6): 43-45. (English translation from Russian). ISSN: 0005-1055.

WECHSLER, MARTIN; SHERIDAN, PÁRIAC; SCHÄUBLE, PETER. 1997. Multi-Language Text Indexing for Internet Retrieval. In: 5th RIAO Conference on Computer-Assisted Information Searching on the Internet; 1997 June 25-27; Montreal, Canada. 217-232. Available WWW: http://www-ir.inf.ethz.ch/Public-Web-Pages/sheridan/papers.

WEIGAND, HANS. 1997. A Multilingual Ontology-based Lexicon for News Filtering—The TREVI Project. In: IJCAI Workshop on Ontologies and Multilingual NLP; 1997 August 23; Nagoya, Japan. Available WWW: http://crl.nmsu.edu/Events/IJCAI/.

WELLISCH, HANS. 1973. Linguistic and Semantic Problems in the Use of English-Language Information Services in Non-English-Speaking Countries. International Library Review. 1973; 5(2): 147-162. ISSN: 0020-7837.

WHITNEY, GRETCHEN. 1990. Language Distribution in Databases: An Analysis and Evaluation. Metuchen, NJ: Scarecrow Press; 1990. 379p. ISBN: 0-8108-2323-3.

WILKINSON, ROSS. 1997. Chinese Document Retrieval at TREC-6. In: Proceedings of the 6th Text REtrieval Conference (TREC-6); 1997 November 19-21; National Institute of Standards and Technology (NIST), Gaithersburg, MD. Available WWW: http://trec.nist.gov/pubs/trec6/t6_proceedings.html.

WOOD, DAVID N. 1967. The Foreign-Language Problem Facing Scientists and Technologists in the United Kingdom: Report of a Recent Survey. Journal of Documentation. 1967; 23(2): 117-130. ISSN: 0022-0418.

WOOD, DAVID N. 1974. Access to Information in Foreign Languages—An Experiment. BLL Review. 1974; 2(1): 12-14. ISSN: 0305-6503.

YAMABANA, KIYOSHI; MURAKI, KAZUNORI; DOI, SHINICHI; KAMEI, SHIN-ICHIRO. 1998. A Language Conversion Front-End for Cross-Linguistic Information Retrieval. In: Grefenstette, Gregory, ed. Cross-Language Information Retrieval. Boston, MA: Kluwer Academic; 1998. ISBN: 0-7923-8122-X. Available WWW: http://www.rxrc.xerox.com/research/mlttDMHead/CLIR/SIGIR96CLIR.html.

YANG, YIMING; BROWN, R.D.; FREDERKING, ROBERT E.; CARBONELL, JAIME G.; GENG, Y.; LEE, D. 1997. Bilingual-Corpus Based Approaches to Translingual Information Retrieval. In: 2nd Workshop on Multilinguality in the Software Industry: The AI Contribution; 1997 August; Nagoya, Japan.

ZISSMAN, MARC A. 1996. Comparison of Four Approaches to Automatic Language Identification of Telephone Speech. IEEE Transactions on Speech and Audio Processing. 1996; SAP-4(1): 31-44. ISSN: 1063-6676.

III

Applications

Section III provides chapters in two applications areas, computer supported cooperative work and electronic publishing. The chapter on "Computer Supported Cooperative Work in Information Search and Retrieval" is by Michael B. Twidale of the University of Illinois, Urbana-Champaign and David M. Nichols of the University of Lancaster, United Kingdom. The chapter on "Electronic Scholarly Journal Publishing" is by Robin P. Peek of Simmons College and Jeffrey P. Pomerantz of Syracuse University.

Michael B. Twidale and David M. Nichols open their chapter on "Computer Supported Cooperative Work in Information Search and Retrieval" by explaining the limits of the literature covered for the chapter. They provide an overview of CSCW indicating the potential for library and information science researchers. They discuss the types of CSCW systems in terms of time-space quadrants: same time, same place; same time, different place; different time, same place; and different time, different place. CSCW systems include technological support for meetings, and shared drawing and collaborative writing.

Within the context of MUDs (Multi-User Dungeon) and MOOs (MUD, Object-Oriented) Twidale and Nichols discuss awareness (i.e., of what one's colleagues are doing), workflow (computerized systems that support the way that offices process work), organizational memory (collective memory of expertise of members of an organization), CSCW and the World Wide Web (where the Web provides an infrastructure for supporting collaborative work at low cost), toolkits (of software for the prototyping and testing of new applications of CSCW), computer-supported collaborative learning (CSCL), and computer-mediated communication (CMC).

In the section titled "Analytical CSCW," the authors treat ethnography, requirements capture, and evaluation of CSCW systems. In the section on "Collaborative Work and LIS," they put library activities into appropriate time-space quadrants. This section covers libraries and organizational CSCW, information retrieval and CSCW, remote reference, context establishment (as it applies to digital libraries), information visualization, and digital libraries. The section on "User-User Collaboration" covers annotations and ratings (associated with documents), matchmaking (users becoming aware of other users with similar interests), and the implications for privacy in the CSCW context. In concluding, Twidale and Nichols note that the "substantial body of LIS knowledge on organizing information structures for usability (access) by others and supporting information searchers in collaborative interactions (e.g., reference work) has great potential to inform CSCW research and development."

Robin P. Peek and Jeffrey P. Pomerantz open their chapter, "Electronic Scholarly Journal Publishing," by observing that while publications that reference the use of electronic scholarly journals have spanned more than three decades and almost every academic discipline, their chapter is limited to milestone works in the evolution of these journals. In a section on "Nontraditional Models" they examine various writers' visions of dissemination of scholarly information as well as proposals for maintenance and policy making. In the next section they identify historically significant experiments and projects, noting that several journals that appeared to be failures were really experiments, intended to be short-lived. The section on "Acceptance by the Scholarly Community" covers issues including journal content, interfaces, formats and delivery, and, ultimately, user and social implications.

Generally, the authors found that knowledge about journals (electronic and otherwise) and scholars' relationships to them is inconsistent. Traditional publishers have either not pursued systematic evaluation of the uses of their experiments and projects or have elected not to make the information public. It is apparent that the relationship between publishing and the scholarly community has destabilized. While there is considerable discussion by advocates of electronic scholarly publishing regarding how the process should change, the authors found that surprisingly little research provides insights into variables that will influence the ultimate acceptance of electronic journals by the academic community.

7

Computer Supported Cooperative Work in Information Search and Retrieval

Michael B. Twidale
University of Illinois, Urbana-Champaign

David M. Nichols
University of Lancaster, UK

AIMS

This review considers how research in collaborative technologies can inform research and development in library and information science (LIS). We review the area of computer supported cooperative work (CSCW). As this is a substantial body of work, we only attempt to provide an overview, giving pointers to more detailed information. We have chosen articles that contain thorough reviews of certain subtopics, illustrate certain approaches, and are particularly accessible to a reader from outside the area. This allows us to bring up to date a number of surveys of CSCW undertaken in the early 1990s. The intention is to indicate the technologies developed in CSCW and some of the modes of analysis that have proven effective. We then consider how these technologies have been and might be applied in LIS and how they can interact with the existing body of knowledge and ongoing research in that field to improve the design of effective computerized information systems.

Although we focus on literature from outside conventional LIS, we wish to acknowledge at the outset that collaboration is not a new idea to the field. After all, what is a traditional library with carefully designed signage and access points to cataloging and indexing sources (even if embodied in the medium of paper, paint, and index cards rather than more glamorous technologies) but an interface to an information system? What is a reference desk but an interface to support collaborative working and learning? Before we get too swept up in the potential of exciting new technologies (a danger that as computer

Annual Review of Information Science and Technology (ARIST), Volume 33, 1998
Martha E. Williams, Editor
Published for the American Society for Information Science (ASIS)
By Information Today, Inc., Medford, NJ

scientists we are only too aware) we need to ground this review in an understanding that librarians have already been doing something directly analogous for many years. With careful analysis and evolution of the design of physical artifacts and conventional face-to-face collaborative interactions, libraries have made much progress. The flow of information should be two-way; existing practice can inform the design of computer systems not only for libraries but also for other contexts where people must navigate an immense information space and work with specialists to understand their complex task. Librarians should be wary of the brash parochialism of some computer scientists who may see a "primitive" low-tech structure and instantly plan how it can be replaced by glitzy but unproven technologies in search of application. Nevertheless, these technologies do offer intriguing possibilities for supporting different kinds of information retrieval and for supporting the usability, usefulness, and acceptability of digital libraries.

The Case for Collaboration

CSCW looks at how computing technologies can be developed to enable groups of people to get their work done. Note that in addition to referring to computer supported cooperative work, the word collaborative is also used. The resulting products are also known as groupware, particularly when referring to commercial applications of CSCW research. CSCW is based on the rather obvious principle that most people do not work alone, but rather interact with other people (a principle nonetheless that much existing software seems to ignore). People are usually part of an organization and work with others in that and other organizations in order to complete tasks. However, until the advent of work in CSCW, most computer systems could be charged as embodying the implicit assumption that people worked alone and needed systems that would help them do so better. Indeed, in some cases, the need to work with other people (e.g., to ask for help or to share the workload) was regarded as something of a failure, and progress was seen in the design of a system that allowed them to accomplish their goals on their own. Examples occur in research ranging from computer-based tutoring systems to information retrieval (IR). Research in artificial intelligence (AI) and intelligent agents extends this approach, aiming to accomplish some subgoals of a task by a division of labor between software rather than between people. Clearly, where such approaches succeed in practical applications, they are very desirable. CSCW is a complementary approach, most effective where it is not currently feasible to replace human-human cooperation.

There are three ways to view collaborative work and computer support for it in the context of research applications in LIS:

- Libraries are organizations and CSCW can be used in them as in other information-intensive organizations, (such as banks, insurance companies, and hospitals) where CSCW research has traditionally focused.
- The search for information is often just a part of people's work, and in this broader context people collaborate and may already use CSCW tools. Thus the information search process should take into account the potential of CSCW to mesh more effectively with people's wider activities.
- The search for information is often itself a collaborative activity involving interaction with colleagues, other users, and reference librarians. CSCW may help this process and provide for new forms of collaborative work to operate in new contexts of search, including digital libraries.

It is this last aspect, collaborative searching, that we consider in most depth in the later parts of this review. Information search and retrieval has collaborative aspects that we believe are often not considered sufficiently by information systems designers. Hence it is our belief that researchers and systems developers may usefully draw on the concepts and methods already tested in CSCW. In this review, we consider a range of kinds of collaborative work and technologies that might be employed to improve the effectiveness of information systems. Note that we see this work as strongly related to the aims of interface designers in that it relies on the resulting collaborative systems having usable interfaces. MARCHIONINI & KOMLODI in this volume examine the issues of interfaces in great detail.

In this review we use the term *collaboration* extensively. It is important to be clear about its meaning. In LIS, the term is often used to mean collaboration between organizations in order to share resources or information and to unite collections, catalogs, and so forth. This kind of collaboration can be considered strategic. By contrast, we focus on collaborations between individuals within or across organizations. These interactions are often ad hoc, may last only short periods of time, and may be best described as tactical. Tactical collaborations may be planned or occur spontaneously. They can be hindered or helped by technology. They may also be a part of a strategic inter-organizational collaborative project. Collaborative work is not a panacea; it may involve conflict as well as cooperation (EASTERBROOK). A system that assumes uncomplicated harmonious synoptic work is unlikely to be used for long. In computer science, the term collaborative is sometimes also used in work on agents (small programs that interact with each other to achieve larger goals). We do not review here agent technology and inter-agent collaboration.

VISIONARY ARTICLES IN LIS

Much of this review cites computer science articles that illustrate concepts with potential for LIS. However, it is important to acknowledge that visionary papers considering the potential of the collaborative viewpoint were published in LIS well before the technologies caught up. It is intriguing to note that many of the ideas relating to collaboration and digital libraries reviewed here as state of the art (or even somewhat futuristic) are previewed in the 1964 paper by SWANSON:

- Full-text retrieval (envisioned as via microfilm)
- Requests based on previous use of the database
- Recovery of materials seen previously by the user, or used by another specified person
- Matchmaking of users by their usage of common materials
- Discovery of groups of books that are frequently used together to inform supplemental cataloging
- Analysis of the variation of such book groups over time
- Reuse of prior searches to enable the creation of a private "demand library" thus reducing the need for users to hoard books
- User annotations
- Retrieval of similar works by common users, or recorded judgments by users
- Different interfaces to the system for different contexts of use
- Incremental feedback of intermediate search results
- The privacy issues of collaboration

We elaborate on these ideas in subsequent sections. Swanson's approach to the issue of raising agendas for the design of computerized catalogs has much to recommend it. He chose to focus on the needs of users as informed by his research and understanding of the topic, fully expecting that the capabilities of information systems (and especially computer hardware) would eventually catch up in terms of functionality and cost. They certainly have. His speculations of costs of approximately $20 million (in 1964 dollars) can perhaps now be realized in high-end personal computers costing little more than $2000 (in 1998 dollars). It is puzzling that so many of his more intriguing ideas seem to have been ignored, or at best rarely implemented.

It seems that much subsequent systems development has been technology-led rather than rooted in careful analysis of user needs. The library world appears to have been focused on the practical implementation of full-scale working systems. There is, of course, nothing wrong with that. However, there does not appear to have been as much speculative development of library systems and interfaces in a research context of proof-by-construction and discovery-by-building as has been used to great effect in other areas of computer science, including CSCW. The process of scenario-based design (CARROLL, 1995a, 1995b) is a powerful mechanism for envisioning potential technologies and how they can be developed and integrated into the work practice efficiently and effectively.

Another visionary article is that by TAYLOR in 1968. This classic analysis of the traditional reference interview has wider implications for the design of systems to enhance both human-human and human-computer interaction as part of the problem-solving process. Taylor states that

> we view the inquiry not as a command, but rather as an adaptive self-organizing system in which the question is open-ended and dynamic. In fact . . . the inquirer's original question may change during the search, as he adapts to the feedback of the search process (TAYLOR, p. 188).

We concur with Taylor's viewpoint and use it to advocate the design of systems that actively provide support for the search process. This means supporting an evolving information need over both time and space, involving both solitary computer use and interaction with others. Taylor notes the difficulties that inquirers have in articulating their need, including the fact that "inquirers seldom ask at first for what they want" (p. 185). The skills of a reference librarian are required to obtain a rich picture of the inquirer, including personal background and context of the query. We return later to the issue of supporting the timely and efficient acquisition of context.

Taylor also notes the additional expertise that the librarian brings to the negotiation process with the inquirer. This includes not only where to look (physical information resources), but also whom to ask (human information resources). It also includes the acquisition and use of context, including previous interactions with the user, what the user has independently tried so far, and whom they have already talked to. These are all techniques that potentially can be supported, although probably should not be automated, in CSCW systems.

Perhaps most intriguing is Taylor's mention in passing that the "work by Engelbart and others at the Stanford Research Institute on the augmentation of human intellect by computers may generate interesting systems sometime in the future, but appears to have little pertinence at this time to the problems under consideration here" (pp. 193-194). Engelbart's research in the 1960s (ENGELBART; ENGELBART & ENGLISH) is one of the key foundations of CSCW systems development. Thus, 30 years after Taylor's paper, we are making the case that the successors to Engelbart's work have reached the stage where they are indeed pertinent.

This discussion of the work of Taylor and Swanson is intended to emphasize that we are not advocating the adoption of collaborative technologies because they are available and are in need of application somewhere. Rather, we are concerned that a consideration by LIS researchers of the issues of collaborative technology will allow them to draw on research within LIS to inform the design of information systems to support collaborative work where that is the most effective and efficient way for people to achieve their aims. The process of doing this involves a combination of technology-driven and user-driven design, as illustrated by these papers. It includes exploiting newly available technologies, analyzing user needs by careful studies of what people actually do rather than what they are meant to do, developing prototypes, and setting research agendas for further analysis and desired functionality.

OVERVIEW OF CSCW

The rest of the review is in two parts. The first surveys existing practice in CSCW, noting technologies, concepts, and methods that in our opinion offer the best potential for insights for an LIS researcher. We attempt to provide a sampling of articles that will be of interest to a reader, particularly one from an LIS background who has not previously encountered CSCW. In the interest of brevity we do not attempt to be exhaustive, nor to elaborate all of the issues raised. The second part, beginning with the section "Collaborative Work and LIS," considers how that knowledge can be applied in LIS.

The term computer supported cooperative work (CSCW) was coined by Cashman and Greif for a workshop in 1984 (GREIF). However, the earlier research by Engelbart involved the development of many features studied in CSCW and research continued in a number of fields including computer science, sociology, psychology, and linguistics. In CSCW, as in other areas of computer science, publication in refereed conferences is a major part of academic activity, so many of the key publications are in conference proceedings. The first conference on CSCW was held in 1986 in Austin, Texas (ASSOCIATION FOR COMPUTING MACHINERY). Other conferences where CSCW papers are published include: The European Conference on Computer Supported Cooperative Work (ECSCW), The Hawaii International Conference on System Sciences (HICSS), The ACM Symposium on User Interface Software and Technology (UIST), and The Conference on Human Factors in Computing Systems (CHI). This list re-emphasizes that collaborative working and interface design are strongly interwoven.

The major journal is *Computer Supported Cooperative Work: The Journal of Collaborative Computing*. In the first issue in 1992, SCHMIDT & BANNON provide a useful clarification of the nature of CSCW as a research area. Many CSCW papers are also published in *Communications of the ACM, ACM Transactions on Office Information Systems,* and the *International Journal of Human-Computer Studies* (renamed from the *International Journal of Man-Machine Studies* in 1994). A number of useful survey articles on CSCW were published in the early 1990s, including RODDEN and ELLIS ET AL. (see KIES ET AL. for a recent overview). Various books of readings also provide a good overview, including BAECKER, GALEGHER ET AL., GREENBERG, and GREIF. GRUDIN (1994a) provides a more recent historical overview that examines the variation in focus among researchers originating in different disciplines as well as variations among researchers in North America, Europe, and Japan. Our aim is to give an overview for newcomers to the field while also providing some more recent references than those in the survey articles mentioned above.

One useful way of categorizing the various kinds of CSCW systems is by determining the place and time of the collaborative interactions supported. This visual categorization by time-space quadrants was originated by JOHANSEN and has been much copied. Collaboration can be between people in the same place (co-located) or different places (remote). Collaboration can be at the same time (synchronous) or separated in time (asynchronous). Figure 1 illustrates the quadrants. Examples from the various quadrants are:

- Same time, same place: meeting support tools
- Same time, different place: video conferencing

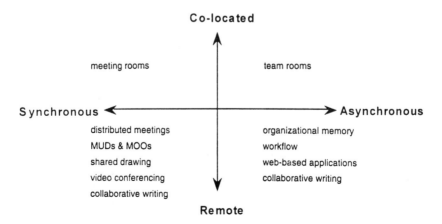

Figure 1. The CSCW spatial and temporal quadrants

- Different time, same place: a design team's shared room containing specialized equipment
- Different time, different place: email systems

As a way to begin understanding the space of actual and possible systems, the quadrant overview is useful, but it is difficult to categorize systems because many provide functions belonging in different quadrants. This is particularly true of systems intended to mesh with different organizational contexts and a variety of ways of working, since most real work activity does not fall into a single quadrant (GRUDIN, 1994a).

TYPES OF CSCW SYSTEMS

A number of types of systems have been developed to support different kinds of collaborative interaction. An outsider to the computing literature needs to proceed with caution. Systems are developed to investigate a problem space. They may work successfully in the laboratory, but still be a long way from commercial deployment. In order to succeed in the marketplace of ideas, some systems and types of systems enjoy considerable hype, only to be deflated by studies that show that they work poorly in practice and then have been superseded by newer technologies. One must allow for extremes of both optimism and pessimism. It is one of the ironies of research that as a technology becomes successful, it figures less in the research literature, and discussion and investigation returns to the difficult applications that have not yet been developed to that level of acceptance. There are some considerable successes in collaborative technologies, such as the World Wide Web, email, and increasing corporate use of video conferencing.

In this section, we outline some of the main types of systems described in the literature. We do not aim to be exhaustive, but rather to give a flavor of activity in CSCW. The types are roughly ordered according to figure 1, progressing counterclockwise. Although we include team rooms (physical locations providing technologies for intermittent working between team members) in that figure as an example of asynchronous co-located work, we shall ignore this quadrant to focus on applications in the other three, where the bulk of research has been concentrated. The rise and fall in prominence of various CSCW types in the literature over time perhaps indicates that systems development in computer science research seems to be driven as much by fashion as by real or perceived needs of functionality. For various types of systems we note some potential LIS implications.

Meeting Support

The huge number of meetings held and the large amount of time spent in them worldwide creates a great interest in improving their effectiveness and efficiency by adding appropriate technology to the meeting room. The costs of assembling participants in the same place at the same time drives the desire to support distributed and even asynchronous meetings. In addition to the CSCW literature, there is a substantial body of work on group decision support systems. JESSUP & VALACICH give a good overview.

MARK ET AL. (1997b) describe a modern meeting support system, DOLPHIN, as well as reviewing related work. Systems may focus on supporting meetings where all participants are physically present in the same room. Each participant may have a computer with the monitor recessed into the desk in order to allow eye contact with other participants. Systems may include support for anonymous brainstorming (everyone types in ideas, which are accumulated for collective discussion and refinement) and different methods of voting. One member may take the floor and highlight or edit the collective display. This is similar to standing at the front of the meeting room and using a whiteboard, flip chart, or overhead transparencies, but allows greater speed and flexibility in both manipulating computational representations such as diagrams or concept maps and in handing control to another member.

Systems intended to support distributed meetings may also include live video links and suitable displays. A distributed meeting may link participants located in different meeting rooms, or participants in their own offices. Both require the use of specialized hardware and software with, in general, more sophisticated features available in special rooms to support distributed meetings. The issues of turn-taking, floor control, sketching at a distance, and telepointing (pointing to or within a document) become more complicated in a distributed meeting. Studies of these tools have shown that important but subtle issues in human communication must be addressed if people are to be comfortable with their use.

For example, a remote participant who appears as a small image on a monitor may be easier to ignore than a local onsite participant. Perhaps virtual representations of remote participants should be life-size to help the impression of equal access. On the other hand, status is important in real meetings and equal access may not always be appropriate. This example reveals how an unconsidered technological fix to a problem may be inadvisable compared to first gaining a more detailed understanding of what people do and why, then using that knowledge, in developing assistive technologies. This approach has been undertaken by researchers in computer-mediated communication (CMC), considered later. As another example, frequently in remote video arrangements (including those on people's desks for person-to-person meetings) the camera is mounted on top of the computer monitor. Although this allows the capture of the user's face, it fails to account for the crucial effect of gaze in communication. The user may be looking into the eyes of the remote user as represented on the monitor, while the image sent to the remote user will show downcast eyes. In Western cultures, the apparent avoidance of eye contact conveys impressions of failure to engage, or even dishonesty. Thus users may have a vague feeling of disquiet about the quality of their remote interaction without necessarily knowing why.

A substantial amount of research in CSCW has investigated the synchronous remote collaboration quadrant. Within that area, many researchers have tried to understand the importance of video links. Providing a video link is relatively expensive, so it is useful to know how well it supports the interaction. Although some studies have shown that video is relatively less important than audio (GALE), TANG & ISAACS show that video was considered by users to be very important and particularly effective in supporting the process of collaboration. Tang and Isaacs explain this difference partly by their concentration on the process of interaction, and partly by the greater authenticity of their experiment, which involved longer-term observation of pre-existing groups going about their regular work. Their experiment also shows that audio quality was a major issue in usability; they advocate degrading video performance, if necessary, in favor of preserving audio quality.

BRINCK & GOMEZ built on the research on Cruiser, a video communications system (KRAUT ET AL.). Observations of the use of Cruiser found that a major disadvantage was its lack of a way of easily sharing the artifacts that people often use in face-to-face meetings, such as drawings, graphs, and photographs. These they term "conversational props": elements that add communicative realism to conversations and that need to be re-inserted into remote conversations. An example is the sharing of a high quality X-ray image in a remote conversation between physicians. In order to understand the desired functionality, Brinck and Gomez studied the use of office whiteboards in face-to-face meetings. They say, "Our goal was not to build an electronic duplicate of a physical whiteboard, but instead to discover the communication intent . . . and to use that information to inform the design of an electronic medium which supports the use of conversational props" (p. 171). This typifies a common and successful method; observe existing work practice in order to understand its underlying structure and use this knowledge to inform innovative design. It does not mean the slavish imitation of the structures of existing practice in systems to support remote working. It is an approach that recurs throughout this review, especially in the more successful research reported.

The study by Brinck and Gomez revealed that whiteboards are more than drawing spaces; considerable amounts of text are produced and rich semantics are used. Conventional physical whiteboards do not support these kinds of features very well. An electronic whiteboard may even be an improvement, supporting the selection of commonly used elements from a palette of objects and easier revision and rearrangement of structure. In particular, users may save objects of importance for future use. This and related research on whiteboards and other props emphasizes their role in supplementing conversation, a theme that reappears when we consider collaboration in libraries.

KARSENTY studied help-giving interactions between expert and novice word processor users. This kind of interaction has many manifestations, including technical software support over the telephone and help given to users of catalogs and bibliographic databases in libraries (see the section on remote reference). Ideally, when the expert is not in the same place as the learner, the system should provide functionalities to enable an approximation of side-by-side interaction. We assume that the latter is the ideal, but is not always possible or economic. Karsenty's experimental comparison of co-located and remote dialogs led to three recommendations: (1) greater integration of the system with the available communication facilities, as it was found that novices' current goals were often too poorly specified for experts to supply appropriate help; (2) more structure to users' messages, especially their goal and request descriptions; and (3) development of interaction-based approaches (similar to TAYLOR'S dynamic feedback in support of the search process) because it is futile to aspire to single-pass help dialogs.

WATSON & SASSE examined the usability and effectiveness of a remote language-teaching system that involved multicast conferencing over the Internet using video, audio, and a shared whiteboard. Audio was key in this application and video was more valuable psychologically than functionally. The researchers determined that a downgraded video connection is acceptable, thus reinforcing the finding of TANG & ISAACS, and that full-duplex audio is more important. Interestingly, students' subjective and objective evaluations, especially of audio quality, did not correlate. Students used the whiteboard more than in a conventional classroom, possibly because they were less intimidated by having a remote tutor. The system allowed simultaneous reading, writing, speaking, and listening, which are not easily achieved in conventional lessons. Thus a new form of interaction with desirable pedagogical effects can arise from an accident of the technology and its context of use.

The (sometimes discordant) research results reported here raise important methodological issues that are discussed in the section on analytical CSCW. LIS implications include remote reference, as well as support for activities common to many organizations. Synchronous and asynchronous technologies can support meetings and collaboration within distributed organizations (such as a metropolitan central library and its satellite branch libraries) and among institutions (including other libraries, schools, universities, corporations, and various levels of government).

Shared Drawing and Collaborative Writing

Shared drawing tools were an early area of research in CSCW but appear to have less apparent immediate application in LIS, justifying only a brief mention here. Their aim is to support collaborative design, where two or more people gather around a table or a drawing board, pencils in hand, and participate in the design process. The bulk of work on CSCW in this context has been to support synchronous remote shared drawing as part of design, either on the desktop or via shared whiteboards (ISHII ET AL.; SCRIVENER ET AL.). An important finding is that the systems must support the kind of fluid interactions that occur in this extremely creative activity and help people overcome the constraints of remoteness. The focus on actual design activities revealed the importance of the integration of computer support with the other artifacts that people use (desks, blueprints, previous designs, previous drafts of the current design). These issues of fluidity and integration are applicable in all collaborative applications.

Co-authoring is clearly a major activity among researchers, not only in the sciences but also in business. The paper may be collectively written from scratch, or pass through a series of revisions and editing as it moves through the hierarchy of an organization. Support may be for synchronous collaborative writing at a distance, where two authors discuss and revise a document as they would sitting together at the same desk. Support may also be asynchronous, where different authors alternately draft and redraft a document. Useful reviews of the state of the art are in RADA, SHARPLES, and SHARPLES & GEEST. A recent study by TAMMARO ET AL. shows that, although collaborative writing was an early area of investigation in CSCW, the task is complex and existing software is still problematic. Their findings indicate that current tools are effective for well-defined tasks performed by experienced users, but otherwise the tools need improvement to be more generally usable. The most immediate implication for LIS is that when authors write collaboratively at a distance (as in the case of this review itself), the information search part of the writing process will probably also be distributed. Thus it is important to consider how information systems can help remote co-authors in their information searching.

MUDs and MOOs

The Multi-User Dungeon (MUD) concept has grown and developed since its origin as a computer game at the University of Essex in 1979. MUDs are a form of remote synchronous communication, mostly involving text-based interactions. Participants navigate a textually constructed virtual space, interacting with other people that they meet in various locations. An influential extension is the MUD, Object-Oriented (MOO) from Xerox PARC. A MOO allows users to extend the virtual environment by creating objects, locations, and behaviors that are then available to other users. DOURISH outlines the history of MUDs and MOOs and their relationship to CSCW research. Although initially developed for recreation, and still mostly used that way, conversations in MUDs can have a serious purpose. MUDs and MOOs are studied in computer-mediated communication (CMC) and are gaining attention as venues for learning, as a form of computer supported collaborative Learning (CSCL) (BRUCKMAN; O'DAY ET AL.). Potential LIS uses include synchronous remote reference and their implications as part of new ways of teaching and learning (including CSCL) for libraries' involvement in that process.

Awareness

An important prerequisite of smoothly operating cooperation in an organization is an awareness of what one's colleagues are doing. This can help in knowing, for example, when it is appropriate to disturb someone and ask for or offer help, and in gaining an overall sense of progress on many concurrent activities, including strategic changes in the organization. Awareness is best maintained in close physical proximity and may require substantial social interaction in order to achieve the desired quality of interaction (DOURISH & BELLOTTI; MARK ET AL., 1997a).

Even being on a different floor in the same building can reduce the degree of awareness and consequently the effectiveness of collaborative work (KRAUT & GALEGHER). Clearly, remote teams split between offices in different locations and teleworkers lack some traditional awareness options. Awareness research in CSCW attempts to remedy this problem using sound, video, and active badges (wearable devices that broadcast wearers' locations in a building) (GUTWIN ET AL.; HARPER, 1996). It is not surprising that, while these awareness technologies hold great potential for including remote members in a group, they also raise important issues of privacy (e.g., HUDSON & SMITH and a later section in this review).

KRAUT ET AL. consider the use of remote video for informal communications. They note the difficulties with supporting eye contact and with people moving out of camera range. Although their technology (VideoWindow) provided life-size images, the psychological distance between remotely connected users was greater than between co-located users. Their study emphasizes the importance of human factors in systems design. The Cruiser system was developed to support, for remote users, the serendipitous interactions that can occur while walking down a corridor. Clearly it is important for such a system to address issues of privacy and access. This is accomplished by a policy of reciprocal views: no one can look into someone else's office without also being seen. A user can be warned that someone is about to look in and may indicate a wish not to be disturbed. Effectively, a whole new social protocol must be developed that can be influenced by (but need not replicate) the protocols of face-to-face interactions in other people's offices (BLY ET AL.; FISH ET AL.).

DOURISH ET AL. (1996a) describe their experiences with using media spaces (integrated sets of CSCW tools located in people's offices) as part of their normal work activities over a period of three years. Admittedly, they are describing their own experiences, so the findings may not be representative, but compared to the usual short-term controlled experiments, a long-term study can uncover the adaptations people make to technologies and how they integrate them into their work as they grow accustomed to their use. For example, Dourish et al. found that over time, users learn how to cope with the lack of direct eye contact and develop other ways of maintaining an awareness of another participant's attention.

Note that physical proximity is not only a factor in maintaining collaborations, but also in initiating them. As KRAUT & GALEGHER discovered in the case of scientific collaboration, physical proximity affords the kind of casual social interactions that can lead to the discovery of mutual interests and the beginning of formal collaborative work. Other ways of intellectual matchmaking are possible, as we note in a later section.

The importance of taking awareness issues into account when attempting to support any form of remote work is not unique to LIS, and should not be ignored.

Workflow

Workflow systems are computerized systems that support the way that offices process work, for example how a bank processes a loan application. Other terms used are office modeling and task modeling. In a paper-based environment, this involves the passing of forms and duplicates from desk to desk as different people work on different aspects of the task. In a computerized environment, some or all of the process can be handled by the passing of electronic messages, the use of electronic forms onscreen, and electronic tracking of the whole process (ABBOTT & SARIN; BOWERS ET AL.; PRINZ & KOLVENBACH; SUCHMAN, 1983). A number of studies reveal serious problems with workflow systems, often caused by their overly constraining nature. Systems may embody rules of the typical work process but, as is noted in the section on ethnography below, people often have to deal with exceptions and work around the rules. With paper and written (or just understood) sets of rules, this is possible. When the rules are embodied in the computer system, the computer's inflexibility can paralyze the working of an office and drive users to subvert, lie to, or abandon the system. This behavior need not be caused by fear of the system or Luddism, but just the worker's sincere wish to do the job effectively.

Many workflow systems, including the COORDINATOR system (WINOGRAD), are influenced by speech act theory (WINOGRAD & FLORES). This theory has been the subject of considerable criticism and debate (BANNON; SUCHMAN, 1994). The overly constraining nature of the early versions of workflow systems has led them to be abused as "naziware" (DOURISH ET AL., 1996b).

Harper, in his study of knowledge work in the International Monetary Fund (HARPER, 1998; HARPER & SELLEN), claims a trade-off between the suitability of asynchronous groupware for supporting knowledge work and the amount of professional judgment used. In a library context, this would predict greater suitability for, say, interlibrary loan and acquisitions processing than for reference interactions and collection development.

Organizational Memory

The idea of organizational memory is an outgrowth of the various management theories that attempt to gain an understanding of an organization by using anthropomorphizing analogies such as the learning organization (SENGE). Organizational memory has become a major focus for researchers from many disciplines (WALSH & UNGSON). The effect of radical business restructuring activities of the early 1990s, such as business process reengineering, was that layers of middle management were removed. This resulted not only in the movement of decision-making responsibility to lower levels of the organization, but also in the loss of the knowledge and expertise of middle managers who lost their jobs and left the organization. The aim of organizational memory is both to record some of the expertise of members of an organization and to allow an organization to make more effective use of the data it necessarily collects in computer files as part of doing business. The attempts to classify and catalog this disparate information clearly parallel some of the traditional activities of librarians.

One interesting example of an organizational memory application is the Answer Garden (ACKERMAN), which attempts to grow expertise by its usage. Computer applications often provide a file called Frequently Asked Questions (FAQ). It is a useful starting point for novices to a system. Although novices may still need to consult a human expert, the FAQ serves as a useful mechanism for saving the time of both novices and experts. Note that the ideal FAQ would be user-specific, addressing all and only the questions of that user. One of the ironies of an FAQ is that its utility to an individual can decrease as the information contained in it grows—the more questions it contains, the harder it is for a user to find whether his or her question is there. Novices may not know the terminology or classification schemes used to organize information about the whole subject area. The Answer Garden extends the FAQ idea by making it easier for novices to search and, if they do not find answers to their questions, to use the Answer Garden to request specific help. The Answer Garden determines who should receive the request, based on the nature of the problem, and the expertise areas and availability of the possible experts. Thus the novice does not need to know who would be the best person to ask. As well as forwarding the response to the novice, both question and answer are added back into the Answer Garden with the hope that this piece of information may help subsequent users. The Answer Garden can be regarded as an attempt to embody in a system a small part of the expertise of an individual, much as a reference librarian develops a store of answers to often-asked questions.

A later version of Answer Garden (ACKERMAN & MCDONALD) extended the system following studies of its use. These studies emphasized the importance of context in understanding an answer. The new system provides an escalation agent to support the search for the person likely to have the knowledge to respond to the request. Escalation is a concept from software support help lines. If the person taking the call is unable to deal with it, it is forwarded to someone with more expertise. In general, however, major problems remain in addressing issues of usability, usefulness, and acceptability to enable organizational memory systems to be widely used in practice (HUGHES ET AL., 1996a).

CSCW and the World Wide Web

The extremely rapid growth of the World Wide Web has created an infrastructure for supporting collaborative interactions at relatively low cost. This enables researchers to move more rapidly from laboratory-based prototypes to versions suitable for worldwide testing and even deployment. In order to exploit and study this potential, a number of research groups are developing toolkits to exploit Web protocols for collaborative work. Web-based collaborative software includes NetMeeting from Microsoft and Collabra from Netscape. Commercial CSCW applications, such as Lotus Notes, may also be adapted for use across the Web, as in the case of Lotus Domino. DIX considers the advantages to using the Web, including standards and protocols that enable use of the Web at minimal cost, compatibility across different hardware platforms, and extensibility in implementing updated functionalities and standards. The overwhelming advantage (both causing and caused by the other factors) is that so many people already use the Web, ensuring that it is worthwhile to continue using and adapting it. This is the critical mass issue identified by GRUDIN (1989) that is crucial in the success of collaborative systems. A large pool of potential users is available to try out any new system with relatively easy installation, and these users span organizational boundaries. The main disadvantage is the basic client-server architecture of the Web. In particular, the HTTP protocol is stateless, that is, it does not store information between requests; therefore the Web cannot support synchronous collaboration as readily as asynchronous. Solutions include the use of cookies and Javascript and the development of specific applications (BENTLEY ET AL.). TREVOR ET AL. review these options and propose their own system as a potential solution. Increasingly, library catalogs, bibliographic databases, etc. provide Web-based access. Thus a cost-effective way of providing collaborative features is to include some of them in a web-based platform, adding value to the core functionalities of the existing databases.

The following three subsections relate to matters that can be applied anywhere in the CSCW quadrant.

Toolkits

In order to provide technologies for different work environments, researchers are developing CSCW construction toolkits. The toolkits allow the easy combination of functionalities to fit the needs of a particular work context, or for the rapid prototyping and testing of new applications. This last point is significant as a method for exploring the potential of collaborative technology in a particular context. In this review we advocate the analysis-synthesis approach, coupling detailed study of how people use the existing features of the system and what they would like to be able to do, with explorations of what is currently technically possible. This is where experimentation with a toolkit can be especially productive. One can try out a certain activity (say remote reference) with different combinations and configurations of functionalities in order to understand which seem to offer the greatest return for the least cost and complexity. The exploration may also give insights into additional functionalities, not available in the toolkit, that appear to address the problems that arise. These can then set agendas for future research.

Functionalities provided by toolkits include those outlined above: shared editing, shared drawing, whiteboards, live audio, and video links. Toolkits may also allow end users to be involved in tailoring general applications to their own needs. However, end users cannot be assumed to be experts in design and may find it difficult to develop easy-to-use combinations of options. Further, a work group may have difficulty adjusting to common support functions (e.g., awareness, informal learning, help-giving) if individuals have tailored their personal workstations in a unique manner. Examples of toolkits include those by R.D. HILL ET AL. (1994), KAPLAN ET AL., PRAKASH & SHIM, ROSEMAN & GREENBERG, and SMITH & RODDEN.

Computer Supported Collaborative Learning

Although some papers on computer supported collaborative learning (CSCL) are published in CSCW journals and conference proceedings, CSCL can be considered a separate area that owes as much to education research as to computer science. It has dedicated conferences, such as CSCL95 (SCHNASE & CUNNIUS) and CSCL97 (HALL ET AL.), and books (HILTZ; KOSCHMANN; O'MALLEY). Although CSCL software has many similarities to CSCW software, the focus on supporting the learning process, construction of shared understanding, and novice users involves a different emphasis. Since many of the potential applications of CSCW in LIS have aspects of learning, help-giving and novice use, and may also occur in an educational context, it is worth studying research in CSCL for useful insights.

Computer-Mediated Communication

Computer-mediated communication (CMC) is also a research area in its own right. The focus of the research is to support the process of communication by detailed analyses of how it occurs, both by microanalyses of conversations and discovery of communication patterns of individuals with others over long periods of time. There have been two *ARIST* chapters, by RICE in 1980 and STEINFIELD in 1986. Useful introductions can also be found in DAFT & LENGEL, FULK & STEINFIELD, HAYTHORNTHWAITE ET AL., JONES, KIESLER, and MCGRATH & HOLLINGSHEAD.

Substantial research has been done in CMC to understand how people use technologies that are now widespread, such as email, mailing lists, and bulletin boards. Usage is studied for different groups and over time so that the effects of learning, expertise-building, and acculturation into the new medium can be observed, as well as global learning as new norms such as "netiquette" develop and evolve. CMC research has led to studies of the growth of electronic communities that naturally use the technologies available to them. By contrast, CSCW researchers tend to concentrate on the development and the problems of deployment of more expensive and glamorous high-tech applications such as shared video. Anyone considering the use of the CSCW technologies outlined in this review would be well advised to study the detailed analyses of CMC for insights into the issues that arise when people use technologies as part of their work rather than just to test out a new system.

ANALYTICAL CSCW

The backgrounds of CSCW researchers vary widely. The advantages of interdisciplinary research are the different perspectives of participants, their focus on different aspects of the overall problem, and the synergies that usually arise from their interactions. Human-computer interaction research and the design and development of more usable interfaces have been substantially enriched by the involvement of cognitive psychologists. Clearly, if one is attempting to design a system that is easy to learn, understand, and use, the insights from psychological theory and its methods for gaining a deeper understanding of individual behavior can play an important role. CSCW researchers are additionally challenged to design systems that fit people's work practices and their interactions with other people within and across organizations. Thus the insights from sociology, both theories and methods, play an equally important role. The alternative is to continually develop elegant systems with amazing functionalities that either no one wants or no one can bear to use because they don't fit with how people actually work. Consequently, any consideration of the application of collaborative technologies in LIS should take into account the studies of how people work together both with and without collaborative technologies, in order to avoid some of the mistakes of early attempts.

The disadvantages of interdisciplinary research result from the difficulty of the researchers learning to work together. This can be caused by differences in world view, research priorities, methods, and terminology. There is even the danger of two subfields developing. Papers in CSCW conferences and journals can be split roughly into those on synthesis (building systems) by computer scientists and those on analysis (understanding users and their work) by social scientists. This is clearly an exaggeration, but we believe it contains a germ of truth. Recent CSCW conferences have had two concurrent sessions that vaguely fit the categories of analysis and synthesis. It would be possible to go to such a conference and attend only the synthesis sessions and talk to computer scientists or attend only the analysis sessions and talk to social scientists. We regard this as particularly unfortunate. Nevertheless, there is a growing understanding of the importance and power of interdisciplinary research, as well as an evolving understanding of how to conduct it (BOWKER ET AL.).

Ethnography

Ethnography, a method used in sociology and anthropology, has been especially prominent in CSCW research. The theory and practice of ethnography is complex and subtle and beyond the scope of this review. In basic terms, the researcher observes what people do in the actual work setting, attempting to understand that work in its own context and describe what people actually do rather than what they "ought" or are "meant" to do. The goal is to describe work activities from the perspective of the participants rather than that of an outsider (such as a systems developer). Useful overviews of ethnography can be found in BENSON & HUGHES and GARFINKEL. Ethnographic techniques have also been coupled with insights and methods from cognitive and social psychology (HUTCHINS). Although we focus here on sociology because of its perhaps unexpected interaction with computer science, that is not to say that the actual and potential contribution of psychology should be ignored (FINHOLT & TEASLEY).

SUCHMAN (1987) has been widely cited in the CSCW literature in advocating the ethnographic approach to studying work practice to reveal the easily overlooked ways that people engage in complex problem-solving. If these issues are not taken into account, systems will be designed that support an overly simplified version of the work practice and thus may fail to mesh with how people actually work. The following subsections give examples of different uses of ethnography.

Exception handling. SUCHMAN (1983) shows how supposedly routine activities involve considerable judgment and problem-solving, including negotiation with co-workers. SCHMIDT & BANNON consider the key issue in CSCW to be articulation work: the coordination, scheduling, and error-recovery activities that enable people to get the job done and, most importantly, allow them a means to handle the inevitable contingencies and exceptions of everyday life. A poorly designed system will automate typical work practices, but may be unusable because it does not allow for handling exceptions. The number of exceptions tends to grow over time, so an inflexible system will grow increasingly obsolete. A system should not be a rigid controlling structure that forces users to work in only one way, thus leading to the frequently observed irritating inflexibilities of workers being unable to serve their customers because "the computer won't let me do that." Schmidt and Bannon use working-to-rule as evidence for the existence and importance of exception handling. This form of industrial action (where workers follow precisely the official procedures but do no more, and in particular show no initiative in dealing with exceptions to those defined procedures) can quickly lead to an office or factory grinding to a halt.

BUTTON & HARPER studied two distinct systems, one for police crime reporting and one for manufacturing sales and invoicing, and found that problems with each system were caused by the significant difference between design assumptions of how work was (or ought to be) done based on the documentation and codes of practice, and the much more reactive and complex (and responsive and effective) actual detail of activity. Their research shows how a more detailed prior analysis of work practice could have informed more effective systems design.

Cooperation and competition. ORLIKOWSKI studied the use of Lotus Notes by a large firm of consultants. Although the tool provided many potentially useful features, there were significant problems due to the fact that the culture and reward structure of the organization encouraged consultants to compete with each other. Consequently, a tool to support cooperation was not as useful as had been anticipated because the benefits of cooperating were outweighed in the competitive climate.

Paperwork. A number of ethnographic studies (HARPER & SELLEN; HUGHES ET AL., 1996b; LUFF ET AL.) reveal the complex ways in which paper is used. A paper form can be annotated, duplicated, or have other bits of paper stapled, clipped, or stuck to it. Boxes for form entry can be used for entering exceptional information that does not belong there, but does not belong anywhere else either. This flexibility of use of paper allows people to adapt to changing circumstances and exceptions. This is important to understand because it helps explain why the often-promised paperless office never seems to appear, and acts as a warning to systems developers of the kinds of functionalities that should be supported in their applications, including making allowance for occasions when people will opt to use paper because it is more efficient.

Systems design. Perhaps the most problematic but potentially most rewarding contribution of ethnography is in direct collaboration between ethnographers and computer scientists during the systems development process (HUGHES ET AL., 1993; SOMMERVILLE ET AL., 1992a). Unfortunately, interdisciplinary collaboration is difficult for reasons mentioned above. For example, the traditional ethnographic approach is descriptive and focuses on being nonjudgmental, whereas a computer scientist may expect prescriptive information in order to help decide what to build. This methodological tension pervades the working relationship. As a consequence, it has been proposed that a variant of traditional ethnography be developed to support the needs of interdisciplinary work and the time constraints of design (HUGHES ET AL., 1994; D. SHAPIRO). Despite the difficulties, there are various fruitful and ongoing collaborations between social scientists and computer scientists (BUTTON; CRABTREE ET AL.; HUGHES ET AL., 1992; PYCOCK & BOWERS; SCHATZ ET AL.; SOMMERVILLE ET AL., 1992b). Descriptions of these collaborations emphasize the importance of taking time to understand the other researchers' different outlooks and terminology.

The analytical work in CSCW can help in several other ways, as the next two sections illustrate.

Requirements Capture

Requirements capture is an aspect of software engineering (SOMMERVILLE) that involves determining what people want a new computer system to do. It is important to know what the system will actually be used for, as opposed to idealizations of what people do. These idealizations can be derived from work practice manuals or interviews of managers who may have only an overview of how their subordinates work and, even if they once undertook the tasks themselves, may be out of date on the technologies and the results of cumulative small changes in the nature of the work. Even asking a person who does the work may not be sufficient. People are inclined to oversimplify and to respond in terms of an idealization of what they are meant to do rather than what they actually do. Observations of work practice can reveal exceptions to the idealization and how they are resolved.

A specific approach called participatory design (PD) has been developed to address the complexity of understanding work practice (BJERKNES ET AL.; GREENBAUM & KYNG). Originating in Scandinavia, PD was partly a response to labor laws that required that workers or their representatives (usually trade unions) be involved in the process of introducing new technology. PD attempts to involve intended users in the design process, particularly during requirements capture. In addition to fulfilling desirable social purposes (and/or legal requirements), it can lead to a more effective, efficient and usable system. Researchers and developers outside Scandinavia, especially in the United States, have been investigating the extent to which PD can be applied in different social and organizational cultures (BLOMBERG ET AL.; MULLER & KUHN), including in the design of digital libraries (NEUMANN & STAR).

Evaluation of CSCW Systems

Although several studies of collaborative systems yielded disappointing results, (e.g., KIRKWOOD ET AL.), they were extremely useful in deepening understanding of the importance of the work context. GRUDIN (1989; 1994b) produced a number of highly influential papers on the problems of introducing CSCW systems into organizations. He identified a set of factors that can contribute to the success or failure of the process. One factor is identification of those who benefit from the introduction of the new technology. If the new system imposes extra work for many people in order to benefit others, people will naturally be reluctant to use it. Managers may require workers to use a disliked system, but workers may still be able to sabotage it by blaming it for all the problems that inevitably arise. If the system can be designed so that everyone using it benefits somewhat, then acceptance and adoption will be far more likely to occur.

Grudin's analysis has many parallels with the ongoing debate about the productivity paradox of computing (LANDAUER): the fact that organizations have spent billions of dollars on computers to support office staff, often with little or no resultant improvement in productivity. PLOWMAN ET AL. review a large number of workplace studies and consider the different ways in which the results can contribute to the systems design process. Not all the news is bad. For example, a study by BIKSON & EVELAND of meeting support technology at the World Bank reveals many successes. The authors apply sociotechnical systems theory to account for these successes and generate predictors for subsequent implementations of technology into organizations.

TWIDALE ET AL. (1994) explore several issues and complications of CSCW evaluation and advocate ethnographic techniques for addressing some problems. Because the purpose of a CSCW system is to support work situated in a complex social environment, a controlled laboratory experiment may fail to uncover aspects of actual use that could have a serious effect on overall usefulness, usability, or acceptability. Although experiments are the standard activity for science, their results in CSCW can be somewhat misleading. This is because

CSCW is in part an engineering discipline where artifacts are created out of an immense design space. They are not natural phenomena that justify detailed, expensive, and time-consuming scientific study, but rather are systems that can be (and are) endlessly redesigned. A rigorous experiment may show that a certain feature (e.g., video) makes no difference, but the results will be influenced by how the video technology was implemented, or used, or how easy people found to use it, or the experimental task that people were given. Further, the real effects may only emerge in days, weeks, or months of authentic use, not in a one-hour experiment. CSCW systems are intended to help people in their everyday lives, yet as systems designers frequently discover, surprisingly little is known about how everyday work is done. Hence systems that perform well in a lab can often fail catastrophically in real life (e.g., GRUDIN, 1989).

COLLABORATIVE WORK AND LIS

From a general review of CSCW, we move to an examination of research that relates explicitly to collaborative work involving library and information science (LIS). This includes work with, in, and using libraries and also aspects of information retrieval (IR) that are examples of, or parts of, collaborative work practice. We consider existing systems, experimental systems, and requirements for potential systems, as well as implications for privacy and changing work roles. Figure 2 is an adaptation of figure 1, including examples of current and potential applications to support collaboration in the context of LIS.

We focus here on the potential of CSCW to support library activities that are more specialized (even though they may have parallels with activities in other organizations). We see collaboration occurring in a

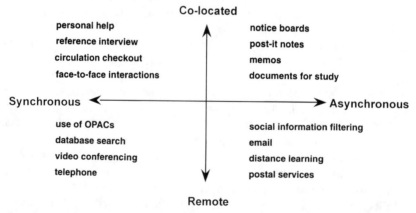

Figure 2. The CSCW spatial and temporal quadrant with LIS examples

library in three ways: (1) among staff members, (2) among users and staff members, and (3) among users.

Libraries and Organizational CSCW

In addition to the conventional staff-staff activities and technologies noted earlier, certain specialist activities have received some consideration, but deserve more. B.J. SHAPIRO & LONG examine library services in the light of business process reengineering and point to the growing importance of team-based work groups. SHAW describes (in rather general terms) various computer technologies that have implications for libraries, including CSCW and collaboratories (distributed shared use of laboratories and research resources). She also notes that libraries will collect the results of collaborative research, and predicts that the notion of authorship will expand as the infrastructure for CSCW develops. Librarians may become involved in the activity of the collaboratories, that is, in supporting the management of virtual blackboards and message systems. Considerations of privacy and ownership arise, especially with documents that evolve over time by collaborative authoring. Questions about how to determine the definitive version of a document, whether this is even a meaningful concept, whether intermediate versions should be kept, and the role of the library as archive all have strong parallels with version control in software engineering (SOMMERVILLE).

Reference librarians collaborate with colleagues in and across institutions when they share particularly tricky or obscure requests, or their process for solving them. Note that in computer science the sharing of "war stories" about debugging and the sharing of suggestions for tackling a difficult problem have been recognized as an important part of software productivity, even if at first glance it appears to be merely unproductive social chat around a coffee machine (ROOT; WEINBERG). ERICKSON & SALOMON found that expert online searchers spent considerable time sharing information at their weekly status meetings. Asynchronous collaboration on reference issues occurs via face-to-face interaction, telephone, letter, publication (such as "The Exchange" in *Reference and User Services Quarterly*; renamed from *RQ* in 1997) or via computer mediation, in direct colleague-to-colleague email or groups such as the Stumpers-L mailing list.

Collaborative learning, whether computer-supported or not, is of growing interest in schools and universities and includes aspects of other popular educational theories such as constructivism, problem-based learning, and situated learning (LAVE & WENGER). It carries implications for use of libraries and library resources and consequently for aspects of bibliographic instruction and support (ASHTON & LEVY).

It is likely to lead to more diverse use of library resources by individuals and groups working on their own projects (rather than the traditional model of a class working through a prescribed set of readings), as well as greater involvement of library personnel in the development and support of curricula.

The following sections consider user-user collaboration in the search for information in more detail.

Information Retrieval and CSCW

MARCHIONINI identifies support for collaboration as a research direction for information retrieval (IR), and as such is one of relatively few researchers to indicate the potential links between IR and CSCW. BATES (1989) proposes berrypicking as a model of interactive searching by individual users. We propose to extend the model to include interactions with other people, such as librarians giving help or friends and colleagues offering suggestions or sharing past experiences. Thus an information search consists of a chain of more intensive visible searching activities over time (compare with TAYLOR's definition of a dynamic inquiry noted earlier). This view raises the need for representations that persist over time, similar to the conversational props for meeting support studied by BRINCK & GOMEZ.

In a subsequent paper, BATES (1990) considers the relationship between a user and a search interface in order to set an agenda for systems development. She describes various levels of functions that can help a user identify and locate information. This analysis reveals a gap in current IR research and development. She notes that the aim of much IR research is to provide a completely automatic search for the user. By contrast, she advocates that more attention be paid to developing functions to support the user rather than to automating the task. We concur with her analysis and add that the more intermediate levels of support that she delineates should include easy access and recourse to human help when necessary. Furthermore, her recommended levels of support (including explicit representation of plans and goals) are precisely those that can also support a more efficient collaborative interaction. The conventional IR focus on automation, Bates contends, is unfortunate for several reasons:

- At times the user may want to be in control of the search process.
- Full automation may currently be impossible, by analogy with some of the wilder claims of AI in the 1980s.
- Intermediate research results of the automation effort, while of great scholarly interest and vital to progress

toward the ultimate goal of automation, may not be usable.

- Simpler, semi-automated mechanisms may be more tractable, usable, empowering, and fit better with existing practice (including help-giving).
- These simpler mechanisms may yield interesting IR research avenues, although the research may be less glamorous and therefore less likely to attract funding.

It seems that much IR research fits this aim of automation. Although it seems that most IR research assumes that the user works alone (or wants to), some examples involving the representation of other users' experiences are noted by SMITH & WARNER. If the goal of IR research is automation of individual searching, then resort to collaboration (e.g., asking for help) will be seen as a failure to be remedied (by an even more sophisticated IR system), rather than an activity that itself would benefit from technological support. Note that this is not to disparage the IR approach, but rather to account for the relative lack of concern for collaborative work that has led to the surprisingly small overlap between CSCW and IR. People often do collaborate to cope with failure (such as not finding what they want), and systems that can avoid such failures are definitely desirable. Collaboration is costly in time and effort (and usually money), and systems to minimize those costs are preferable.

Remote Reference

Only a small proportion of the many possible forms of collaboration in the information search process occur in synchronous and co-located situations. The gold standard of the face-to-face reference interview must be reconciled with the reality of distributed networked users of information services. NARDI & O'DAY performed an ethnographic study of reference librarians as a way of understanding which aspects of the work realistically could and could not be supported by the use of intelligent agents. Remote reference is a topic that deserves an *ARIST* chapter in its own right; see FERGUSON & BUNGE and SLOAN for reviews.

MARTIN gives an early example of distance collaboration: the telephone reference interview. With the advent of collaborative technologies, variants on this theme are possible. SWIGGER ET AL. explicitly address CSCW as a research focus, using remote information searching almost arbitrarily as a representative task to investigate issues of generic relevance to CSCW. Although their later work focuses more on possible contributions of collaborative technologies to information searching, their approach serves as evidence that the exchange of ideas can be two-way: that studying technological support in an information searching context not only can be informed by CSCW but also can give valuable insights into general CSCW research.

A later study by SWIGGER & HARTNESS investigated remote synchronous support of mediated searching. The tools provided were various text input/output screens designed to support different aspects of a search dialog. The end-user and the search intermediary used the screens to interact with each other and to present the results of the intermediary's searches on a range of databases. Surprisingly, the experiments showed that the remote collaborative interface was actually superior to face-to-face interaction. This could be accounted for by the fact that the interface was imposed on novice end users and its structure may have helped them understand the nature of the interaction and how they were to participate in it.

Perhaps the simplest way of introducing remote reference is by email (ABELS; BUSHALLOW-WILBER ET AL.; HAHN), which can easily be integrated into newly developed Web-based searching environments. The advantages of simplicity and low setup cost must be offset by the lack of structured support for the work activity. The same is true of many CSCW contexts. Sometimes it is sensible to begin using a technology that is familiar and easy to use, but basic (such as email) to support the work practice, and then to evaluate the resultant interaction to determine what is missing and what needs to be provided in terms of more sophisticated functionality.

GLEADHILL describes a Web-based system, derived from ACKERMAN's Answer Garden, that provides an electronic inquiry and reference service for a university library. The system is intended to supplement the inquiry desk for users who want help at their preferred time and location, or who are reluctant to bother a librarian, despite the staff's best endeavors to be approachable. The growing database of previously asked questions, suitably organized, means that frequently asked questions are already available, while giving new users an insight into the range and quality of information available either via the system or face-to-face in the traditional manner.

In addition to text, live video conferencing offers intriguing possibilities for supporting remote reference. The ability of the end-user and librarian to see each offers a smoother transition from the status quo in terms of familiarity and ease of use, even though it requires more sophisticated hardware and software and much greater bandwidth. Video has been explored by LESSICK ET AL., MORGAN, and SUGIMOTO ET AL. The findings from the CSCW research on use of video, noted above, especially the crucial importance of audio quality, should be considered in designing a suitable practical configuration.

It is becoming clear that simply using a communication medium such as email is inadequate to support the detailed context-dependent interactions that occur in some library practice (TWIDALE ET AL., 1997a). Study of interactions between librarians and users reveals the problems inherent in many help-giving sessions. For example, the act of walking over to seek help at the reference desk can cause the user to forget the context of the problem, including previous searches. Observations of librarian-user interactions show that a common activity is reconstruction of the sequence of actions that led to the impasse (TWIDALE ET AL., 1997a). This reconstruction is subject to the limitations of the user's memory and vocabulary.

Communication media can be used to support users in many ways: an FAQ is very different from video conferencing. PROCTOR ET AL. (1998) characterize these differences in terms of effectiveness, availability, and responsiveness: for example, an FAQ may rate highly for responsiveness and availability but be unpredictable in its effectiveness. PROCTOR ET AL. (1997) use the term genres for various forms of interactions. Their prototype network reference consultation support system integrates several genres, including email, text conferencing, audio, and video. Their prototype also enhances the underlying communication facilities by allowing a librarian to take control of a user's remote session to demonstrate interactively features of the database that the user is accessing. This approach introduces notions of control and turn-taking that flow naturally in face-to-face dialog but which must be included explicitly in software.

The notion of taking control of another user's session is also present in the C-TORI system (HOPPE & ZHAO), which allows synchronous collaborative searching, including cooperative query formulation, cooperative browsing of results, and sharing of search histories. C-TORI also uses a WYSIWIS (What You See Is What I See) mode to allow one user to couple the other's environment so that two can share the same interaction. For reusing previous work, C-TORI has a shared history mechanism that allows elements of a user's query history to be copied and merged with histories of other members of a group.

Context Establishment

Remote asynchronous collaborative work, of the kind that can be expected in digital libraries, necessarily requires that information about the work be recorded and communicated. In the case of information searching this implies that some record be stored of the evolving information need, the search process, and the search product. The record is needed to establish the context of a new interaction, and to re-establish the context of an interaction that resumes later. Often this record may be a simple free-text description by the user, but computerized environments offer the potential for detailed recording of a user's actions. Automatic recording has clear advantages in that a user's own memory may be partial or inaccurate. The disadvantages are less obvious and are described in the section on privacy. Many systems provide a record of a user's actions (usually in the form of "these queries produced these hits") but these are usually only partial records and they are not digital objects that can be edited, communicated, or annotated without losing their structure.

Once a system supports the creation of such an interaction history, it can be used in many ways (HOPPE & ZHAO). Single-user uses include re-use of earlier searches, error recovery, navigation, reminding, and user modeling (LEE). A record of search activity frees users from having to remember low-level goal-stack details (e.g., actions already tried, which inform dynamic replanning) and enables them to concentrate on more strategic elements of the search process. A search object can be stored, highlighted, edited, annotated, replayed, and re-executed: typically the kinds of activities that occur in tutorial and help-giving interactions (LEMAIRE & MOORE). Thus the communication of context, rather than just communication, emerges as a key requirement of a more supportive environment.

Recording-based support for asynchronous interactions has been referred to as a WYSNIWIST (What You See Now is What I Saw Then) paradigm (MANOHAR & PRAKASH). In a multimedia collaborative environment, this can extend to audio and video annotations in addition to replaying interactions via the computer interface. A variant of this approach is to record the same information but present it back to users in a slightly different format, for example, in a visualization that allows easier recognition of certain aspects of the interaction. The ARIADNE system (TWIDALE & NICHOLS, 1996; 1998; TWIDALE ET AL., 1995) replays a user's interaction with a database as a two-dimensional visualization that can be edited, annotated, and communicated.

One potential use of recorded searches would be for library staff to collect a set of examples (common mistakes, good strategies, etc.) that could be sent to users who exhibit typical problems. These examples, as executable entities, would be much more powerful than paper-based descriptions. This approach has similarities to user-oriented transaction log analysis (SANDORE) and moves closer to user-modeling approaches in which the system automatically detects familiar patterns in users' behavior.

Information Visualization

Work on information visualization is mostly intended to support a single user, although it may also be used collaboratively around a shared screen (WHITE & MCCAIN). Synchronous query formulation can also be realized by interacting in a virtual reality environment where both information and users can be visualized (BENFORD & MARIANI; CHALMERS). BENFORD ET AL. describe the VR-VIBE system that provides explicit support for cooperative IR. Their research is strongly rooted in the computer science traditions of CSCW and virtual reality (VR). As noted earlier, collaboration relies on awareness of the activities of others. When VR is used to support CSCW, awareness can be supported by embodiment: providing virtual bodies for users. The constraints of memory, bandwidth, and processing power led to the use of "blockies"—very simple cartoon-like representations of users that convey position and spatial orientation using only a few polygons, which are computationally inexpensive. Communication is provided synchronously over a live audio channel and asynchronously through annotations attached to documents.

VR-VIBE is not a practical system in its current form, but an exploration of possibilities of radically different interfaces. As such, it is a powerful example of the computer science research approach of building in order to learn, discover, and refine the problem area. It is also an example of how a consideration of the issues and needs of LIS applications can feed back into general computer science research issues, in this case the design of VR environments. In the study of VR-VIBE, BENFORD ET AL. note that relevance decisions and the marking of objects as significant or boring by users are highly likely to be subjective. Although this is not surprising to librarians, it led the designers to reassess the functionalities that may be necessary in collaborative VR systems in general. The prior implicit assumption was that a VR environment should provide an objective view of the world. The VR-VIBE study revealed that there may sometimes be a need for subjectivity in VR applications.

Digital Libraries

There are now a significant number of digital library projects worldwide (FOX ET AL., 1995; KESSLER; LESK; SCHATZ ET AL.; WOLF ET AL.). As the *ARIST* review on social informatics by BISHOP & STAR reveals, there is a growing awareness that digital library initiatives should not be solely technology-driven. Just as a recognition of the practical, commercial importance of taking account of the needs of users led to the growth of human-computer interaction and the growing analysis of work practice as part of CSCW, so digital libraries research and development should take greater account of the usefulness and usability of digital libraries (FOX ET AL., 1993) and the organizational context of that use (ELLIOTT & KLING; KLING & ELLIOT). Development techniques such as user-centered iterative design (VAN HOUSE ET AL.) can help this process. Techniques such as ethnography and social theory (SCHIFF ET AL.) have provided new insights into the needs and practices of users. Developers must also make use of the expertise that a long tradition of analysis in LIS can bring to bear on new manifestations of traditional problems.

ROBERTSON ET AL. examine the possibilities for Web-based collaborative library use in a corporate setting. Their system supported dialogs between researchers and librarians via Web pages in an attempt to move away from the company's older system of remote reference via telephone and email. Study of the work setting revealed its highly collaborative nature and the open-ended incremental nature of a stream of results (dialogs throughout a research interaction rather than one-shot questions and answers). The system aimed to support incremental delivery of results and recorded usage data for accounting purposes. Research interactions were made visible to take advantage of work already done and to support general awareness (e.g., the forming of interest groups). The developers consider the importance of creating a sense of place where researchers and clients go to check the status of requests.

Studies of user activity both with existing digital libraries and with conventional paper-based systems can examine a range of activities, from search and retrieval (BARRY) to annotation (MARSHALL) and note-making (O'HARA ET AL.). O'DAY & JEFFRIES conducted an ethnographic study of the uses of search results by regular clients of professional information intermediaries in a commercial context. They found that all the clients not only acted as intermediaries in their turn, but also often created new information artifacts by transforming and enhancing the search results before passing them on. This study illustrates the power of ethnography to reveal the broader context of work, in this case emphasizing that the retrieval of information is not an end in itself but part of a wider set of activities. Digital library developers should be aware of this wider context in order to maximize system effectiveness. The study by O'Day and Jeffries emphasizes the importance of technologies for supporting the communication of search results, particularly after the results have been further processed by the searchers. LEVY & MARSHALL examine some of the assumptions underlying the development of certain digital library projects. In particular, they question the widespread assumption that digital libraries are to be used by individuals working alone.

MARSHALL ET AL. illustrate concepts of community memory (see the section on organizational memory) and how it is acquired, understood, and used. They consider the implications for digital library design. Note that community memory is much more ephemeral and rapidly evolving than the information usually stored in a traditional library. A lot of it consists of procedural knowledge that enables people to get their work done. Much of it is informal, pragmatic, heuristic, and approximate, or involves coping behavior rather than definitive and well-researched statements. Some of it may be wrong, or at least out of date. Nevertheless, community memory can be of great use in helping people in their work. It can contribute both as a particular kind of information and work practice that a digital library ought to support and as a supporting mechanism that allows the digital library to work—the community memory of how to use it.

EHRLICH & CASH (1994) also consider support for corporate memory to be part of digital library research. They studied a customer-support organization using Lotus Notes as an environment for sharing information between analysts helping users over the telephone. They point out interesting parallels between remote customer support and remote reference interviews, implying that support of the latter can be informed by studies of the former (see PENTLAND). Ehrlich and Cash identify three myths about information access that can inform the development of digital libraries:

(1) Customers understand their own problems, but do not know how to fix them.

The study revealed that often the problem as understood by the customer was frequently not the real problem and that the job of the analyst was to uncover this underlying problem.

(2) Customers would use online information if it were available.

This myth can almost be a premise justifying the development of a digital library. If it is indeed a myth, then the digital library is unlikely to be successful. This would not be because customers are lazy, but because locating answers to their questions in a vast quantity of information is so difficult.

(3) Customer support analysts can work from home.

Ehrlich and Cash show how the analysts work collaboratively to help their customers. Because corporate history databases are collectively created artifacts, it is important to know the name of the analyst who wrote each item of information, and details about the author in order to judge reliability and recency. They advocate face-to-face contact between analysts in order to use the stored information more effectively. Direct contact also offers the opportunity to gather information that was not recorded by the author.

EHRLICH & CASH (1999) stress the importance of intermediaries whose role they say is likely to last despite predictions of disintermediation. They advocate technologies such as agents, not to replace human intermediaries, but as tools for greater effectiveness. They also note the invisibility of collaborative activities to management, again leading to the danger of assumptions that the work can be done equally well at home. By contrast, the analysts in the organization studies were very sensitive to each others' whereabouts. Some used "gopher-net, peeking over cubicle walls, even standing on chairs to see who was free" (p. 158). Face-to-face sessions in offices, cubicles, hallways, and lunch rooms were used to address problems together and test hypotheses. Analysts found it useful to get second opinions. Ehrlich & Cash claim that "what these professionals were aware of, and what many researchers miss, is that while an individual can query the system, making use of that information is a collaborative activity" (p. 159). Their study emphasizes the importance of peer support and reliance on local experts. It also raises a number of concerns with using the various technologies outlined above for supporting remote work. They show the high quality of face-to-face interaction that can easily be lost.

PAEPCKE studied information workers in a single company. He identified the ways information was shared, including different styles of working. Much of the work he observed has parallels with that of reference librarians in helping users find information, or acting as contact brokers; effecting introductions between a person needing help and the appropriate expert (see the section on matchmaking). The knowledge possessed and traded in the technological environment that Paepcke studied is heterogeneous, constantly changing, and poorly classified. It is less like carefully cataloged library books and more like the librarians' knowledge of how to choose among, use, and integrate many databases and information systems.

All this research reinforces the importance of understanding how people use existing technology (including the books, organization, and human resources of conventional libraries) in order to inform the design of features for digital libraries to enhance current work practice and support new ways of working. It is also helpful to look for analogous work activities in other contexts, including remote customer support.

USER-USER COLLABORATION

Although the World Wide Web/Internet is widely recognized for enabling low-cost publishing of documents, it also enables low-cost publishing of document fragments, evaluations, annotations, and metadata. While a traditional library's contents are static (the items remain the same for each successive access), a digital library's contents can be dynamic. In a previous *ARIST* review KANTOR (1994) describes the "feedback of exogenous information" and mentions examples of annotations and links (between documents). A seminal article by KOENIG describes a variety of user-supplied data, including query terms and evaluations. KING ET AL. outline a proposal for a "self-enriching library" (although it does not appear to have been implemented) to which users can contribute links, evaluative commentary, and datasets. Their idea is based on the proposition that, unlike traditional libraries, digital libraries can both accept information from and dispense information to users, and thus be improved and enriched through use.

Implementation of systems that are improved by, or rely on, user feedback have been largely reported in the computer science literature. The user feedback has been predominantly numerical ratings because they are easier to process computationally than free-text annotations. Although the ideas of annotation and rating are not new, the novel aspect of these systems is that one user's feedback can be computationally processed to enhance the system for others, even though the users may not know of each other's existence.

Annotations and Ratings

In the Tapestry system developed at Xerox PARC, users can attach annotations to the items they view, including ratings, free-text comments, and other indicators (GOLDBERG ET AL.). Because annotations can be supplied at any time—perhaps even years after receipt of the document—each annotation is stored as a separate document containing a link back to the original document. Users set up standing queries that can refer to annotation fields; thus they can ask to receive documents that have been endorsed by other known users.

In Tapestry, annotations are attached to a whole document. By contrast, in the ComMentor system (RÖSCHEISEN ET AL.), annotations can be attached at points within electronic documents. The annotations are accessed by buttons positioned within the text of the document. Moreover, annotations are associated with groups of users, so that a given reader sees only those annotations relevant to his or her own group. An alternative approach is found in the URN system (BREWER & JOHNSON), which allows users to insert, delete, and rate the keywords associated with documents.

A rating is an indication of the usefulness, interest, or quality of a document as viewed by a user (see ALLEN). Ratings may be supplied deliberately by a user (explicit feedback), or computed by the system on the basis of the interest users show in a document (implicit feedback).

Explicit ratings are usually supplied on a several-point scale; for instance, MALTZ uses a scale of terrible, ok, good, and great. A rating system has a priming problem (variously described as the "day one," "cold start," or "critical mass" problem), in that early users do not see the benefits of supplying ratings and so stop contributing. As fewer ratings are added, the benefit of the system to a user falls, fewer users are active, and the number of ratings can quickly fall to near-zero. These systems serve as examples of the need to consider the costs and benefits of cooperative systems (GRUDIN, 1989). One potential partial solution is to create a population of software agents (or "virtual users") that rate one specific topic (e.g., books on cyberspace) highly and ignore everything else (MAES).

Implicit feedback yields inferred ratings that do not rely on special action by users, but on indirect (and therefore rather ambivalent) clues. The system may count the number of times a document is opened for reading, relative to the number of times its summary is displayed, or record average time spent reading a document (NICHOLS ET AL.). The PHOAKS system (TERVEEN ET AL.) identifies significant mentions of URLs from Usenet messages and rates recommended resources according to the number of mentions.

One way to use document ratings is to aggregate the ratings for each document into an overall quality score. The rating can be displayed during online inspection of document details, or used to adjust the likelihood of the item being retrieved during a search. This approach may be useful within a group of people who share a similar interest, but will be relatively useless for users at large, because many documents are of great interest to a few people and of no interest to the rest. Another use of ratings is to create filters such as "show me the articles that Jane Doe liked" (MALTZ), which allow a user to share his or her expertise with other users.

A more effective option is to use ratings values to identify pairs of searchers with similar interests. This is variously known as collaborative filtering, social filtering, or recommender systems (OARD). This idea appears to have been first suggested (in computational terms) in 1962 by KOCHEN & WONG, who proposed a system for automatically passing details of interesting retrievals to other appropriate users. Binary relevance judgments were used to identify pairs of users who tended to show interest in the same documents, with the links being stored as a binary matrix.

One current example is the GroupLens system (KONSTAN ET AL.), which allows collaborative filtering of Usenet Netnews articles by allowing users to assign ratings on a five-point scale. A profile is constructed using the document ratings contributed by one user. Users with highly similar profiles are identified, and an item can then be recommended to a user if other similar users have already approved of it. SHARDANAND & MAES describe the Ringo system (which was subsequently renamed HOMR and then Firefly), which uses a similar approach to make personalized recommendations about music albums and artists. They use the term social information filtering. W.C. HILL ET AL. (1995) prefer the term community of use in describing a similar explicit rating scheme for recommending videos. Calculations of the similarity of users can also be used for purposes such as matchmaking (see below).

Inferred ratings can be regarded as document wear. Physical objects naturally show signs of wear caused by usage, but many digital objects do not reflect whether (and by whom) they have been used. It is possible to recreate the implicit information of the well-thumbed, often-used text on a library shelf that conveys its popularity by degree of wear and falls open at a particularly popular page. Usage is just one kind of information that can be recorded, but it illustrates how the implicit power of paper can be overlooked in the implementation of a digital equivalent. Indications of wear can serve as a starting point for recovering useful functionality and introducing new functionality that is unfeasible without digitization.

The variety of history-enriched digital objects includes edit wear and read wear (HILL & HOLLAN). That is, a document can record and display information, or metadata, on its history of edits and reading patterns (BÖHM & RAKOW). A library database that records and uses searches can be regarded as a history-enriched digital object. Concepts such as browse wear and borrow wear can be used not only for collection management but also as additions to existing history-of-use information to facilitate searching. There remains the open question posed by KANTOR (1993) as to whether such functions add more value than they cost to build and maintain. Systems such as those described above are proliferating rapidly; recent reviews can be found in OARD and TWIDALE ET AL. (1997b).

The personalization of content is an issue that goes beyond LIS. The marketing community has realized that individualized advertising may be more effective than mass-marketing techniques. Thus the term one-to-one marketing was coined (PEPPERS & ROGERS). The central message for vendors is to integrate all their information systems to enable their customer-related knowledge to be deployed in highly targeted marketing aimed at increasing customer loyalty. With the appropriate information at their fingertips, they can make recommendations based on any implicit ratings they hold. For example, they can use information derived from purchase records to suggest products to one customer based on purchases by other customers with similar buying patterns.

Many of the research projects that we mention may seem far removed from practical application in any library, digital or not. It is therefore interesting to note that many of the recommending features described are already being used (in somewhat rudimentary form) in online commerce. For example, the online bookstore Amazon.com needs to ensure that its customers can find what they want (and also find what they do not yet know they want). This requires careful design of the interface, a Web-based system that facilitates page navigation, use of different search engines and button clicks, and form filling for ordering. It requires the provision of standard library catalog functions for author, title, and subject searching.

Amazon.com also accommodates the leisure shopper, the person who browses the shelves of a bookshop looking for something to buy, or who welcomes advice or recommendations. The system builds profiles of registered users based on their purchases over time. The profiles can be used for more targeted marketing, say of a new book about to be published by an author whose books a customer has bought in the past. If the customer searches from the same machine (e.g., a home computer) or uses an account- or registration-based system, it is possible to collect information on his or her searching behavior. This can be used to compile information about near misses (books almost bought), as well as usability information about the interface itself.

Collaborative filtering and recommending can be provided in different ways. For example, on finding a book of interest, the user may receive the information "Customers who bought this book also bought . . ." followed by a list of other book links. This feature assumes that books bought together by previous customers are likely to appeal to the current customer. Amazon.com also invites customers and authors to write reviews of books and rate them. Recommendations can then be based on the similarity of their ratings to those of other raters, as with the research systems described earlier.

Although these examples may stretch the concept of collaboration, the systems and techniques described in this section are potentially very important because they enable virtual communities to help their members without some of the restrictions of space, time, or even personal identity. They permit a digital library, if its users so wish, to respond to requests such as "Show me some articles that are new to me and that people with similar interests to me have found interesting."

Matchmaking

One of the questions inherent in user-user collaboration is that of how the users become aware of each other. In a physical library, presence in the same area may indicate similar interests, and an accidental meeting with another user could be the start of a collaborative relationship (NICHOLS & TWIDALE). The major limiting factor in this scenario is the requirement for co-location and synchronicity (CHANG & RICE), whereas the digital library promotes remote asynchronous interactions. Matchmaking, or introducing people with similar interests, may be a useful service for a digital library for several reasons:

- Personal networking to gain awareness of the activities of others is known to be a powerfully efficient mechanism, for example in academia leading to the formation of invisible colleges (CRANE).
- Traditional forms of matchmaking, such as attending international conferences, may be too difficult or expensive for new entrants to a research field.
- People working on similar projects may be unaware of each other (FONER & CRABTREE), particularly if they have backgrounds in different subject areas.
- Other people can be useful filters and sources of recommendations (NICHOLS ET AL.) that can help prevent needless repetition of effort.
- Some people, especially those new to a field, are unaware of word-of-mouth information in a subject area (FONER & CRABTREE).

Locating people with similar interests can be considered equivalent to matching queries with documents: personal profiles can just as easily be compared with each other as with a stream of documents (see AHUVIA & ADELMAN; FONER & CRABTREE; STREETER & LOCHBAUM). In collaborative filtering systems, user profiles provide a mechanism for introducing users to potential collaborators. This form of matchmaking is based on similarity of users' document evaluations or usage patterns and is less subject to any self-reporting biases than the scenario of the social introduction agency.

Implications for Professional Librarianship

SWANSON'S 1964 article, already cited as being visionary about many aspects of advanced functionality, also touches on implications of computerized systems for the profession of librarianship. Swanson notes the fear that discussions of automation can engender, but says "Librarians who accept systems analysis and mechanization as legitimate subjects to be studied and mastered will fall heir to the responsibility of planning future libraries and to planning tasks that machines will perform. There will be no threat to, nor question of, their professional status" (p. 125). Although technological developments discussed in this review are usually described from the end-user's point of view, it is important to consider the implications for library staff. FOWELL & LEVY describe these changes as contributing to a new model of professional practice for librarians that they term networked learner support. This is the delivery of training and help via computer networks to both library staff members as part of their continuing professional development and to library users.

Privacy

New technologies inevitably have social impacts. The impacts of collaborative technologies are likely to be greater because the technologies can have an immediate effect on how people work and interact with one another. KLING provides a good introduction to the broader issue of social implications. Here we consider only the issue of privacy. BELLOTTI & SELLEN discuss the privacy implications of a range of CSCW technologies. In the context of information access and retrieval and digital libraries, a major implication of the move to remote and asynchronous interactions is that computers will be storing increasing amounts of personal information about library users. In principle, a digital library can record everything from borrowing physical books, through searches, purchases, and the reading of individual pages (NICHOLS).

The general principle in CSCW is a trade-off on a continuum: sacrificing privacy permits increased collaborative functionality. It remains to be seen where people wish to locate themselves along this continuum. They will wish to have control over the process and choose different privacy-functionality options for different kinds of work, in a manner analogous to (but much more sophisticated than) the choice of levels of privacy afforded by shared file systems.

In digital libraries, anonymous recording of usage can allow recommending activities. If named recording is permitted, additional functionality such as matchmaking becomes possible. The principle also applies in the case of nontechnological systems. Telling colleagues about one's current project in the hope of getting feedback, or even asking a librarian for help clearly involves a loss of privacy that may be regarded as undesirable and unacceptable in certain contexts and circumstances.

Librarians have a long tradition of protecting the privacy of users. It may be that the benefits of collaborative functionalities are considered insufficient to outweigh the actual, perceived, or assumed potential loss of privacy. Users have several valid concerns which can lead to their refusal to use a given collaborative feature:

- Loss of privacy from using the feature
- Fear of signing a blank check (although the loss of privacy entailed in using the feature is acceptable to the user because it affords a certain collaborative benefit, the user does not trust that the information will not be used for some undeclared reason)
- Fear of setting a precedent (although the privacy/benefit tradeoff is acceptable, and the organization is trusted to make only appropriate use of the information, the user fears that by countenancing this minor, seemingly benign and voluntary erosion of privacy, it will be harder to oppose subsequent variants with more malign consequences)

The collection over time of customer purchase statistics has been common practice in commerce for many years. With online purchasing it is possible to acquire far more information, including a larger part of the purchasing process: not only what users bought but also near misses (items considered for purchase and rejected) and how users navigated through screens of options. With sufficiently sophisticated data mining, the retailer can obtain valuable information (PEPPERS & ROGERS). Again, this information can be used to improve service to the customer directly, for example by recommending books the customer might like. It seems that people either tolerate or expect loss of privacy in a commercial context, or that they are unaware of it. In a library context, even without the commercial imperative to sell more books, there is a strong professional imperative to provide better access. Recommending options may be valuable for libraries in much the same way as they are for bookstores. However, librarians are much more sensitive to the issue of privacy and the potential for abuse.

One common approach to dealing with privacy problems is cryptography (see BOOKSTEIN), a technique employed by many Web-based systems for concealing credit card details. As more CSCW applications are deployed on the Internet, it can be expected that more will include similar features for dealing with other types of personal information, including details of information searching activities. However, cryptography can not allay all concerns about privacy. Once information is collected for the most noble of reasons, it can be hard to refuse to release it for reasons that run counter to protection of the user's privacy. If librarians fear that collecting usage and searching data means they might be forced to hand the data over to, say the FBI, then they may decide not to collect the data at all, despite the advantages its use would offer for improving service to users. Encryption would not help this scenario. It can reduce the threat of unauthorized access, but not prevent additional access that the library is subsequently forced to provide. Making the data anonymous would solve this problem somewhat, but that means certain forms of detailed recommending would not be possible. This may be an acceptable compromise. Even with anonymous data, there is still the possibility of the data being correlated with external data to reveal details about individuals.

Privacy issues are complicated by cultural responses. The different approaches of the European Union (EU) and the United States are good examples (BENNETT & RAAB). The EU favors legislation and the United States favors private-sector agreements. In the United States there seems to be greater tolerance for the accumulation and exploitation of personal information by the private sector (defenders cite private enterprise issues such as freedom from interference by restrictive legislation and regulation) than by similar accumulation in the public sector (including various kinds of libraries). When collaborative functions for digital libraries and other databases are considered in a North American context (see Bennett & Raab for a discussion of differences between the United States and Canada), greater concern about privacy may be evident in public-sector libraries than in private-sector information centers and marketing departments. Even in the private sector, though, concerns about privacy are being voiced (HOFFMAN ET AL.) and written privacy policies now appear on various commercial Web sites.

CONCLUSION

Although it is hard to comprehend major transitions while they are underway, the emerging information society, or information economy, seems to be a combination of technological innovations and implementations that have the potential for supporting new ways of working and living. Research in CSCW concentrates on technologies to support people working together to solve problems. A particular interest is supporting people separated by distance, helping establish distributed teams that can draw on a wider pool of expertise. Various studies of collaborative work and the use of technologies reveal the difficulties that can arise if technologies are introduced without an understanding of the work context and the way people work. We believe that many of these technologies can be used to support the information search and retrieval process, provided careful account of the process is made in systems development.

A consideration of collaborative work in the context of LIS can take several forms. A library viewed as an organization includes people working together who may or may not benefit from using existing CSCW technology. The search for information by the users of a library is just part of their work, and that broader activity often includes collaborative work that should be better supported within the information search infrastructure. Finally, and in our view most importantly, the search for information itself often involves collaboration and would benefit from more explicit support for it.

In some ways the approach of CSCW runs counter to the approach of much IR research. In IR, the development of more powerful and easier-to-use systems can be regarded as a classic attempt at automation: trying to provide functionalities an end user will be able to use without the bother and expense of consulting a human intermediary. By contrast, much of the work in professional librarianship can be regarded as cooperative work (not necessarily computer supported) with a rich history of practice, analysis, and theory. These insights and perspectives should be used in designing collaborative technologies to further enhance the reach and kinds of support for information search and retrieval. However, this should be a two-way traffic in ideas: not only should the theory and technologies of CSCW be used to improve support and functionality in libraries, but the theory and practical insights from existing collaborative work in libraries should also be used to inform CSCW research. This can be done by providing a library work context of use for collaborative systems that is distinctly under-represented in the CSCW literature. Further, the substantial body of LIS knowledge on organizing information structures for usability (access) by others and supporting information searchers in collaborative interactions (e.g., reference work) has great potential to inform CSCW research and development.

BIBLIOGRAPHY

ABBOTT, KENNETH R.; SARIN, SUNIL K. 1994. Experiences with Workflow Management: Issues for the Next Generation. In: Furuta, Richard; Neuwirth, Christine, eds. CSCW '94: Proceedings of the Conference on Computer Supported Cooperative Work; 1994 October 22-26; Chapel Hill, NC. New York, NY: ACM; 1994. 113-120. ISBN: 0-89791-689-1.

ABELS, EILEEN G. 1996. The E-Mail Reference Interview. RQ. 1996; 35(3): 345-358. ISSN: 0033-7072.

ACKERMAN, MARK S. 1994. Augmenting the Organizational Memory: A Field Study of Answer Garden. In: Furuta, Richard; Neuwirth, Christine, eds. CSCW '94: Proceedings of the Conference on Computer Supported Cooperative Work; 1994 October 22-26; Chapel Hill, NC. New York, NY: ACM; 1994. 243-252. ISBN: 0-89791-689-1.

ACKERMAN, MARK S.; MCDONALD, DAVID W. 1996. Answer Garden 2: Merging Organizational Memory with Collaborative Help. In: Ackerman, Mark S., ed. CSCW '96: Proceedings of the Conference on Computer Supported Cooperative Work; 1996 November 16-20; Cambridge, MA. New York, NY: ACM; 1996. 97-105. ISBN: 0-89791-765-0.

AHUVIA, AARON C.; ADELMAN, MARA B. 1992. Formal Intermediaries in the Marriage Market: A Typology and Review. Journal of Marriage and the Family. 1992; 54(2): 452-463. ISSN: 0022-2445.

ALLEN, ROBERT B. 1990. User Models: Theory, Method, and Practice. International Journal of Man-Machine Studies. 1990; 32(5): 511-543. ISSN: 0020-7373.

ASHTON, SARAH; LEVY, PHILIPPA. 1998. Networked Learner Support in Higher Education: Initiatives in Professional Development and Research for a New Role. Journal of the American Society for Information Science. 1998; 49(9): 850-853. ISSN: 0002-8231.

ASSOCIATION FOR COMPUTING MACHINERY. 1986. CSCW '86: Proceedings of the Conference on Computer Supported Cooperative Work; 1986 December 3-5; Austin, TX. New York, NY: ACM; 1986. 386p. OCLC: 15913327.

BAECKER, RONALD M., ed. 1993. Readings in Groupware and Computer Supported Cooperative Work: Assisting Human-Human Collaboration. San Mateo, CA: Morgan Kaufmann; 1993. 882p. ISBN: 1-55860-241-0.

BANNON, LIAM. 1995. Editorial: Commentaries and a Response on the Suchman-Winograd Debate. Computer Supported Cooperative Work: The Journal of Collaborative Computing. 1995; 3(1): 29. ISSN: 0925-9724.

BARRY, CHRISTINE. 1996. The Digital Library: The Needs of Our Users. Paper Presented at the International Summer School on the Digital Library; 1996 August 5; Tilburg University, The Netherlands. Available from the author.

BATES, MARCIA J. 1989. The Design of Browsing and Berrypicking Techniques for the Online Search Interface. Online Review. 1989; 13(5): 407-424. ISSN: 0309-314X.

BATES, MARCIA J. 1990. Where Should the Person Stop and the Information Search Interface Start? Information Processing and Management. 1990; 26(5): 575-591. ISSN: 0306-4573.

BELLOTTI, VICTORIA; SELLEN, ABIGAIL. 1993. Design for Privacy in Ubiquitous Computing Environments. In: De Michelis, Giorgio; Simone, Carla; Schmidt, Kjeld, eds. Proceedings of the 3rd European Conference on Computer-Supported Cooperative Work (ECSCW'93); 1993 September 13-17; Milan, Italy. Dordrecht, The Netherlands: Kluwer Academic Publishers; 1993. 77-92. ISBN: 0-7923-2447-1.

BENFORD, STEVE; MARIANI, JOHN A. 1995. Virtual Environments for Data Sharing and Visualisation: Populated Information Terrains. In: Sawyer, Peter, ed. Interfaces to Database Systems (IDS94): Proceedings of the 2nd

International Workshop on Interfaces to Database Systems; 1994 July 13-15; Lancaster, UK. New York, NY: Springer-Verlag; 1995. 168-182. ISBN: 3-540-19910-1.

BENFORD, STEVE; SNOWDON, DAVE; GREENHALGH, CHRIS; INGRAM, ROB; KNOX, IAN; BROWN, CHRIS. 1995. VR-VIBE: A Virtual Environment for Co-operative Information Retrieval. Computer Graphics Forum. 1995; 14(3): C-349-C-360. ISSN: 0167-7055.

BENNETT, COLIN; RAAB, CHARLES D. 1997. The Adequacy of Privacy: The European Union Data Protection Directive and the North American Response. The Information Society. 1997; 13(3): 245-264. ISSN: 0197-2243.

BENSON, DOUGLAS; HUGHES, JOHN A. 1983. The Perspective of Ethnomethodology. London, UK: Longman; 1983. 205p. ISBN: 0-582-29584-X.

BENTLEY, RICHARD; HORSTMANN, THILO; TREVOR, JONATHON. 1997. The World Wide Web as Enabling Technology for CSCW: The Case of BSCW. Computer Supported Cooperative Work: The Journal of Collaborative Computing. 1997; 6(2/3): 111-134. ISSN: 0925-9724.

BIKSON, TORA K.; EVELAND, J.D. 1996. Groupware Implementation: Reinvention in the Sociotechnical Frame. In: Ackerman, Mark S., ed. CSCW '96: Proceedings of the Conference on Computer Supported Cooperative Work; 1996 November 16-20; Cambridge, MA. New York, NY: ACM; 1996. 428-437. ISBN: 0-89791-765-0.

BISHOP, ANN PETERSON; STAR, SUSAN LEIGH. 1996. Social Informatics of Digital Library Use and Infrastructure. In: Williams, Martha E., ed. Annual Review of Information Science and Technology: Volume 31. Medford, NJ: Information Today, Inc. for the American Society for Information Science; 1996. 301-401. ISSN: 0066-4200; ISBN: 1-57387-033-1.

BJERKNES, GRO; EHN, PELLE; KYNG, MORTEN, eds. 1987. Computers and Democracy : A Scandinavian Challenge. Aldershot, UK: Avebury; 1987. 434p. ISBN: 0-566-05476-0.

BLOMBERG, JEANETTE; KENSING, FINN; DYKSTRA-ERICKSON, ELIZA-BETH, eds. 1996. PDC'96: Proceedings of the Participatory Design Conference. Palo Alto, CA: Computer Professionals for Social Responsibility; 1996. 268p. Available from: CPSR, P.O. Box 717, Palo Alto, CA 94302-0717.

BLY, SARA A.; HARRISON, STEVE R.; IRWIN, SUSAN. 1993. Media Spaces: Bringing People Together in a Video, Audio and Computing Environment. Communications of the ACM. 1993; 36(1): 28-47. ISSN: 0001-0782.

BÖHM, KLEMENS; RAKOW, THOMAS C. 1994. Metadata for Multimedia Documents. SIGMOD Record. 1994; 23(4): 21-26. ISSN: 0163-5808.

BOOKSTEIN, ABRAHAM. 1996. Bibliocryptography. Journal of the American Society for Information Science. 1996; 47(12): 886-895. ISSN: 0002-8231.

BOWERS, JOHN; BUTTON, GRAHAM; SHARROCK, WES. 1995. Workflow from Within and Without. In: Marmolin, Hans; Sundblad, Yngve; Schmidt, Kjeld, eds. Proceedings of the 4th European Conference on Computer-Supported Cooperative Work (ECSCW'95); 1995 September 10-14; Stockholm, Sweden. Dordrecht, The Netherlands: Kluwer Academic Publishers; 1995. 51-66. ISBN: 0-7923-3697-6.

BOWKER, GEOFFREY C.; STAR, SUSAN LEIGH; TURNER, WILLIAM; GAS-
SER, LES, eds. 1997. Social Science, Technical Systems, and Cooperative
Work. Mahwah, NJ: Lawrence Erlbaum Associates; 1997. 470p. ISBN: 0-
8058-2402-2.

BREWER, ROBERT S.; JOHNSON, PHILIP M. 1994. Toward Collaborative
Knowledge Management within Large, Dynamically Structured Systems.
Honolulu, HI: Collaborative Software Development Laboratory, Depart-
ment of Information and Computer Sciences, University of Hawaii; 1994.
(Technical Report CSDL-TR-94-02). Available WWW: ftp://
ftp.ics.hawaii.edu/pub/tr/ics-tr-94-02.pdf.

BRINCK, TOM; GOMEZ, LOUIS M. 1992. A Collaborative Medium for the
Support of Conversational Props. In: Turner, Jon; Kraut, Robert, eds.
CSCW '92: Proceedings of the Conference on Computer Supported Coop-
erative Work; 1992 October 31-November 4; Toronto, Canada. New York,
NY: ACM; 1992. 171-178. ISBN: 0-89791-542-9.

BRUCKMAN, AMY. 1998. Community Support for Constructionist Learning.
Computer Supported Cooperative Work: The Journal of Collaborative
Computing. 1998; 7(1/2): 47-86. ISSN: 0925-9724.

BUSHALLOW-WILBER, LAURA; DEVINNEY, GEMMA; WHITCOMB, FRITZ.
1996. Electronic Mail Reference Service: A Study. RQ. 1996; 35(3): 359-363.
ISSN: 0033-7072.

BUTTON, GRAHAM, ed. 1993. Technology in Working Order: Studies of
Work, Interaction and Technology. London, UK: Routledge; 1993. 264p.
ISBN: 0-415-06839-8.

BUTTON, GRAHAM; HARPER, RICHARD. 1996. The Relevance of "Work
Practice" for Design. Computer Supported Cooperative Work: The Journal of Collaborative Computing. 1996; 4(4): 263-280. ISSN: 0925-9724.

CARROLL, JOHN M. 1995a. How to Avoid Designing Digital Libraries: A
Scenario-Based Approach. SIGOIS Bulletin. 1995; 16(2): 5-7. ISSN: 0894-
0819.

CARROLL, JOHN M., ed. 1995b. Scenario-Based Design: Envisioning Work
and Technology in System Development. New York, NY: Wiley; 1995.
408p. ISBN: 0-471-07659-7.

CHALMERS, MATTHEW. 1995. Design Perspectives in Visualising Complex
Information. In: Spaccapietra, Stefano; Jain, Ramesh, eds. Visual Database
Systems 3: Visual Information Management: Proceedings of the 3rd IFIP
2.6 Working Conference on Visual Database Systems; 1995 March 27-29;
Lausanne, Switzerland. London, UK: Chapman & Hall; 1995. 103-111.
ISBN: 0-412-72170-8.

CHANG, SHAN-JU; RICE, RONALD E. 1993. Browsing: A Multidimensional
Framework. In: Williams, Martha E., ed. Annual Review of Information
Science and Technology: Volume 28. Medford, NJ: Learned Information,
Inc. for the American Society for Information Science; 1993. 231-276. ISSN:
0066-4200.

CRABTREE, ANDY; TWIDALE, MICHAEL B.; O'BRIEN, JON; NICHOLS,
DAVID M. 1997. Talking in the Library: Implications for the Design of
Digital Libraries. In: Allen, Robert B.; Rasmussen, Edie, eds. Proceedings
of the 2nd ACM International Conference on Digital Libraries; 1997 July

23-26; Philadelphia, PA. New York, NY: ACM; 1997. 221-228. ISBN: 0-89791-868-1.

CRANE, DIANA. 1972. Invisible Colleges: Diffusion of Knowledge in Scientific Communities. Chicago, IL: University of Chicago Press; 1972. 213p. ISBN: 0-226-11857-6.

DAFT, RICHARD L.; LENGEL, ROBERT H. 1986. Organizational Information Requirements, Media Richness and Structural Design. Management Science. 1986; 32(5): 554-571. ISSN: 0025-1909.

DIX, ALAN. 1997. Challenges for Cooperative Work on the Web: An Analytical Approach. Computer Supported Cooperative Work: The Journal of Collaborative Computing. 1997; 6(2/3): 135-156. ISSN: 0925-9724.

DOURISH, PAUL. 1998. Introduction: The State of Play. Special Issue on Interaction and Collaboration in MUDs. Computer Supported Cooperative Work: The Journal of Collaborative Computing. 1998; 7(1/2): 1-7. ISSN: 0925-9724.

DOURISH, PAUL; ADLER, ANNETTE; BELLOTTI, VICTORIA; HENDERSON, AUSTIN. 1996a. Your Place or Mine? Learning from Long-Term Use of Audio-Video Communication. Computer Supported Cooperative Work: The Journal of Collaborative Computing. 1996; 5(1): 33-62. ISSN: 0925-9724.

DOURISH, PAUL; BELLOTTI, VICTORIA. 1992. Awareness and Coordination in Shared Workspaces. In: Turner, Jon; Kraut, Robert, eds. CSCW '92: Proceedings of the Conference on Computer Supported Cooperative Work; 1992 October 31-November 4; Toronto, Canada. New York, NY: ACM; 1992. 107-114. ISBN: 0-89791-542-9.

DOURISH, PAUL; HOLMES, JIM; MACLEAN, ALLAN; MARQVARDSEN, PERNILLE; ZBYSLAW, ALEX. 1996b. Freeflow: Mediating between Representation and Action in Workflow Systems. In: Ackerman, Mark S., ed. CSCW '96: Proceedings of the Conference on Computer Supported Cooperative Work; 1996 November 16-20; Cambridge, MA. New York, NY: ACM; 1996. 190-208. ISBN: 0-89791-765-0.

EASTERBROOK, STEVE, ed. 1993. CSCW: Cooperation or Conflict? New York, NY: Springer-Verlag; 1993. 211p. ISBN: 0-387-19755-9.

EHRLICH, KATE; CASH, DEBRA. 1994. Turning Information into Knowledge: Information Finding as a Collaborative Activity. In: Schnase, John L.; Leggett, John J.; Furuta, Richard K.; Metcalfe, Ted, eds. Proceedings of Digital Libraries '94: The 1st Annual Conference on the Theory and Practice of Digital Libraries; 1994 June 19-21; College Station, TX. College Station, TX: Texas A&M University; 1994. 119-125. Also available WWW: http://www.csdl.tamu.edu/DL94/paper/lotus.html.

EHRLICH, KATE; CASH, DEBRA. 1999. The Invisible World of Intermediaries: A Cautionary Tale. Computer Supported Cooperative Work: The Journal of Collaborative Computing. 1999; 8(1/2): 147-167. ISSN: 0925-9724.

ELLIOTT, MARGARET; KLING, ROB. 1997. Organizational Usability of Digital Libraries: Case Study of Legal Research in Civil and Criminal Courts. Journal of the American Society for Information Science. 1997; 48(11): 1023-1035. ISSN: 0002-8231.

ELLIS, C.A.; GIBBS, S.J.; REIN, G.L. 1991. Groupware: Some Issues and Experiences. Communications of the ACM. 1991; 34(1): 38-58. ISSN: 0001-0782.

ENGELBART, DOUGLAS C. 1962. Augmenting Human Intellect: A Conceptual Framework. Menlo Park, CA: Stanford Research Institute; 1962. 134p. OCLC: 8671016.

ENGELBART, DOUGLAS C.; ENGLISH, WILLIAM K. 1968. A Research Center for Augmenting Human Intellect. In: Proceedings of the Fall Joint Computer Conference; 1968 December 9-11; San Francisco, CA. Washington, DC: Thompson Books; 1968. 395-410. (AFIPS Conference Proceedings: Volume 33). OCLC: 35419608.

ERICKSON, THOMAS; SALOMON, GITTA. 1991. Designing a Desktop Information System: Observations and Issues. In: Robertson, Scott P.; Olson, Gary M.; Olson, Judith S., eds. CHI '91: Proceedings of the Association for Computing Machinery Special Interest Group on Computer-Human Interaction (ACM/SIGCHI) Conference on Human Factors in Computing Systems; 1991 April 27-May 2; New Orleans, LA. New York, NY: ACM; 1991. 49-54. ISBN: 0-201-51278-5.

FERGUSON, CHRIS D.; BUNGE, CHARLES A. 1997. The Shape of Services to Come: Values-Based Reference Service for the Largely Digital Library. College and Research Libraries. 1997; 58(3): 252-265. ISSN: 0010-0870.

FINHOLT, THOMAS A.; TEASLEY, STEPHANIE D. 1998. The Need for Psychology in Research on Computer-Supported Cooperative Work. Social Science Computer Review. 1998; 16(1): 40-52. ISSN: 0894-4393.

FISH, ROBERT S.; KRAUT, ROBERT E.; ROOT, ROBERT W.; RICE, RONALD E. 1993. Video as a Technology for Informal Communication. Communications of the ACM. 1993; 36(1): 48-61. ISSN: 0001-0782.

FONER, L.; CRABTREE, I.B. 1996. Multi-Agent Matchmaking. BT Technology Journal. 1996; 14(4): 115-123. ISSN: 1358-3948.

FOWELL, SUSAN P.; LEVY, PHILIPPA. 1995. Developing a New Professional Practice: A Model for Networked Learner Support in Higher Education. Journal of Documentation. 1995; 51(3): 271-280. ISSN: 0022-0418.

FOX, EDWARD A.; AKSCYN, ROBERT M.; FURUTA, RICHARD K.; LEGGETT, JOHN J., eds. 1995. Special Issue on Digital Libraries. Communications of the ACM. 1995; 38(4): 22-96. ISSN: 0001-0782.

FOX, EDWARD A.; HIX, DEBORAH; NOWELL, LUCY T.; BRUENI, DENNIS J.; WAKE, WILLIAM C.; HEATH, LENWOOD S.; RAO, DURGESH. 1993. Users, User Interfaces, and Objects: Envision, a Digital Library. Journal of the American Society for Information Science. 1993; 44(8): 480-491. ISSN: 0002-8231.

FULK, JANET; STEINFIELD, CHARLES, eds. 1990. Organizations and Communication Technology. Newbury Park, CA: Sage Publications; 1990. 328p. ISBN: 0-8039-3530-7.

GALE, STEPHEN. 1990. Human Aspects of Interactive Multimedia Communication. Interacting with Computers. 1990; 2(2): 175-189. ISSN: 0953-5438.

GALEGHER, JOLENE; KRAUT, ROBERT E.; EGIDO, CARMEN, eds. 1990. Intellectual Teamwork: Social and Technological Foundations of Cooperative Work. Hillsdale, NJ: Lawrence Erlbaum Associates; 1990. 542p. ISBN: 0-8058-0533-8.

GARFINKEL, HAROLD. 1967. Studies in Ethnomethodology. Englewood Cliffs, NJ: Prentice-Hall; 1967. 288p. OCLC: 356659.

GLEADHILL, DAPHNE. 1997. Does the Nerd Have the Answer? Library Technology. 1997; 2(2): 35-36. ISSN: 1362-1122.

GOLDBERG, DAVID; NICHOLS, DAVID M.; OKI, BRIAN M.; TERRY, DOUGLAS. 1992. Using Collaborative Filtering to Weave an Information Tapestry. Communications of the ACM. 1992; 35(12): 61-70. ISSN: 0001-0782.

GREENBAUM, JOAN; KYNG, MORTEN, eds. 1991. Design at Work: Cooperative Design of Computer Systems. Hillsdale, NJ: Lawrence Erlbaum Associates; 1991. 294p. ISBN: 0-8058-0611-3.

GREENBERG, SAUL, ed. 1991. Computer Supported Cooperative Work and Groupware. London, UK: Academic Press; 1991. 416p. ISBN: 0-12-299220-2.

GREIF, IRENE, ed. 1988. Computer-Supported Cooperative Work: A Book of Readings. San Mateo, CA: Morgan Kaufmann; 1988. 783p. ISBN: 0-934613-57-5.

GRUDIN, JONATHAN. 1989. Why Groupware Applications Fail: Problems in Design and Evaluation. Office Technology and People. 1989; 4(3): 245-264. ISSN: 0167-5710.

GRUDIN, JONATHAN. 1994a. Computer-Supported Cooperative Work: Its History and Participation. Computer. 1994; 27(5): 19-26. ISSN: 0018-9162.

GRUDIN, JONATHAN. 1994b. Groupware and Social Dynamics: Eight Challenges for Developers. Communications of the ACM. 1994; 37(1): 92-105. ISSN: 0001-0782.

GUTWIN, CARL; ROSEMAN, MARK; GREENBERG, SAUL. 1996. A Usability Study of Awareness Widgets in a Shared Workspace Groupware System. In: Ackerman, Mark S., ed. CSCW '96: Proceedings of the Conference on Computer Supported Cooperative Work; 1996 November 16-20; Cambridge, MA. New York, NY: ACM; 1996. 258-267. ISBN: 0-89791-765-0.

HAHN, KARLA. 1997. An Investigation of an E-mail-Based Help Service. College Park, MD: University of Maryland; 1997. (CLIS Technical Report No. 97-03). Available WWW: http://oriole.umd.edu/research/reports/tr97/03/9703.html.

HALL, ROGERS; MIYAKE, NAOMI; ENYEDY, NOEL, eds. 1997. Proceedings of the 2nd International Conference on Computer Support for Collaborative Learning. Mahwah, NJ: Lawrence Erlbaum Associates; 1997. 315p. ISBN: 0-8058-3262-9.

HARPER, RICHARD. 1996. Why People Do and Don't Wear Active Badges: A Case Study. Computer Supported Cooperative Work: The Journal of Collaborative Computing. 1996; 4(4): 297-312. ISSN: 0925-9724.

HARPER, RICHARD. 1998. Inside the IMF: An Ethnography of Documents, Technology and Organizational Action. San Diego, CA: Academic Press; 1998. 305p. ISBN: 0-12-325840-5.

HARPER, RICHARD; SELLEN, ABIGAIL. 1995. Collaborative Tools and the Practicalities of Professional Work at the International Monetary Fund. In: Katz, Irvin R.; Mack, Robert; Marks, Linn; Rosson, Mary Beth; Nielsen, Jakob, eds. CHI '95: Proceedings of the Association for Computing Machinery Special Interest Group on Computer-Human Interaction (ACM/

SIGCHI) Conference on Human Factors in Computing Systems; 1995 May 7-11; Denver, CO. New York, NY: ACM; 1995. 122-129. ISBN: 0-89791-694-8.

HAYTHORNTHWAITE, CAROLINE; WELLMAN, BARRY; GARTON, LAURA. 1998. Work and Community via Computer-Mediated Communication. In: Gackenbach, J., ed. Psychology and the Internet. San Diego, CA: Academic Press; 1998. 199-226. ISBN: 0-12-271950-6.

HILL, R.D.; BRINCK, T.; ROHALL, S.L.; PATTERSON, J.F.; WILNER, W. 1994. The Rendezvous Architecture and Language for Constructing Multi-User Applications. ACM Transactions on Computer Human Interaction. 1994; 1(2): 81-125. ISSN: 1073-0516.

HILL, WILLIAM C.; HOLLAN, JAMES D. 1994. History-Enriched Digital Objects: Prototypes and Policy Issues. The Information Society. 1994; 10(2): 139-145. ISSN: 0197-2243.

HILL, WILLIAM C.; STEAD, LARRY; ROSENSTEIN, MARK; FURNAS, GEORGE W. 1995. Recommending and Evaluating Choices in a Virtual Community of Use. In: Katz, Irvin R.; Mack, Robert; Marks, Linn; Rosson, Mary Beth; Nielsen, Jakob, eds. CHI '95: Proceedings of the Association for Computing Machinery Special Interest Group on Computer-Human Interaction (ACM/SIGCHI) Conference on Human Factors in Computing Systems; 1995 May 7-11; Denver, CO. New York, NY: ACM; 1995. 194-201. ISBN: 0-89791-694-8.

HILTZ, STARR ROXANNE. 1994. The Virtual Classroom: Learning without Limits via Computer Networks. Norwood, NJ: Ablex Publishing Corp.; 1994. 384p. ISBN: 0-89391-928-4.

HOFFMAN, DONNA L.; NOVAK, THOMAS P.; PERALTA, MARCOS A. 1999. Information Privacy in the Marketplace: Implications for the Commercial Uses of Anonymity on the Web. The Information Society. 1999. (In press). ISSN: 0197-2243.

HOPPE, H. ULRICH; ZHAO, JIAN. 1994. C-TORI: An Interface for Cooperative Database Retrieval. In: Karagiannis, Dimitris, ed. Database and Expert Systems Applications: Proceedings of the 5th International Conference (DEXA'94); 1994 September 7-9; Athens, Greece. New York, NY: Springer-Verlag; 1994. 103-113. ISBN: 0-387-58435-8.

HUDSON, SCOTT E.; SMITH, IAN. 1996. Techniques for Addressing Fundamental Privacy and Disruption Tradeoffs in Awareness Support Systems. In: Ackerman, Mark S., ed. CSCW '96: Proceedings of the Conference on Computer Supported Cooperative Work; 1996 November 16-20; Cambridge, MA. New York, NY: ACM; 1996. 248-257. ISBN: 0-89791-765-0.

HUGHES, JOHN A.; KING, VAL; MARIANI, JOHN A.; RODDEN, TOM; TWIDALE, MICHAEL B. 1996a. Paperwork and Its Lessons for Database Systems: An Initial Assessment. In: Shapiro, Dan; Tauber, Michael; Traunmueller, Roland, eds. The Design of Computer Supported Cooperative Work and Groupware Systems. New York, NY: Elsevier; 1996. 43-66. ISBN: 0-444-81998-3.

HUGHES, JOHN A.; KING, VAL; RODDEN, TOM; ANDERSEN, HANS. 1994. Moving Out from the Control Room: Ethnography in System Design. In: Furuta, Richard; Neuwirth, Christine, eds. CSCW '94: Proceedings of the

Conference on Computer Supported Cooperative Work; 1994 October 22-26; Chapel Hill, NC. New York, NY: ACM; 1994. 429-439. ISBN: 0-89791-689-1.

HUGHES, JOHN A.; KRISTOFFERSEN, STEINAR; O'BRIEN, JON; ROUNCEFIELD, MARK. 1996b. "When Mavis Met IRIS": Ending the Love Affair with Organisational Memory. In: Dahlbom, Bo; Ljunberg, Fredrik; Nuldén, Urban; Simon, Kai; Sorensen, Carsten; Stage, Jan, eds. Proceedings of the 19th Information Systems Research Seminar in Scandinavia (IRIS 19); 1996 August 10-13; Lökeberg, Sweden. Gothenberg, Sweden: University of Gothenberg; 1996. 767-787. (Gothenberg Studies in Informatics). ISBN: 91-972942-0-9.

HUGHES, JOHN A.; RANDALL, DAVID; SHAPIRO, DAN. 1992. Faltering from Ethnography to Design. In: Turner, Jon; Kraut, Robert, eds. CSCW '92: Proceedings of the Conference on Computer Supported Cooperative Work; 1992 October 31-November 4; Toronto, Canada. New York, NY: ACM; 1992. 115-122. ISBN: 0-89791-542-9.

HUGHES, JOHN A.; RANDALL, DAVID; SHAPIRO, DAN. 1993. From Ethnographic Record to System Design. Computer Supported Cooperative Work: The Journal of Collaborative Computing. 1993; 1(3): 123-141. ISSN: 0925-9724.

HUTCHINS, EDWIN. 1995. Cognition in the Wild. Cambridge, MA: MIT Press; 1995. 381p. ISBN: 0-262-08231-4.

ISHII, HIROSHI; KOBAYASHI, MINORU; ARITA, KAZUHO. 1994. Iterative Design of Seamless Collaborative Media. Communications of the ACM. 1994; 37(8): 83-97. ISSN: 0001-0782.

JESSUP, LEONARD M.; VALACICH, JOSEPH S., eds. 1993. Group Support Systems: New Perspectives. New York, NY: Macmillan; 1993. 365p. ISBN: 0-02-360625-8.

JOHANSEN, ROBERT. 1988. Groupware: Computer Support for Business Teams. New York, NY: Free Press; 1988. 205p. ISBN: 0-02-916491-5.

JONES, STEVEN G., ed. 1995. Cybersociety: Computer-Mediated Communication and Community. Thousand Oaks, CA: Sage Publications; 1995. 241p. ISBN: 0-8039-5676-2.

KANTOR, PAUL B. 1993. The Adaptive Network Library Interface: A Historical Overview and Interim Report. Library Hi Tech. 1993; 11(3): 81-92. ISSN: 0737-8831.

KANTOR, PAUL B. 1994. Information Retrieval Techniques. In: Williams, Martha E., ed. Annual Review of Information Science and Technology: Volume 29. Medford, NJ: Learned Information, Inc. for the American Society for Information Science; 1994. 53-90. ISBN: 0-938734-91-1.

KAPLAN, SIMON M.; TOLONE, WILLIAM J.; BOGIA, DOUGLAS P.; BIGNOLI, CELSINA. 1992. Flexible, Active Support for Collaborative Work with ConversationBuilder. In: Turner, Jon; Kraut, Robert, eds. CSCW '92: Proceedings of the Conference on Computer Supported Cooperative Work; 1992 October 31-November 4; Toronto, Canada. New York, NY: ACM; 1992. 378-385. ISBN: 0-89791-542-9.

KARSENTY, LAURENT. 1997. Effects of the Amount of Shared Information on Communication Efficiency in Side by Side and Remote Help Dialogues.

In: Hughes, John A.; Prinz, Wolfgang; Rodden, Tom; Schmidt, Kjeld, eds. Proceedings of the 5th European Conference on Computer Supported Cooperative Work (ECSCW'97); 1997 September 7-11; Lancaster, UK. Dordrecht, The Netherlands: Kluwer Academic Publishers; 1997. 49-64. ISBN: 0-7923-4638-6.

KESSLER, JACK. 1996. Internet Digital Libraries: The International Dimension. Boston, MA: Artech House; 1996. 265p. ISBN: 0-89006-875-5.

KIES, JONATHAN K.; WILLIGES, ROBERT C.; ROSSON, MARY BETH. 1998. Coordinating Computer-Supported Cooperative Work: A Review of Research Issues and Strategies. Journal of the American Society for Information Science. 1998; 49(9): 776-791. ISSN: 0002-8231.

KIESLER, SARA B., ed. 1997. Culture of the Internet. Mahwah, NJ: Lawrence Erlbaum Associates; 1997. 463p. ISBN: 0-8058-1635-6.

KING, GARY; KUNG, H.T.; GROSZ, BARBARA; VERBA, SIDNEY; FLECKER, DALE; KAHIN, BRIAN. 1994. The Harvard Self-Enriching Library Facilities (SELF) Project. In: Schnase, John L.; Leggett, John J.; Furuta, Richard K.; Metcalfe, Ted, eds. Proceedings of Digital Libraries '94: The 1st Annual Conference on the Theory and Practice of Digital Libraries; 1994 June 19-21; College Station, TX. College Station, TX: Texas A&M University; 1994. 134-138. Also available WWW: http://www.csdl.tamu.edu/DL94/paper/harvard.html.

KIRKWOOD, A.; FURNER, S.; ABLARD, W.; CLARK, B.; DICKERSON, KEITH; MERCER, A.; O'DONNELL, S.; SIU, Y.; WILLIAMS, OWEN. 1993. Usability Trialling for CSCW Technology: Lessons from a Structured Messaging Task. In: Diaper, Dan; Sanger, Colston, eds. CSCW in Practice: An Introduction and Case Studies. New York, NY: Springer-Verlag; 1993. 163-176. ISBN: 0-387-19784-2.

KLING, ROB, ed. 1996. Computerization and Controversy: Value Conflicts and Social Choices. 2nd edition. San Diego, CA: Academic Press; 1996. 961p. ISBN: 0-12-415040-3.

KLING, ROB; ELLIOT, MARGARET. 1994. Digital Library Design for Organizational Usability. SIGOIS Bulletin. 1994; 15(2): 59-70. ISSN: 0894-0819.

KOCHEN, MANFRED; WONG, E. 1962. Concerning the Possibility of a Cooperative Information Exchange. IBM Journal of Research and Development. 1962; 6(2): 270-271. ISSN: 0018-8646.

KOENIG, MICHAEL E. D. 1990. Linking Library Users: A Culture Change in Librarianship. American Libraries. 1990; 21(9): 844-849. ISSN: 0002-9769.

KONSTAN, JOSEPH A.; MILLER, BRADLEY N.; MALTZ, DAVID; HERLOCKER, JONATHAN L.; GORDON, LEE R.; RIEDL, JOHN. 1997. GroupLens: Applying Collaborative Filtering to Usenet News. Communications of the ACM. 1997; 40(3): 77-87. ISSN: 0001-0782.

KOSCHMANN, TIMOTHY, ed. 1996. CSCL: Theory and Practice of an Emerging Paradigm. Mahwah, NJ: Lawrence Erlbaum Associates; 1996. 353p. ISBN: 0-8058-1345-4.

KRAUT, ROBERT E.; FISH, ROBERT S.; ROOT, ROBERT W.; CHALFONT, BARBARA L. 1993. Informal Communication in Organizations: Form, Function and Technology. In: Baecker, Ronald M., ed. Readings in

Groupware and Computer Supported Cooperative Work. San Mateo, CA: Morgan Kaufmann; 1993. 287-314. ISBN: 1-55860-241-0.

KRAUT, ROBERT E.; GALEGHER, JOLENE. 1990. Patterns of Contact and Communication in Scientific Research Collaboration. In: Galegher, Jolene; Kraut, Robert E.; Egido, Carmen, eds. Intellectual Teamwork: Social and Technological Foundations of Cooperative Work. Hillsdale, NJ: Lawrence Erlbaum Associates; 1990. 149-171. ISBN: 0-8058-0534-6.

LANDAUER, THOMAS K. 1995. The Trouble with Computers: Usefulness, Usability, and Productivity. Cambridge, MA: MIT Press; 1995. 425p. ISBN: 0-262-12186-7.

LAVE, JEAN; WENGER, ETIENNE. 1991. Situated Learning: Legitimate Peripheral Participation. Cambridge, UK: Cambridge University Press; 1991. 138p. ISBN: 0-521-41308-7.

LEE, ALISON. 1992. Investigations into History Tools for User Support. Toronto, Canada: University of Toronto; 1992. 242p. (Ph.D. dissertation). ISBN: 0-315-73815-4.

LEMAIRE, BENOÎT; MOORE, JOHANNA. 1994. An Improved Interface for Tutorial Dialogues: Browsing a Visual Dialogue History. In: Adelson, Beth; Dumais, Susan; Olson, Judith, eds. CHI '94: Proceedings of the Association for Computing Machinery Special Interest Group on Computer-Human Interaction (ACM/SIGCHI) Conference on Human Factors in Computing Systems; 1994 April 24-28; Boston, MA. New York, NY: ACM; 1994. 16-22. ISBN: 0-201-76557-8.

LESK, MICHAEL E. 1997. Practical Digital Libraries: Books, Bytes, and Bucks. San Francisco, CA: Morgan Kaufmann; 1997. 297p. ISBN: 1-55860-459-6.

LESSICK, SUSAN; KJAER, KATHRYN; CLANCY, STEVE. 1997. Interactive Reference Services (IRS) at UC Irvine: Expanding References Service beyond the Reference Desk. Available WWW: http://www.ala.org/acrl/paperhtm/a10.html.

LEVY, DAVID M.; MARSHALL, CATHERINE C. 1995. Going Digital: A Look at Assumptions Underlying Digital Libraries. Communications of the ACM. 1995; 38(4): 77-84. ISSN: 0001-0782.

LUFF, PAUL; HEATH, CHRISTIAN; GREATBATCH, DAVID. 1992. Tasks-in-Interaction: Paper and Screen Based Documentation in Collaborative Activity. In: Turner, Jon; Kraut, Robert, eds. CSCW '92: Proceedings of the Conference on Computer Supported Cooperative Work; 1992 October 31-November 4; Toronto, Canada. New York, NY: ACM; 1992. 163-170. ISBN: 0-89791-542-9.

MAES, PATTIE. 1994. Agents That Reduce Work and Information Overload. Communications of the ACM. 1994; 37(7): 31-40. ISSN: 0001-0782.

MALTZ, DAVID A. 1994. Distributing Information for Collaborative Filtering on Usenet Net News. Cambridge, MA: Massachusetts Institute of Technology; 1994. 71p. (M.S. thesis). OCLC: 31314097.

MANOHAR, NELSON R.; PRAKASH, ATUL. 1995. The Session Capture and Replay Paradigm for Asynchronous Collaboration. In: Marmolin, Hans; Sundblad, Yngve; Schmidt, Kjeld, eds. Proceedings of the 4th European Conference on Computer-Supported Cooperative Work (ECSCW'95); 1995

September 10-14; Stockholm, Sweden. Dordrecht, The Netherlands: Kluwer Academic Publishers; 1995. 149-164. ISBN: 0-7923-3697-6.

MARCHIONINI, GARY. 1992. Interfaces for End-User Information Seeking. Journal of the American Society for Information Science. 1992; 43(2): 156-163. ISSN: 0002-8231.

MARCHIONINI, GARY; KOMLODI, ANITA. 1998. Design of Interfaces for Information Seeking. In: Williams, Martha E., ed. Annual Review of Information Science and Technology: Volume 33. Medford, NJ: Information Today, Inc. for the American Society for Information Science; 1998. 89-130. ISBN: 1-57387-065-X.

MARK, GLORIA; FUCHS, LUDWIN; SOHLENKAMP, MARKUS. 1997a. Supporting Groupware Conventions through Context Awareness. In: Hughes, John A.; Prinz, Wolfgang; Rodden, Tom; Schmidt, Kjeld, eds. Proceedings of the 5th European Conference on Computer Supported Cooperative Work (ECSCW'97); 1997 September 7-11; Lancaster, UK. Dordrecht, The Netherlands: Kluwer Academic Publishers; 1997. 253-268. ISBN: 0-7923-4638-6.

MARK, GLORIA; HAAKE, JORG M.; STREITZ, NORBERT A. 1997b. Hypermedia Use in Group Work: Changing the Product, Process, and Strategy. Computer Supported Cooperative Work: The Journal of Collaborative Computing. 1997; 6(4): 327-368. ISSN: 0925-9724.

MARSHALL, CATHERINE C. 1997. Annotation: from Paper Books to the Digital Library. In: Allen, Robert B.; Rasmussen, Edie, eds. Proceedings of the 2nd ACM International Conference on Digital Libraries; 1997 July 23-26; Philadelphia, PA. New York, NY: ACM; 1997. 131-140. ISBN: 0-89791-868-1.

MARSHALL, CATHERINE C.; SHIPMAN, FRANK M., III; MCCALL, RAYMOND J. 1994. Putting Digital Libraries to Work: Issues from Experience with Community Memories. In: Schnase, John L.; Leggett, John J.; Furuta, Richard K.; Metcalfe, Ted, eds. Proceedings of Digital Libraries '94: The 1st Annual Conference on the Theory and Practice of Digital Libraries; 1994 June 19-21; College Station, TX. College Station, TX: Texas A&M University; 1994. 126-133. Also available WWW: http://www.csdl.tamu.edu/DL94/paper/marshall.html.

MARTIN, NANNETTE P. 1986. Cooperative Online Searching: The Emporia/Kansas State Experience. College & Research Libraries News. 1986; 47(11): 719-721. ISSN: 0099-0086.

MCGRATH, JOSEPH EDWARD; HOLLINGSHEAD, ANDREA B. 1994. Groups Interacting with Technology: Ideas, Evidence, Issues, and an Agenda. Thousand Oaks, CA: Sage Publications; 1994. 180p. ISBN: 0-8039-4897-2.

MORGAN, ERIC LEASE. 1996. See You See A Librarian Final Report. Available WWW: http://sunsite.berkeley.edu/~emorgan/see-a-librarian/index.html.

MULLER, MICHAEL J.; KUHN, SARAH. 1993. Participatory Design: Guest Editors' Introduction. Communications of the ACM. 1993; 36(4): 24-28. (Special Issue on Participatory Design). ISSN: 0001-0782.

NARDI, BONNIE A.; O'DAY, VICKI L. 1996. Intelligent Agents: What We Learned at the Library. Libri. 1996; 46(2): 59-88. ISSN: 0024-2667.

NEUMANN, LAURA J.; STAR, SUSAN LEIGH. 1996. Making Infrastructure: The Dream of a Common Language. In: Blomberg, Jeanette; Kensing, Finn; Dykstra-Erickson, Elizabeth, eds. Proceedings of the Participatory Design Conference (PDC'96). Palo Alto, CA: Computer Professionals for Social Responsibility; 1996. 231-240. Available from: CPSR, P.O. Box 717, Palo Alto, CA 94302-0717.

NICHOLS, DAVID M. 1998. Implicit Rating and Filtering. In: 5th DELOS Workshop: Filtering and Collaborative Filtering; 1997 November 10-12; Budapest, Hungary. Le Chesnay, France: European Research Consortium for Informatics and Mathematics (ERCIM); 1998. 31-36. ISBN: 2-912335-04-3.

NICHOLS, DAVID M.; TWIDALE, MICHAEL B. 1997. Matchmaking and Privacy in the Digital Library: Striking the Right Balance. In: Davies, Clare; Ramsden, Anne, eds. Electronic Library and Visual Information Research—ELVIRA 4: Proceedings of the 4th UK/International Conference on Electronic Library and Visual Information Research; 1997 May 6-7; Milton Keynes, UK. London, UK: Aslib; 1997. 31-38. ISBN: 0-85142-401-5.

NICHOLS, DAVID M.; TWIDALE, MICHAEL B.; PAICE, CHRIS D. 1997. Recommendation and Usage in the Digital Library. Lancaster, UK: Computing Department, Lancaster University; 1997. 14p. (Technical Report CSEG/2/97). Available WWW: http://www.comp.lancs.ac.uk/computing/research/cseg/projects/ariadne/docs/recommend.html.

O'DAY, VICKI L.; BOBROW, DANIEL; BOBROW, KIMBERLY; SHIRLEY, MARK; HUGHES, BILLIE; WALTERS, JIM. 1998. Moving Practice: From Classrooms to MOO Rooms. Computer Supported Cooperative Work: The Journal of Collaborative Computing. 1998; 7(1/2): 9-45. ISSN: 0925-9724.

O'DAY, VICKI L.; JEFFRIES, ROBIN. 1993. Information Artisans: Patterns of Results Sharing by Information Searchers. In: COOCS '93: Proceedings of the Conference on Organizational Computing Systems; 1993 November 1-4; Milpitas, CA. New York, NY: ACM; 1993. 98-107. ISBN: 0-89791-627-1.

O'HARA, KENTON; SMITH, FIONA; NEWMAN, WILLIAM; SELLEN, ABIGAIL. 1998. Student Readers Use of Library Documents: Implications for Library Technologies. In: Karat, Clare-Marie; Lund, Arnold; Coutaz, Joelle; Karat, John, eds. CHI '98: Proceedings of the Association for Computing Machinery Special Interest Group on Computer-Human Interaction (ACM/SIGCHI) Conference on Human Factors in Computing Systems; 1998 April 18-23; Los Angeles, CA. New York, NY: ACM; 1998. 233-240. ISBN: 0-201-30987-4.

O'MALLEY, CLAIRE, ed. 1995. Computer Supported Collaborative Learning. New York, NY: Springer-Verlag; 1995. 303p. ISBN: 0-387-57740-8.

OARD, DOUGLAS W. 1997. The State of the Art in Text Filtering. User Modeling and User-Adapted Interaction. 1997; 7(3): 141-178. ISSN: 0924-1868.

ORLIKOWSKI, WANDA J. 1992. Learning from Notes: Organizational Issues in Groupware Implementation. In: Turner, Jon; Kraut, Robert, eds. CSCW '92: Proceedings of the Conference on Computer-Supported Cooperative

Work; 1992 October 31-November 4; Toronto, Canada. New York, NY: ACM; 1992. 362-369. ISBN: 0-89791-542-9.

PAEPCKE, ANDREAS. 1996. Information Needs in Technical Work Settings and Their Implications for the Design of Computer Tools. Computer Supported Cooperative Work: The Journal of Collaborative Computing. 1996; 5(1): 63-92. ISSN: 0925-9724.

PENTLAND, BRIAN T. 1992. Organizing Moves in Software Support Hot Lines. Administrative Science Quarterly. 1992; 37(4): 527-548. ISSN: 0001-8392.

PEPPERS, DON; ROGERS, MARTHA. 1993. The One-to-One Future: Building Relationships One Customer at a Time. New York, NY: Currency Doubleday; 1993. 443p. ISBN: 0-385-42528-7.

PLOWMAN, LYDIA; ROGERS, YVONNE; RAMAGE, MAGNUS. 1995. What Are Workplace Studies for? In: Marmolin, Hans; Sundblad, Yngve; Schmidt, Kjeld, eds. Proceedings of the 4th European Conference on Computer-Supported Cooperative Work (ECSCW'95); 1995 September 10-14; Stockholm, Sweden. Dordrecht, The Netherlands: Kluwer Academic Publishers; 1995. 309-324. ISBN: 0-7923-3697-6.

PRAKASH, ATUL; SHIM, HYONG SOP. 1994. DistView: Support for Building Efficient Collaborative Applications Using Replicated Objects. In: Furuta, Richard; Neuwirth, Christine, eds. CSCW '94: Proceedings of the Conference on Computer Supported Cooperative Work; 1994 October 22-26; Chapel Hill, NC. New York, NY: ACM; 1994. 153-164. ISBN: 0-89791-689-1.

PRINZ, WOLFGANG; KOLVENBACH, SABINE. 1996. Support for Workflows in a Ministerial Environment. In: Ackerman, Mark S., ed. CSCW '96: Proceedings of the Conference on Computer Supported Cooperative Work; 1996 November 16-20; Cambridge, MA. New York, NY: ACM; 1996. 199-208. ISBN: 0-89791-765-0.

PROCTOR, ROB; GOLDENBERG, ANA; DAVENPORT, ELISABETH; MCKINLAY, ANDY. 1998. Genres in Support of Collaborative Information Retrieval in the Virtual Library. Interacting with Computers. 1998; 10(2): 157-172. ISSN: 0953-5438.

PROCTOR, ROB; MCKINLAY, ANDY; GOLDENBERG, ANA; DAVENPORT, ELISABETH; BURNHILL, PETER; CANNELL, SHEILA. 1997. Enhancing Community and Collaboration in the Virtual Library. In: Peters, Carol; Thanos, Costantino, eds. Proceedings of the European Conference on Research and Advanced Technology for Digital Libraries (ECDL'97); 1997 September 1-3; Pisa, Italy. Berlin, Germany: Springer; 1997. 25-40. ISBN: 3-540-63554-8.

PYCOCK, JAMES; BOWERS, JOHN. 1996. Getting Others to Get It Right: An Ethnography of Design Work in the Fashion Industry. In: Ackerman, Mark S., ed. CSCW '96: Proceedings of the Conference on Computer Supported Cooperative Work; 1996 November 16-20; Cambridge, MA. New York, NY: ACM; 1996. 219-228. ISBN: 0-89791-765-0.

RADA, ROY, ed. 1996. Groupware and Authoring. London, UK: Academic Press; 1996. 369p. ISBN: 0-12-575005-6.

RICE, RONALD E. 1980. The Impacts of Computer-Mediated Organizational and Interpersonal Communication. In: Williams, Martha E., ed. Annual Review of Information Science and Technology: Volume 15. White Plains,

NY: Knowledge Industry Publications, Inc. for the American Society for Information Science; 1980. 221-249. ISSN: 0066-4200; ISBN: 0-914236-65-2.

ROBERTSON, SCOTT; JITAN, SHERIF; REESE, KATHY. 1997. Web-Based Collaborative Library Research. In: Allen, Robert B.; Rasmussen, Edie, eds. Proceedings of the 2nd ACM International Conference on Digital Libraries; 1997 July 23-26; Philadelphia, PA. New York, NY: ACM; 1997. 152-160. ISBN: 0-89791-868-1.

RODDEN, TOM. 1991. A Survey of CSCW Systems. Interacting with Computers. 1991; 3(3): 319-354. ISSN: 0953-5438.

ROOT, ROBERT W. 1988. Design of a Multi-Media Vehicle for Social Browsing. In: CSCW '88: Proceedings of the Conference on Computer Supported Cooperative Work; 1988 September 26-29; Portland, OR. New York, NY: ACM; 1988. 25-38. ISBN: 0-89791-282-9.

RÖSCHEISEN, MARTIN; MORGENSEN, CHRISTIAN; WINOGRAD, TERRY. 1995. Beyond Browsing: Shared Comments, SOAPs, Trails, and Online-Communities. Computer Networks and ISDN Systems. 1995; 27(6): 739-749. ISSN: 0169-7552.

ROSEMAN, MARK; GREENBERG, SAUL. 1996. Building Real-Time Groupware with GroupKit, a Groupware Toolkit. ACM Transactions on Computer-Human Interaction. 1996; 3(1): 66-106. ISSN: 1073-0516.

SANDORE, BETH. 1993. Applying the Results of Transaction Log Analysis. Library Hi Tech. 1993; 11(2): 87-97. ISSN: 0737-8831.

SCHATZ, BRUCE; MISCHO, WILLIAM H.; COLE, TIMOTHY; BISHOP, ANN PETERSON; HARUM, SUSAN; JOHNSON, ERIC; NEUMANN, LAURA; CHEN, HSINCHUN; NG, DORBIN. 1999. Federated Search of Scientific Literature: A Retrospective on the Illinois Digital Library Project. IEEE Computer. 1999. (In press). ISSN: 0018-9162.

SCHIFF, LISA R.; VAN HOUSE, NANCY A.; BUTLER, MARK H. 1997. Understanding Complex Information Environments: A Social Analysis of Watershed Planning. In: Allen, Robert B.; Rasmussen, Edie, eds. Proceedings of the 2nd ACM International Conference on Digital Libraries; 1997 July 23-26; Philadelphia, PA. New York, NY: ACM; 1997. 161-168. ISBN: 0-89791-868-1.

SCHMIDT, KJELD; BANNON, LIAM. 1992. Taking CSCW Seriously: Supporting Articulation Work. Computer Supported Cooperative Work: The Journal of Collaborative Computing. 1992; 1(1/2): 7-40. ISSN: 0925-9724.

SCHNASE, JOHN L.; CUNNIUS, EDWARD L., eds. 1995. Proceedings of CSCL '95: The 1st International Conference on Computer Support for Collaborative Learning; 1995 October 17-20; Bloomington, IN. Mahwah, NJ: Lawrence Erlbaum Associates; 1995. 405p. ISBN: 0-8058-2243-7.

SCRIVENER, S.A.R.; CLARK, S.M.; KEEN, N. 1994. The Looking Glass Distributed Shared Workspace. Computer Supported Cooperative Work: The Journal of Collaborative Computing. 1994; 2(3): 137-157. ISSN: 0925-9724.

SENGE, PETER M. 1990. The Fifth Discipline: The Art and Practice of the Learning Organization. New York, NY: Doubleday/Currency; 1990. 424p. ISBN: 0-385-26094-6.

SHAPIRO, BETH J.; LONG, KEVIN BROOK. 1994. Just Say Yes: Reengineering Library Users Services for the 21st Century. Journal of Academic Librarianship. 1994; 20(5-6): 285-290. ISSN: 0099-1333.

SHAPIRO, DAN. 1994. The Limits of Ethnography: Combining Social Sciences for CSCW. In: Furuta, Richard; Neuwirth, Christine, eds. CSCW '94: Proceedings of the Conference on Computer Supported Cooperative Work; 1994 October 22-26; Chapel Hill, NC. New York, NY: ACM; 1994. 417-428. ISBN: 0-89791-689-1.

SHARDANAND, UPENDRA; MAES, PATTIE. 1995. Social Information Filtering: Algorithms for Automating "Word of Mouth". In: Katz, Irvin R.; Mack, Robert; Marks, Linn; Rosson, Mary Beth; Nielsen, Jakob, eds. CHI '95: Proceedings of the Association for Computing Machinery Special Interest Group on Computer-Human Interaction (ACM/SIGCHI) Conference on Human Factors in Computing Systems; 1995 May 7-11; Denver, CO. New York, NY: ACM; 1995. 210-217. ISBN: 0-89791-694-8.

SHARPLES, MIKE, ed. 1993. Computer Supported Collaborative Writing. New York, NY: Springer-Verlag; 1993. 222p. ISBN: 0-387-19782-6.

SHARPLES, MIKE; GEEST, THEA VAN DER, eds. 1996. The New Writing Environment: Writers at Work in a World of Technology. New York, NY: Springer-Verlag; 1996. 274p. ISBN: 3-540-76011-3.

SHAW, DEBORA. 1994. Libraries of the Future: Glimpses of a Networked, Distributed, Collaborative, Hyper, Virtual World. Libri. 1994; 44(3): 206-223. ISSN: 0024-2667.

SLOAN, BERNIE. 1997. Service Perspectives for the Digital Library Remote Reference Services. Available WWW: http://alexia.lis.uiuc.edu/~sloan/e-ref.html.

SMITH, GARETH; RODDEN, TOM. 1993. Using an Access Model to Configure Multi-User Interfaces. In: Kaplan, Simon, ed. COOCS '93: Proceedings of the Conference on Organizational Computing Systems; 1993 November 1-4; Milpitas, CA. New York, NY: ACM; 1993. 289-298. ISBN: 0-89791-627-1.

SMITH, LINDA C.; WARNER, AMY J. 1984. A Taxonomy of Representations in Information Retrieval System Design. Journal of Information Science. 1984; 8: 113-121. ISSN: 0165-5515.

SOMMERVILLE, IAN. 1995. Software Engineering. 5th edition. Harlow, UK: Addison Wesley; 1995. 649p. ISBN: 0-201-42765-6.

SOMMERVILLE, IAN; RODDEN, TOM; SAWYER, PETE; BENTLEY, RICHARD. 1992a. Sociologists Can Be Surprisingly Useful in Interactive Systems Design. In: Bauersfeld, Penny; Bennett, John; Lynch, Gene, eds. CHI '92: Proceedings of the Association for Computing Machinery Special Interest Group on Computer-Human Interaction (ACM/SIGCHI) Conference on Human Factors in Computing Systems; 1992 May 3-7; Monterey, CA. New York, NY: ACM; 1992. 341-353. ISBN: 0-201-53344-X.

SOMMERVILLE, IAN; RODDEN, TOM; SAWYER, PETE; BENTLEY, RICHARD; TWIDALE, MICHAEL B. 1992b. Integrating Ethnography into the Requirements Engineering Process. In: IEEE International Symposium on Requirements Engineering (RE'93); 1993 January 4-6; San Diego, CA. Los Alamitos, CA: IEEE Computer Society Press; 1992. 165-173. ISBN: 0-8186-3120-1.

STEINFIELD, CHARLES W. 1986. Computer-Mediated Communication Systems. In: Williams, Martha E., ed. Annual Review of Information Science and Technology: Volume 21. White Plains, NY: Knowledge Industry Publications, Inc. for the American Society for Information Science; 1986. 167-202. ISSN: 0066-4200; ISBN: 0-86729-209-1.

STREETER, LYN A.; LOCHBAUM, KAREN E. 1988. Who Knows: A System Based on Automatic Representation of Semantic Structure. In: Proceedings of RIAO 88 Conference on User-Oriented Content-Based Text and Image Handling; 1988 March 21-24; Cambridge, MA. Paris, France: CID; 1988. 380-388. OCLC: 18671148.

SUCHMAN, LUCY A. 1983. Office Procedures as Practical Action: Models of Work and System Design. ACM Transactions on Office Information Systems. 1983; 1(4): 320-328. ISSN: 0734-2047.

SUCHMAN, LUCY A. 1987. Plans and Situated Actions: The Problem of Human-Machine Communication. Cambridge, UK: Cambridge University Press; 1987. 203p. ISBN: 0-521-33739-9.

SUCHMAN, LUCY A. 1994. Do Categories Have Politics? The Language/Action Perspective Reconsidered. Computer Supported Cooperative Work: The Journal of Collaborative Computing. 1994; 2(3): 177-190. ISSN: 0925-9724.

SUGIMOTO, SHIGEO; GOTOU, SEKEI; ZHAO, YANCHUN; SAKAGUCHI, TETSUO; TABATA, KOICHI. 1995. Enhancing Usability of Network-Based Library Information System—Experimental Studies of a User Interface for OPAC and of a Collaboration Tool for Library Services. In: Shipman, Frank M., III; Furuta, Richard K.; Levy, David M., eds. Proceedings of Digital Libraries '95: The 2nd Annual Conference on the Theory and Practice of Digital Libraries; 1995 June 11-15; Austin, TX. College Station, TX: Texas A&M University; 1995. Also available WWW: http://www.csdl.tamu.edu/DL95/papers/sugimoto/sugimoto.html.

SWANSON, DON R. 1964. Dialogues with a Catalog. Library Quarterly. 1964; 34: 113-125. ISSN: 0024-2519.

SWIGGER, KATHLEEN M.; HARTNESS, KEN. 1996. Cooperation and Online Searching via a Computer-Supported Cooperative Problem Solving Environment. Journal of the American Society for Information Science. 1996; 47(5): 370-379. ISSN: 0002-8231.

SWIGGER, KATHLEEN M.; THOMAS, TOM; SWIGGER, KEITH. 1992. Communication Competencies: A Model for Characterizing Computer-Supported Cooperative Problem Solving. Denton, TX: Department of Computer Science, University of North Texas; 1992. (Technical Report TR92). Available from the author.

TAMMARO, S.G.; MOSIER, J.N.; GOODWIN, N.C.; SPITZ, G. 1997. Collaborative Writing Is Hard to Support: A Field Study of Collaborative Writing. Computer Supported Cooperative Work: The Journal of Collaborative Computing. 1997; 6(1): 19-51. ISSN: 0925-9724.

TANG, JOHN C.; ISAACS, ELLEN. 1993. Why Do Users Like Video? Studies of Multimedia-Supported Collaboration. Computer Supported Cooperative Work: The Journal of Collaborative Computing. 1993; 1(3): 163-196. ISSN: 0925-9724.

TAYLOR, ROBERT S. 1968. Question-Negotiation and Information Seeking in Libraries. College & Research Libraries. 1968; 29(3): 178-194. ISSN: 0010-0870.

TERVEEN, LOREN; HILL, WILL; AMENTO, BRIAN; MCDONALD, DAVID; CRETER, JOSH. 1997. PHOAKS: A System for Sharing Recommendations. Communications of the ACM. 1997; 40(3): 59-62. ISSN: 0001-0782.

TREVOR, JONATHAN; KOCH, THOMAS; WOETZEL, GERD. 1997. MetaWeb: Bringing Synchronous Groupware to the World Wide Web. In: Hughes, John; Prinz, Wolfgang; Rodden, Tom; Schmidt, Kjeld, eds. Proceedings of the 5th European Conference on Computer Supported Cooperative Work (ECSCW'97); 1997 September 7-11; Lancaster, UK. Dordrecht, The Netherlands: Kluwer Academic Publishers; 1997. 65-80. ISBN: 0-7923-4638-6.

TWIDALE, MICHAEL B.; CHAPLIN, DAMON; CRABTREE, ANDY; NICHOLS, DAVID M.; O'BRIEN, JON; ROUNCEFIELD, MARK. 1997a. Collaboration in Physical and Digital Libraries. London, UK: British Library Research and Innovation Centre; 1997. 137p. ISBN: 0-7123-3324-X.

TWIDALE, MICHAEL B.; NICHOLS, DAVID M. 1996. Collaborative Browsing and Visualisation of the Search Process. Aslib Proceedings. 1996; 48(7-8): 177-182. ISSN: 0001-253X.

TWIDALE, MICHAEL B.; NICHOLS, DAVID M. 1998. Designing Interfaces to Support Collaboration in Information Retrieval. Interacting with Computers. 1998; 10(2): 177-193. ISSN: 0953-5438.

TWIDALE, MICHAEL B.; NICHOLS, DAVID M.; PAICE, CHRIS D. 1997b. Browsing Is a Collaborative Process. Information Processing and Management. 1997; 33(6): 761-783. ISSN: 0306-4573.

TWIDALE, MICHAEL B.; NICHOLS, DAVID M.; SMITH, GARETH; TREVOR, JONATHAN. 1995. Supporting Collaborative Learning during Information Searching. In: Schnase, John. L; Cunnius, Edward L., eds. Proceedings of CSCL '95: The 1st International Conference on Computer Support for Collaborative Learning; 1995 October 17-20; Bloomington, IN. Mahwah, NJ: Lawrence Erlbaum Associates; 1995. 367-374. ISBN: 0-8058-2243-7.

TWIDALE, MICHAEL B.; RANDALL, DAVID; BENTLEY, RICHARD. 1994. Situated Evaluation for Cooperative Systems. In: Furuta, Richard; Neuwirth, Christine, eds. CSCW '94: Proceedings of the Conference on Computer Supported Cooperative Work; 1994 October 22-26; Chapel Hill, NC. New York, NY: ACM; 1994. 441-452. ISBN: 0-89791-689-1.

VAN HOUSE, NANCY A.; BUTLER, MARK H.; OGLE, VIRGINIA; SCHIFF, LISA. 1996. User Centered Iterative Design for Digital Libraries. D-Lib Magazine. 1996 February. ISSN: 1082-9873. Available WWW: http://www.dlib.org/dlib/february96/02vanhouse.html.

WALSH, JAMES P.; UNGSON, GERARDO RIVERA. 1991. Organizational Memory. Academy of Management Review. 1991; 16(1): 57-91. ISSN: 0363-7425.

WATSON, A.; SASSE, A. 1996. Assessing the Usability and Effectiveness of a Remote Language Teaching System. In: Proceedings of the World Conference on Educational Multimedia and Hypermedia (ED-MEDIA'96); 1996 June 17-22; Boston, MA. Charlottesville, VA: AACE; 1996. 685-690. Available from: AACE, PO Box 2966, Charlottesville, VA 22902.

WEINBERG, GERALD M. 1971. The Psychology of Computer Programming. New York, NY: Van Nostrand Reinhold; 1971. 288p. OCLC: 216809.

WHITE, HOWARD D.; MCCAIN, KATHERINE W. 1997. Visualization of Literatures. In: Williams, Martha E., ed. Annual Review of Information Science and Technology: Volume 32. Medford, NJ: Information Today, Inc. for the American Society for Information Science; 1997. 99-168. ISSN: 0066-4200; ISBN: 1-57387-047-1.

WINOGRAD, TERRY. 1988. A Language/Action Perspective on the Design of Cooperative Work. Human Computer Interaction. 1988; 3(1): 3-30. ISSN: 0737-0024.

WINOGRAD, TERRY; FLORES, FERNANDO. 1986. Understanding Computers and Cognition: A New Foundation for Design. Norwood, NJ: Ablex Publishing Corp.; 1986. 207p. ISBN: 0-89391-050-3.

WOLF, MILTON T.; ENSOR, PAT; THOMAS, MARY AUGUSTA, eds. 1998. Information Imagineering: Meeting at the Interface. Chicago, IL: American Library Association; 1998. 255p. ISBN: 0-8389-0729-6.

8 Electronic Scholarly Journal Publishing

ROBIN P. PEEK
Simmons College

JEFFREY P. POMERANTZ
Syracuse University

INTRODUCTION

Perhaps no other segment of the publishing industry has received as much scrutiny as the scholarly journal. Even before an electronic alternative was considered viable, dissatisfaction with elements of the traditional printed journal was evident. The literature is replete with complaints chiefly focused on subscription costs and the length of time from submission of manuscript to publication. Electronic distribution of journals has been seen by some as the possible solution to these concerns. This discussion has now spanned decades, but only recently is there evidence of a tentative embrace of the scholarly journal in electronic form. In 1998, most of the major publishing houses are offering some form of electronic product aimed at the academic marketplace. The purpose of this chapter is to review the literature that has led to this possible transformation of scholarly publishing.

Reviewing this literature proved to be exceptionally complicated because the literature is so broadly dispersed across disciplines. Few disciplines have ignored the possibility of an electronic alternative to traditional paper-based publishing. In reviewing the large number of citations located, we found a surprising amount of redundancy in the literature. In part this is a reflection of the parochial view that the average academic or practitioner maintains regarding the professional literature he or she consults. Therefore it is not uncommon for a writer in one discipline to present an idea, unaware that the same idea had been presented earlier by another writer in another discipline, or for one writer to publish essentially the same ideas within a number of disciplines or areas that could be affected by changes in the scholarly publishing process. Another surprise is the number of electronic jour-

Annual Review of Information Science and Technology (ARIST), Volume 33, 1998
Martha E. Williams, Editor
Published for the American Society for Information Science (ASIS)
By Information Today, Inc., Medford, NJ

nals that are claimed to be the first ever created. Among other things, in this review we hope to clarify the historical discrepancy.

While there are hundreds of references to electronic scholarly publishing, many articles concern merely the fact that such a medium exists. Frequently this literature fails to go beyond the initial "gee whiz" phase that is common with the introduction of a new technology. Quite naturally, many works published electronically speak at length to this topic. At this time a debate is taking place regarding the proper place of scholarly work in an electronic environment (DENNING & ROUS; KLING & COVI; SCHAUDER). One valid concern is the stability of these works. In any writing that cites references, an underlying premise is that the work cited is locatable, within reason, by the reader. Granted, some materials such as conference proceedings and reports may not be easily found, such as the report to the National Science Foundation (SHERIDAN ET AL.), which is available only through the MIT archives. Despite all efforts, the print world still provides a higher level of assurance that a work is obtainable than does the current electronic world. We, therefore, are caught in a bit of a dilemma, because to ignore electronically produced works would not be consistent with the spirit of the chapter at hand, while at the same time, we must also cite works that can be accessed in the future.

In this chapter we focus on the scholarly journal, which traditionally has been seen as the most practical vehicle by which researchers are able to communicate their findings to others (PEEK, 1996b). Hence, scholarly journals also have been referred to as scholarly communication. In the print world, the wedding of these two concepts would have little consequence for a literature review. In the electronic world, however, the advent of computer-mediated communication (CMC) has thrown the long-standing definition of scholarly communication into turmoil because the CMC literature has explored how researchers use computer networks to communicate with each other, independent of print journals.

Further, the overarching concept of scholarly communication becomes more problematic in contemporary times as the time delay in getting scholarly works to print detracts from the usefulness of the print medium as a vehicle for disseminating scholarly research. GUÉDON states that "printed scholarly journals . . . act more like archival and legitimizing tools than like communication tools. Print technology implies long publication delays . . . The main consequence is that the communication function of journals has essentially broken down" (GUÉDON, p. 79). Therefore, in this chapter we focus only on literature directly related to the publishing of scholarly journals, although some of the works we cite refer to both electronic journals and CMC. The cited sources are in English, mostly originating from the United States and Great Britain.

As we examined the literature, it became clear that no published work had yet provided a comprehensive historical context for the evolution of the scholarly electronic journal. We begin, therefore, with a brief history of the development of the idea of the scholarly journal in formats other than print. Next we discuss models, visions, and possible scenarios for the future of scholarly publishing, which tend to focus on dissemination and management structures of the publishing process. Then we identify electronic publishing experiments and projects representing the large number of electronic journals that have come online. We then discuss the acceptance of electronic journals by the academic community. Finally, we present an overview of the status of research on electronic scholarly journals. Space limitations have required the exclusion of related discussions about copyright and managerial concerns such as archival practices and long-term retrieval.

BACKGROUND

Activities in this field now span more than three decades, beginning with the first experiments in electronic scholarly publishing in the 1960s. However, little was published on the subject of electronic publication, scholarly or otherwise, until the early 1970s. One much earlier article, however, is considered to have set the stage for the coming changes in thought concerning publication formats: BUSH's famous 1945 article "As We May Think." In this article, Bush proposes the memex, a sort of interactive desk making use of pieces of microfilm that the user could organize into "trails . . . exactly as though the physical items had been gathered together . . . to form a new book." (BUSH, p. 107). At that time, dissatisfaction with the utility of print for scholarly uses was already becoming evident (PEEK & BURSTYN). The problem faced by the scholarly community was the decreasing effectiveness of print as a publication medium; as new technologies produced new data storage media, these were drafted into service as solutions to this problem. Bush's memex reflected the idea that microfilm provides a greater degree of interactivity than print, now a debatable proposition.

The first paper journal to be published in an electronic format was *Chemical Titles*, a current-awareness publication of the Chemical Abstracts Service (CAS), in 1962, followed by *Chemical-Biological Activities* in 1965, both of which were produced on magnetic tape (BARKER ET AL.). *Chemical Titles* is still in production; *Chemical-Biological Activities* went out of production in the early 1990s. In 1972, ten years after the first issue of *Chemical Titles*, SONDAK & SCHWARTZ (1972; 1973) published what is generally acknowledged to be the first article to propose a paperless version of a scholarly journal (see LANCASTER, 1995b). Sondak and Schwartz's paperless journal was to be produced on magnetic tape for library subscribers and on microfilm for individual subscribers. The journal on magnetic tape did not succeed, however, and there is no literature explaining why. One could speculate that the journal on magnetic tape did not provide a sufficient degree of interactivity, and that the computer hardware being used at the time did not offer sufficient speed and ease of use to make such journals appealing. Another explanation could be that the scholarly community was not yet ready to accept a journal in any format other than paper.

It is not clear who first proposed a scholarly journal produced exclusively in an electronic format, as several authors arrived at this same idea during the middle to late 1970s. In 1975, in a report to the National Science Foundation, SENDERS ET AL. propose mass storage of journal articles on computer disks. They are also the earliest to describe the drawbacks of the electronic medium for storage of published scholarly works: a great deal of computer memory is required, access time may be slow, and the articles themselves must be read-only so as to prevent alteration. They mention that, prior to 1975, the National Science Foundation conducted a feasibility study for development of an Editorial Processing Centre, "an electronic system for the preparation of scientific journals" (SENDERS ET AL., p. 55). In 1978, ROISTACHER proposes a virtual journal, to be established by scholars with access to a time-sharing computer; he credits the term virtual journal to Robert I. Bell of UCLA's Campus Computing Network (p. 24).

The earliest experiment in electronic scholarly publishing was the Electronic Information Exchange System (EIES), which was carried out at the New Jersey Institute of Technology from 1976 to 1981 (TUROFF; TUROFF & HILTZ, 1982). Even now, EIES remains one of the most visionary and revolutionary efforts with regard to its treatment of the general concept of publication. At its inception, EIES had only one model for all of its publications, based on traditional print publications; however, over time and with use, four distinct forms of electronic journals evolved. (1) Newsletters were based on traditional print newsletters for members of special-interest groups and professional societies; they were produced on a regular schedule and were not peer-reviewed. (2) The Unrefereed Free for All format was totally unrefereed, in that any subscriber to the EIES system could submit papers, as well as comments on other submitted papers. This format resembles HARNAD's (1990) Scholarly Skywriting model in that scholarly work was submitted for critique prior to a formal editorial and publication process, and ideas could be exchanged freely and quickly. (3) The Classical Model, with Variations format duplicated in all essentials the traditional process of scholarly publication in print. The first publication to follow this model was the Mental Workload project, which began in 1979 (SHERIDAN ET AL.), and was "advertised, refereed, edited, copyrighted, and mass distributed—just as are traditional journals" (TUROFF & HILTZ, 1982, p. 197).

Finally, the (4) Tailored and Structured 'Journals' format only super-ficially resembled traditional print journals, and indeed represented, at the time, an entirely new form of publication. The first journal in this area was *Legitech,* a forum used by state science legislation advisors and federal representatives, which started in January 1978 (TUROFF & HILTZ, 1980). A *Legitech* user would submit a request for information to the forum, and other users would submit responses. Each user could then choose whether to receive future responses. When a certain critical mass of responses had been posted, a user could compile a brief con-taining the original inquiry and all responses to it, essentially a tran-script of a lengthy online conversation; this brief was then published in a publicly accessible notebook. The organization of user discussions on *Legitech* is comparable to that of today's listserv or Usenet newsgroup, and the compiled brief is an archive of the entire contents of a discus-sion.

NONTRADITIONAL MODELS

Dissemination

Concerns about specific management practices are central to all discussions of the changing manner in which scholars produce and disseminate their work. The literature on management of electronic publishing and archiving describes models that can be expressed as the questions How? and Who?: the first set of models suggest how dissemi-nation should be implemented and the second set suggest who is responsible for maintenance and policy making. The opportunities afforded by electronic publishing challenge all parts of the manage-ment process from peer review to long-term preservation of the record. The distinction between scholarly publishing and scholarly communi-cation that is so clear in the world of print-based publication, where published works are what is contained in a journal and communication is everything else, becomes blurred in the arena of electronic scholarly publishing. In the sense that everything produced in a networked environment is available to every user with access to the network, it is all published material. However, the material is not necessarily re-viewed. Further, the managers of the networked environment may choose to impose differing degrees of review on different materials, just as some listservs today are moderated and some are not. Moreover, the greater the degree of moderation of particular materials, the closer to an approximation of peer review; indeed, the managers of a particular networked environment may make the arbitrary decision that *these* moderated materials are in fact publications, but that *those* are not.

HARNAD (1990) defines Scholarly Skywriting as the "almost instan-taneous" process of interactive communication that is made possible by the technology of networked environments. Harnad's Skywriting is technically nothing more than email, as it possesses the potential to allow close to real-time conversations among the members of large groups. The use of the word skywriting makes explicit the idea that a networked environment provides a format in which scholars can "get their ideas up there" and, like skywriting, have their words viewed by an enormously large number of people.

Harnad suggests that, in the print medium, "the archiving of scientific ideas is *already* on a continuum, with varying degrees of formality, reliability, and even of peer validation," and that therefore "it is natural to transpose all of this into the electronic dimension as well." To implement this continuum in the electronic environment, Harnad proposes "bi-directional quality control mechanisms": the vertical dimension is "a pyramidal hierarchy of email groups" in which read/write access is provided "based on the contributors' degree of expertise, specialization, and their record of contributions in a given field" (1990, p. 343); the horizontal dimension takes the material that has been produced at all levels of the hierarchy, subjects it to a traditional peer-review process, and electronically archives it. Harnad suggests that "scholarly inquiry in this new medium . . . is likely to become a lot more participatory" (p. 344) as scholars can exchange ideas at a speed approaching that of natural conversation.

Similar to Harnad, GUÉDON envisions the Seminar becoming the primary mode of scholarly communication and publishing, encompassing both of these concepts. A Seminar is a subject-specific discussion group allowing scholars easy access to each other, as well as providing a vehicle for the rapid flow of ideas, rather than having to wait for "the slow, jerky process of putting small, discrete articles inside slightly larger packages called *journal issues*" (GUÉDON, p. 82). The Seminar is conceived of as an "eco-museum" approach to scholarship: an individual Seminar would contain both information specific to a field of scholarly inquiry and information intended to make that field comprehensible to an outsider. As Guédon puts it, "the territory [i.e., scholarly inquiry] crisscrosses itself along a multiplicity of perspectives, each of which corresponds to the interrogation of a particular group addressed to another" (p. 84). Scholars need not write exclusively for their peers in their narrowly focused field, but could communicate to scholars in other fields, using the Seminar as the forum. Links could be established across a single Seminar and between Seminars, thus bridging the gap between differing fields of study. This approach treats scholarly inquiry as an immense hypertext, with any one information source linking to many others.

Neither Guédon nor Harnad discusses the issues involved in actually managing the proposed electronic environment. Their models serve as ideals or abstract concepts upon which actual electronic publishing projects can be built. Harnad did, however, go one step further on June 27, 1994, when he posted his now-famous Subversive Proposal to the electronic discussion list VPIEJ-L (hosted by the Virginia Polytechnic Institute and State University) (see OKERSON & O'DONNELL). This proposal suggests that every author of esoteric works in the world (Harnad defines esoteric as "non-trade, no-market scientific and scholarly publication") establish public FTP archives. Further, Harnad suggests that with the establishment of such an archive, the "transition from paper publication to purely electronic publication (of esoteric research) would follow suit almost immediately" (see OKERSON & O'DONNELL, p. 11).

A related idea is GARDNER's (1990) Electronic Archive which, like Harnad's FTP archive, is founded on the premise that the article is the fundamental unit of scholarly publication. Retaining the article as the fundamental unit, both Gardner's and Harnad's archives simply change the method of access to the article. However, while Harnad's FTP archive leaves it to users to know about and access articles on their own, Gardner's Electronic Archive formalizes the process of dissemination. Gardner's Archive publishes one or more articles on demand in any format users specify, from onscreen to bound as a traditional print journal. The Archive *personalizes the journal*. People can get the articles they want as they are published, based on their own definition of their professional needs" (GARDNER, 1990, p. 336); rather than purchasing every article published by a particular publisher under a particular journal title, users can select only articles they wish to purchase. Gardner points out that this idea is similar to the print publication of separates, a scheme with which several academic societies had already experimented.

Gardner does not discuss the review process that an article must undergo in order to be accepted into the Electronic Archive, but there is no reason the traditional review process for print publications (or any variation) cannot be used. Harnad addresses this issue slightly when he says that "NO scholar would ever consent to WITHDRAW any preprint of his from the public eye after the refereed version was accepted for paper 'PUBLICation'" [emphasis Harnad's]. This suggests that the scholar would voluntarily submit preprints for review by every interested scholar in the world (not to mention simply everyone, scholar or not, with access to an FTP connection). Once an article is published in print, Harnad goes on to say, "everyone would, quite naturally, substitute the refereed, published reprint for the unrefereed preprint" (see OKERSON & O'DONNELL, p. 12). Ignoring the obvious copyright issues involved in a scholar making available a work that was published elsewhere, Harnad leaves it to the authors to make their own works accessible in the FTP archive. Gardner, on the other hand, says that once the article is accepted into the Electronic Archive, the editorial process should not differ significantly from the traditional editorial process for print publication, although, as one might expect, he suggests the use of electronic delivery methods—specifically, fax and email—instead of the postal service. Indeed, the only significant departure from the traditional publication process that Gardner suggests is the use of automated software to perform cataloging and indexing functions: assigning a call number to the article, establishing links to other articles in the archive that the author has cited, assigning indexing terms and keywords to the article, and sending mail (electronic and paper) to archive subscribers who, judging by their previous publishing requests, may be interested in the newly published article.

Inspired by Gardner's Electronic Archive is Mani's model of the MEGAJOURNAL (MANI; PEEK & BURSTYN). The MEGAJOURNAL, as a central repository for all published articles in a specific scholarly field, is a cross between a peer-reviewed scholarly journal and an archive. This model differs in scope from Harnad's and Gardner's archives but is the same in that it is discipline-specific rather than universal. The organization of the MEGAJOURNAL is reminiscent of the "bi-directional quality control mechanisms" (HARNAD, 1990, p. 343) of HARNAD's Scholarly Skywriting model in that it "will have a hierarchical, pyramid structure; the apex being formed by the papers which go into today's high-quality printed journals and the lowest . . . being formed by contributions that . . . constitute some of today's conference and workshop papers" (MANI, introduction). The MEGAJOURNAL also allows for interdisciplinary pursuits with the ease of Guédon's Seminars due to the fact that "interdisciplinary pyramids can be created by just appropriate pointers to the papers in the areas from which the interdisciplinary area is formed" (MANI, section d).

A further refinement of this same concept is the Acquisition-On-Demand model of the Coalition for Networked Information (CNI). Like the MEGAJOURNAL, the Acquisition-On-Demand model is proposed as a discipline-specific archive; BAILEY (1992) states that "it would be theoretically possible to construct a monolithic, universal article archive," like Harnad's FTP archive, but that it "appears to be both unlikely and undesirable in this decade" to do so (p. 78). Individual articles are stored on one or more file servers, which can be accessed on demand and priced according to use. Bailey states that there is no reason electronic publications must be tied to fixed publication schedules like print journals; that electronic publications can be released at irregular intervals. Thus the traditional concept of journals may vanish entirely, and publication may simply mean accessing a single article from the archive (BAILEY, 1992, p. 79). This is fundamentally no different from the concepts behind Harnad's and Gardner's archives, as both posit user access to individual articles as intrinsic to the nature of the archive and thus to the consequent breakdown of traditional journal structure. The movement from Harnad's FTP archive and Gardner's Electronic Archive to the MEGAJOURNAL and CNI's Acquisition-On-Demand model exemplifies the conceptual development of an increasingly specific implementation of an essentially similar model.

Maintenance and Policy Making

HURTADO states that academic institutions must collaborate on electronic publishing projects in order to exchange expertise and experience as well as to avoid the all-too-common problem among noncommunicating users of new technologies of reinventing the wheel. Hurtado therefore suggests that a consortium of universities jointly create a forum for not-for-profit academic publication because "it is generally conceded that university presses set the standard of quality in academic publications" (p. 206). In addition to the universities in these consortia, Hurtado stresses the importance of including academic societies for their expertise in the dissemination of research in journals published by the societies themselves. Regardless of what other organizations join the consortia, Hurtado says that only academic institutions and societies should have voting privileges, thus ensuring that the consortia are run by those who best understand the needs of scholarly publication: the scholars themselves. The consortia should be multidisciplinary or cross-disciplinary, although specific disciplines may set up special forums unique to their own needs. Additionally, the consortia should be international in scope, just as the Internet is international. This raises new issues of governance because the laws that govern the Internet (such as they are) and the maintenance of its hardware are regulated at the national level.

OKERSON's (1992) Circle of Gifts proposes a model of electronic publishing that, to a certain extent, already exists. The Circle of Gifts, unlike other models, does not involve either a single archive or a single entity that maintains the archive; instead, individual organizations provide unique services to each other, and are repaid with other unique services. Published information is owned by the scholars or institutions that created it or funded its creation, and owners can distribute this information as they see fit. Similar to many interlibrary loan services, the services provided by The Circle are free to member organizations, charged on a cost-recovery basis "to the extended scholarly community; and sold at cost plus to for-profit purchasers" (p. 93). Overarching the Circle of Gifts model is the research cooperative, essentially an agreement between participating organizations, that, like a library consortium, states common goals and services. Like Hurtado's model, Okerson's Circle of Gifts requires cooperation among academic institutions and possibly academic societies toward the common end of electronic publication.

Alternatively, YOUNG proposes a Corporation for Scholarly Publishing (CSP). This model of networked scholarly publication is funded and governed by a combination of government, commercial, academic, foundation, and private agencies. The primary source of funding is federal subsidies, making the CSP analogous to the Corporation for Public Broadcasting. The CSP is responsible for the dissemination of scholarly research, "especially that research that is performed through federally administered grants and contracts" (YOUNG, p. 101). Essentially, this model proposes that academic scholarship be federally subsidized, an idea that might not be well received outside academic circles. An additional drawback of this model is that it places the federal government in competition with commercial industries. Young himself admits that "publication of research funded by federal sources in a Corporation for Scholarly Communication might . . . divert valuable material from the commercial and society scholarly publishers' products" (p. 101). This raises issues of how to govern the distribution of scholarly publications, which currently is more or less governed by publishers' sales of reprints and by fair use laws. Further, and more ominously, if the federal government were to fund scholarly publishing, the CSP, like the National Endowment for the Arts, would have the ability to select which avenues of research to be published should be funded and which should not.

EXPERIMENTS AND PROJECTS

At first glance, it may appear that the history of electronic scholarly publishing as represented in Table 1 is littered with the corpses of failed efforts. This is not truly the case because these are experiments: investigations or trials of different aspects of electronic scholarly publishing, intended to be of a limited duration, with mistakes and failures meant to be as illuminating as successes. Projects, on the other hand, are endeavors that are intended to be ongoing.

Network Delivery Experiments

Network delivery experiments are divided into two categories: (1) those that published original material, including EIES and BLEND, and (2) those that converted previously published print material into electronic formats, including CORE, STELAR, TULIP, and Red Sage (Table

1). Experiments that published original material were conceived of as explorations "of an electronic communication network as an aid to writing, submitting and refereeing papers, and also as a medium for other types of scientific and technical communication" (SHACKEL, 1982, p. 227). Experiments that converted previously published print material were conceived of as controlled environments in which to explore alternative methods of access to scholarly work. The difference in stated intent is worth noting: experiments that published original material were concerned with new methods of scholarly communication, whereas experiments that converted previously published print material into electronic formats were concerned with new methods of distribution.

The group of experiments that published original material further divides into two subcategories: those that published material exclusively electronically, and those that published material simultaneously in both electronic and print formats. Like the experiments that converted previously published print material, ELVYN, the only dual-publishing experiment listed in Table 1, was exploring alternate methods of access to scholarly material. At the time that these experiments were taking place, the economic viability as well as the stability of the electronic medium for scholarly publication was still being widely questioned by the scholarly community. The publishers involved in these experiments were "seek[ing] to supply each customer library with a format suiting its own particular needs" (WOODWARD & ROWLAND), or letting user demand determine the feasibility of pursuing electronic publishing.

It should be mentioned that the interfaces for these experiments were remarkably consistent in functionality. The major differences were in technical details: methods of access to and presentation of materials, inclusion or lack of inclusion of graphics with textual material, and complexity of search capabilities. Interfaces are discussed in greater depth in a subsequent section.

Network Delivery Projects

The development of the World Wide Web was a boon to electronic journal projects. As noted above, much of the literature on electronic publishing experiments states that one difficulty of implementation was the fact that, at the time the experiment was underway, no format in existence could easily and cleanly integrate text and graphics into a viewable page. Ironically, the later experiments were being conducted at the same time that the World Wide Web (with graphics capability) was being invented. It was not until the mid-1990s, however, that the

Table 1. Network Delivery Experiments

Name of Project	Dates of Operation	Interface	Institutions Involved	Scope
Electronic Information Exchange System (EIES)	1976-1981	Project-specific	New Jersey Institute of Technology	Original material
Birmingham and Loughborough Electronic Network Development (BLEND)	1980-1985	NOTEPAD	British Library R&DD et al.[1]	Original material
CORE	1991-1995	XSCEPTER (X-Window SCientific Electronic Publishing and TExt Retrieval)	Cornell University et al.[2]	Print material converted to electronic
STELAR	1991-1995	WAIS, WWW	NASA et al.[3]	Print material converted to electronic
The University Licensing Project (TULIP)	1991-1996	Institution-specific	Elsevier Science et al.[4]	Print material converted to electronic

[1]British Library Research & Development Department (BL R&DD), The University of Birmingham, Loughborough University
[2]Cornell University, Bellcore, American Chemical Society (ACS), Chemical Abstracts Service (CAS), Online Computer Library Center (OCLC)
[3]National Aeronautics and Space Administration (NASA), American Astronomical Society (AAS), The Astronomical Society of the Pacific, American Institute of Physics (AIP), The Library of Congress, The National Science Foundation (NSF), University of North Carolina at Chapel Hill
[4]Elsevier Science, Carnegie Mellon University, Cornell University, Georgia Institute of Technology, Massachusetts Institute of Technology, University of California, University of Michigan, University of Tennessee, University of Washington, Virginia Polytechnic Institute and State University (Virginia Tech)

Table 1. Network Delivery Experiments (cont.)

Name of Project	Dates of Operation	Interface	Institutions Involved	Scope
ELVYN	1992-1995	Institution-specific: SGML, PostScript, TeX	British Library R&DD et al.[5]	Dual publishing
Red Sage	1992-1996	RightPages	AT&T Bell Labs et al.[6]	Print material converted to electronic

[5]British Library Research and Development Department (BL R&DD), Institute of Physics Publishers (IoPP), Standing Conference of National and University Libraries (SCONUL), Imperial College of Science, Technology and Medicine of University College London, University of Hertfordshire, University of Exeter, Cavendish Lab of University of Cambridge, Loughborough University, The University of Manchester, University of Oxford, Harwell Laboratory of the Atomic Energy Authority, Chalmers University of Technology Sweden

[6]AT&T Bell Labs, Springer-Verlag, University of California San Francisco (UCSF)

World Wide Web entered the mainstream of public consciousness, so those in charge of the experiments may not even have known about its existence.

At some point in their development, all the early electronic publishing projects moved to a Web-based format. There is no literature that documents this period, so statistics are difficult to find. According to PEEK (1996), the NewJour archives as of September 1996 contained 1,272 electronic journal titles, and the current archives, from July 30, 1995 to December 1, 1995, contained 625 titles. As of this writing, in mid-September 1998, the NewJour archives contains 6,365 titles. Because NewJour is not confined to scholarly journal titles, the number of Web-based scholarly electronic journals is clearly less than the numbers stated here. Nevertheless, the limitations of space prevent us from addressing all of the Web-based scholarly electronic journals currently in existence. Rather, the electronic journals listed in Table 2 are some of the earliest to be published on the Bitnet and Internet that have since migrated to the Web. Because they were early comers to the electronic format, these journals also received more press than those that went online later. As more journals were published electronically, the change became less noteworthy; therefore there is little literature on electronic publishing projects past the early 1990s.

Table 2 Early Network Delivery Projects

Name of Project	Date Begun	Institutions Initially Involved
Comserve	1986	Communication Institute for Online Scholarship (CIOS)
Postmodern Culture	1990	University of Virginia's Institute for Advanced Technology in the Humanities
Psycoloquy	1990	American Psychological Association (APA)
Public-Access Computer Systems Review (PACS-Review)	1990	University of Houston Libraries
High-Energy Physics—Theory (HEP-TH)	1991	American Physical Society (APS) et al.[1]
Online Journal of Current Clinical Trials (OJCCT)	1992	American Association for the Advancement of Science (AAAS)
Interpersonal Computing and Technology Journal (IPCT-J)	1993	Association for Educational Communications and Technology et al.[2]

[1]American Physical Society (APS), Los Alamos National Laboratory, National Science Foundation (NSF)
[2]Association for Educational Communications and Technology (AECT), Georgetown University, University of Maryland, Baltimore County, Northern Arizona University

All of the electronic journals listed in Table 2 currently have Web-based interfaces, but they bear the marks of their humble pre-Web beginnings, for example in their text-only archives. The earliest network delivery projects and journals include Comserve, *PostModern Culture, Psycoloquy, Public-Access Computer Systems Review (PACS-Review)*, High-Energy Physics—Theory (HEP-TH), *Online Journal of Current Clinical Trials (OJCCT)*, and *Interpersonal Computing and Technology*

Journal (IPCT-J). All of the journals are peer-reviewed and continue to publish.

The first project, starting in 1986, was Comserve, funded by the Communication Institute for Online Scholarship (CIOS) as a forum for the communication discipline (HARRISON & STEPHEN, 1994; STEPHEN & HARRISON, 1993a, 1994). Comserve is a collection of several public and private so-called hotlines, or forums for computer-mediated communication, not all of which were intended to contain journal-quality publishable material (STEPHEN & HARRISON, 1994). Comserve's hotlines bear a strong resemblance to GUÉDON's proposed Seminars. Originally, Internet users interacted with the hotlines via email, through automated processes, although Bitnet users had access to a menu-driven interface. Today, Comserve has both a World Wide Web interface and an email interface. Ironically, by 1990, Comserve was so popular, and was being accessed so often, that "a number of changes . . . were then enacted in an attempt to *discourage* contact and experimentation from network users who were not primarily invested in the communication discipline" (STEPHEN & HARRISON, 1994, p. 769).

One of the hotlines in Comserve was the *Electronic Journal of Communication/La Revue Electronique de Communication (EJC/REC)*, which was organized by the CIOS in 1990 to be a "risk[y] test of the ability of the networks to support scholarly communities"; it has since become the official scholarly journal of the CIOS (HARRISON & STEPHEN, 1994; STEPHEN & HARRISON, 1993a, 1994). *EJC/REC* is a peer-reviewed scholarly journal that differs from traditional print publications only in its method of distribution, which is via an email distribution list.

Similar in nature is *Psycoloquy*, which owes its initial existence almost entirely to the efforts of Harnad. *Psycoloquy* was established as an FTP archive as suggested in Harnad's Subversive Proposal. At some point, Gopher, listserv, and Usenet interfaces were provided to the same material that was available via FTP. Today *Psycoloquy* is an international, interdisciplinary Web-based journal sponsored by the American Psychological Association (APA). A future generation, called *HYPER-Psycoloquy*, is under development at the time of this writing.

In a similar vein is the High-Energy Physics—Theory (HEP-TH) archive. HEP-TH uses an entirely automated process for submission and indexing of articles. The archive also contains bulletin board-like functionality by which "researchers who might not ordinarily communicate with one another can quickly set up a virtual meeting ground, and ultimately disband if things do not pan out" (GINSPARG, 1996, p. 3 of 8). The HEP-TH archive is not intended to contain exclusively journal articles, but rather is designed to be, like Comserve, a forum for scholarly communication, reminiscent of Guédon's Seminars.

The *Online Journal of Current Clinical Trials* (*OJCCT*) is noteworthy because it was the first electronic journal that was published by a traditional publisher and the first to incorporate graphics. The journal struggled through its first year until the American Association for the Advancement of Science (AAAS) was successful in lobbying *Index Medicus* and Medline to index the journal (PEEK, 1994).

OJCCT is not the only one of these electronic journals to be included by indexing and abstracting services. *Postmodern Culture* is indexed in Arts & Humanities Search. The *Electronic Journal of Communication/La Revue Electronique de Communication* (*EJC/REC*) (in Comserve), *Public-Access Computer Systems Review* (*PACS-Review*), and *Interpersonal Computing and Technology Journal* (*IPCT-J*) are indexed in ERIC.

CD-ROM Delivery Projects

An interesting characteristic of the CD-ROM publishing projects is that they are projects, not experiments: all the projects listed in Table 3 are still in operation at the time of this writing. This may be interpreted as a statement about the permanence of CD-ROM media. More likely, however, it is an indication of the maturity of electronic scholarly publishing: by the time these CD-ROM projects were begun in the early 1990s (with the exception of ADONIS, which was begun a full decade before the rest), electronic publishing was reasonably well established and accepted by the scholarly community. Jasperse, in an article about the 100 Rivers on Disk project, requested all users to evaluate software that was then being distributed on $3\frac{1}{2}$-inch or $5\frac{1}{4}$-inch diskettes (JASPERSE, 1991, p. 4), but the project was ultimately released on CD-ROM as a part of The *New Zealand Journal of Marine and Freshwater Research*. In a later article, Jasperse indicates that the opinions of users of 100 Rivers on Disk "that paper journals be *replaced* by CD-ROM journals was highly skewed toward undesirability . . . yet, *supplementing* paper journals with CD-ROM and/or an online database was highly skewed toward desirability" (JASPERSE, 1994, pp. 779-780).

With the CD-ROM delivery projects, as with the network delivery experiments, come a wide range of interface implementations. The most extreme solution is that of the ADONIS project, which involves proprietary software and three proprietary cards that are installed in a dedicated workstation specifically to run the ADONIS CD-ROMs (the workstation was intended to be useful for other library purposes as well) (STERN & CAMPBELL, 1989). The *New Zealand Journal of Marine and Freshwater Research* (the first scholarly CD-ROM database to be produced outside of the United States or Great Britain) does not require a dedicated workstation, but does have its own interface that provides hypertext-style access to the material (JASPERSE, 1994). Likewise,

Table 3. CD-ROM Delivery Projects

Name of Project	First Issue Date	Interface	Institutions Involved	Scope
ADONIS	1980	dedicated workstation	Academic Press et al.[1]	Print material (journal titles from all publishers involved) converted to electronic
New Zealand Journal of Marine and Freshwater Research (NZJMFR)	1992	Hypertext by Romware authoring software	Royal Society of New Zealand	Dual publishing of pre-existing journal
CD-ROM Acrobat Journals Using Networks (CAJUN)	1993	Adobe Acrobat, network delivery	John Wiley & Sons et al.[2]	Print material (9 Wiley Computer Science journals & 1 book series) converted to electronic
ExtraMED	1994	Idealist	Informania Ltd., World Health Organization (WHO)	Dual publishing of specialized journals, many not indexed by indexing services

[1] Academic Press, Blackwell Scientific Publications, Elsevier Science, Pergamon Press, Springer-Verlag, John Wiley & Sons
[2] John Wiley & Sons, Electronic Publishing Research Group at the University of Nottingham, Electronic Publishing Solutions, Merlin Open Systems

Blackwell Scientific Publishers developed its own interface for ExtraMED. The CAJUN project takes a different tack entirely by presenting material in the commercially available Adobe Acrobat software (.pdf extension) file format (SMITH ET AL.). As with the network delivery experiments, the interfaces of the CD-ROMs are all different, but the functionality remains fairly consistent: all allow searching of articles by author, title, subject, or other metadata field.

ACCEPTANCE BY THE SCHOLARLY COMMUNITY

When first introduced, electronic scholarly journals met with considerable resistance from the academic community. The principal reasons were common to electronic publishing in general: the superior portability of paper over electronic formats, the lack of a common interface, the poor quality of viewing technologies (BAILEY, 1994; GRENQUIST). The academic community has had these and other concerns about electronic journals, some similar to those in the mainstream press and others unique to academia.

Journal Content

The most intriguing argument against the usefulness of the electronic scholarly journal calls into question the intellectual validity of scholarly work published in an electronic format. According to this argument, the decrease in time taken to publish a work electronically from the time required to publish a work in print diminishes the rigor of the review process, and thus the intellectual weight of the resultant scholarly work (KLING & COVI). This argument falls short when one suggests, as GARDNER (1990) does in his proposal for an Electronic Archive, that the process of peer review for an electronic scholarly journal is conducted in precisely the same manner as the traditional review process for a print journal. According to this counterargument, it takes no less time for an author to write an article than it ever did, and it takes no less time for reviewers to critique it than it ever did. However, the speed of transmission between author and reviewer is increased by the use of electronic forms of communication, such as email, and the speed of publication is increased by eliminating the time-consuming printing process. Ultimately, it is only the publication format that is changed, and the content suffers not at all.

Lack of content has always been a factor weighing against acceptance of the electronic journal by the scholarly community. Many of the early electronic publishing experiments published only journal titles produced by a single publisher, thus restricting the amount of material available in the electronic medium. The availability of material is summed up by LYNCH's (1995) discussion of the TULIP experiment. Lynch states that "because Elsevier did not completely dominate scholarly publishing in any discipline," TULIP failed to achieve the critical mass of subject-specific information required to make the use of the materials compelling for subject specialists (p. 12). He concludes that "production of future electronic information systems, if they are to achieve real user acceptance, must achieve critical mass" (p. 22). The same statement could be made about most of the early experiments; indeed, the Mental Workload experiment in EIES was, in the end, evaluated to be less than a complete success because "the twenty or so actual participants did not in fact generate enough 'publishable' material" (SHERIDAN ET AL., p. 73). An experiment such as STELAR, which was confined to astrophysics literature, had a focus narrow enough that it could potentially have achieved critical mass. Unfortunately, none of the available literature about STELAR addresses this issue.

Interfaces

Another major factor that limited the usability of the early experiments was the interface. Most of the experiments relied on proprietary interfaces that users were required to learn before they could access the published material. Some experiments, such as EIES, involved multiple interfaces. The Mental Workload experiment included systems similar to current electronic email, chat, and bulletin board operations (SHERIDAN ET AL.). The *Legitech* experiment had a system similar to current listserv functionality (JOHNSON-LENZ ET AL.) Like EIES, TULIP had its own interfaces, but unlike EIES, and complicating matters further, the participating TULIP institutions were given the latitude to develop interfaces specifically to meet their own unique requirements. All of the TULIP interfaces necessarily shared similar functionalities, including the ability to search, browse, view, print, save, and fax individual articles, but there was no standardization (BORGHUIS ET AL.). In a similar vein, proprietary interfaces were developed for the CORE and Red Sage projects, but unlike EIES and TULIP, these interfaces took the intent of the projects into consideration from the outset, rather than allowing the interfaces to evolve as the projects evolved.

Few experiments used any sort of standardized software for their interface. STELAR made use of the newly invented World Wide Web as an interface, and it also made use of a proprietary X Windows-based WAIS client (VAN STEENBERG). Participating ELVYN libraries were allowed to develop their own delivery mechanisms, which ranged from proprietary software to the World Wide Web (ELVYN). BLEND was the only project to use a standard interface exclusively by adopting the commercially available NOTEPAD software (SHACKEL & PULLINGER).

In short, this wide variety in interface design can be considered a major factor contributing to the disappointing results of the experiments. Certainly it is true that at the time these experiments were underway, computers were not as widespread in academia as they are today, and therefore some scholars would have had a serious learning curve merely to use the equipment effectively (BORGHUIS ET AL., p. 73). More important is convenience: users will employ the means that is most convenient for accessing the information they need (SHERIDAN ET AL.).

Formats and Delivery

Another issue in many of the early experiments and projects is the format in which text and graphics were presented. Literature on the CORE, TULIP, and Red Sage experiments, for example, states that they presented the entire page in bitmap image format. The bitmap format was one of the earliest formats in which to store image data, and was therefore an obvious choice at the time these projects were starting. There is, however, some vagueness in the literature: it is uncertain whether the word bitmap refers to files in bitmap format (that is, with a .bmp extension), or whether it merely indicates any digitally rendered image. At any rate, bitmap (.bmp) files are extremely large, and take a long time to download and display on a monitor. Bitmaps are therefore impractical for any sort of networked environment, especially when speed of access is a consideration. Today, the newer formats used to store image data, improvements in data compression, and increased speed of telecommunication have made speed nearly a non-issue. Beyond these concerns, BAILEY (1992) states that text-only formats are inadequate for the electronic publication of scholarly research, and that a new format is required that will allow for the integration of text with color images, tables, charts, and other graphics. The subsequent popularization of the World Wide Web, and the Web's ability to integrate formats, allows publication of multimedia materials with an ease that was merely hoped for even five years ago, and that will undoubtedly continue to improve.

A more serious problem with storing pages of text as image files is that such images are not searchable, as the page would be if it were stored as text. Each file, as an image, must be indexed separately, and thus progress is not really made from the print format. The TULIP experiment hit on a compromise in which each page image was converted to text using optical character recognition (OCR) software, and this OCR-generated text was made available. Unfortunately, "the uncorrected ASCII text was unusable for viewing, since it omitted or misinterpreted the equations, Greek letters, and other nontextual information, and made numerous errors in recognizing the text itself" (LYNCH, 1995, p. 15). Thus it appears that these experiments were victims of insufficient technology.

In a study conducted on ELVYN, InfoTrain, and Café Jus, ROWLAND ET AL. (1997) found that the inadequacy of Internet infrastructure is a factor undermining the acceptance of electronic journals. The authors note that "users in Europe are well aware of the need to do their netsurfing in the morning, when it is the middle of the night in North

America" (p. 72). However, they also found that users were fairly tolerant of the slow delivery of information. They caution that because the network is slow and congested, publishers must minimize the number of screens that users must navigate in order to get from the site's initial page to an article of interest.

In this same study, the authors also suggest that use of Adobe Acrobat's Portable Document Format (.pdf) could possibly reduce the acceptability of electronic journals. While electronic journals must be designed for viewing on a computer screen, Adobe Acrobat and similar viewers are based on the traditional vertical format of paper publishing, not the horizontal format of a computer screen. PEEK ET AL. found that most traditional publishers are choosing proprietary formats instead of the HTML format used on the Web. Although these proprietary formats do maintain original page integrity, ROWLAND ET AL. (1997) suggest that this appearance factor may undermine acceptance by users.

User and Social Implications

Over time, the electronic journal in purely electronic display format has come to be more widely accepted by the scholarly community. In WARKENTIN's recent survey of Germanists in Canada, a field the author claims is very conservative and traditional, only 36% of respondents subscribed to or used electronic journals, yet 58% indicated they would be willing to submit an article to an electronic journal. Hence, he states, the "majority are willing to give qualified support to the idea of 'electronic' scholarship" (p. 42). Curiously, greater support for electronic journals was offered by those with more than 20 years in the profession than those with 11 to 20 years. Indeed, students made use of electronic journals least of any group in the field; doctoral students were not prepared to cite electronic journals in their dissertations for fear that a member of their dissertation committee would object.

Other studies indicate that there is little resistance to electronic publishing in the scholarly community. In BUTLER's survey of sociologists of science who had published works in electronic journals, 21% indicated that they believed their contributions to electronic publications were viewed by their colleagues as equal in importance to their contributions to print publications. Of those surveyed, 43% indicated that they believed their electronic contributions were viewed as less important than their print publications. Butler attributes this latter figure to a persecution complex on the part of contributors to electronic journals, based on the responses of 63% who indicated that they believed that their colleagues viewed electronic publications as "not 'real' publication," although only 9% could provide any solid facts to support this belief. In support of Butler's conclusion is the fact that many educational institutions now view electronic publications as valid supporting material for tenure requirements (KELLEY ET AL.).

It is apparent that the relationship between publishing and the scholarly community has destabilized. However, there is surprisingly little research that provides insights into the impact of these possibly changed relationships on the academic community. As SILVERMAN observes, one problem with this literature is that it presumes a universal academic community, ignoring how each discipline develops its own truth. Further, much of the work to date has been exceedingly optimistic, with critics focusing on mechanical issues such as long-term storage and retrieval. Little research focuses on possible negative consequences to scholarship. As Silverman states, "the electronic journal promises to make it evident when a paper is of utter nonconsequence to the community by spawning no reactions, or hostile and nonconfirming ones. This publicness will be somewhat like the ratings that appear in movie reviews" (p. 63).

HURD ET AL. offer some key questions about interactive electronic journals. "If a manuscript or document is dynamic, what is the 'archival' version? Which is the copyrighted version? Who is responsible for updating text? Who is (are) the author(s)?" (p. 105). Despite these questions, the authors state that as long as electronic journals are identical to print journals, their utility and use will be limited.

There is evidence, however, that electronic journals are making inroads into the mainstream of scholarly work. Using citation analysis on data collected in February 1996, HARTER (1998) says the "top-five most highly cited ejournals are *Bulletin of the American Mathematical Society (BAMS), Online Journal of Current Clinical Trials (OJCCT), PACS Review, Digital Technical Journal,* and *Psycoloquy*" (p. 509). However, the study concluded that electronic journals (ejournals) have made limited impact in the research process. But Harter also concluded that three journals, *OJCCT, PACS Review,* and *Psycoloquy* show considerable promise and may eventually become key journals in their respective fields.

RESEARCH AND DEVELOPMENT

Earlier in this chapter we describe the evolution of scholarly electronic journals and present models that have been proposed as alternative forms of scholarly communication. Few of these models have been implemented to any extent, with the exception of preprint databases that have gained acceptance in high-energy physics, a field that had relatively early access to computers when compared to other academic disciplines. This lack of implementation is not surprising, given the nature of the funding sources of the projects and experiments undertaken to date. Further, the experiments have been developed primarily by amateurs as labors of love. BORWEIN & SMITH observe that "the current diversity of form in electronic scholarly publication will not last as amateur burnout occurs, and amateurs are replaced by traditional publishing companies" (p. 143).

Perhaps several factors combined have affected the uneven knowledge about journals (electronic or otherwise) and the scholars' relationship (present and future) to the journals. Advocates for electronic journals, frequently the editors themselves, probably have little time to conduct research on scholarly electronic publishing. Indeed, their field of expertise may be outside the realm of social and behavioral research. Traditional publishers have either not pursued systematic evaluation of the uses of their experiments and projects or have elected not to make the information public. Doctoral students may be reluctant to pursue such topics for dissertations because of committee disapproval or methodological uncertainty in the measurement of parameters in an electronic environment.

Despite many references on the subject, an understanding of the influence of electronic journals on scholarship is still not well-developed. The literature is filled with discussions about publishing costs and delays, shortcomings of interfaces, rigor of peer review, and acceptance of electronic journal publication in tenure and promotion processes. Yet little research focuses on actual uses of scholarly journals, print or electronic, or for that matter, what scholars really want.

With the exception of databases such as those of the Institute for Scientific Information (ISI), which provides information on article citations, knowledge about the behavior of users of scholarly journals is quite shallow. Although scholars complain about the slowness of journal publishing, it is unclear how many scholars, and in which disciplines, are concerned. If the issue is legitimate, then scholars should embrace electronic versions of journals as alternatives to print versions that appear weeks or months later. Then again, if improvement in publication speed of electronic over print versions is negligible or nonexistent, the motivation may be far less.

Another area that bears examination is the possible variance between journals published by academic societies and journals published strictly for institutional purchase. Advocates for electronic journal publishing have focused primarily on the high-cost journals to which fewer and fewer institutions are able to subscribe. We found no significant discussion about scholars' perspectives on the journals that they receive directly as members of academic societies. Although projects like the new Digital Library of the Association for Computing Machinery (ACM) will certainly provide insights into these behaviors, the ACM is obviously predisposed toward computing. It is not clear whether scholars in other disciplines will be as interested in receiving or viewing online the same journals they receive in print. It is also possible that if institutions subscribe to online versions of society journals, scholars may decide to discontinue memberships if their primary reason for belonging to a society is to obtain the journal.

Without knowledge of actual behaviors in usage of scholarly journals in general, there is little basis for making comparisons. Knowledge of faculty versus student use is particularly deficient because, according to NIMIJEAN, students typically have been overlooked. Most studies focus on faculty populations; if students are also surveyed, the results are often collapsed in a manner that obscures the specifics of student responses. The role of student use is important because the way in which students are socialized about the use of electronic journals could play a critical role in journal acceptance. If faculty members indicate that references to electronic journals are unacceptable, then students may view such journals as having less quality than the print versions. Alternatively, if research finds high acceptance of electronic journals by students, then acceptance may be generational, and the new generation of students may play a significant role in the evolution of electronic scholarly journals.

Much of the research points to the failure to develop an effective interface or the slowness of the equipment as a major deterrent to acceptance of electronic journals. The universal nature of the World Wide Web, as well as improvements in the technological infrastructure at many colleges and universities, has removed this barrier for some members of the academic community. The problem is determining the size of this population. For example, we know of a small college in Boston that has a Web site mounted on a commercial provider, but only the librarian has Internet access and an email account. While this may be an anomaly, it does generate concerns about the readiness of the international academic community to embrace electronic scholarship.

At the beginning of this chapter we state our intent to examine only literature on the electronic scholarly journal and not on computer-mediated communication (CMC) by scholars. We find it difficult to discern the extent to which findings in CMC research reveal future uses of electronic scholarly journals. Certainly CMC has blurred the boundaries of scholarly communication and may ultimately play a significant role in determining the willingness of scholars to embrace electronic journals and to effect significant changes in the traditional peer-review process.

CONCLUSION

The future of the electronic scholarly journal remains unclear. While there are pockets of innovation, much of the publishing vista remains the same. However, it is premature to conclude that the future of scholarly publishing can be based on the present situation. Regrettably, because we know little about the psychological or technological readiness of scholars to embrace electronic journals, predictions prove difficult.

Some research findings must viewed in the proper context. Speed of retrieval, interface design, and quality of the viewing experience are hardly complaints limited to the genre of electronic journals. Why would any scholar wish to view electronic journals, or any other electronic information, if the overall technology cannot provide a satisfactory experience? It is not surprising that the future of electronic scholarly journals may be seen by some as bleak.

It is possible that every viable alternative model for the publication of scholarly work has been proposed over the course of three decades. These models provide evidence that there is dissatisfaction with the traditional scholar-publisher-library relationships. Had the Internet not emerged, it seems unlikely that alternative forms of scholarship would have found expression. Yet despite the attention that scholarly electronic journals have generated in almost every discipline, there is a limited base of research on electronic journals from which to draw. Therefore it is difficult to determine from the available research how interested the majority of scholars are in changing the scholarly publishing process.

BIBLIOGRAPHY

ABELS, EILEEN G.; LIEBSCHER, PETER; DENMAN, DANIEL W. 1996. Factors That Influence the Use of Electronic Networks by Science and Engineering Faculty at Small Institutions. Part I. Queries. Journal of the American Society for Information Science. 1996; 47(2): 146-158. ISSN: 0002-8231.

AMIRAN, EYAL; ORR, ELAINE; UNSWORTH, JOHN. 1991. Refereed Electronic Journals and the Future of Scholarly Publishing. In: Hewitt, Joe A., ed. Advances in Library Automation and Networking: A Research Annual: Volume 4. Greenwich, CT: JAI Press Inc.; 1991. 25-33. ISBN: 1-55938-188-4.

AMIRAN, EYAL; UNSWORTH, JOHN. 1991. Postmodern Culture: Publishing in the Electronic Medium. The Public-Access Computer Systems Review. 1991; 2(1): 67-76. ISSN: 1048-6542. Available WWW: http://info.lib.uh.edu/pr/v2/n1/amiran.2n1.

ARNOLD, KENNETH. 1993. The Scholarly Monograph Is Dead, Long Live the Scholarly Monograph. In: Okerson, Ann, ed. Scholarly Publishing on the Electronic Networks: The New Generation: Visions and Opportunities in Not-for-Profit Publishing: Proceedings of the 2nd Symposium; 1992 December 5-8; Washington, DC. Washington, DC: Association of Research Libraries, Office of Scientific and Academic Publishing; 1993. 73-79. ISBN: 0-918006-61-9. Available WWW: http://www.arl.org/scomm/symp2/Arnold.html.

ASSOCIATION OF UNIVERSITIES AND COLLEGES OF CANADA; CANADIAN ASSOCIATION OF RESEARCH LIBRARIES. 1996. The Changing

World of Scholarly Communication Challenges and Choices for Canada: Final Report of the AUCC-CARL/ABRC Task Force on Academic Libraries and Scholarly Communication. 1996 November. Available WWW: http://www.aucc.ca/english/sites/aucccarl.htm.

BADGER, ROBERT C.; MCKAY, BEATRICE L. 1996. Springer-Verlag's Electronic Projects. The Serials Librarian. 1996; 28(1/2): 181-184. ISSN: 0361-526X.

BAILEY, CHARLES W., JR. 1992. The Coalition for Networked Information's Acquisition-on-Demand Model: An Exploration and Critique. Serials Review. 1992 Spring and Summer; 18(1/2): 78-81. ISSN: 0098-7913.

BAILEY, CHARLES W., JR. 1994. Scholarly Publishing on the Internet, the NREN, and the NII: Charting Possible Futures. Serials Review. 1994 Fall; 20(3): 7-16. ISSN: 0098-7913.

BARDEN, PHIL. 1990. ADONIS—The British Library Experience. Interlending and Document Supply. 1990; 18(3): 88-91. ISSN: 0264-1615.

BARKER, FRANCES H.; WYATT, BARRY K.; VEAL, DOUGLAS C. 1972. Report on the Evaluation of an Experimental Computer-Based Current-Awareness Service for Chemists. Journal of the American Society for Information Science. 1972 March-April; 23(2): 85-99. ISSN: 0002-8231.

BERGE, ZANE L.; COLLINS, MAURI P. 1996. IPCT Journal Readership Survey. Journal of the American Society for Information Science. 1996 September; 47(9): 701-710. ISSN: 0002-8231.

BIGGS, MICHAEL; HUITFELDT, CLAUS. 1997. Philosophy and Electronic Publishing. The Monist. 1997; 80(3): 348-367. ISSN: 0026-9662. Available WWW: http://hhobel.phl.univie.ac.at/mii/mii/node5.html.

BISHOP, ANN PETERSON; STAR, SUSAN LEIGH. 1996. Social Informatics of Digital Library Use and Infrastructure. In: Williams, Martha E., ed. Annual Review of Information Science and Technology: Volume 31. Medford, NJ: Information Today, Inc. for the American Society for Information Science; 1996. 301-401. ISSN: 0066-4200; ISBN: 1-57387-033-1.

BORGHUIS, MARTHYN; BRINCKMAN, HANS; FISCHER, ALBERT; HUNTER, KAREN; VAN DER LOO, ELEONORE; MORS, ROB TER; MOSTERT, PAUL; ZIJLSTRA, JACO. 1996. TULIP Final Report. New York, NY: Elsevier Science; 1996. 368p. ISBN: 0-444-82540-1. Available WWW: http://www.elsevier.nl/homepage/about/resproj/trmenu.htm.

BORWEIN, JONATHAN; SMITH, RICHARD. 1997. On-line Journal Publication: Two Views from the Electronic Trenches. Canadian Journal of Communication. 1997 Summer/Fall; 22(3/4): 135-152. ISSN: 0705-3657.

BUSH, VANNEVAR. 1945. As We May Think. The Atlantic Monthly. 1945 July; 175: 101-108. ISSN: 0160-6514. Available WWW: http://www.isg.sfu.ca/~duchier/misc/vbush/vbush-all.shtml.

BUTLER, H. JULENE. 1995. Where Does Scholarly Electronic Publishing Get You? Journal of Scholarly Publishing. 1995 July; 26(4): 234-246. ISSN: 1198-9742.

CAJUN. CD-ROM Acrobat Journals Using Networks Project. Website: http://cajun.cs.nott.ac.uk/.

CAMPBELL, ROBERT M.; STERN, BARRIE T. 1987. ADONIS—A New Approach to Document Delivery. Microcomputers for Information Management. 1987 June; 4(2): 87-107. ISSN: 0742-2343.

COLLINS, MAURI P.; BERGE, ZANE L. 1994. IPCT Journal: A Case Study of an Electronic Journal on the Internet. Journal of the American Society for Information Science. 1994 December; 45(10): 771-776. ISSN: 0002-8231.

DENNING, PETER J.; ROUS, BERNARD. 1995. The ACM Electronic Publishing Plan. Communications of the ACM. 1995; 38(4): 97-100. ISSN: 0001-0782. Available WWW: http://info.acm.org/pubs/epub_plan.html.

DROTT, M. CARL. 1995. Reexamining the Role of Conference Papers in Scholarly Communication. Journal of the American Society for Information Science. 1995 May; 46(4): 299-305. ISSN: 0002-8231.

EGAN, DENNIS E.; LESK, MICHAEL E.; KETCHUM, R. DANIEL; LOCHBAUM, CAROL C.; REMDE, JOEL R.; LITTMAN, MICHAEL; LANDAUER, THOMAS K. 1991. Hypertext for the Electronic Library? CORE Sample Results. In: Hypertext '91: Association for Computing Machinery (ACM) 3rd Conference on Hypertext Proceedings; 1991 December 15-18; San Antonio, TX. New York, NY: ACM; 1991. 299-312. ISBN: 0-89791-461-9.

ELVYN. Project ELVYN: Implementing an Electronic Version of a Journal. Available WWW: http://info.lboro.ac.uk/departments/dils/elvyn.

ENSOR, PAT; WILSON, THOMAS. 1997. Public-Access Computer Systems Review: Testing the Promise. The Journal of Electronic Publishing. 1997; 3(1). ISSN: 1080-2711. Available WWW: http://www.press.umich.edu:80/jep/03-01/pacs.html.

ENTLICH, RICHARD. 1995. Electronic Chemistry Journals: Elemental Concerns. The Serials Librarian. 1995; 25(3/4): 111-123. ISSN: 0361-526X.

ENTLICH, RICHARD; GARSON, LORRIN; LESK, MICHAEL E.; NORMORE, LORRAINE; OLSEN, JANETTE R.; WEIBEL, STUART L. 1994. Making a Digital Library: The Contents of the CORE Project. Available WWW: http://www.lesk.com/mlesk/chem94/chtx.html.

ENTLICH, RICHARD; GARSON, LORRIN; LESK, MICHAEL E.; NORMORE, LORRAINE; OLSEN, JANETTE R.; WEIBEL, STUART L. 1995. Making a Digital Library: The Chemistry Online Retrieval Experiment: A Summary of the CORE Project (1991-1995). D-Lib Magazine. 1995 December. ISSN: 1082-9873. Available WWW: http://www.dlib.org/dlib/december95/briefings/12core.html.

GAINES, BRIAN R.; CHEN, LEE LI-JEN; SHAW, MILDRED L. G. 1997. Modeling the Human Factors of Scholarly Communities Supported through the Internet and World Wide Web. Journal of the American Society for Information Science. 1997 November; 48(11): 987-1003. ISSN: 0002-8231.

GARDNER, WILLIAM. 1990. The Electronic Archive: Scientific Publishing for the 1990s. Psychological Science. 1990 November; 1(6): 333-341. ISSN: 0956-7976.

GARDNER, WILLIAM. 1992. Prospects for the Electronic Publication of Scientific Journals. Current Directions in Psychological Science. 1992; 1(2): 75-78. ISSN: 0963-7214.

GASS, JAMES E.; BROTZMAN, LEE E.; WARNOCK, ARCHIBALD; KOVALSKY, DEBBIE; GIOVANE, FRANK J. 1993. STELAR: An Experiment in the Electronic Distribution of Astronomical Literature. In: Okerson, Ann, ed. Scholarly Publishing on the Electronic Networks: The New Generation: Visions and Opportunities in Not-for-Profit Publishing: Proceedings of the 2nd Symposium; 1992 December 5-8; Washington, DC. Washington, DC: Association of Research Libraries, Office of Scientific and Academic Publishing; 1993. 43-51. ISBN: 0-918006-61-9. Available WWW: http://www.arl.org/scomm/symp2/STELAR.html.

GINSPARG, PAUL. 1994a. After Dinner Remarks. APS Meeting at LANL. 1994 October 14. Available WWW: http://xxx.lanl.gov/blurb/pg14Oct94.html.

GINSPARG, PAUL. 1994b. First Steps towards Electronic Research Communication. Computers in Physics. 1994 July/August; 8(4): 390. ISSN: 0894-1866. Available WWW: http://xxx.lanl.gov/ftp/hep-th/papers/macros/blurb.tex (TeX format); http://xxx.lanl.gov/blurb/blurb.ps.Z (PostScript format).

GINSPARG, PAUL. 1996. Winners and Losers in the Global Research Village: Invited Contribution for Conference Held at UNESCO Headquarters; 1996 February 19-23; Paris, France. 1996 February 21. Available WWW: http://xxx.lanl.gov/blurb/pg96unesco.html.

GRENQUIST, PETER. 1997. Why I Don't Read Electronic Journals: An Iconoclast Speaks Out. The Journal of Electronic Publishing. 1997 September; 3(1). ISSN: 1080-2711. Available WWW: http://www.press.umich.edu/jep/03-01/Iconoclast.html.

GRYCZ, CZESLAW JAN. 1991. Economic Models for Disseminating Scholarly Information. DLA Bulletin. 1991 Summer; 11(1): 1, 3-4, 24. ISSN: 0272-037X.

GRYCZ, CZESLAW JAN. 1992. Economic Models for Networked Information. Serials Review. 1992 Spring and Summer; 18(1/2): 11-136. (Special issue). ISSN: 0098-7913.

GUÉDON, JEAN-CLAUDE. 1996. The Seminar, the Encyclopedia, and the Eco-Museum as Possible Future Forms of Electronic Publishing. In: Peek, Robin P.; Newby, Gregory B., eds. Scholarly Publishing: The Electronic Frontier. Cambridge, MA: The MIT Press; 1996. 71-89. ISBN: 0-262-16157-5.

HARNAD, STEVAN. 1990. Scholarly Skywriting and the Prepublication Continuum of Scientific Inquiry. Psychological Science. 1990 November; 1(6): 342-344. ISSN: 0956-7976. Available WWW: www.cogsci.soton.ac.uk/~harnad/Papers/Harnad/harnad90.skywriting.html.

HARNAD, STEVAN. 1991. Post-Gutenberg Galaxy: The Fourth Revolution in the Means of Production of Knowledge. The Public-Access Computer Systems Review. 1991; 2(1): 39-53. ISSN: 1048-6542. Available WWW: http://info.lib.uh.edu/pr/v2/n1/harnad.2n1.

HARNAD, STEVAN. 1997. How to Fast-Forward Learned Serials to the Inevitable and the Optimal for Scholars and Scientists. The Serials Librarian. 1997; 30(3/4): 73-81. ISSN: 0361-526X.

HARRISON, TERESA M.; STEPHEN, TIMOTHY D. 1992. On-Line Disciplines: Computer-Mediated Scholarship in the Humanities and Social Sciences. Computers and the Humanities. 1992; 26(3): 181-193. ISSN: 0010-4817.

HARRISON, TERESA M.; STEPHEN, TIMOTHY D. 1994. The Case of EJC/ REC: A Model for Producing, Consuming, and Delivering Electronic Journals Electronically. In: Proceedings of the 1993 International Conference on Refereed Electronic Journals; 1993 October 1-2; Winnipeg, Manitoba. Winnipeg, Manitoba: University of Manitoba Libraries, University of Manitoba; 1994. ISBN: 0-919932-02-9; OCLC: 30665009.

HARRISON, TERESA M.; STEPHEN, TIMOTHY D. 1995. The Electronic Journal as the Heart of an Online Scholarly Community. Library Trends. 1995 Spring; 43(4): 592-608. ISSN: 0024-2594.

HARRISON, TERESA M.; STEPHEN, TIMOTHY D. 1996. Computer Networking and Scholarly Communication in the Twenty-First-Century University. Albany, NY: State University of New York Press; 1996. 468p. ISBN: 0-7914-2854-0.

HARRISON, TERESA M.; STEPHEN, TIMOTHY D.; WINTER, JAMES. 1991. Online Journals: Disciplinary Designs for Electronic Scholarship. The Public-Access Computer Systems Review. 1991; 2(1): 25-38. ISSN: 1048-6542. Available WWW: http://info.lib.uh.edu/pr/v2/n1/harrison.2n1.

HARTER, STEPHEN P. 1996. The Impact of Electronic Journals on Scholarly Communication: A Citation Analysis. The Public-Access Computer Systems Review. 1996; 7(5). ISSN: 1048-6542. Available WWW: http://info.lib.uh.edu/pr/v7/n5/hart7n5.html.

HARTER, STEPHEN P. 1998. Scholarly Communication and Electronic Journals: An Impact Study. Journal of the American Society for Information Science. 1998; 49(6): 507-516. ISSN: 0002-8231.

HARTER, STEPHEN P.; KIM, HAK JOON. 1996a. Accessing Electronic Journals and Other E-publications: An Empirical Study. College & Research Libraries. 1996 September; 57(5): 440-456. ISSN: 0010-0870.

HARTER, STEPHEN P.; KIM, HAK JOON. 1996b. Electronic Journals and Scholarly Communication: A Citation and Reference Study. In: Whitney, Gretchen, ed. ASIS Mid-Year 1996: Proceedings of the Mid-Year Meeting of the American Society for Information Science; 1996 May 20-22; San Diego, CA. Medford, NJ: Information Today, Inc. for ASIS; 1996. 299-315. ISBN: 1-57387-028-5. Available WWW: http://php.indiana.edu/~harter/ harter-asis96midyear.html.

HILTZ, STARR ROXANNE; TUROFF, MURRAY. 1993. The Network Nation: Human Communication via Computer. Revised edition. Cambridge, MA: MIT Press; 1993. 557p. ISBN: 0-262-08219-5.

HITCHCOCK, STEVE; CARR, LESLIE; HALL, WENDY. 1996. A Survey of STM Online Journals 1990-95: The Calm before the Storm. In: Mogge, D., ed. Directory of Electronic Journals, Newsletters and Academic Discussion Lists. 6th edition. Washington, DC: Association of Research Libraries; 1996. 7-32. ISSN: 1057-1337; OCLC: 35717736.

HITCHCOCK, STEVE; CARR, LESLIE; HALL, WENDY. 1997. Web Journals Publishing: A UK Perspective. Serials. 1997 November; 10(3): 285-299.

ISSN: 0953-0460. Available WWW: http://journals.ecs.soton.ac.uk/uksg.htm.

HURD, JULIE M.; WELLER, ANN C.; CRAWFORD, SUSAN Y. 1996. The Changing Scientific and Technical Communications System. In: Crawford, Susan Y.; Hurd, Julie M.; Weller, Ann C. From Print to Electronic: The Transformation of Scientific Communication. Medford, NJ: Information Today, Inc.; 1996. 97-114. ISBN: 1-57387-030-7.

HURTADO, LARRY W. 1996. A Consortium for Refereed Electronic Journals. In: Peek, Robin P.; Newby, Gregory B., eds. Scholarly Publishing: The Electronic Frontier. Cambridge, MA: The MIT Press; 1996. 201-213. ISBN: 0-262-16157-5.

JACOBS, MICHAEL; LUCIER, RICHARD E.; BADGER, ROBERT C. 1993. The Red Sage Project: A Press Release. In: Okerson, Ann, ed. Scholarly Publishing on the Electronic Networks: The New Generation: Visions and Opportunities in Not-for-Profit Publishing: Proceedings of the 2nd Symposium; 1992 December 5-8; Washington, DC. Washington DC: Association of Research Libraries, Office of Scientific and Academic Publishing; 1993. 119-121. ISBN: 0-918006-61-9. Available WWW: http://www.arl.org/scomm/symp2/RedSage.html.

JASPERSE, JAAP A. 1991. New Zealand Science Journals on CD-ROM: How It Can Be Done—Now! New Zealand Libraries. 1991 March; 46(9): 2-4. ISSN: 0028-8381.

JASPERSE, JAAP A. 1993. NZ Science Published on Trial CD-ROM. New Zealand Libraries. 1993 March; 47: 95-96. ISSN: 0028-8381.

JASPERSE, JAAP A. 1994. Primary Science on CD-ROM: The New Zealand Experiment. Journal of the American Society for Information Science. 1994 December; 45(10): 777-784. ISSN: 0002-8231.

JOA, HARALD. 1997. A Case Study in E-Journal Developments: The Scandinavian Position. Against the Grain. 1997 February; 9: 43-44, 46-47. ISSN: 1043-2094.

JOHNSON-LENZ, PETER; JOHNSON-LENZ, TRUDY; SCHER, JULIAN M. 1978. How Groups Can Make Decisions through Computerized Conferencing. Bulletin of the American Society for Information Science. 1978 June; 4(5): 15-17. ISSN: 0095-4403.

KELLEY, DONALD R.; GRAHAM, PETER S.; FARRIS, GEORGE F.; SCHOCHET, GORDON J.; VANDERBILT, DAVID H.; WASSERMAN, MARLIE P.; WHICKER, MARCIA L.; COONEY, ROBERT F. 1997. Report of the Committee on Electronic Publishing and Tenure. New Brunswick, NJ: Rutgers—The State University of New Jersey; 1997 June 12. Available WWW: http://aultnis.rutgers.edu/texts/ept.html.

KENNEDY, H.E. 1986. Information Delivery Options over Three Decades. Information Services & Use. 1986; 6: 135-151. ISSN: 0167-5265.

KEYHANI, ANDREA. 1993. The Online Journal of Current Clinical Trials: An Innovation in Electronic Journal Publishing. Database. 1993 February; 16: 14-23. ISSN: 0162-4105.

KLING, ROB; COVI, LISA. 1995. Electronic Journals and Legitimate Media in the Systems of Scholarly Communication. The Information Society. 1995; 11: 261-271. ISSN: 0197-2243. Available WWW: http://www.ics.uci.edu/~kling/klingej2.html.

KLING, ROB; LAMB, ROBERTA. 1996. Analyzing Alternative Visions of Electronic Publishing and Digital Libraries. In: Peek, Robin P.; Newby, Gregory B., eds. Scholarly Publishing: The Electronic Frontier. Cambridge, MA: The MIT Press; 1996. 17-54. ISBN: 0-262-16157-5.

KOENIG, JOHN A.; ORR, DOUGLAS B.; OZIL, EROL; RODGERS, DAVID L. 1992. The AMS Electronic Publishing Experiment: A New Vision of the Scientific Journal. Available WWW: http://www.arl.org/scomm/symp2/Koenig.html.

LANCASTER, F. W. 1978. Toward Paperless Information Systems. New York, NY: Academic Press; 1978. 179p. ISBN: 0-12-436050-5.

LANCASTER, F. W. 1995a. Attitudes in Academia toward Feasibility and Desirability of Networked Scholarly Publishing. Library Trends. 1995 Spring; 43(4): 741-752. ISSN: 0024-2594.

LANCASTER, F.W. 1995b. The Evolution of Electronic Publishing. Library Trends. 1995 Spring; 43(4): 518-527. ISSN: 0024-2594.

LANGSTON, LIZBETH. 1996. Scholarly Communication and Electronic Publication: Implications for Research, Advancement, and Promotion. In: Duda, Andrea L., ed. Untangling the Web: Proceedings of the Conference Sponsored by the Librarians Association of the University of California, Santa Barbara and Friends of the UCSB Library; 1996 April 26; Santa Barbara, CA. Santa Barbara, CA: University of California, Santa Barbara Library; 1996. Available WWW: http://www.library.ucsb.edu/untangle/langston.html.

LESK, MICHAEL E. 1991. The CORE Electronic Chemistry Library. In: Bookstein, A.; Chiaramella, Y.; Salton, G.; Raghavan, V., eds. SIGIR '91: Proceedings of the Association for Computing Machinery/Special Interest Group on Information Retrieval (ACM/SIGIR) 14th Annual International Conference on Research and Development in Information Retrieval; 1991 October 13-16; Chicago, IL. New York, NY: ACM; 1991. 93-112. ISBN: 0-89791-448-1.

LIEBSCHER, PETER; ABELS, EILEEN G.; DENMAN, DANIEL W. 1997. Factors That Influence the Use of Electronic Networks by Science and Engineering Faculty at Small Institutions. Part II. Preliminary Use Indicators. Journal of the American Society for Information Science. 1997 June; 48(6): 496-507. ISSN: 0002-8231.

LORIMER, ROWLAND; GILBERT, JOHN H.V.; PATRICK, RUTH J. 1997. Scholarly Communication in the Next Millennium: Selected Papers from Canada's Policy Conference. Canadian Journal of Communication. 1997 Summer/Autumn; 22(3/4): 39-47. ISSN: 0705-3657.

LUCIER, RICHARD E.; BADGER, ROBERT C. 1994. Red Sage Project. The Serials Librarian. 1994; 24(3/4): 129-134. ISSN: 0361-526X.

LUCIER, RICHARD E.; BRANTLEY, PETER. 1995. The Red Sage Project: An Experimental Digital Journal Library for the Health Sciences: A Descriptive Overview. D-Lib Magazine. 1995 August. ISSN: 1082-9873. Available WWW: http://www.dlib.org/dlib/august95/lucier/08lucier.html.

LYNCH, CLIFFORD A. 1994. Scholarly Communication in the Networked Environment: Reconsidering Economics and Organizational Missions. Serials Review. 1994 Fall; 20(3): 23-30. ISSN: 0098-7913.

LYNCH, CLIFFORD A. 1995. The TULIP Project: Context, History, and Perspective. Library Hi Tech. 1995; 13(4): 8-24. ISSN: 0737-8831.

MANI, GANESH. 1990. Electronic Archival of Scientific Journals: The MEGAJOURNAL. Psycoloquy. 1990; 1(1-7). ISSN: 1055-0143. Available WWW: ftp://ftp.princeton.edu/pub/harnad/Psycoloquy/1990.volume.1/psyc.arch.1.1-7.90.

MATYLONEK, JOHN C.; GREEN, JAMES L.; LISS, EVELYN; DUNCAN, ANDY. 1997. HortBase: An Example of Professional Societies' Roles in Electronic Information Systems. In: Logan, Elisabeth; Gluck, Myke, eds. Electronic Publishing: Applications and Implications. Medford, NJ: Information Today, Inc.; 1997. 95-105. ISBN: 1-57387-036-6.

MCKNIGHT, CLIFF. 1993. Electronic Journals—Past, Present. . . and Future? Aslib Proceedings. 1993; 45(1): 7-10. ISSN: 0001-253X.

MCKNIGHT, CLIFF. 1995. Digital Library Research at Loughborough: The Last Fifteen Years. In: Shipman, Frank M., III; Furuta, Richard K.; Levy, David M., eds. Proceedings of Digital Libraries '95: The 2nd Annual Conference on the Theory and Practice of Digital Libraries; 1995 June 11-13; Austin, TX. College Station, TX: Texas A&M University; 1995. 65-70. Available WWW: http://www.csdl.tamu.edu/DL95/papers/mcknight/mcknight.html.

MCKNIGHT, CLIFF. 1997. Designing the Electronic Journal: Why Bother? Serials. 1997 July; 10(2): 184-188. ISSN: 0953-0460.

MCKNIGHT, CLIFF; MEADOWS, ARTHUR JACK; PULLINGER, DAVID J.; ROWLAND, FYTTON. 1994. ELVYN—Publisher and Library Working Towards the Electronic Distribution and Use of Journals. In: Schnase, John L.; Leggett, John J.; Furuta, Richard K.; Metcalfe, Ted, eds. Proceedings of Digital Libraries '94: The 1st Annual Conference on the Theory and Practice of Digital Libraries; 1994 June 19-21; College Station, TX. College Station, TX: Texas A&M University; 1994. 6-11. Available WWW: http://www.csdl.tamu.edu/DL94/paper/mcknight.html.

MILLER, ERIC J. 1995. The Design and Implementation of XSCEPTER, an X-Windows Graphical User Interface to the CORE Project. Annual Review of OCLC Research. 1995. ISSN: 0894-198X. Available WWW: http://www.oclc.org/~emiller/publications/xscepter/.

NIMIJEAN, RICHARD. 1997. And What about Students? The Forgotten Role of Students in the Scholarly Communication Debate. Canadian Journal of Communication. 1997 Summer/Fall; 22(3/4): 179-196. ISSN: 0705-3657.

OAKESHOTT, PRISCILLA. 1985. The "BLEND" Experiment in Electronic Publishing. Scholarly Publishing. 1985 October; 17(1): 25-36. ISSN: 0036-634X.

ODLYZKO, ANDREW M. 1996. Tragic Loss or Good Riddance? The Impending Demise of Traditional Scholarly Journals. In: Peek, Robin P.; Newby, Gregory B., eds. Scholarly Publishing: The Electronic Frontier. Cambridge, MA: The MIT Press; 1996. 91-101. ISBN: 0-262-16157-5.

OKERSON, ANN. 1992. The Missing Model: A "Circle of Gifts." Serials Review. 1992 Spring and Summer; 18: 92-96. ISSN: 0098-7913.

OKERSON, ANN. 1994. Oh Lord, Won't You Buy Me A Mercedes Benz or, There Is a There There. Surfaces. ISSN: 1188-2492. Available WWW: http://tornade.ere.umontreal.ca/~guedon/Surfaces/vol4/okerson.html.

OKERSON, ANN; O'DONNELL, JAMES J., eds. 1995. Scholarly Journals at the Crossroads: A Subversive Proposal for Electronic Publishing: An Internet Discussion about Scientific and Scholarly Journals and Their Future. Washington, DC: Association of Research Libraries; 1995. 242p. ISBN: 0-918006-26-0.

OLSEN, JANETTE R. 1992. Implications of Electronic Journal Literature for Scholars. Ithaca, NY: Cornell University; 1992. 102p. (Ph.D. dissertation). Available: UMI, Ann Arbor, MI. (UMI order no.: AA69236073).

OLSEN, JANETTE R. 1994. Electronic Journals: Implications for Scholars. Learned Publishing. 1994 July; 7(3): 167-176. ISSN: 0953-1513.

PEEK, ROBIN P. 1994. Where Is Publishing Going? A Perspective on Change. Journal of the American Society for Information Science. 1994 December; 45(10): 730-736. ISSN: 0002-8231.

PEEK, ROBIN P. 1996a. Electronic Publishing Grows Up. Journal of the American Society for Information Science. 1996 September; 47(9): 665-668. ISSN: 0002-8231.

PEEK, ROBIN P. 1996b. Scholarly Publishing: Facing the New Frontiers. In: Peek, Robin P.; Newby, Gregory B., eds. Scholarly Publishing: The Electronic Frontier. Cambridge, MA: The MIT Press; 1996. 3-15. ISBN: 0-262-16157-5.

PEEK, ROBIN P.; BURSTYN, JOAN N. 1991. In Pursuit of Improved Scholarly Communications. In: Burstyn, Joan N., ed. Desktop Publishing in the University. Syracuse, NY: Syracuse University Press; 1991. 99-120. ISBN: 0-8156-8116-X.

PEEK, ROBIN P.; NEWBY, GREGORY B., eds. 1996. Scholarly Publishing: The Electronic Frontier. Cambridge, MA: The MIT Press; 1996. 363p. ISBN: 0-262-16157-5.

PEEK, ROBIN P.; POMERANTZ, JEFFREY P.; PALING, STEPHEN. 1998. The Traditional Scholarly Journal Publishers Legitimize the Web. Journal of the American Society for Information Science. (In press). ISSN: 0002-8231.

PULLINGER, DAVID J. 1984. The BLEND Network and Electronic Journal Project. Program. 1984 July; 18(3): 263-264. ISSN: 0033-0337.

ROES, HANS. 1995. Electronic Journals: A Survey of the Literature and the Net. Journal of Information Networking. 1995; 2(3): 169-186. ISSN: 0966-9248. Available WWW: http://cwis.kub.nl/~dbi/users/roes/articles/ej_join.htm.

ROGERS, SHARON J.; HURT, CHARLENE S. 1990. How Scholarly Communication Should Work in the 21st Century. College & Research Libraries. 1990 January; 51(1): 5-8. ISSN: 0010-0870.

ROISTACHER, RICHARD C. 1978. The Virtual Journal. Computer Networks. 1978; 2: 18-24. ISSN: 0376-5075.

ROWLAND, FYTTON. 1997. Print Journals: Fit for the Future? Ariadne. 1997; 7. ISSN: 1361-3200. Available WWW: http://www.ariadne.ac.uk/issue7/fytton.

ROWLAND, FYTTON; BELL, IAN; FALCONER, CATHERINE. 1997. Human and Economic Factors Affecting the Acceptance of Electronic Journals by Readers. Canadian Journal of Communication. 1997; 22(3/4): 61-75. ISSN: 0705-3657.

ROWLAND, FYTTON; MCKNIGHT, CLIFF; MEADOWS, ARTHUR JACK, eds. 1995. Project ELVYN: An Experiment in Electronic Journal Delivery: Facts, Figures and Findings. London, England: Bowker Saur; 1995. 181p. ISBN: 1-85739-161-6.

ROWLAND, FYTTON; MCKNIGHT, CLIFF; MEADOWS, ARTHUR JACK. 1996. ELVYN: The Delivery of an Electronic Version of a Journal from the Publisher to Libraries. Journal of the American Society for Information Science. 1996 September; 47(9): 690-700. ISSN: 0002-8231.

SCHAUDER, DONALD E. 1994. Electronic Publishing of Professional Articles: Attitudes of Academics and Implications for the Scholarly Communication Industry. Journal of the American Society for Information Science. 1994; 45(2): 73-100. ISSN: 0002-8231.

SCHOONBAERT, DIRK. 1996. Experiences with ExtraMED, an Electronic Full-Text Biomedical Journal Collection on CDROM. The Electronic Library. 1996 June; 14(3): 251-255. ISSN: 0264-0473.

SENDERS, JOHN W. 1977. An On-line Scientific Journal. The Information Scientist. 1977 March; 2(1): 3-9. ISSN: 0020-0263.

SENDERS, JOHN W.; ANDERSON, C.M.B; HECHT, C.D. 1975. Scientific Publication Systems: An Analysis of Past, Present and Future Methods of Scientific Communication. Washington, DC: National Science Foundation; 1975. 181p. NTIS: PB242259.

SHACKEL, BRIAN. 1982. Plans and Initial Progress with BLEND—An Electronic Network Communication Experiment. International Journal of Man-Machine Studies. 1982; 17(2): 225-233. ISSN: 0020-7373.

SHACKEL, BRIAN. 1983. The BLEND System: Programme for the Study of Some "Electronic Journals". Journal of the American Society for Information Science. 1983 January; 34(1): 22-30. ISSN: 0002-8231.

SHACKEL, BRIAN. 1991. BLEND-9: Overview and Appraisal. London, England: British Library Research and Development Department; 1991. 116p. ISBN: 0-7123-3231-6.

SHACKEL, BRIAN; PULLINGER, DAVID J. 1984. BLEND-1: Background and Developments. London, England: British Library; 1984. 155p. (Library and Information Science Research Report no. 29). ISBN: 0-7123-3042-9.

SHACKEL, BRIAN.; PULLINGER, DAVID J.; MAUD, T.I.; DODD, W.P. 1983. The BLEND-LINC Project on "Electronic Journals" after Two Years. Aslib Proceedings. 1983 February; 35(2): 77-91. ISSN: 0001-253X.

SHERIDAN, T.; SENDERS, JOHN W.; MORAY, N.; STOKLOSA, J.; GUILLAUME, J.; MAKEPEACE, D. 1981. Experimentation with a Multi-Disciplinary Teleconference and Electronic Journal on Mental Workload: Report to the National Science Foundation Division of Science Information Access Improvement. Cambridge, MA: Massachusetts Institute of Technology; 1981 June. 329p. OCLC: 34520190.

SILVERMAN, ROBERT J. 1996. The Impact of Electronic Journals on the Academic Community. In: Peek, Robin P.; Newby, Gregory B., eds. Scholarly Publishing: The Electronic Frontier. Cambridge, MA: The MIT Press; 1996. 55-69. ISBN: 0-262-16157-5.

SMITH, PHILIP N.; BRAILSFORD, DAVID F.; EVANS, DAVID R.; HARRISON, LEON; PROBETS, STEVE G.; SUTTON, PETER E. 1993. Journal Publishing with Acrobat: The CAJUN Project. Electronic Publishing. 1993 December; 6(4): 481-493. ISSN: 0894-3982. Available WWW: http://cajun.cs.nott.ac.uk/cgi-bin/getpaper?paper=compsci/epo/papers/samples/smith.pdf (Adobe Acrobat format).

SONDAK, NORMAN E.; SCHWARTZ, RICHARD J. 1972. The Paperless Journal. Available from: American Institute of Chemical Engineers.

SONDAK, NORMAN E.; SCHWARTZ, RICHARD J. 1973. The Paperless Journal. Chemical Engineering Progress. 1973 January; 69(1): 82-83. ISSN: 0360-7275.

SPINK, AMANDA; SCHAMBER, LINDA. 1997. Use of Book Reviews by Scholars: Implications for Electronic Publishing. In: Logan, Elisabeth; Gluck, Myke, eds. Electronic Publishing: Applications and Implications. Medford, NJ: Information Today, Inc.; 1997. 113-119. ISBN: 1-57387-036-6.

STEPHEN, TIMOTHY D.; HARRISON, TERESA M. 1993a. Comserve: An Electronic Community for Communication Scholars. In: Okerson, Ann, ed. Scholarly Publishing on the Electronic Networks: The New Generation: Visions and Opportunities in Not-for-Profit Publishing: Proceedings of the 2nd Symposium; 1992 December 5-8; Washington, DC. Washington DC: Association of Research Libraries, Office of Scientific and Academic Publishing; 1993. 123-132. ISBN: 0-918006-61-9. Available WWW: http://www.arl.org/scomm/symp2/Comserve.html.

STEPHEN, TIMOTHY D.; HARRISON, TERESA M. 1993b. Online Academic Centers: Building a Community of Scholars Electronically. Media Information Australia. 1993 February; 67: 71-75. ISSN: 0312-9616.

STEPHEN, TIMOTHY D.; HARRISON, TERESA M. 1994. Comserve: Moving the Communication Discipline Online. Journal of the American Society for Information Science. 1994 December; 45(10): 765-770. ISSN: 0002-8231.

STERN, BARRIE T.; CAMPBELL, ROBERT M. 1988. ADONIS: The Story So Far. In: Oppenheim, Charles, ed. CD-ROM: Fundamentals to Applications. London, England: Butterworths; 1988. 181-219. ISBN: 0-408-00746-X.

STERN, BARRIE T.; CAMPBELL, ROBERT M. 1989. ADONIS—Publishing Journal Articles on CD-ROM. Advances in Serials Management. 1989; 3: 1-60. ISBN: 0-89232-965-3.

STERN, BARRIE T.; COMPIER, HENK C.J. 1990. ADONIS—Document Delivery in the CD-ROM Age. Interlending and Document Supply. 1990 July; 18(3): 79-87. ISSN: 0264-1615.

STORY, GUY A.; O'GORMAN, LAWRENCE; FOX, DAVID; SCHAPER, LOUISE LEVY; JAGADISH, H.V. 1992. The RightPages Image-Based Electronic Library for Alerting and Browsing. Computer. 1992 September; 25: 17-25. ISSN: 0018-9162.

TULIP—The University Licensing Program. Website: http://www.elsevier.nl/homepage/about/resproj/tulip.shtml.

TUROFF, MURRAY. 1978. The EIES Experience: Electronic Information Exchange System. Bulletin of the American Society for Information Science. 1978 June; 4(5): 9-10. ISSN: 0095-4403.

TUROFF, MURRAY; HILTZ, STARR ROXANNE. 1980. Electronic Information Exchange and Its Impact on Libraries. In: Lancaster, F. Wilfrid, ed. The

Role of the Library in an Electronic Society: Papers Presented at the 1979 Clinic on Library Applications of Data Processing; 1979 April 22-25; Urbana, IL. Urbana-Champaign, IL: Graduate School of Library Science, University of Illinois; 1980. 117-134. ISBN: 0-87845-053-X.

TUROFF, MURRAY; HILTZ, STARR ROXANNE. 1982. The Electronic Journal: A Progress Report. Journal of the American Society for Information Science. 1982 July; 33(4): 195-202. ISSN: 0002-8231.

UNIVERSITY OF CALIFORNIA SAN FRANCISCO. 1996. Red Sage Electronic Journal Project. Available WWW: http://www.ckm.ucsf.edu/projects/RedSage.

VALAUSKAS, EDWARD J. 1997. Waiting for Thomas Kuhn: First Monday and the Evolution of Electronic Journals. The Journal of Electronic Publishing. 1997; 3(1). ISSN: 1080-2711. Available WWW: http://www.press.umich.edu:80/jep/03-01/FirstMonday.html.

VAN STEENBERG, MICHAEL E. 1994. NASA STELAR Experiment. The Serials Librarian. 1994; 24(3/4): 135-151. ISSN: 0361-526X.

WARKENTIN, ERWIN. 1997. Consumer Issues and the Scholarly Journal. Canadian Journal of Communication. 1997 Summer/Autumn; 22(3/4): 39-47. ISSN: 0705-3657.

WEIBEL, STUART L.; MILLER, ERIC J.; GODBY, C. JEAN. 1993. The CORE Project: Technical Shakedown Phase and Preliminary User Studies. Annual Review of OCLC Research, 1992-1993. Available WWW: http://www.oclc.org/~emiller/publications/core.html.

WHEELER, DAVID L. 1997. A Scholar Outlines a Plan to Use Electronic Publishing to Change Peer Review. The Chronicle of Higher Education. 1997 February 28; 43(25): A28. ISSN: 0009-5982.

WOODWARD, HAZEL; ROWLAND, FYTTON. 1994. ELVYN: The Delivery of an Electronic Version of a Journal from the Publisher to Libraries. 1994. Available WWW: http://www.lboro.ac.uk/departments/dils/elvyn/join.html.

YOUNG, PETER R. 1992. National Corporation for Scholarly Publishing: Presentation and Description of the Model. Serials Review. 1992 Spring and Summer; 18: 100-101. ISSN: 0098-7913.

Introduction to the Index

Index entries have been made for names of individuals, corporate bodies, subjects, geographic locations, and author names included in the text pages and for author and conference names from the bibliography pages. The page numbers referring to the bibliography pages are set in italics, and are listed after the page numbers relating to the text pages. This format allows one to distinguish references to bibliographic materials from references to text.

Acronyms are listed either under the acronym or under the fully spelled-out form, depending on which form is more commonly used and known. In either case a cross reference from the alternative form is provided. Postings associated with PRECIS, for example, would be listed under PRECIS as readers are generally less familiar with the full name "Preserved Context Index System." In a few cases, such as names of programs, systems, and programming languages, there is no spelled-out form either because there is none or because the meaning has been changed or is no longer used.

The Index is arranged on a word-by-word basis. The sort sequence places special characters first, followed by alpha characters, then numbers. Thus, O'Neill would precede Oakman and 3M Company would file after the Zs. Government organizations are generally listed under country name, with *see* references provided from names of departments, agencies, and other subdivisions. While index entries do correspond precisely in spelling and format, they do not follow the typographical conventions used in the text. Author names, which are all upper case in the text, and both programming languages and software packages (such as expert system shells), which are in small caps in the text, are in upper and lower case or normal upper case in the Index.

Subject indexing is by concepts rather than by words. When authors have used different words or different forms of the same word to express the same or overlapping concepts, the terminology has been standardized. An effort has been made to use the form of index entries for concepts that appear in previous *ARIST* Indexes and in the 1994 *ASIS Thesaurus of Information Science and Librarianship.** See also* references are used for overlapping or related (but not synonymous) concepts; *see* references are used to send the reader to the accepted form of a term used in the Index.

---

* Milstead, Jessica L., ed. 1994. *ASIS Thesaurus of Information Science and Librarianship.* Medford, NJ: Learned Information, Inc., for the American Society for Information Science; 1994. 139p. ISBN: 0-938734-80-6.

The Index was prepared by Debora Shaw, using the MACREX Plus Indexing Program, version 5.10 developed by Hilary and Drusilla Calvert and distributed in the United States by Bayside Indexing. The overall direction and coordination of the Index were provided by Martha E. Williams. Comments and suggestions should be addressed to the Editor.

Index*

---

*Italicized page numbers refer to Bibliography pages.

Introduction to the Cumulative Keyword and Author Index of *ARIST* Titles: Volumes 1-33

The following section is a Cumulative Keyword and Author Index (both single word and multiword terms have been used) to *ARIST* chapters for Volumes 1 through 33. Terms are largely based on the titles of *ARIST* chapters, with editing for consistency. It has been produced to assist users in locating specific topics and author names (in bold when at the entry position) for all *ARIST* volumes to date. The index terms are sorted alphabetically. Multiple forms (e.g., adjective, verb, and noun forms) of the same word have been combined, and *see* and *see also* references are provided. The sort word is followed by the author(s) name(s) and the *ARIST* citation. This Cumulative Keyword and Author Index was totally reworked in Volume 30 and the new indexing procedures have been employed in succeeding volumes.

Cumulative Keyword and Author Index of *ARIST* Titles: Volumes 1-33

Abstracting and Indexing Services *see* Secondary Information Systems and Services

Acquisition and Use of Information

 Choo, Chun Wei and Ethel Auster. Environmental Scanning: Acquisition and Use of Information by Managers. **28**, p279

Adams, Peter D. Lerner, Rita G., Ted Metaxas, John T. Scott, Peter D. Adams and Peggy Judd. Primary Publication Systems and Scientific Text Processing. **18**, p127

Adams, Scott and Judith A. Werdel. Cooperation in Information Activities through International Organizations. **10**, p303

ADI (American Documentation Institute)

 Cuadra, Carlos A. Introduction to the ADI Annual Review. **1**, p1

Adkinson, Burton W. Berninger, Douglas E. and Burton W. Adkinson. Interaction between the Public and Private Sectors in National Information Programs. **13**, p3

Agriculture

 Frank, Robyn C. Agricultural Information Systems and Services. **22**, p293

Aines, Andrew A. and Melvin S. Day. National Planning of Information Services. **10**, p3

Allen, Bryce L. Cognitive Research in Information Science: Implications for Design. **26**, p3; Kinnucan, Mark T., Michael J. Nelson and Bryce L. Allen. Statistical Methods in Information Science Research. **22**, p147

Allen, Thomas J. Information Needs and Uses. **4**, p3

Alper, Bruce H. Library Automation. **10**, p199

Alsberg, Peter A. Bunch, Steve R. and Peter A. Alsberg. Computer Communication Networks. **12**, p183

American Institute of Physics Staff. Techniques for Publication and Distribution of Information. **2**, p339

Amsler, Robert A. Machine-Readable Dictionaries. **19**, p161

Analysis Methods

 Sugar, William. User-Centered Perspective of Information Retrieval Research and Analysis Methods. **30**, p77

Annual Review

 Cuadra, Carlos A. Introduction to the ADI Annual Review. **1**, p1

Annual Review Staff. New Hardware Developments. **1**, p191

Applications *see also* Information Services; Information Systems and Services; Information Technology

 Baruch, Jordan J. Information System Applications. **1**, p255;

 Beard, Joseph J. Information Systems Application in Law. **6**, p369;

About the Editor. . .

Professor Martha E. Williams assumed the Editorship of the *ANNUAL REVIEW OF INFORMATION SCIENCE AND TECHNOLOGY* with Volume 11 and has produced a series of books that provide unparalleled insights into, and overviews of, the multifaceted discipline of information science.

Professor Williams holds the positions of Director of the Information Retrieval Research Laboratory and Professor of Information Science in the Coordinated Science Laboratory (CSL) as well as Professor of Information Science in the Graduate School of Library and Information Science and affiliate of the Computer Science Department at the University of Illinois, Urbana-Champaign, Illinois. As a chemist and information scientist Professor Williams has brought to the Editorship a breadth of knowledge and experience in information science and technology.

She has served as a Director and Chairman of the Board of Engineering Information, Inc.; she was founding editor of *Computer-Readable Databases: A Directory and Data Sourcebook*; is editor of *Online & CDROM Review* (Learned Information, Ltd., Oxford, England); and is Program Chairman for the National Online Meetings, which are organized by Information Today, Inc. She was appointed by the Secretary of Health, Education and Welfare, Joseph Califano, to be a member of the Board of Regents of the National Library of Medicine (NLM) in 1978 and has served as Chairman of the Board. She has been a member of the Numerical Data Advisory Board of the National Research Council (NRC), National Academy of Sciences (NAS). She was a member of the Science Information Activities task force of the National Science Foundation (NSF), was chairman of the Large Database subcommittee of the NAS/NRC Committee on Chemical Information, and was chairman of the Gordon Research Conference on Scientific Information Problems in Research in 1980.

Professor Williams is a Fellow of the American Association for the Advancement of Science, Honorary Fellow of the Institute of Information Scientists in England, recipient of the 1984 Award of Merit of the American Society for Information Science (ASIS) and recipient of the 1995 Watson Davis Award of ASIS. She is a member of, has held offices in, and/or is actively involved in various committees of the American Association for the Advancement of Science (AAAS), the American Chemical Society (ACS), the Association for Computing Machinery (ACM), and the American Society for Information Science (ASIS). She has published numerous books and papers and serves on the editorial boards of several journals. She is the founder and President of Information Market Indicators, Inc., and consults for many governmental and commercial organizations.

Other Recent ASIS Titles
Published by Information Today, Inc.

ARIST 32
Annual Review of Information Science and Technology
Edited by Martha E. Williams

Contents of Volume 32 include:

* Evaluation of Information Retrieval Systems, by Stephen P. Harter and Carol A. Hert
* Visualization of Literatures, by Howard D. White and Katherine W. McCain
* Indexing Images, by Edie M. Rasmussen
* Data Mining and Knowledge Discovery, by Walter J. Trybula
* Content Evaluation of Databases, by Péter Jacsó
* Chemical Structure Handling by Computer, by Gregory Paris
* Information Ethics, by Martha Montague Smith
* Legal Informatics: Application of Information Technology in Law, by Sandra Erdelez and Sheila O'Hara

1997/500 pp/hardbound/ISBN 1-57387-047-1
$79.95 ASIS Members $99.95 Non-Members

Historical Studies in Information Science
Edited by Trudi Bellardo Hahn and Michael Buckland

Contrary to popular belief, the field of information science has a broad history spanning nearly a century. *Historical Studies in Information Science* focuses on the progression of this dynamic and evolving industry by looking at some of its pioneers. This informative volume concentrates on the following areas: Historiography of Information Science; Paul Otlet and His Successors; Techniques, Tools and Systems; People and Organizations; Theoretical Topics; and Literature.

1998/317pp/hardbound/ISBN 1-57387-062-5
$31.60 ASIS Members $39.50 Non-Members

Information Management for the Intelligent Organization
Second Edition
Chun Wei Choo

The intelligent organization is one that is skilled at marshalling its information resources and capabilities, transforming information into knowledge, and using this knowledge to sustain and enhance its performance in a restless environment. The objective of this newly updated and expanded book is to develop an understanding of how an organization may manage its information processes more effectively in order to achieve these goals. This book is a must read for senior managers and administrators, information managers, information specialists and practitioners, information technologists, and anyone whose work in an organization involves acquiring, creating, organizing, or using knowledge.

1998/272 pp/hardbound/ISBN 1-57387-057-9
$31.60 ASIS Members $39.50 Non-Members

To order directly from the publisher, include $3.95 postage and handling for the first book ordered and $3.25 for each additional book. Catalogs also available upon request.

Information Today, Inc.
143 Old Marlton Pike, Medford, NJ 08055 • (609)654-6266

Knowledge Management for the Information Professional

Edited by T. Kanti Srikantaiah and Michael Koenig

Written from the perspective of the information community, *Knowledge Management for the Information Professional* examines the business community's recent enthusiasm for "Knowledge Management" (KM). With contributions from 26 leading KM practitioners, academics, and information professionals, editors Srikantaiah and Koenig bridge the gap between two distinct perspectives, and equip information professionals with the tools to make a broader and more effective contribution in developing KM systems and creating a knowledge management culture within their organizations.

August 1999/hardbound/ISBN 1-57387-079-X
$35.60 ASIS Members $44.50 Non-Members

Intelligent Technologies and the Special Library of the Future

F. W. Lancaster and Linda Smith

The work described in this book was from research conducted with a grant from the Special Libraries Association. Authors Lancaster and Smith take on the formidable task of reining in the scope of information on Artificial Intelligence and related technologies. Their goal is to be able to advise the special libraries community on what can be applied today and what one might reasonably expect to be applicable to library and information services in the near future.

September 1999/hardbound/ISBN: 1-57387-063-3
$31.60 ASIS Members $39.50 Non-Members

Proceedings of the Conference on the History and Heritage of Science Information Systems

Edited by Mary Ellen Bowden, Trudi Bellardo Hahn, and Robert V. Williams

The conference on the History and Heritage of Science Information Systems was held on October 23-25, 1998 in Pittsburgh, PA, prior to the ASIS annual meeting. The conference papers explored the history and heritage of the nature, development, and influence of all types of science information systems worldwide. It was co-sponsored by ASIS, the ASIS SIG History and Foundations of Information Science (SIG/HFIS), and the Chemical Heritage Foundation. This was the first conference to explore this topic and should be of great interest to both historians and current practitioners.

October 1999/softbound/ISBN 1-57387-080-3
$31.60 ASIS Members $39.50 Non-Members

Selecting or Designing an Integrated Library System

Denise Bedford

The process of selecting or designing an Integrated Library System consists of a series of important decisions. Each of the book's seven chapters details a part of the process, offering advice and both positive and negative experiences from many institutions, as well as comments from commercial and institutional designers of automated systems. The author consulted with organizations currently in the process of a procurement, and also with developers and commercial suppliers involved in the procurement process.

November 1999/hardbound/ISBN 1-57387-064-1
$31.60 ASIS Members $39.50 Non-Members

To order directly from the publisher, include $3.95 postage and handling for the first book ordered and $3.25 for each additional book. Catalogs also available upon request.

Information Today, Inc.
143 Old Marlton Pike, Medford, NJ 08055 • (609)654-6266

Electronic Publishing: Applications and Implications

Edited by Elisabeth Logan and Myke Gluck

This book addresses some of the most perplexing issues related to the widening use of electronic media as a supplement to, or substitute for, paper-based print. These issues include access rights, preservation, standards, and copyright, among others. The book also provides a look at some proposals, prototypes, and processes in electronic publishing.

1997/160 pp/hardbound/ISBN 1-57387-036-6
$27.95 ASIS Members $34.95 Non-Members

From Print to Electronic: The Transformation of Scientific Communication

Susan Y. Crawford, Julie M. Hurd, and Ann C. Weller

In the age of digital libraries, a network-based information infrastructure, and "Bigger Science," what are the implications for informal communication, publishing, peer review, and vast data sets shared by international groups of investigators, and other elements of the system? Based on findings in the three specialties, outcome models are projected on electronic versions of paper-based communication, research results refereed or unrefereed, electronic invisible colleges, and organizational changes for the information professions.

1997/118 pp/hardbound/ISBN 1-57387-030-7
$31.60 ASIS Members $39.50 Non-Members

Entertainment Technology and Tomorrow's Information Services

Thomas E. Kinney

Clearly, the emerging U.S. National Information Infrastructure (NII) is being created as much to support interactive television, video-on-demand, multimedia CDs, video games, virtual reality theme parks, and other digital entertainment services as it is to deliver what most of us recognize as "information." Directed mainly at professionals involved with the development and delivery of information services, this book explores how that entertainment orientation—as reflected in specific emerging technologies—is likely to shape the information services of tomorrow.

1995/128 pp/hardbound/ISBN 1-57387-006-4
$27.95 ASIS Members $34.95 Non-Members

Advances in Classification Research–Vol. 8
Proceedings of the 8th ASIS SIG/CR Classification Research Workshop

Edited by Efthimis N. Efthimiadis

Advances in Classification Research, Volume 8, is a compilation of papers prepared for the 8th ASIS SIG/CR Workshop on Classification Research, held at the 60th ASIS Annual Meeting in Washington, D.C. on November 1-6, 1997.

Volume 8 concentrates on such important developments as:
- Classification Systems as Boundary Objects in Diverse Information Ecologies, by Hanne Albrechtsen & Elin Jacob
- Automatic Categorization of Statute Documents, by Thomas Curran & Paul Thompson
- Knowledge Class—A Dynamic Structure for Subject Access on the Web, by Xia Lin & Lois Mai Chan
- The Word Association Test in the Methodology of Thesaurus Construction, by Marianne Lykke Nielsen

To order directly from the publisher, include $3.95 postage and handling for the first book ordered and $3.25 for each additional book. Catalogs also available upon request.

Information Today, Inc.
143 Old Marlton Pike, Medford, NJ 08055 • (609)654-6266

- Automatic Text Categorization Using Neural Networks, by Miguel Ruiz & Padmini Srinivasan
- End-User Searching of Web Resources: Subject Needs and Zero-Hits, by Peiling Wang & Line Pouchard

1998/106pp/softbound/ISBN 1-57387-061-7
$31.60 ASIS Members $39.50 Non-Members

Advances in Classification Research—Vol. 7

Edited by Paul Solomon
Advances in Classification Research, Volume 7, is a compilation of papers prepared for the 7th ASIS SIG/CR Workshop on Classification Research, held in Baltimore, Maryland, at the 59th ASIS Annual Meeting on Sunday, October 20, 1996.

1997/138pp/softbound/ISBN 1-57387-045-5
$31.60 ASIS Members $39.50 Non-Members

Advances in Classification Research—Vol. 6

Edited by Ray Schwartz
Advances in Classification Research, Volume 6, is a compilation of papers prepared for the 6th ASIS SIG/CR Workshop on Classification Research, held in 1995.

1998/255pp/softbound/ISBN 1-57387-046-3
$31.60 ASIS Members $39.50 Non-Members

Advances in Classification Research—Vol. 5

Edited by Raya Fidel, Barbara H. Kwasnik, Clare Beghtol, and Philip J. Smith
Advances in Classification Research, Volume 5, is a compilation of the papers presented at the 5th ASIS SIG/CR Workshop on Classification Research, held in Alexandria, Virginia, at the ASIS Annual Meeting on Sunday, October 16th, 1994.

1996/296 pp/softbound/ISBN 1-57387-039-0
$31.60 ASIS Members $39.50 Non-Members

Advances in Classification Research—Vol. 4

Edited by Raya Fidel, Barbara H. Kwasnik, Clare Beghtol, and Philip J. Smith
Topics presented in Advances in Classification Research, Volume 4 focus on methods for creating and exploiting classification structures, using classification for designing retrieval tools and for the elicitation and representation of knowledge, and concept representation and the design of tools for a variety of settings to help information seekers explore such representations.

1994/190 pp/softbound/ISBN 0-938734-97-0
$31.60 ASIS Members $39.50 Non-Members

Advances in Classification Research—Vol. 1-3

Volume 1—1991/172 pp/softbound/ISBN 0-938734-53-9
Volume 2—1992/227 pp/softbound/ISBN 0-938734-67-9
Volume 3—1994/233 pp/softbound/ISBN 0-938734-79-2

$31.60 each ASIS Members $39.50 each Non-Members

To order directly from the publisher, include $3.95 postage and handling for the first book ordered and $3.25 for each additional book. Catalogs also available upon request.

Information Today, Inc.
143 Old Marlton Pike, Medford, NJ 08055 • (609)654-6266